D1507387

THE COMMONWEALTH IN THE 1980s

Also edited by A. J. R. Groom and Paul Taylor

FUNCTIONALISM
INTERNATIONAL ORGANIZATIONS: A Conceptual Approach

Also by A. J. R. Groom

THE MANAGEMENT OF BRITAIN'S EXTERNAL RELATIONS
  (*editor with Robert Boardman*)
BRITISH THINKING ABOUT NUCLEAR WEAPONS
THE STUDY OF WORLD SOCIETY: A London Perspective (*with
  J. W. Burton, A. V. S. De Reuck and C. R. Mitchell*)
INTERNATIONAL RELATIONS THEORY: A Critical Bibliog-
  raphy (*editor with C. R. Mitchell*)
BRITAIN BETWEEN EAST AND WEST: Concerned Independence
  (*with J. W. Burton, Margot Light, C. R. Mitchell and D. Sandole*)
STRATEGY AND CONFLICT IN THE MODERN WORLD

Also by Paul Taylor

INTERNATIONAL COOPERATION TODAY
THE LIMITS OF INTEGRATION IN THE EUROPEAN
  COMMUNITIES
A SURVEY OF INTERNATIONAL INSTITUTIONS (*editor*)

THE COMMONWEALTH IN THE 1980s

Challenges and Opportunities

Edited by

A. J. R. Groom

*University of Kent at Canterbury
and Centre for the Analysis of Conflict*

and

Paul Taylor

*London School of Economics
and Political Science*

MACMILLAN

© A. J. R. Groom and Paul Taylor 1984

First published 1984 by
THE MACMILLAN PRESS LTD
London and Basingstoke
Companies and representatives
throughout the world

Printed in Hong Kong

Filmset by Latimer Trend & Company Ltd, Plymouth

British Library Cataloguing in Publication Data
Groom, A. J. R.
The Commonwealth in the 1980s.
1. Commonwealth of Nations
I. Title   II. Taylor, Paul, *1939–*
909'.09712410828   DA18

ISBN 0–333–30073–4

Contents

Notes on the Contributors   vii
Preface   xi

PART I   THE FRAMEWORK

1   The Continuing Commonwealth: its Origins and Character-
    istics
    A. J. R. Groom and Paul Taylor   3

2   The Commonwealth Secretariat
    Margaret Doxey   15

3   Regionalism and the Commonwealth
    A. E. Thorndike   40

PART II   FUNCTIONAL DIMENSIONS

4   The Commonwealth Youth Programme and Youth-oriented
    Activities
    L. S. Trachtenberg   55

5   Education
    Ruth Butterworth (with a Note on Regional Examination
    Councils by *L. S. Trachtenberg*)   65

6   The Arts: an Emerging Dimension
    A. J. R. Groom   83

7   Science and Technology: the Commonwealth Dimension
    Kaye Turner   94

8   Commonwealth Co-operation in the Field of Health
    John Martin   107

9   Military Ties
    William Gutteridge   116

10 Law of the Commonwealth
    Alfred M. Kamanda   125

v

11   The Residual Legatee: Economic Co-operation in the
     Contemporary Commonwealth
     Arthur Kilgore and James Mayall   140

12   By Way of Comparison: French Relations with Former
     Colonies
     R. J. Harrison   166

PART III   HIGH POLITICS

13   Continuity without Consensus: the Commonwealth Heads
     of Government Meetings, 1971–81
     Michael O'Neill   185

14   Conflict Management in the Commonwealth
     C. R. Mitchell   225

15   Migration in the Commonwealth
     Hugh Tinker   244

16   The Existing Dependencies
     L. S. Trachtenberg   260

PART IV   CONCLUSIONS

17   The Commonwealth as an International Organisation
     A. J. R. Groom   293

18   The Commonwealth in the 1980s: Challenges and
     Opportunities
     Paul Taylor   305

Appendices
A   *The Commonwealth – Members and Organisations*   327
B   *The Agreed Memorandum on the Commonwealth Secretariat*   338
C   *The Declaration of Commonwealth Principles*   346
D   *Commonwealth Statement on Apartheid in Sport (The Gleneagles
     Agreement)*   348
E   *The Lusaka Declaration of the Commonwealth on Racism and
     Racial Prejudice*   350
F   *The Melbourne Declaration*   353

Bibliography   355
Index of Authors, Politicians, etc.   362
Index of Subjects   365

Notes on the Contributors

Dr Ruth Butterworth is Associate Professor in Political Studies, University of Auckland. She was formerly Research Officer, Royal Institute of Public Administration, and Deputy Personnel Manager, Simpson (Piccadilly) Ltd. She is the author of numerous papers on the politics of education and information, and on Southern African affairs.

Dr Margaret Doxey was born and educated in Britain. She has taught economics and international relations at South African and Canadian universities and worked in industry and government in Britain. She has been Professor of Political Studies at Trent University, Ontario, since 1976, and is the author of *Economic Sanctions and International Enforcement* (2nd edition published by Macmillan for the Royal Institute of International Affairs in 1980). She has also contributed articles on aspects of international organisation to *International Affairs, International Journal, International Organization*, the *Year Book of World Affairs*, and other periodicals.

Dr A. J. R. Groom is Reader in International Relations at the University of Kent at Canterbury and Co-Director of the Centre for the Analysis of Conflict. He previously taught at University College London. He is the author (or co-author) of several books, including *British Thinking about Nuclear Weapons, Britain between East and West* and *Strategy and Conflict in the Modern World*, and co-editor of five volumes of original essays.

William Gutteridge is Professor Emeritus of International Studies at the University of Aston in Birmingham. He taught previously at Sandhurst and Lanchester Polytechnic in Coventry. His books include *Armed Forces in New States, Military Institutions and Power in New States, The Military in African Politics, Military Regimes in Africa, European Security, Nuclear Weapons and Public Confidence* (co-editor), and *The Dangers of New Weapon Systems* (co-editor).

Dr R. J. Harrison taught politics at Victoria University, Wellington, from 1957 to 1967 and was a well-known broadcaster and television commentator in New Zealand. Following a developing interest in European politics and European integration, he returned to England in 1967 and is now Senior Lecturer at the University of Lancaster. He is the author of *Europe in Question*, *Pluralism and Corporatism* and a large number of articles and reviews. He spent 1981–2 as Visiting Fellow, Victoria University, Wellington.

Dr Alfred M. Kamanda was born in Sierra Leone. He is presently Senior Lecturer in Law at the Polytechnic of Central London. He was previously Legal Officer at the ILO, Principal Secretary in the Foreign Office of Sierra Leone and High Commissioner of Sierra Leone in London as well as Professor of International Law at Leuven, Belgium.

Arthur Kilgore is a research student and tutor in international organisations, in the Department of International Relations at the London School of Economics.

Dr John Martin is a medical graduate of Queen's University, Belfast. Following a year in Bangladesh he undertook postgraduate studies in community health at the London School of Hygiene and Tropical Medicine. He has worked as a community physician in the East End of London and as a consultant to the Medical Division of the Commonwealth Secretariat. Since 1979 Dr Martin has been working as Adviser on Primary Health Care to the Government of Zambia.

James Mayall is Senior Lecturer in International Relations at the London School of Economics. He has published widely on the theory of international relations, and is the author of a volume on international relations in Africa.

Dr C. R. Mitchell has taught international relations at University College London, at Southampton University and at the University of Surrey. He is currently Senior Lecturer at The City University, London, where he continues research into various forms of conflict management and dispute settlement. He is the author of *The Structure of International Conflict* (Macmillan, 1981), *Peacemaking and the Consultant's Role* and numerous articles and reviews on social and international conflict.

Dr Michael O'Neill is Lecturer in the Department of Political Studies at Sheffield City Polytechnic. His research interest lies in the post-colonial relationship with a developing interest in the attitudes and approaches of French politicians to their former colonies.

Dr Paul Taylor is Lecturer in International Relations at the London School of Economics and Political Science. He has published widely on international organisations and on the European Communities, and teaches these subjects.

Dr A. E. Thorndike is currently Head of the Department of International Relations and Politics at the North Staffordshire Polytechnic, Stoke-on-Trent. He is a specialist in Caribbean and Central American political affairs, several articles on which have been published.

Hugh Tinker is Professor of Politics in the University of Lancaster and formerly Director of the Institute of Race Relations. He is the author of a number of books on South and South-East Asia, including three on the emigrant communities from India, Pakistan and Bangladesh, and of *Race, Conflict and the International Order: from Empire to United Nations* (Macmillan, 1977).

Kaye Turner is currently a Research Fellow at the Institute of African Studies at the University of Zambia. She is working on urban community research. A New Zealander, Kaye Turner has co-edited *Women and the Law in New Zealand*.

L. S. Trachtenberg is Associate Director of Studies of the University of Southern California's UK Program. He is currently completing a PhD on the United Nations at the London School of Economics and Political Science.

Preface

We came to this book virtually by accident. As teachers of international organisation and international relations we had paid no more than the scantist regard to the Commonwealth. Our research interest in the topic was excited more by its supposed negative qualities than by its positive ones. Like most people of our age group, born just before the Second World War, we had no sense of being 'Commonwealth men' – a breed that has now nearly died out. On the contrary, our instincts were that the Commonwealth was a contemporary manifestation of a dubious past: it generated discomforting thoughts of imperialism, national service in dangerous faraway places, and old-fashioned and tetchy Colonel Blimps. However, John Goormaghtigh and Jean Siotis, who were then directing the Centre for Research on International Institutions in Geneva, persuaded us that it was time for an academic team to have a new look at the Commonwealth. We are grateful to them for starting us off on what is probably the best kind of academic voyage: one on which one gains both enlightenment, and sympathy for the subject.

If we started off in half a mind that we were on to an academic demolition job, the project has turned out very differently – and not only for ourselves but also for several of the team who shared our scepticism about the Commonwealth. We have ended up with a view of the Commonwealth which is quite different from that with which we started, in part because the contemporary Commonwealth is different in many ways from its earlier self. Indeed, our earlier image is only faintly recognisable in the stuff and institutions of the contemporary Commonwealth. Above all we have become convinced that the quality of relations between its members is an impressive asset in approaching a range of contemporary problems, and that there is considerable scope for the extension of its role even where its present contribution is, perhaps, from some points of view, rather small scale. We have come to see merit in the way it conducts its business and to see its promise for growth. Despite its failures and its weaknesses the contemporary Commonwealth contributes significantly to the wellbeing of contemporary world society as we see it. It is eminently worth having and cherishing.

We were concerned to describe and explain the contemporary Commonwealth as an international organisation, a task which we believe has not been attempted before in a book. By 'contemporary Commonwealth' we mean the Commonwealth since the mid-1960s, when it ceased to be the British Commonwealth and became the Commonwealth of independent states, of which Britain is a member amongst others. This overall purpose explains the arrangement of the volume: in the first section the origins and institutions are examined, and in the second are considered the range of functional dimensions, that is, the organisation of specific activities among Commonwealth members, primarily at the non-governmental level. A third section examines the more important political problems among member governments, and it is here that the style and diplomacy of the Commonwealth Heads of Government Meetings are discussed, as well as a selection of 'high' political issues. In a final section we offer our conclusions.

A number of themes recur throughout the various chapters, and these also are the product of our concern with the Commonwealth as an international organisation. We were concerned to discover the nature of the members' interest in the organisation, as compared with that in other organisations at the universal or regional level; the extent to which distinctive structures and processes of the Commonwealth could be identified in international society; and the nature of the Commonwealth's response to a number of recent challenges, such as the demand for a new international economic order, British accession to the European Communities, and the process of decolonisation and its associated problems. In other words emphasis has been placed on the comparative evaluation of the Commonwealth in relation to other organisations so that is distinctive qualities could emerge more clearly.

Our team have co-operated with us in an extremely helpful manner. They have been tolerant, perhaps too tolerant, of their editors, and we are grateful for their co-operation and what we have learned from them. An enterprise of this nature is also heavily dependent on the secretarial staff who helped us at the University of Kent, the late Pat Sutherland, Sarah Wood and Mary Thomas; and at the London School of Economics, Gill Portwine and Marie Williams. Their willing efforts have been greatly appreciated.

And lastly, but probably first, we would like to thank our wives Antoinette and Janetta for tolerating the various diversions inevitably associated with an enterprise such as this.

A. J. R. GROOM
PAUL TAYLOR

Part I
The Framework

1 The Continuing Commonwealth: Its Origins and Characteristics

A. J. R. GROOM and PAUL TAYLOR

The focus of this volume is on the contemporary Commonwealth – an institution that has evolved from an imperial past through a complete metamorphosis of values and practice. Yet the seeds of the present lie in that past. The imperial phase ended with the formal acknowledgement of the reality of the sovereign equality of the dominions. If there was to be unity it would be unity in diversity, and by consent, not by command. Moreover, the diversity increased as non-British peoples demanded independence but were prepared to acknowledge a modicum of unity. This unity lost most of its political content in terms of the capacity for concerted action, but not entirely so, despite the conflicts engendered during the process of decolonization. In part this was due to the continued evolution and flourishing of many non-governmental ties after independence. These ties often reflected shared interests, but they could also have a neo-colonial aspect. The relatively peaceful accession to independence of the Indian sub-continent obviated any need for a sharp discontinuity of such ties and their continued existence gave a degree of relevance to continued political ties. A Commonwealth based on transactions in functional and non-governmental dimensions existed and it made necessary a political Commonwealth which was no mere face-saving device or sentimental illusion. Prime Minister Nehru also pointed to a supportive role for the Commonwealth in the management of contemporary world problems. He felt that it brought a 'touch of healing' to a sick world.[1]

The Indian precedent was followed virtually throughout the Empire in the next quarter of a century, but it was a period of Commonwealth evolution marked by great political turbulence. Britain still assumed a leadership role and its leadership was challenged by increasing pressures towards transforming the Commonwealth into a loose, equal and non-structured association, and by the scepticism and anxiety of African governments over British policy in Southern Africa. The subsequent British disillusionment with the Commonwealth caused other members to reflect on the value of the association and the form it should take. It was a sort of catharsis which led, in the mid-seventies, to the contemporary Commonwealth. The Anglo-African confrontation also led to the creation of the Secretariat, which has contributed significantly to the metamorphosis of the *British* Commonwealth into a Commonwealth which is no longer Anglocentric but belongs to all its members in their different ways.

Despite its nebulous character the Commonwealth is real, significant and relevant to the attempted solution of a wide range of contemporary problems. It encompasses a network of ties at governmental and non-governmental levels in virtually every domain; it has grown out of and facilitates an impressive movement of goods, services, ideas and people in a remarkably non-coercive framework. However, because the Commonwealth lacks a constitution and the network of ties is informal and diverse, its magnitude, behaviour and effects are hard to quantify and evaluate. Moreover, because of its colonial past it is an unfashionable subject; it cannot however be ignored, not only because of what it does, but also because of the manner in which it does it. The way of conducting business is a matter of evolving practice that has no constitutional definition, though the practice can be described and, while the Commonwealth is devoid of a constitution, it does have explicit principles which reflect its values. The behaviour of Commonwealth governments may too often fall short of these principles, but they stand as *desiderata* with which all Commonwealth governments necessarily wish to be associated. In January 1971 the Commonwealth Heads of Government Meeting in Singapore formulated *The Declaration of Commonwealth Principles* to which in 1977 they added a statement on *Apartheid in Sport* and, in 1979, *The Lusaka Declaration of the Commonwealth on Racism and Racial Prejudice*.[2]

It is pertinent that, despite the fierce intra-Commonwealth disagreement over Southern Africa at the 1971 Singapore meeting of Heads of Government, they were able to agree 'on a set of ideals which are subscribed to by all members and provide a basis for peace, understanding and goodwill among all mankind'. The essential points of the Declaration stressed the voluntary nature of the association, its non-exclusivity and the promotion of equal rights between member states and for their citizens. Racial prejudice was called a 'dangerous sickness' which would be 'vigorously combat[ted] at home and eschewed abroad'. All forms of colonial domination and racial oppression would be opposed and governments pledged themselves to the progressive removal of the wide disparities in wealth. 'In pursuing these principles the members of the Commonwealth believe that they can provide a constructive example of the multinational approach which is vital to peace and progress in the modern world. The association is based on consultation, discussion and co-operation.'[3]

The Declaration reveals quite clearly that the Commonwealth has no aspirations for integration of a supra-national kind but seeks permanent inter-governmental co-operation in a variety of forms over a wide range of issues. It espouses Western liberal notions of human rights and political processes, although the Commonwealth houses some disfiguring regimes. Nevertheless, the standard has been set, even if it is not always kept.

The opposition to racial prejudice and discrimination is a different matter, since its eradication has been a Commonwealth action policy and not merely a mouthing of high-sounding principles. From the parting of company between the Commonwealth and the Republic of South Africa (RSA) to the present, the Commonwealth has been active on this issue, with Southern Africa in the forefront. Specifically, the Commonwealth helped to keep Britain on the straight and narrow path over Rhodesia. On the larger issue of the RSA, members agreed to combat discrimination by abjuring measures which in their 'own judgement directly contribute to the pursuit or consolidation of this evil policy'. Thus the Commonwealth has no mandatory power to impose a policy on its members but it has demonstrated that collectively it can stay the hand of a member state if it is united and determined. It is, however, also the case that the Commonwealth states in the OAU have generally occupied a more moderate position on such issues as Rhodesia than their radical colleagues, as in the weeks immediately following UDI in 1965.

Southern Africa was not the only great Commonwealth theme in the sixties and seventies. The Commonwealth has worked long and hard on the worsening economic plight of its poorer members and achieved a relative degree of success. From the Singapore meeting sprang the Commonwealth Fund for Technical Co-operation (CFTC) which has made invaluable contributions. The Commonwealth Secretariat has been a fertile source of ideas and support for the North-South dialogue and the Commonwealth framework has been used for broaching questions prior to their presentation in wider fora and for further examination if no results have been achieved elsewhere. In this the Commonwealth decision-making process has proved helpful – frank, free, informal, flexible, and consensual in an atmosphere tinged with fellow-feeling. Again, it has often performed the useful role of acting as a bridge between the more radical developing states and the developed world.

It is hardly surprising, given the events in Southern Africa in the 1970s, that the Commonwealth's commitment 'to rid the world of the evils of racism and racial prejudice' should be re-iterated in two further documents. These were the statement on *Apartheid in Sport* issued at the Heads of Government Meeting in 1977 and *The Lusaka Declaration of the Commonwealth on Racism and Racial Prejudice* of August 1979.[4] The declaration on apartheid in sport was intended to defuse the issue and to de-politicize Commonwealth sport, although it did not entirely succeed and a code of conduct in relation to sporting links with the RSA based on the 1977 'Gleneagles' Agreement proved necessary. The Lusaka Declaration was essentially a reaffirmation, at a critical and tense time in the Rhodesian dispute, of principles previously agreed. However, another African problem could not be ignored – that of the conduct of Idi Amin's regime in Uganda.

It is a fundamental principle of the Commonwealth that there can be no discussion of the internal affairs of a member without the consent of that member state. On the other hand there is an assumption that each member's conduct of its internal affairs will be such as not to cause basic offence to other member states. It was because such a state of affairs did not obtain in the RSA that the Commonwealth parted company with it. In a technical sense the long Commonwealth involvement with the Rhodesian problem was also intervention in Britain's internal affairs, but the British did not deny the legitimacy of such an intervention although they did seek to ensure that they alone were responsible for policy (despite the fact that they sometimes tried to shirk their responsibilities). With Amin's Uganda the principle was breached and the Secretary-General put the case well:

There has been in the Commonwealth, of course, as in the international community, a long and necessary tradition of non-
interference in the internal affairs of other states. No Commonwealth

country (indeed, who anywhere in the world?) is above reproach in some respect or other. If these traditions were not to be respected there would be no end to recrimination and censoriousness. How to strike the balance of political judgement between the two extremes of declamation and silence is sometimes difficult – but it would be entirely illusory to believe that such a judgement could, or indeed should, be avoided altogether. There will be times in the affairs of the Commonwealth when one member's conduct will provoke the wrath of others beyond the limits of silence. Any other relationship would be so sterile as to be effete. What we must work for is an ethic which constrains meddling but which also inhibits excesses of the kind that demand and justify protest from without.

There never will be unanimity that criticism or complaint is legitimate comment, not improper interference. But the truth is that, although the line may be indefinable, all the world will know when it is crossed.[5]

It was crossed in the case of Uganda. President Amin had sinned against two precepts that Canadian Prime Minister Trudeau had identified as distinctively 'Commonwealth':

The first was the obvious dedication of Commonwealth leaders to the betterment of their peoples. At the Conference there were not propounded – or vigorously defended – schemes or programmes designed for the glory of the state: we were concerned with the dignity of individual human beings and the improvement of the lot of ordinary men and women. The second distinction was a willingness on the part of all of us to believe that, should the policies of other Commonwealth governments sometimes appear misdirected or lead to disappointment, this is as a result of error, or inefficiency or lack of discipline; it is not the consequence of purposeful intent. In short, within the Commonwealth there is a willingness to help one another, and a willingness to believe that that help is genuinely offered.[6]

As Arnold Smith once pointed out,[7] the Commonwealth has relatively few hard principles but many useful habits – which make the Commonwealth effective, if difficult to define.

The Commonwealth is a voluntary association of those states which have experienced some form of British rule who wish to work together to further their individual and common interests. Not all states, on emerging from British rule, have chosen to join the Commonwealth, and not all states, once members of the Commonwealth, have remained in the association. Although there has been a presumption that newly-independent countries would join, pressure to do so has been persuasive rather than coercive and no sanctions have been made against those states which did not join or those which left. However, the case of the RSA was different, since that country was and remains in clear violation of Commonwealth principles and sanctions have been implemented in various ways. Amin's Government, too, was given a cold shoulder in Commonwealth settings, although the people of Uganda remained in the Commonwealth 'fraternity'.

This sense of fraternity, which has survived many buffetings, has two elements: the first is a 'distant cousin' syndrome and the second is a sense of common interest. The distant cousin analogy suggests that Commonwealth governments and peoples react to each other in new circumstances in a different way from non-Commonwealth governments and peoples. Just as on meeting a distant cousin for the first time a person will observe the rules of family ties and behaviour by sharing information and affording help in a more open relationship than would be expected with a total stranger, so Commonwealth 'distant cousins' do not approach each other negatively, but positively and in a co-operative and friendly manner. There is a sense of 'we-feeling' that pervades Commonwealth relations, that includes a notion of Commonwealth interest, and even international community interest, over and above the pursuit of self-interest. Even where disputes arise between Commonwealth members the aim is, at the very least, to discuss issues in an independent and catalytic manner if this will help and if it is desired. It is to be supportive of the parties rather than to be partisan.

The generally supportive nature of the Commonwealth is illustrated by the decision-making process. The Commonwealth can only recommend: it cannot command or coerce. Its informality in negotiation is exemplified by the seminar-like Heads of Government Meetings (CHOGMs) with their frequent interjections, the general avoidance of set speeches and the usually friendly, even 'matey' atmosphere which, although sometimes interrupted by tension, nevertheless permits the frank discussion of delicate issues. Heads of government can 'let themselves go' with a peer group without fear that advantage will be taken. This is a situation rare in their experience to which they attach sufficient importance to devote a week or more of their time. There is often no particular end in view, but any decisions, if decisions are required and desired, will be taken by consensus and in private. And they usually return home having found the meeting fertile in ideas. New members are socialised into the ways of the Commonwealth by the

Heads of Government Meetings, which set and reflect the tone at other levels; by the Secretariat and its activities, which have an important inductive role for new members and new governments; and, finally, by the existence of non-governmental ties which often precede independence and even at that time instil into participants the informal, frank and consensual way of doing business. Indeed, the Commonwealth is not only about the business that it does, but also about the way in which it does business.

The informality, frankness and co-operative spirit are aided substantially by a common working language and compatible administrative practice. The role of English is important because language constitutes a paradigm which is shared and which has a subtle but pervasive influence that facilitates bridge-building. However, 'Speaking English is a Commonwealth fact; it is not part of any Commonwealth ideology; it is one channel for easy communication, and a precious one in functional terms. It is not a badge of identity.'[8] With the use of English and compatible administrative procedures 'progress' is given a head start. Yet to participate in this process is in no sense to deny participation in other organizations. Although the Commonwealth commands loyalty, it does not command exclusive loyalty. Indeed, one of its virtues is its diversity, and practically all Commonwealth countries also have strong regional or other extra-Commonwealth ties.

Although the Commonwealth was once British, and in its past it was certainly Anglocentric, the touchstone of the emergence of the contemporary Commonwealth was that Britain had no special rights or privileges, duties or responsibilities, although it is difficult to conceive of a Commonwealth without Britain surviving for long. The existence of the Secretariat made the passing of the *British* Commonwealth easier, as did British policy. Mr Heath, in Singapore, asserting his determination to follow British interests despite Commonwealth objections, stated Britain's claim for equality:

> It is assumed that there will be equality between members as neither Britain nor any other member seek or obtain a privileged position; second it is assumed that nothing is involved in membership which impairs the right of a member to take its own decisions in its own jurisdiction.[9]

Functionally Britain plays a more central role, especially at the non-governmental level, although at the governmental level the Secretariat has become a central force and there is much regional activity within the

Commonwealth. Thus the divergence of Commonwealth members due to the dissolving of the British tie has been counterbalanced by Commonwealth regional and pan-Commonwealth ties. The Commonwealth maintains its coherence both despite Britain's new role and because of it, since it meets felt needs.

The Commonwealth is used by all its members, but it is held dearest by those who have few other avenues into the world. In particular, it enables small countries to act on a worldwide stage in a familiar and supportive setting without the encumbering and overwhelming framework, formality, intrigues and bureaucracy of the United Nations and its agencies. Even in questions of high politics in the Commonwealth there is a welcome element of fraternity. It is a political and functional forum in which governments can try out ideas, test policies and get feedback on their standing in a worldwide context and in a friendly and frank fashion which is available virtually nowhere else. Commonwealth heads of government particularly value their meetings for these purposes. For small countries the Commonwealth is an invaluable and flexible source of trustworthy and relevant information, help and research, whether from other members or from the Secretariat, whereas for medium powers, such as Australia or Canada, it is a manageable forum for a worldwide policy and an invaluable entrée into global politics. Above all, the Commonwealth is a North-South bridge and one of the few acceptable bridges for all parties which has already been trod to ameliorate North-South problems with some degree of success. As Mr Ramphal has suggested, 'the Commonwealth cannot negotiate for the world; but it can help the world to negotiate'.[10]

Yet the Commonwealth is more than governments 'helping the world to negotiate', it is also a relationship between people and peoples. Its ties at the non-governmental level give it a substance that is denied to many regional organisations manufactured by governments but so frequently ignored by people. However, it is here that the Commonwealth is still somewhat Anglocentric, although this is changing, especially with the growth of Commonwealth regions and as patterns of transactions lose their Anglocentricity. The British Commonwealth has largely gone through its metamorphosis to the contemporary Commonwealth at this level too. It reflects the whole gamut of human relations in a diverse institutional framework, based on a network of ties growing out of a shared experience which has given rise to a sense of community. The community and association thrive in a complex institutional framework.

There were several timid attempts to give the 'official', that is governmental, Commonwealth a formal institutional framework in the time of the dominions, but these came to nothing. In the mid-sixties the situation changed when the feeling grew that it was no longer acceptable for Britain to act as a Secretariat, particularly for CHOGMs, at a time when Britain's policy in Southern Africa was being strongly questioned. The newly independent countries wished to maintain an association with each other as well as with Britain and a clearly 'pan-Commonwealth' institutionalization was necessary to facilitate this and to remove any taint of continued subservience to Britain. The British did not demur, recognising that the role had changed, and the Commonwealth Prime Ministers agreed, in July 1964, to establish a Secretariat.

There were initially differing conceptions of the role of the Secretariat but it quickly became a major actor in the political, economic and other functional affairs of the official Commonwealth. While the Secretaries-General have always paid scrupulous regard to the sovereignty of Commonwealth governments, the Secretary-General has become a major political figure not only within but also beyond the Commonwealth. Governments have chosen their Secretaries-General wisely, Arnold Smith and Shridath Ramphal having the different but necessary qualities for a changing role, and Secretaries-General have developed their competences to fill felt needs in a process of task expansion and spillover of considerable proportions. These competences have been developed not only in high politics such as Rhodesia but also in economic affairs, where the CFTC has been such a success, and also in the North-South dimension where the Commonwealth has helped the world to negotiate and Mr Ramphal has played an important personal role. The functions of the Secretariat also touch upon many aspects of the external relations of the smaller Commonwealth countries, since the Secretariat is an understanding, efficient, and trustworthy source of information, research, aid and support. In addition, the divisions of the Secretariat play a role in Commonwealth ministerial meetings which are often a prelude to meetings at an United Nations Specialised Agency.

The Secretariat is responsible in its work to the Secretary-General who is in turn responsible to the member governments. Since the governments work on a basis of consensus then so must the Secretary-General. Both he and his staff are responsible to the Commonwealth as a whole and therefore they neither seek nor accept instructions from individual governments, a stipulation that governments are pledged to respect, although there is a necessary and frequently-used right to consultation. The Secretariat is not itself a career Secretariat, its members being seconded from other functions (often with member governments), and the Secretary-General has the services of a high quality staff, despite the usual strictures of geographical distribution as well as competence. The Secretariat has the very important blessing of a single working language and usually compatible administrative practices among its recruits and, perhaps as significantly, among its clientele.

The Commonwealth is a trans-regional organisation but its ties in no way exclude the participation of member governments in non-Commonwealth regional organizations such as the European Community, ASEAN and ECOWAS. Indeed, the Secretariat may help member governments in their participation in or relationship with such organisations. However, the Commonwealth has its own regional organisations such as the Caribbean Community, the South Pacific Forum, and the Asia-Pacific regional meetings of Heads of Government. These regional activities appear not to be divisive of the Commonwealth as a whole. The Secretariat is an important conduit and actor to ensure that this remains so. It is noteworthy that Britain does not participate in the extra-European regional groupings, thus exemplifying the absence of Anglocentricity in the contemporary Commonwealth. In various functional dimensions the Commonwealth is regionalising fast, and this seems a likely trend for the 1980s. It is a reflection of the growth in size and activities of the Commonwealth, and the Secretariat has been well able to respond both to Commonwealth regional and pan-Commonwealth concerns. Similar trends are also evident in the 'unofficial' Commonwealth.

A recommendation that the unofficial Commonwealth should have a degree of official recognition in the shape of a non-Governmental Organizations (NGO) desk in the Commonwealth Secretariat has not commended itself to governments or to the Secretariat.[11] It came at an inopportune moment financially, when the Secretariat was struggling to find the means to continue its existing range of activities, including the CFTC and, in any case, it did not reflect the priorities of the Secretary-General. Moreover, there are ideological problems, since Commonwealth NGOs are mainly to be found in the developed Commonwealth and, overall, they reflect a higher degree of Anglocentricity than other aspects of the Commonwealth. Yet the range of Commonwealth organisations need each other and are dependent upon each other for the most efficient fulfilment of their tasks. Such co-operation, however, is essentially informal with ties between divisions of the Secretariat and appropriate INGOs and NGOs.

The unofficial Commonwealth is, however, far from being anarchic.[12]

It is a network which, while it has nodal points, does not have a centre. It is a living organism in which parts of the network flourish and parts decay. It has not been conceived as a coherent whole and does not behave as such, thus leading on occasion to duplication and inefficiencies, or worse, with undermanned and under-financed bodies struggling to survive. Yet not always: other parts of the network are expanding and are fruitfully complementary, providing a precious element of unity and diversity. What gives the hundreds of bodies the quality of a network is their unplanned but collective ability to evolve, in the face of new demands and a changing environment, in a recognisably Commonwealth fashion. A common historical background, a common working language and compatible administrative practices are some explanatory factors. A sense of a psycho-social community and perceived interests in common are likewise important, but the quintessence of the Commonwealth network is its flexible and consensual approach to decision-making and its relative success in preventing institutional values from dominating human values. It responds to felt needs in a pragmatic manner and, while there is no formal coherent whole, a pragmatic set of responses emerging out of a sense of community can give coherence where it is felt necessary.

In the succeeding chapters these characteristics are explored in a wide range of contexts, both at governmental and non-governmental level. They are amply illustrative of the adaptability of the Commonwealth, and of its considerable potential in view of its unusual qualities, for helping to meet challenges posed in contemporary world society. It is indeed aptly described as a bond that held.

NOTES AND REFERENCES

1. Prime Minister Nehru of India in a speech to the Indian Constituent Assembly on the continued membership of republican India in the Commonwealth, 16 May 1949, quoted in Ali A. Mazrui, *The Anglo–African Commonwealth* (Oxford: Pergamon, 1967) pp. 137–8.
2. See Appendix E.
3. Ibid.
4. Ibid.
5. *Report of the Commonwealth Secretary-General* (London: Commonwealth Secretariat, 1977) pp. 13–14.
6. Pierre E. Trudeau, 'The Commonwealth after Ottawa', *Round Table*, January 1974, p. 38.
7. In an address to the Royal Commonwealth Society in London shortly after taking office as Secretary-General.

8. Shridath Ramphal, *One World to Share* (London: Hutchinson, 1979) p. 242.
9. *The Times*, 16 January 1971.
10. Shridath Ramphal, *One World to Share*, p. 123.
11. *From Grassroots to Governments*, Report of advisory committee on relationships between official and unofficial Commonwealth (London: Commonwealth Secretariat, 1978).
12. For a description of Commonwealth organisations see the Secretariat's publication *Commonwealth Organisations*, 2nd edn (London: Commonwealth Secretariat, 1979) part of which can be found in Appendix A.

2 The Commonwealth Secretariat

MARGARET DOXEY

Over the past three decades the proliferation of international institutions and the increasing range and complexity of the issues with which they grapple have stimulated considerable scholarly interest in the character and role of international secretariats.[1] There have been excellent case studies of particular institutions and of individual Secretaries-General and valuable analytical work of a comparative nature.[2] But until very recently the Commonwealth, which has been well served by historians, was generally overlooked by international relations scholars; its significance was derided; its survival doubted; many texts on international organisation failed to mention it at all.[3] Over the last fifteen years this neglect has become progressively less justifiable, and the book of which this chapter forms a part indicates a growing awareness of the importance of the new Commonwealth as an institution worthy of study. While the association still has distinctive qualities, the establishment of a Commonwealth Secretariat in 1965 moved it structurally more into line with other international institutions, as well as giving greater cohesion to the multiplicity of Commonwealth links and impetus to the development of new areas of co-operation. At the same time, other international organisations – even those which were set up to fulfil more specifically goal-oriented functions – have tended in practice to resemble the Commonwealth. Martin Wight commented in 1969 that the Commonwealth was 'a ruminant, not a carnivore, in the international jungle'.[4] Continuing the metaphor, one could say that the few carnivores have proved relatively toothless and that ruminants abound. International organisations, typically, are not decision-making, action-oriented bodies. At the political level they provide frameworks or contexts in which issues are discussed, bargaining takes place, coalitions develop, priorities are set. There are few signs anywhere of a significant trend to supranationalism; even in the European Communities, member governments are reluctant to relinquish formal sovereignty to community organs. At the functional level international secretariats have operational roles which they fulfil with varying degrees of efficiency and economy.

This chapter deals specifically with the Commonwealth Secretariat: its organisation, resources, functions and achievements. First, however, it is useful to sketch the background to its inauguration.

Prior to 1965, the Commonwealth had no formal machinery: its major organisational features were Prime Ministers' Meetings (renamed Heads of Government Meetings in 1971) serviced by the British Cabinet Office. Between these meetings, which on average were held at eighteen-month intervals, there were other ministerial meetings and continuing consultation on a government-to-government basis. General liaison and information work was handled by the Commonwealth Relations Office (CRO) a British government department.[5]

A former Secretary to the British Cabinet has pointed out that the first Prime Ministers' Meeting, held in 1944, set a style of informality quite different from the very formal Imperial Conferences.[6] This new style was carried forward in subsequent Prime Ministers' Meetings which were held in private with no pre-arranged agenda, no moving of formal resolutions and no voting. Agreed communiqués, couched in very general terms, were published at the end of the meetings. Further conventions were also developed: there were no formal decisions on 'Commonwealth' policies; no discussion of the internal affairs of member states without their consent; no discussion of intra-Commonwealth disputes except with the consent of the parties.[7]

This machinery of collective consultation at the Prime Ministerial level, operating on procedural norms of confidentiality, informality and consensus, successfully met the challenge of handling the transition from 'old' to 'new' Commonwealth. In the first place, it confirmed and reinforced the substantive norms of equality between members, codified in the Statute of Westminster. Secondly, it allowed Commonwealth members to adopt a republican form of government (India being the first to do so); since 1949 the British monarch has had symbolic significance as Head of the Commonwealth, while retaining, of course, constitutional responsibilities as head of state in Britain and thirteen of the other seventeen monarchies within the Commonwealth. Thirdly, it supported new and important norms of multi-racialism and non-intervention as well as the right to self-determination which was implicit in the whole evolution of the association.[8]

At the 1944 Prime Ministers' Meeting the Australian Prime Minister suggested a continuing secretariat or council for the Commonwealth but his proposal had few attractions for the Canadian and South African governments, who feared it might mean centralisation and a loss of autonomy; nor at that time for the British government which did not want to lose – or share – control.[9] In the decades which followed, however, as the Commonwealth changed drastically in composition and character, it became clear that its needs could no longer be satisfactorily served by Whitehall. With the independence of India, Pakistan and Ceylon (now Sri Lanka), the enhanced middle-power status of Canada and Australia, and the decline in the use of the term 'Dominion', both reorganisation and renaming were necessary. The India Office was wound-up in 1947 and in the same year the Commonwealth Relations Office (CRO) superseded the Dominions Office as an autonomous department. Its role was to advise ministers on all aspects of policy affecting other members of the Commonwealth, to co-ordinate the work of British government departments in so far as other Commonwealth governments were concerned, to arrange for consultation when necessary and to act as a channel for information.[10] Responsibility for dependent territories remained with the Colonial Office, which handled virtually all the major sets of negotiations for independence in the decades which followed. From 1962, the CRO and the Colonial Office had a single secretary of state. But by the mid-sixties, decolonisation had proceeded to a point where the Colonial Office could be absorbed into the CRO as a Dependent Territories Division. 'Aid' had already been administratively 'hived-off' to the Department of Technical Co-operation, which in 1964 became the Ministry of Overseas Development. Of greater importance for Commonwealth organisation, however, was the report of the (Plowden) Committee on Representational Services Overseas[11] whose recommendation for the eventual merger of the CRO and the Foreign Office (FO) was accepted by the British government. A unified diplomatic service was established in 1965 and in October 1968 the CRO was absorbed by the FO, which then became the Foreign and Commonwealth Office (FCO).[12] In Whitehall, Commonwealth work is now spread between the various departments of the FCO, and only a small unit (the Commonwealth Co-ordination Department) maintains liaison with the Commonwealth Secretariat and advises ministers on constitutional matters regarding dependent territories. There is no separate Minister for Commonwealth Affairs.

The drastic reorganisation of the Whitehall machinery serving the Commonwealth which was foreshadowed by the Plowden Report underlined the need for a distinctive Commonwealth agency. It would obviously be impossible for an amalgamated Foreign and Commonwealth Office to carry on the work of the CRO, and indeed the time was past when any British government department – even one charged only with this function – could usefully act as a 'Commonwealth' office or present an authentic 'Commonwealth' image. It could not be an effective clearing-house for information; still less could it generate or support any new, specifically Commonwealth activities without an inevitable British bias. Its personnel, however dedicated to the ideal of the Commonwealth, would be British nationals, and their prime loyalty would properly be due to the British government.[13]

By the mid-sixties, too, emphases had changed. Commonwealth defence was a thing of the past; Commonwealth preference was of dwindling importance with Britain seeking EEC membership; decolonisation was producing new members in increasing numbers. Ghana and Malaysia became independent in 1957, Nigeria in 1960; twelve more states joined the Commonwealth between 1962 and 1965 for a total of twenty-three in all, with the prospect of continuing expansion.[14] These new Commonwealth countries faced urgent problems of nation building and modernisation in circumstances of poverty, inadequate resources and a lack of trained personnel in all fields of endeavour. They were also anxious to shed any vestiges of subordinate status. For the Commonwealth to remain relevant to them it had to satisfy national pride as well as national need; to reinforce sovereignty and be seen to do so. For these reasons the time was ripe for new machinery in the form of a small secretariat, serving the whole of the Commonwealth, which would not only take over the functions which Whitehall had performed but also provide for its members a new range of services appropriate to the need of the times. The 1964 Prime Ministers' Meeting responded to proposals put forward by Ghana, Nigeria, Trinidad and Uganda and instructed officials to 'consider the best basis for establishing a Commonwealth Secretariat' which could perform these tasks, as well as serving as 'a visible symbol of the spirit of co-operation which animates the Commonwealth'.[15] Accordingly, a conference of senior Commonwealth officials, chaired by the British Cabinet Secretary met in London early in 1965 and its report went to the Prime Ministers' Meeting held in July of the same year. At that meeting (which was marked by lengthy and acrimonious discussions over Rhodesia), the decision was taken to establish the Secretariat, and Arnold Smith, a senior Canadian diplomat, was chosen as the first Commonwealth Secretary-General. For the first time in the history of the association, there was now a Commonwealth agency, staffed by Commonwealth servants and supported by all Commonwealth governments.[16]

LOCATION

Marlborough House, London, a royal palace which the Queen had made available for Commonwealth use since 1962, became the new Secretariat's main headquarters. The British government gave the Secretariat legal personality and inviolability of premises, archives and communications and has continued to pay for the maintenance of Marlborough House. While London was not necessarily the first choice of all members, some of whom would perhaps have liked to move the centre of the Commonwealth away from Britain in order to diminish Anglocentricity, it was obviously a sensible location. Historically, the Commonwealth was British and Britain is the one member which has enjoyed a special responsibility for the relationship with each of the others. Moreover, all Commonwealth governments maintain diplomatic representation in London at the High Commissioner (ambassadorial) level. The London base for the Secretariat has not precluded the holding of meetings in different Commonwealth countries – a practice which has become standard. The Secretariat has also encouraged the development of a regional focus for Commonwealth activities where appropriate. For instance regional health centres have been established in East and West Africa and in the Caribbean and Regional Heads of Government Meetings were held in Sydney in 1978, in New Delhi in 1980 and in Suva in 1982, attended by leaders of Asian and Pacific Commonwealth countries and the Secretary-General.

THE AGREED MEMORANDUM

An agreed memorandum, published separately, set out the basis on which the Secretariat was to be constituted and the scope of its activities.[17]

On the one hand, Britain wanted a limited role for the new bureau[18] and there was general concern that information about an individual member should not be circulated without its approval. India, too, opposed an active Secretariat, but Canada and the African members were disposed to see it play a purposeful role. Consensus was maintained by flexible directives. The Agreed Memorandum indicated that the 'organisation and functions of the Secretariat would support the essential character of the Commonwealth as an association which enables countries in different regions of the world ... to exchange opinions in a friendly, informal and intimate atmosphere' (para. 4); it would serve all Commonwealth governments collectively but would not 'arrogate to itself executive functions' (para. 6). At the same time, it was to play a constructive role expanding its staff and functions 'pragmatically, in the light of experience' and subject to governmental approval (para. 7).

RESOURCES

Financial

Each member agreed to make a financial contribution towards the cost of the Secretariat, and scales of contribution to the general fund (based on population and national income) were set out in the Agreed Memorandum. These have been adjusted as membership has increased and in 1966 the minimum rate for countries with a population with less than one million was reduced from 1.5 per cent to 0.75 per cent (now paid by twenty members). In 1980–81, Britain's share was 30 per cent, Canada's 17.81 per cent, Australia's 9.93 per cent, India's 3.26 per cent and New Zealand and sixteen others' 1.50 per cent. Over half the cost of the Secretariat is therefore met by the four remaining 'old' Commonwealth members. With the exception of India, which contributed 4.3 per cent in 1979–80, no other member contributes more than 1.5 per cent, while nineteen with less than one million people pay 0.75 per cent. Nauru and Tuvalu as special members each make a contribution of £1000 per annum, and St Vincent's contribution is £2250.

The general fund (regular budget) of the Secretariat has remained small. In 1966–67, its first full year of operation, it was just over £200 000; in 1974–75 it was just over £1 million. By 1980–81 it had grown to £3.25 million, but it must be remembered that the real value of increased financial resources which governments make available is significantly reduced by inflation and currency depreciation.[19] Three special programmes have their own budgets: the Commonwealth Fund for Technical Co-operation (CFTC), the Commonwealth Youth Programme (CYP), and the Commonwealth Science Council (CSC). Resources are pledged to the CFTC and CYP on a voluntary basis while members of the CSC are assessed for contribution on the same basis as for the general fund. All three budgets are administered by the Secretariat: the CFTC in its first year of operation (1971–72) expended £0.2 million; in 1974–75 £2.9 million; in 1980–81 its estimated expenditure was slightly down on the £9.5 million of 1979–80. The CYP budget in 1978–79 was £761 000 and it was also slightly down in 1980;

that of the CSC was £170000 in 1978–79 and in 1980–81 increased to £232740.

Annual budgets for the Secretariat's general fund and for the CSC are considered by a finance committee composed of Commonwealth high commissioners in London and a representative of the British government, and submitted to Commonwealth governments for their approval.

Personnel

The chief officer of the Secretariat is the Secretary-General who is appointed for five years by Commonwealth heads of government, to whom he has individual right of access. The Agreed Memorandum conferred on him a rank equal to that of a senior high commissioner (para. 33) but in practice he ranks higher. He is treated as an equal at Heads of Government Meetings and takes precedence at ministerial meetings. He is assisted by two deputy Secretaries-General and two assistant Secretaries-General. The deputies are appointed by Commonwealth governments acting through their representatives in London: one is responsible for political affairs and the other for economic affairs. The two assistant Secretaries-General have responsibility for social affairs and the Commonwealth Fund for Technical Co-operation. For these and other senior (diplomatic) posts governments are invited to nominate candidates but other applicants can also be considered. Nominations and applications are not restricted to civil servants. Appointments are usually for three to five-year terms and the appointees enjoy diplomatic privileges and immunities. The Secretary-General has authority to make these senior appointments, as well as junior appointments, although government clearance is required where a selected candidate was not nominated by government. There is no career service, but reappointment is possible. The objectives for all appointments are efficiency, integrity and a balance of representation from different parts of the Commonwealth. Staff are expected, in terms of the Agreed Memorandum to be 'strictly impartial in the discharge of their functions and to place loyalty to the Commonwealth as a whole above all other considerations' (para. 37). In 1966 the total staff of the Secretariat was forty-one, of whom eleven were senior diplomatic officers; at 31 March 1980 the number of established posts for the Secretariat, CFTC, CYP and CSC was 417, but staff strength was 352, of whom 53 held senior appointments. Approximately 40 per cent of the staff were women.

The problems faced by international bureaucracies are well-known:

competing national loyalties, sacrifice of merit to 'balance' in appointments and promotion; language difficulties; different bureaucratic
styles.[20] The Commonwealth Secretariat could not expect to be spared
these problems, but in many ways it has been able to minimise them. Its
relatively small size makes personal interaction easy and at the senior
level there is no question of making a lifetime career of the Secretariat.
The secondment principle has enabled very able staff to be recruited for
short periods of service at the end of which they return to their own
countries and their own careers. This allows the Commonwealth to take
precedence during their time at Marlborough House and reduces the
possible development of entrenched positions and of inter-office
jealousies and rivalries.[21] The need to bring staff to the Secretariat from
as many parts of the Commonwealth as possible was particularly
pressing in view of the preponderance of new states within the
association; there could be no question of the Secretariat being a CRO in
disguise. In fact a wide geographical representation of staff has been
maintained. At the time of writing the Secretary-General comes from
Guyana; Deputy and Assistant Secretaries-General from Bangladesh,
Britain, Canada and Nigeria; directors of divisions from Cyprus,
Ghana, India, Malaysia, New Zealand, Sierra Leone and Sri Lanka. The
Medical Adviser comes from Barbados, the Science Adviser from
Canada, and the recently-appointed Adviser on Women and Develop-
ment from Jamaica. In all, twenty-six nationalities are represented
among senior staff.

This mixture of nationalities blends more easily because of the
existence of English as a common working language. The fact that oral
and written communication difficulties are few is an inestimable
advantage not only to the Secretariat but also to the Commonwealth as
a whole, which thereby avoids most of the obstacles to effective
communication which two or more languages present within an
international organisation can cause. At formal meetings, however high
the standard of translation, and however 'simultaneous', there is an
inevitable loss of spontaneity and comprehension, and these difficulties
are compounded in written and oral communication within a bureaucracy. But the Secretariat benefits not only from a common working
language, but also from what may be called a common 'style'. Style is an
elusive quality, but it is one which most senior members of the
Secretariat tend to stress in personal interviews.[22] Commonwealth
'style' derives in the main from similar educational and administrative
traditions and experience; it is also a comparable way of looking at
problems, and a recognisable approach to dealing with them. It seems to

deal in common sense rather than political rhetoric, prefers informality to protocol and performance to theory. It is typically low-key, pragmatic and modest in scale – useful if uncharacteristic bureaucratic attributes. As practised by the Secretariat, Commonwealth style has also developed an emphasis on flexibility and innovation in direct response to need, particularly in areas of activity not covered by other agencies. These features of the Secretariat's work are discussed in more detail later in this chapter.

THE SECRETARY-GENERAL

In any discussion of the Commonwealth Secretariat the role of the Secretary-General merits special consideration. There has been much debate over the relative significance of different factors which determine the effectiveness of executive heads of international bureaux,[23] and useful categories for analysis focus upon the institutional framework, the resources which the Secretary-General (and Secretariat) can draw upon, the personal qualities of the Secretary-General and the character of the external environment in which the organisation must operate.[24] Efforts to ascribe weightings to one category or another are likely to be sterile, for each case will vary. Generally, however, it can be said that in all international agencies the scope for independent action by the chief executive officer is constrained within firm limits set by member governments.

The institutional setting in which the Commonwealth Secretary-General operates and the resources available to the Secretariat have already been described; points to emphasise are the flexibility of the Agreed Memorandum, the Secretary-General's right of access to all heads of government and encouragement to travel widely in the Commonwealth, and the newness of the office which meant that he could operate initially in a milieu unencumbered by bureaucratic precedent and *immobilisme*. This gave scope for creative definition of the office and for expanding the range of tasks and responsibilities which the Secretariat would be allowed to perform.

At the outset it was important that the Secretary-General should win the confidence of Commonwealth governments and not alarm them with indications that he sought to 'arrogate executive functions'. On the other hand, initiatives, if accepted, could lay the foundations for the development of his role. Personal qualities were crucial in this context. The first Secretary-General, elected from a list of six nominees for a five-year period and re-elected for a second term in 1970, successfully met these challenges. Arnold Smith, who had served as Canadian Ambassador to Egypt and Moscow and had considerable UN experience, brought to the Secretariat a firm belief in the value of international co-operation in general, and Commonwealth links in particular, as well as impressive diplomatic and entrepreneurial skills. He succeeded in winning the trust of the 'new' Commonwealth members without offending the 'old', particularly Britain, and skilfully developed precedents for the Secretary-General in the policy making sphere – for instance, in submitting his own nominations for senior appointments, in circulating new applications for membership to existing members (a function previously handled by Whitehall), and in making proposals at Heads of Government Meetings. It was, of course, necessary for him to ensure that he had the support of a number of governments for his proposals before showing his hand, but his initiatives, when accepted or unchallenged, set precedents for the office and raised its profile. It is a measure of his achievement that although the birth of the Commonwealth Secretariat coincided with a very difficult period, when the problems of Southern Africa, and particularly UDI in Rhodesia, threatened to tear the Commonwealth apart, the Secretariat weathered the storm and was soon firmly established as the indispensable core of the Commonwealth. The Commonwealth did not collapse at the different times African members threatened to leave. It is interesting to note that while political tumult raged, functional co-operation continued to develop: for instance, the Commonwealth Fund for Technical Co-operation was established by the 1971 Heads of Government Meeting in Singapore, which is better known for the furore over the British government's proposed sale of arms to South Africa.

In 1975 the appointment of Shridath Ramphal to succeed Arnold Smith as Secretary-General confirmed the confidence in the Secretariat and the office of the Secretary-General which had been built up over the preceding decade. Mr Ramphal had been Minister of Foreign Affairs and Justice in his native Guyana and had been deeply involved in Caribbean politics and in the non-aligned movement. He is a highly articulate spokesman for the Third World from which he comes, and while his diplomatic skills are unquestioned, his background as an active politician gave the Commonwealth office a new and higher profile, which would not have been acceptable to all member governments in 1965. Mr Ramphal, who was reappointed for a second five-year term at the Lusaka Heads of Government Meeting in 1979, has not only given a lead in articulating the needs of the less developed countries, but has played a very active diplomatic role at the summit level of Commonwealth relations; his contribution to a successful outcome of the negotiations for the settlement of the Rhodesian problem in 1979 first at the Lusaka Heads of Government Meeting and subsequently 'in the wings' at the Lancaster House Conference in London has been widely acknowledged.[26]

It is no exaggeration to say that the Secretary-General has become the personification of the Commonwealth at the level of high politics where there are some opportunities for the exercise of constructive leadership. It is also essential for the continuing vitality of functional co-operation that member governments should be chivvied and encouraged to participate in and support the many ventures in economic and social co-operation in which the Commonwealth is engaged and this, too, requires the personal commitment of the Secretary-General. Last but not least, his role in encouraging Commonwealth non-governmental links and in interpreting the association to the world at large should not be undervalued.

FUNCTIONS

In the Agreed Memorandum the functions of the Secretariat were categorised under the headings of 'International', 'economic' and 'general and administrative' and this threefold division was reflected in the Secretariat's original organisational structure. But the demands placed upon it and the expansion of its activities have meant a steady increase in the number of divisions and the addition of other specialised tasks. In 1975 a meeting of senior officials in Canberra endorsed priorities for restructuring the Secretariat, with emphasis on consolidation, economy and efficiency.[27] A further review of its structure and operations was undertaken in the light of discussion of the role of the Commonwealth in the 1980s by senior officials, and at the Heads of Government Meeting in Melbourne in October 1981. The following diagrammatic presentation of the current organisation of the Secretariat shows the allocation of responsibility at the senior level and indicates the wide range of activities in which the Secretary-General and his staff are involved.

Basically the Secretariat performs the following tasks:

(1) it services government and other Commonwealth meetings;
(2) it prepares and commissions papers and studies on questions of common concern for circulation to all members;

(3) it undertakes initiating and co-ordinating roles in fields of economic and social co-operation;

(4) it fulfils a liaison role between members;

(5) it can provide assistance for one or more members in situations where they are negotiating with non-member governments, other international agencies or non-governmental (transnational) actors, particularly multinational corporations;

(6) it can act as a representative of the Commonwealth in relations with other organisations and governments. Action is taken on the directive of Commonwealth governments or, with their approval, on the initiative of the Secretary-General.

A broad distinction is often drawn between the two levels at which the Commonwealth operates: the level of 'high politics' where it is mainly a forum for discussion and the level of 'low politics' or functional co-operation at which it has some of the attributes of a service agency. But consultative processes characterise both levels; some of the practical programmes sponsored and supported by Commonwealth members as a group have originated in and are associated with matters of high politics; and many co-operative links, particularly in the field of education, pre-date the Secretariat, have both governmental and non-governmental facets and were not designed specifically for members who are now classified as 'developing' rather than 'developed'. It is not satisfactory therefore, to draw a hard and fast line between these two levels. What is incontrovertible is that the Secretariat under the leadership of the Secretary-General is now centrally involved at all levels of Commonwealth consultation and co-operation. In the remainder of this chapter some account is given of the major activities in which the Commonwealth is engaged, with primary focus on the Secretariat's role. The division between international affairs (broadly 'high politics') and functional co-operation ('low politics') is used for convenience, but the qualifications noted above should be borne in mind. More detailed accounts of specific Commonwealth programmes are given in later chapters.

INTERNATIONAL AFFAIRS

The Commonwealth approach to matters of 'high politics' – which today include and frequently stress economic problems – emphasises consultation and the exchange of views. Concerted Commonwealth

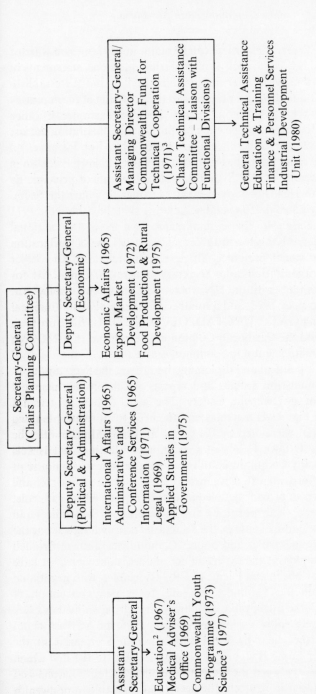

Secretary-General
(Chairs Planning Committee)

Assistant Secretary-General

Education[2] (1967)
Medical Adviser's
Office (1969)
Commonwealth Youth
Programme (1973)
Science[3] (1977)

**Deputy Secretary-General
(Political & Administration)**

International Affairs (1965)
Administrative and
Conference Services (1965)
Information (1971)
Legal (1969)
Applied Studies in
Government (1975)

**Deputy Secretary-General
(Economic)**

Economic Affairs (1965)
Export Market
Development (1972)
Food Production & Rural
Development (1975)

**Assistant Secretary-General/
Managing Director
Commonwealth Fund for
Technical Cooperation
(1971)[3]
(Chairs Technical Assistance
Committee – Liaison with
Functional Divisions)**

General Technical Assistance
Education & Training
Finance & Personnel Services
Industrial Development
Unit (1980)

NOTES

1. Dates of establishment of divisions in brackets.
2. The Commonwealth Education Liaison Unit (CELU) was absorbed by the Secretariat in 1967.
3. The Commonwealth Science Council (CSC) and Commonwealth Fund for Technical Cooperation (CFTC) were integrated more closely with the Secretariat in 1977.

(a) There has been a scientific adviser to the Secretary-General since 1965 who acted as secretary to the CSC.
(b) The Managing Director of the CFTC Became an Assistant Secretary-General in 1977.
4. Directors of divisions generally report to the Secretary-General through the relevant deputy or Assistant Secretary-General.
5. The British (Whitehall) system of administrative routine is used internally in the Secretariat.

action is rare. Nevertheless, there can be major policy issues on which a common stand is needed, such as membership questions, statements of principle, relations with other international bodies, and the establishment of new Commonwealth projects and the provision of the necessary resources for them. A few of many possible examples of such Commonwealth action may be cited for purposes of illustrating the key role of the Secretary-General and his senior staff. For instance, on membership, Arnold Smith has recorded his efforts to keep Pakistan in the Commonwealth in 1972,[28] and notable statements of principle by Commonwealth Heads of Government Meetings to which the Secretariat has contributed drafting and negotiating skills have been the 1971 Singapore Declaration, the commitment to a New International Economic Order at Kingston in 1975, and the 1979 Lusaka Declaration on racism and racial prejudice. In developing relations with other international organisations, the Secretary-General is responsible for maintaining contacts with the UN where the Commonwealth has had observer status since 1975, and a number of other global and regional bodies including GATT, UNCTAD, OECD, the OAU, the European Commission and the Caribbean Community Secretariat (CARICOM) whose membership is entirely 'Commonwealth'.

In support of political and diplomatic initiatives, the Secretariat can prepare or commission studies and reports which provide essential information for government leaders. The general lack of relevant information at high-level meetings and the need for forward-planning by the Secretariat was noted by the Canadian Prime Minister after he had hosted the Ottawa Heads of Government Meeting.[29] It is also obvious that many Commonwealth member governments do not have and cannot afford an extensive network of overseas missions and technical experts to provide detailed analytical reports which can assist them to prepare their positions for international conferences. In fulfilling this function, of course, the Secretariat is providing a service of particular value to smaller and poorer Commonwealth members. An important example was the expert advice and assistance which it gave the African, Caribbean and Pacific (ACP) 'associables' who negotiated as a group with the Yaoundé associates for a new convention of association with the European Community after Britain joined in 1973. The Lomé I agreement was signed in February 1975; the ACP associates were given further help by the Commonwealth Secretariat in the negotiations for Lomé II signed in November 1979. In the first place, through contacts between the Commonwealth Secretary-General and the ACP secretariat in Brussels, the Secretariat was able to prepare or provide technical studies for use in the negotiations.[30] Secondly, a Secretariat staff member, Dr S. K. Rao, was loaned to the ACP Secretariat during the actual negotiations, at Commonwealth Secretariat expense as regards salary, but with travel and other expenses met by UNDP. Informal contacts were maintained throughout the period and active co-operation has continued.

Through reports and studies the Secretariat can also contribute to efforts to ameliorate the serious economic and social ills which plague the world community. That the Secretary-General sees this as a high priority task is apparent from the most cursory reading of his official reports. In pursuit of this goal, in addition to servicing groups set up to prepare a series of studies commissioned by CHOGMs on the New International Economic Order (NIEO), on the Common Fund, and on accelerated industrial development, which have been the basis for new directions in Commonwealth activity as well as providing a resource for UN and other conferences, the Secretariat's Economic Affairs Division has prepared numerous papers, some of restricted circulation, which follow up these reports or provide additional information for member governments.[31]

Among policies and projects in the realm of international affairs in which the Commonwealth and the Secretariat have been centrally engaged, there is little question that the problems of Southern Africa have been dominant. Arnold Smith commented that the crisis over UDI in Rhodesia (now Zimbabwe) 'conditioned much of the first year of the Secretariat's existence'[32] and Rhodesian questions continued to dominate the agenda of all Heads of Government Meetings for the next fifteen years. Moreover the spillover effects of international sanctions against Rhodesia on neighbouring Commonwealth countries, particularly Zambia – and on Mozambique, a non-Commonwealth country, after it became independent in 1975 – produced Commonwealth studies and programmes of direct assistance.[33]

It was inevitable that as Britain's African colonies joined the Commonwealth as fully independent states they would press hard for the end of racial discrimination and for the introduction of majority rule in the white-ruled southern tip of the continent. It was also essential for Britain and the other 'old' Commonwealth countries to respond positively if the association were not to disintegrate. For the Secretary-General this meant a delicate role. On the one hand, he had to identify the new Secretariat positively with the aims of non-discrimination and majority rule which the Commonwealth espoused and, at the same time, he had to avoid a situation in which he was seen as the leader of a group in confrontation with Britain. The establishment of the Secretariat may have meant that Tanzania, for instance, could temporarily sever diplomatic relations with Britain and remain in the Commonwealth; it did not mean that the Secretariat itself could adopt or be seen as adopting an adversarial position towards Britain – or any Commonwealth government. Where common ground is limited, international organisations and those who serve them must seek to extend or enlarge it; they venture off it at their peril. Arnold Smith's task was particularly difficult, given Britain's constitutional responsibility for Rhodesia and British hesitancy concerning an executive role for the Secretariat. Mr Ramphal, ten years later, faced a situation which in some respects was worse: there was full-scale guerrilla war in Rhodesia and weariness in Britain and the US with ineffective sanctions. But his 'domestic' base – the Secretariat – was firmer, and the Commonwealth's role in striving for a negotiated settlement in Rhodesia had been legitimised. There can be no question of giving a detailed account of the fifteen years between UDI and the emergence of an independent Zimbabwe in this context, but one or two milestones can be noted to indicate the responsibilities assumed by the Secretariat.

UDI in 1965 brought British and Commonwealth 'voluntary' sanctions which were made mandatory by the UN Security Council just over a year later. The 1966 Commonwealth Prime Ministers' conference, called in Lagos specifically to discuss Rhodesia, was not a happy occasion. It did, however, set up a high level committee in London composed of high commissioners, a British minister and the Commonwealth Secretary-General to monitor the implementation of sanctions. At the 1966 meeting Commonwealth leaders also took practical steps to organise a programme of assistance and training for Rhodesian Africans.[34] A similar, though smaller-scale, programme for Namibians was set up in 1975. The Sanctions Committee, originally set up at Lagos, was given the power to recommend meetings of heads of government and to recommend further sanctions to governments who could then take them up at the UN Security Council. A link was subsequently established between this Committee and Commonwealth permanent representatives in New York. A subcommittee to aid Zambia was also set up. In 1977 reports of major evasions of oil sanctions led to the commissioning of a study subsequently published by the Secretariat.[35] In turn, this report, and others published by non-governmental organisations, persuaded the British government to set up its own Commission of Inquiry which produced the Bingham Report.[36] In 1977 the Sanctions Committee was renamed the Commonwealth Committee for Southern Africa and it now co-ordinates Commonwealth policy in regard to the whole area.

Mr Ramphal's significant contribution to the Lusaka Heads of Government Meeting in respect of Rhodesia, and to the ensuing Lancaster House Conference, has already been noted. In the tense period following the end of the Lancaster House Conference and the lifting of sanctions, when Rhodesia reverted temporarily to the status of a British colony, there was a continuing role for quiet diplomacy at the highest level and also for the maintenance of a Commonwealth 'presence', particularly through the despatch of a Commonwealth observer group to monitor the election process.

On the many occasions between 1965 and 1980 when matters hung in the balance, the existence of a Commonwealth bureau headed by a skilled diplomat gave substance to the assertion of a Commonwealth responsibility for Zimbabwe and restrained the British government from accepting a settlement with the Smith or Muzorewa regimes, which would not have received the approval of other Commonwealth governments or ended the guerrilla war.[37]

FUNCTIONAL CO-OPERATION

In promoting and sustaining practical co-operative links between members of the Commonwealth for their mutual benefit, the Secretariat is also performing an important role. It is responsible for securing governmental approval and financial support for the initiation, continuation and expansion of activities in health, education, scientific co-operation, technical co-operation and other fields, but it also manages some programmes, monitors their progress and maintains effective liaison between them. The identification of particular needs and of appropriate responses has been a notable feature of the Secretariat's work.

Perhaps the Commonwealth's most successful venture in the field of functional co-operation has been the Commonwealth Fund for Technical Co-operation (CFTC) through which members of the Commonwealth, and particularly the richer countries, Britain, Canada, Australia, New Zealand and Nigeria, voluntarily finance programmes of technical assistance and supply the experts needed to implement them.[38]

The CFTC has steadily expanded its efforts since its inception in 1971 and although there was, for the first time, a drop in the level of pledged support in 1979–80, the position improved in 1980–1 with pledges of increased contributions from a number of member countries including Australia, Canada and Nigeria. It is controlled by a board of representatives, on which all members are represented, which meets twice a year to review operations and agree on budgetary allocations. At the operational level, more detailed guidance is given by a committee of management, chaired by the Secretary-General. The chairman of the board is an ex-officio member of this committee. The managing director of the Fund, who is responsible for day-to-day operations, ranks as an Assistant Secretary-General and is responsible to the Secretary-General. There is close integration of the work of the CFTC with the general work of the Secretariat, and it funds the divisions responsible for export market development, food production and rural development, and studies in government.

The Fund's two major divisions are General Technical Assistance, and Education and Training. General Technical Assistance absorbs more than half of the CFTC's total programme budget, and in 1979 330 experts were assigned to sixty Commonwealth countries, regions and institutions. Their roles were advisory in most cases, and seen as an interim stage in the development of indigenous skills in the area to which they were assigned. Training is a component of all such appointments.

Education and training are relevant, of course, to all Commonwealth assistance to developing countries, and the Education and Training Division of the CFTC is at the core of these efforts. It provides resources for workshops and training courses, especially for middle level personnel (managers and technicians), organises academic exchange programmes and supports the special training programmes for Zimbabweans and Namibians already referred to in this chapter. It also supports training-oriented activities organised by Secretariat divisions concerned with health, education and law.

The CFTC has a 'resident' mobile Technical Assistance Group (TAG): a team of economists, lawyers, fiscal and tax specialists and statisticians, who are available at short notice for urgent short-term assignments. An area of special concern in recent years has been assistance to new Commonwealth governments in their handling of natural resources exploitation, particularly in negotiating with multi-national corporations and in devising the legal and financial framework which best safeguards national interests, but constitutional, economic, statistical and tax advice has also been sought from members of the TAG and a 'bank' of information is being built up in the Secretariat. The work of this Group illustrates the innovative approach which has characterised Secretariat initiatives; it has made available independent expertise on a wide range of important issues where and when it is most needed.[39]

In addition to the CFTC, the Secretariat has responsibility for co-operative programmes in education, health, science, youth matters and legal affairs. Since 1975 there have been new ventures in applied studies in government, food production and rural development, and industrial development, all of which now have divisions in the Secretariat. An Advisor on Women and Development was appointed to head a small unit in 1980. Resources are limited, but there have been no serious problems and no overblown bureaucracy bogged-down in inertia and red tape to reduce or vitiate the efficiency of the programmes. An example of the Secretariat's efforts to keep costs to a minimum and avoid unnecessary bureaucracy is the arrangement worked out by the Education and Training Division with a number of institutions in developing areas which themselves take responsibility for nomination of personnel to courses it supports. A glance at the list of meetings of all kinds at the end of the Secretary-General's 1979 report indicates the very wide scope of functional activity, and the different levels at which it is organised and encouraged: from workshops and seminars, to planning and project review meetings of experts and officials, to meetings at the senior official or ministerial level on a regular or *ad hoc* basis. A pattern of high-level meetings has been developed which is useful: ministers of education, health and law meet triennially; ministers of finance meet annually prior to the International Monetary Fund and World Bank meetings.

It is impossible to do justice to the work of the Secretariat in the limited compass of this chapter. Its major achievements have been to use limited material and human resources in an intelligent, economical manner for immediate practical effect with maximum 'forward spin'. Thus, experts are chosen for their knowledge of local conditions as well as for their theoretical skills, and they are expected to train local people so that the need for imported experts will then fall away. It is particularly useful if the trainee can subsequently train others. Similarly, small-scale workshops are preferred to large set-piece conferences, and, again, a carry-forward of findings and ideas to further sessions maintains momentum and minimises repetition and replication.

It is worth illustrating the distinctive and practical nature of Commonwealth ventures by a few examples. First, there has been recognition of the needs of very small states, mostly islands, which have been joining the Commonwealth in increasing numbers. The Secretary-

General noted in his 1979 report that nine members have populations under 200 000 and at least as many more are coming up to independence. There is a need for their stronger Commonwealth partners, and for the Secretariat, to make available to them special services such as assistance in international representation on a bilateral and collective Commonwealth basis, and in development research. The Heads of Governments meeting at Lusaka endorsed a plan worked out by the Secretariat in consultation with senior officials of Commonwealth countries for a new Industrial Development Unit within the CFTC which differs from larger agencies in that it will identify and formulate projects using complementary Commonwealth resources and assist governments to approach external sources of finance and technology. The unit became operational in February 1980 and is assembling a data-base as well as preparing pre-investment studies and appraising possibilities for joint industrial enterprises.

A second example is provided by recent efforts to improve rural technology. Following a rural technology meet held in Tanzania in September 1977, national appropriate technology committees were set up by seven Commonwealth countries to exchange information on the shortcomings of imported farm equipment and to publicise locally-produced designs. The minimum tillage workshop held in Nigeria in 1979 was a similar enterprise. Information sharing and the development of technology suited to local conditions may be 'small-scale' but this is no disadvantage. Quite the opposite – for it ensures relevance and can be of practical importance.

Examples of timely response to specific requests, can also be cited. In May 1979, for instance, the Secretariat was able to despatch a team of experts headed by Professor Dudley Seers of Sussex University, to survey Uganda's needs for economic reconstruction. The team completed its work in less than two months and its report was used as a basis for approaches to aid agencies. Early in 1980 the Secretariat also arranged for a Commonwealth team of eleven observers, fifty-five assistants and twenty support staff to observe the electoral process and elections throughout Rhodesia and subsequently mounted a five-week course in Salisbury to groom a cadre of diplomats for the new Zimbabwe government. 'Trainers' in this case, were senior diplomats from several Commonwealth countries. The course was organised by the Secretariat's Division for Applied Studies in Government and financed by the CFTC, with the government of Zimbabwe meeting local costs.

Appropriateness of scale, and cost effectiveness are hallmarks of

Commonwealth activity, as well as sharing knowledge and ideas and encouraging self-reliance and mutual help. Although the Commonwealth contribution is small in terms of human and financial resources and in relation to overall global needs, it is valuable in its own right and as a model whose 'ripple effect' cannot be easily measured and should not be underrated.

The Commonwealth Secretariat, like other secretariats striving for welfare-oriented goals, works with, through and on governments. Education of politicians, elites and publics is part of its task which must emphasise consciousness-raising and consensus-building in terms of overall problems and their specific dimensions, and particularly the abuse of human rights and economic and social ills of a regional and global nature which are on both Commonwealth and world agendas. The Commonwealth has no monopoly of problems or solutions but as the Secretary-General has emphasised in his official reports and in his many lucid and compelling speeches, it can contribute to human betterment and community-building.[39] It is an imaginative role for a former empire, which once existed primarily for the benefit of the metropolitan power, to serve on an egalitarian and non-exclusive basis, not only its members but the wider community beyond. There is of course, a danger that too much 'externalisation' could dilute what is distinctive about the Commonwealth so that it ceases to have an identity. There is also a danger that resources will not be forthcoming within the Commonwealth to sustain existing programmes. This would be a serious error of judgment on the part of the richer, developed members for whom the contributions they make to Commonwealth programmes are minuscule in monetary terms but immeasurable in symbolic value.

The Commonwealth is not likely to concern itself with security or defence issues, nor with integration in the sense of closer political union. It can, however, fulfil a variety of useful roles at some levels of high politics and many levels of low politics. For it to do this the Secretariat is indispensable. Its establishment in 1965 marked a new and distinctive phase in what James Cameron has called 'the curious, accidental quality of the Commonwealth'.[40] It has given new shape and cohesion to the association and provided an effective framework for political and economic activities which can draw multilateral support. Provided it is sustained by high quality staff and adequate resources and led by a Secretary-General who succeeds in retaining the confidence and respect of all its members, the Secretariat can strengthen Commonwealth links and continue to serve its members in a variety of practical ways.

NOTES AND REFERENCES

1. In my research on the Commonwealth I have benefited greatly from consultation with senior officials in the Commonwealth Secretariat who have been generous with time and information. In particular, the Secretary-General, Mr Ramphal, and his predecessor Professor Arnold Smith, provided enlightening comments on their office. Responsibility for the chapter, however, is entirely mine.
2. See particularly S. M. Schwebel, *The Secretary-General of the United Nations* (Cambridge, Mass.: Harvard University Press, 1952); Robert W. Cox, 'The Executive Head: an essay on leadership in international organization', *International Organization*, vol. 23, 2, Spring 1969, pp. 205–30; Mark W. Zacher, 'The Secretary-General: some comments on recent research', *International Organization*, vol. 23, 4, Autumn 1969, pp. 932–50; Robert W. Cox, Harold K. Jacobson, *et al.*, *The Anatomy of Influence: decision making in international organization* (New Haven, Conn.: Yale University Press, 1973); B. David Meyers, 'The OAU's Administrative Secretary-General', *International Organization*, vol. 30, 3, Summer 1976, pp. 509–20; Roger A. Rieber, 'Public Information and Political Leadership in International Organizations', *The Year Book of World Affairs*, vol. 30, 1976, pp. 42–68.
3. A notable exception was M. Margaret Ball, *The 'Open' Commonwealth* (Durham N.C.: Duke University Press, 1971). See, too, Hedley Bull, 'What is the Commonwealth?' *World Politics*, vol. 22, 4, July 1959, pp. 577–87, and Martin Wight, 'Is the Commonwealth a Non-Hobbesian Institution?', a paper given in 1959, published in the *Journal of Commonwealth and Comparative Politics*, vol. 16, 2, July 1978, pp. 119–35. Both authors noted the tendency to emphasise 'emotional commitment' rather than analysis in writing on the Commonwealth.
4. 'Is the Commonwealth a Non-Hobbesian Institution?', p. 123.
5. For the earlier history of Whitehall organisation see J. A. Cross, *Whitehall and the Commonwealth: British Departmental Organization for Commonwealth Relations, 1900–1966* (London: Routledge & Kegan Paul, 1967). Lord Garner, a former permanent under-secretary for Commonwealth Relations, has also written an informative study. See Joe Garner, *The Commonwealth Office, 1925–1968* (London: Heinemann, 1978).
6. Lord Normanbrook, 'Meetings of Commonwealth Prime Ministers', *Journal of the Parliaments of the Commonwealth*, 1964, p. 248. See, too, H. Harvey, *Consultation and Co-operation in the Commonwealth* (London: Oxford University Press, for the Royal Institute of International Affairs, 1952); J. D. B. Miller, 'Commonwealth Conferences 1945–1955' in the *Year Book of World Affairs*, vol. 10, 1956, pp. 144–69.
7. J. D. B. Miller notes 'autonomy' as characteristic of Prime Ministers' Meetings rather than the 'unity' stressed at Imperial Conferences. 'Commonwealth Conferences 1945–55', p. 159n.
8. These norms were fully set out in the Declaration of Commonwealth Principles issued after the Heads of Government Meeting in Singapore in 1971. See Appendix C.
9. See J. Garner, *The Commonwealth Office*, p. 266. A permanent bureau for

the Commonwealth was not a new idea and Australia had proposed a secretariat for Imperial Conferences but there was decisive opposition. See B. Vivekanandan, 'The Commonwealth Secretariat', *International Studies* (New Delhi), vol. 9, January 1969, pp. 301–31; Garner, pp. 7–8.

10. The CRO also had responsibility for the Federation of Rhodesia and Nyasaland until 1962 (when a separate Central African Office was set up for two years), Ireland which was not a foreign country in British law, and relations between Britain and the Australian states. See J. D. B. Miller, 'The CRO and Commonwealth Relations', *International Studies* (New Delhi), vol. 2, July 1960, pp. 45–6.

11. *Cmnd* 2276, 1964.

12. Lord Gore-Booth, permanent under-secretary at the FO from 1965–69, who was visiting Bolivia when the announcement of the amalgamation of the two offices was made in March 1968, records his 'complete surprise' at the news. But the surprise was over the timing: he notes that most official thinking had put this merger some four or five years later 'no one had predicted 1968', *With Great Truth and Respect* (London: Constable, 1974, pp. 386–7). See, too, Garner, *The Commonwealth Office*, p. 420.

13. With some candour, in rejecting the idea of a separate overseas Commonwealth service, the Plowden Report noted, *inter alia*, that such a body might tend to advocate the interests of Commonwealth countries and this 'would work to the detriment of Britain's trade requirements in which the promotion of purely British interests must take priority'. *Cmnd* 2276, p. 11.

14. Singapore broke away from Malaysia in 1965. Full details of Commonwealth membership are given in Appendix A.

15. See Arnold Smith with Clyde Sanger, *Stitches in Time: the Commonwealth in World Politics* (Don Mills, Ont.: General Publishing Co., 1981) pp. 4–5. See too Garner, *The Commonwealth Office*, p. 351.

16. Smith gives some details of the Canadian government's initial lack of enthusiasm for the idea of a Secretariat and also notes Australian misgivings (*Stitches in Time*, p. 8). Cross has suggested that there may have been particular dissatisfaction among the new members of the Commonwealth over the handling of the Rhodesian question and a desire to remove agenda control for future Prime Ministers Meetings from Britain. (*Whitehall and the Commonwealth*, pp. 83–4.) But note Garner's statement that the Secretariat idea was 'no less emphatically in British interests' (*The Commonwealth Office*, p. 351).

17. *Cmnd* 2713, July 1965. Garner notes that the Memorandum was effectively the officials' report. (*The Commonwealth Office*, p. 352).

18. This was the CRO line, supported by the FO, Treasury and Board of Trade. See Garner, ibid.

19. This budget figure is comparable with that of the Organisation of African Unity, although Meyers has noted that members of that body have a poor record of paying up. See 'The OAU's Administrative Secretary-General', p. 513. It also compares with the budget of the Latin American Economic System (SELA). Of interest, too, is the comment by 'A' that the 'Secretariats of the Central American Common Market and the Latin American Free Trade Area, financed by the participating countries, have simply been unable to marshal resources commensurate with their mandates'. 'Regional

Organization without Big-Power Participation', *International Journal*, vol. 30, 4, Autumn 1975, p. 770.

20. A study published by the Royal Institute of International Affairs, *The International Secretariat of the Future*, 1944, is still useful as a summary of these problems; it was prepared by a group of former League of Nations officials.

21. The comments of R. W. Cox on NATO are interesting in this connection. See 'The Executive Head: an essay on leadership in international organization', p. 215.

22. Arnold Smith's comments in 'Commonwealth of Nations after Twenty-Five Years of Change', *International Perspectives*, Nov/Dec 1975, p. 45, support this assessment.

23. See, particularly, Cox, 'The Executive Head: . . .'.

24. These categories are used by Meyers in his study of the Secretary-General of the OAU.

25. In his memoir of ten years as the first Secretary-General, Arnold Smith gives a first-hand account of these trials and tribulations and of some notable achievements. See Arnold Smith with C. Sanger, *Stitches in Time: the Commonwealth in World Politics*, particularly pp. 26–33.

26. See the editorial 'Comment' in *Commonwealth*, Feb/March 1980, pp. 1–2 and Mr Ramphal's modest references to his own role as a 'roving Secretary-General' in a speech to the Trilateral Commission in London on 25 March 1980 ('Beyond Trilateralism', issued by the Commonwealth Secretariat).

27. [Sixth] *Report of the Commonwealth Secretary-General*, 1977, p. 72.

28. [Fourth] *Report of the Commonwealth Secretary-General*, 1973, p. xviii. Smith also notes that Pakistan has shown interest in rejoining the Commonwealth on more than one occasion but has met with opposition from India. (*Stitch in Time*, p. 148).

29. Pierre E. Trudeau, 'The Commonwealth After Ottawa', *Round Table*, No. 253, January 1974, pp. 38–41.

30. The Secretariat itself produced studies of STABEX and the problems of the Least developed, Landlocked and Island Developing Countries in the context of the Lomé Convention. Other special studies, for instance on customs cooperation in the Lomé Convention and the processing of natural resources and the industrial development of ACP States, were commissioned through the CFTC and paid for out of its budget.

31. See for instance *Towards a New International Economic Order*, 1977; *The Commonwealth Fund*, 1978, *Co-operation for Accelerating Industrialisation*, 1978. Titles of restricted Secretariat papers are given in Appendix 1 of the [Seventh] *Report of the Commonwealth Secretary-General*, 1979. A full list of publications is issued by the Secretariat at regular intervals.

32. Annual [First] *Report of the Commonwealth Secretary-General*, 1966, p. 5.

33. For details see, *The Front Line States; the Burden of the Liberation Struggle* (London: Commonwealth Secretariat (no date)) and the Secretary-General's *Reports* for 1975, 1977 and 1979.

34. In 1979 the Commonwealth Secretary-General reported that more than 4000 Zimbabweans had been offered 'Study places, scholarships and employment opportunities as a result of . . . contributions from more than twenty-five Commonwealth countries'. [Seventh] *Report*, 1979, p. 26.

35. *Oil Sanctions against Rhodesia*, prepared by Martin Bailey and Bernard Rivers (London: Commonwealth Secretariat, July 1977).
36. T. H. Bingham and S. M. Gray, *Report on the Supply of Petroleum and Petroleum Products to Rhodesia* (London: HMSO (Foreign and Commonwealth Office), 1978).
37. These arguments are developed more fully in the writer's 'Strategies in Multilateral Diplomacy: the Commonwealth, Southern Africa, and the New International Economic Order', *International Journal*, vol. 35, 3, Spring 1980, pp. 329–56.
38. See Chapter 11 below.
39. Roger Rieber's discussion of the Annual Report of the UN Secretary-General as a tool of policy is interesting and relevant in this context. See 'Public Information and Political Leadership in International Organizations'.
40. 'The Club Britain no Longer Wields', *Manchester Guardian Weekly*, 5 August 1979.

3 Regionalism and the Commonwealth

A. E. THORNDIKE

With sixty or so actual or potential Commonwealth members encom-
passing a diversity of interests, it is hardly surprising that the widening
scope of Commenwealth multilateral diplomacy has resulted in regional
groups being formed for various purposes. The sheer growth in numbers
is one factor but another has been the reordering of priorities in this
'fraternal association'[1] as it became a framework for member states to
search for new and more equitable economic relationships and an end to
racialism. Groupings did not emerge, as was feared (and hoped?) by
some, based on distinctions between the 'old' and 'new' Commonwealth, but rather as a response to often very divergent needs and
pressures in different parts of the world.

These regional groups defy generalisation. They range from the
informal to the formal, their objectives from the vague to the specific.
Some are 'non-exclusive', involving alliances and agreements with other
non-Commonwealth states, wherein Commonwealth members often
form a readily identifiable, if not always cohesive, group. In contrast,
others are 'exclusive' to Commonwealth members. While the majority
are formal, some emerge in an *ad hoc* manner at the highest level of
Commonwealth consultation, that of Commonwealth Heads of
Government Meetings (CHOGMs). It was at the 1973 Ottawa
CHOGM that regionalism was first identified and encouraged. As
Commonwealth links deepened and matured, and thereby lessened the
risk of fragmentation, the tangible benefits of regional co-operation
were acknowledged. Regional health secretariats in West and East
Africa followed, and regional representatives of the Secretary-General
were appointed in the Caribbean and Pacific. This process, started by
Arnold Smith, was taken further and faster by his successor Shridath

Ramphal. A Guyanese political leader who for long had preached the cause of regionalism in the Commonwealth Caribbean, he had personally experienced the frustrations of its initial aspirations but also its positive results. His enthusiasm for regionalism bore fruit in the 1977 London CHOGM which 'attached particular value to processes of Commonwealth consultation at the regional level directed to enhancing co-operation on matters of Commonwealth interest and furthering Commonwealth objectives'. The Secretariat was encouraged to 'continue to provide every possible assistance in maximising the benefits of co-operation within and between regions'.[2]

Innovation soon followed with the establishment of Commonwealth Heads of Government Regional Meetings (CHOGRMs) in the Asia and Pacific region which have now been held in Sydney (1978), New Delhi (1980) and Suva (1982) with Port Moresby scheduled for 1984. Although mooted as a result of some restlessness by members of that region with the preoccupation of CHOGMs with African, and specifically Rhodesian, affairs, their success in 'a region as variegated as Asia and the Pacific held a real potential for advancing the cause of a wider harmony by fostering a policy of mutual co-operation in an outward-looking spirit'.[3] Although the main emphasis at the CHOGRMs has been on regional and functional co-operation, particularly for the benefit of the newly-emergent island mini-states of the Pacific, both international and regional political and economic trends have received considerable attention.

Since 1976 the Secretariat has promoted pan-Commonwealth activity through inter-regional links between exclusive groups by occasional meetings of Commonwealth regional organisations. Areas of activity have been identified where the Secretariat could assist the promotion of intra-regional and inter-regional co-operation. Thus any trends toward isolationism and disengagement which occasionally surfaced have been counterbalanced.

The regions are not based on geography, but rather upon the perceived interests and expectations of the participants. Indeed, some regional organisations such as the CHOGRMs straddle different continents, others link distant areas of a continent as with the 'special relationship' between Canada and the Commonwealth Caribbean, while some organisations such as the Caribbean Community (CARICOM) and the South Pacific Forum are geographically limited.

Generally speaking, those regional groups composed exclusively of Commonwealth members exhibit a commonality of outlook based upon a consciousness of a common cultural heritage. Reinforcing this is the considerable mesh of official and unofficial intra-Commonwealth agreements and conventions built up over time, very often on a regional basis, and a cobweb of personal links up to political leader level. However, the majority of Commonwealth groupings are not exclusive to Commonwealth members only, and general observations about the cohesiveness of Commonwealth members within them, their collective (or individual) influence and the existence or otherwise of caucusing and voting patterns are very much harder to make due to their rich diversity of origin, purpose and *modus operandi*. But the fact of exclusivity does not, and will not, guarantee greater success: the East African Community collapsed, whereas ASEAN has developed steadily.

None the less, all the groups bring benefits such as status and solidarity: they also represent at least a psychological means of security to many uncomfortably close to tension such as those in Southern Africa; or bordering a dominant neighbour as is Canada; or subject to territorial claims by another, such as Guyana on its boundary with Venezuela or Kenya in relation to Somalia. This is the essential backcloth to regional co-operation in more specific military, economic and political fields. They can be most usefully analysed through a distinction between the non-exclusive and the exclusive, in their formal and informal manifestations respectively.

NON-EXCLUSIVE FORMAL GROUPS

Not unexpectedly, these vary considerably in their degree of institutionalisation and specificity of concerns. There are military alliances such as NATO and ANZUS which constitute fundamental determinants of defence policy for the Commonwealth members concerned. The latter symbolised a reorientation by Australia and New Zealand towards the USA and away from Britain, which wanted to be a party to the treaty.[4] There are also those dealing with political and economic regional co-operation, namely the OAU, OAS and ASEAN. One of the oldest is the Colombo Plan for Co-operative Economic and Social Development of Asia and the Pacific of 1950. Its regional members, ranging from Afghanistan to Fiji and India, Australia and New Zealand to Vietnam, have benefited from an impressive array of development projects and training programmes. Its aim of socio-economic development of member countries through a co-operative effort involving both developed and less developed states, with full British, Canadian and US participation, has been resolutely pursued. As a result, the plan has not fallen victim to political difficulties.

The Organisation for African Unity (OAU) has involved African Commonwealth states from its inception. But the enthusiasm of Commonwealth leaders for the OAU has never matched that of the francophone members. Commonwealth regionalism, by contrast, suffered a blow with the break-up of the East African Community, and there has been little indication of a Commonwealth caucus either in voting or pressure-group terms compared to the francophone bloc within the OAU. Their support of the OAU's foundation was largely based on a belief that Africa needed to be united against colonialism, racialism and imperialist exploitation, and they have been at the forefront of the struggle against South Africa and its apartheid policies. On the other hand they have sometimes disagreed with more radical approaches to these problems in the UN and the OAU. They also dominate the debate on Namibia (as they did that on Rhodesia) to the point of virtually pillorying those states, such as Ivory Coast and fellow Commonwealth member Malawi, who have either advocated or practised an accommodation with the Pretoria regime. Commonwealth states have not seen the OAU as a mere pressure partner on Southern African issues but also as a medium through which beneficial and positive change could be promoted. Commonwealth leadership was asserted on another negative issue to considerable effect: that of the overthrow of Amin's regime in Uganda.

Of the Commonwealth members of the OAU, Nigeria and (to a lesser extent) Tanzania have played the most active roles. The sheer size and population of Nigeria, coupled with the value of its extensive petroleum assets, makes its involvement a natural one. Its influence is considerable, not only in the OAU and in specialised sub-regional agencies such as the West African Health Community, and the River Niger and Lake Chad Basin Commissions, but also in the influential Lagos-based Economic Community of West African States (ECOWAS), which is working towards a customs union, co-operation in economic activity and common agricultural, industrial and monetary systems involving sixteen states, including the four Commonwealth members in the region (The Gambia, Sierra Leone, Ghana and, of course, Nigeria). It has on more than one occasion attempted to use this to steer the OAU's attention to extra-continental political issues such as that of Palestine.

In the Americas, Commonwealth members are less prominent in terms of numbers but have, nevertheless, made a considerable impact on the Organisation of American States (OAS). While Canada never joined, virtually all Commonwealth Caribbean states have done so at independence for reasons of hemispheric solidarity and, to a lesser extent, economic benefit. The heavy predominance of Iberian nations and the pivotal position of the USA has limited their participation, although Barbados has for long hosted the headquarters of its Caribbean regional office. But the small Caribbean minority has been closely-knit and has effectively used the OAS in two different directions. One has been both to develop a sense of identity with their Latin American neighbours after 300 years of colonialism and to stress that, like themselves, they are Third World communities and should play a role in Third World fora commensurate with their importance. Another has been to generate support and a sense of hemispheric solidarity for those of their number facing territorial claims by neighbours, namely Guyana and Belize. Although both are independent, neither can join the OAS since its rules prevent participation by states faced with such a claim. The Belizean struggle was to enable it to achieve independence in the face of Guatemalan threats. Sustained effort by Belize's Commonwealth colleagues successfully led to all Hispanic states favouring the cause of the beleaguered territory and a very considerable dilution of support for Guatemala (admittedly for wider hemispheric reasons) by the USA. The Caribbean Commonwealth countries also supported the British view of the Falklands dispute within the OAS.

Unfortunately, these activities have not endeared them to many of their Latin American fellow members. Charges of 'bloc voting' and caucus activity are largely hypocritical but those of infectious radicalism and *sotto voce* racialist statements made by (white) Latin Americans to, and about (black) West Indians, have tended to act as a counterforce to the movement to make the OAS less of an instrument of US foreign policy and more of a reflection of common hemispheric Third World interests.[5]

In South-East Asia the context for regional grouping has been characterised as 'collective political defence'.[6] The Association of South-East Asian Nations (ASEAN) was established in 1967. Its membership coalesced slowly as political relations in the region developed. Thus the institutional arrangements were kept very simple, there being no central secretariat until 1973, although there had been small national secretariats since 1967. Not unnaturally, ASEAN tended to react to problems rather than take the initiative, but Razak of Malaysia, through astute diplomacy, fostered a proclamation by ASEAN of a 'Zone of Peace, Freedom and Neutrality' in the area in 1976. Although members' policies over specific issues, such as détente with China following the US lead, contradicted each other, the principle of a region closed as a cold war battleground was established.

The difficulty is that ASEAN remains specifically political in its intent but that cannot be admitted for fear that it will be seen as a mere replacement for the discredited SEATO. To mask itself therefore, a successful economic organisation has been built up to give coherence and legitimacy to the association. 'Dialogues' with Australia, New Zealand and Japan, talks with the EEC, and strong pressure from Lee Kuan Yew of Singapore for regional economic co-operation and a free trade area led to the first ASEAN Heads of Government conference in Bali. This resulted in The Treaty of Amity and Co-operation which replaced the 1967 charter. Economic co-operation was assured and procedures for the peaceful settlement of disputes were established. In line with this a second document, the Bali Concord, was signed, after considerable pressure from the two Commonwealth members. Restating the main principles of the Razak plan, it called for the settlement of intra-regional disputes (thus prompting the Philippines at last to drop their claims to Sabah) and the harmonisation of views and, if possible, action.

Although Singapore has been less than successful in persuading all of the members, especially Indonesia, of the benefits of a preferential trading area, Malaysia has, with Thailand, effectively pressurised others into adopting common policies in response to regional political crises, such as the condemnation of the Vietnamese intervention in Kampuchea in 1979. A measure of its success and prestige, not least because of its Commonwealth members, can be gauged by the reaction of the Vietnamese. From denouncing ASEAN during its 1977 Kuala Lumpur summit meeting as a regional military alliance, it mounted a considerable campaign to improve its relations with the association by 1979, acknowledged its efforts for peace and security in the region and responded to its demands to take steps to stem the flow of human misery from its shores.

Despite the varying degrees of Commonwealth member participation in these non-exclusive formal regional groupings, two general observations may be made. Firstly, there is a high propensity to leadership. Whether this is a function of British-inherited pragmatism, a greater exposure by English-speaking Third World leaders to the rough and tumble of international politics, or a reflection of personality, is difficult to discover. Such Commonwealth leaders as Kaunda (Zambia), Nyerere (Tanzania), Manley (Jamaica), Bishop (Grenada), Razak (Malaysia) and Lee Kuan Yew (Singapore) are very active in international fora despite, in some cases, the weakness of the economies they represent and their lack of military power. Moreover, Commonwealth members readily act as 'conduits of information' to other Commonwealth states not (or less) involved so that consultation, particularly at the highest levels, is widespread and constant.

NON-EXCLUSIVE INFORMAL GROUPS

Non-exclusive informal groups range from broad solidarity coalitions such as the African Caribbean Pacific (ACP) group which negotiated the Lomé Convention with the EEC, to alliances which occasionally emerge in response to a particular regional problem such as the 'front-line states' on Southern African issues. No generalisations can be made of the cohesiveness of Commonwealth members in such groups. Even in the Rhodesian case, while all agreed with the ultimate aim of majority rule, the unity of the front-line states reflected the deep divisions among the Zimbabweans themselves, leaving Mozambique ultimately to play the most important role of all. In contrast, not only did Commonwealth politicians such as Ramphal (Guyana) and Patterson (Jamaica) play crucial leadership roles in the long ACP-EEC negotiations but in doing so they united the Commonwealth members to such an extent that many Francophone states relied heavily on their English-speaking partners to look after their interests.

EXCLUSIVE FORMAL GROUPS

It is here where the greatest degree of institutionalisation is found, some having developed from Secretariat initiatives as with the regional health secretariats in Africa. The two major manifestations are the Caribbean Community (CARICOM) and the South Pacific Forum and their respective associated organisations. Both are nominally more orientated toward economic rather than political concerns, but in practice the distinction is blurred. As for the less institutionalised Caribbean-Canada grouping, this is characterised by a series of cumulative trade, financial and commercial agreements dating over a century. Finally, there is the biannual CHOGRM, the full effects of which are now emerging as being significant.

CARICOM is what remains of a series of experiments in closer union of the scattered territories of the region, the twelve members of which have a combined population of only 4.7 million and which are strung out in a belt of some 1500 miles. Repeated attempts since 1689 fell foul of pronounced feelings of insularity, traditions of separate 'particularist' administrations, sometimes intense personal jealousies at leadership level and individual trading links with the British metropole on which they were all individually dependent for their high-priced exports of sugar and later, bananas. To this should be added a deep-seated lack of identity and social cohesiveness due to a colour-class dichotomy, and considerable differences in constitutional advancement, economic structures and relative growth rates, resulting in a broad division between More Developed (MDC) and Less Developed (LDC).

Despite these divisive influences, an underlying subjective sense of a common heritage and destiny and a desire to give it some institutional form remain. As political unity had failed with the Federation of the West Indies, regional economic integration was the new aim. It began with an agreement between Antigua, Barbados and the then British Guiana, signed in December 1965. Paradoxically, it was largely due to the initiative of British Guiana's Prime Minister Burnham: his territory had not featured in any of the previous attempts at co-operation. The signatories traded very little with each other; nevertheless the agreement had at its base a free trade area for goods produced or processed by themselves. Not unexpectedly, it never became a functional reality but Burnham's continued exertions, not wholly unconnected with his attempt to gain regional approval after his installation as prime minister by Britain and the USA in preference to the Marxist Cheddi Jagan, ultimately led to a conference in Georgetown in 1967. Eleven states agreed to create the Caribbean Free Trade Area (CARIFTA), later joined by a suspicious Jamaica. Although intra-regional trade did not significantly increase nor was agreement reached on, *inter alia*, a regional air carrier, it provided, through its council of ministers, a method by which the MDCs could hammer out a common line to be taken in their negotiations with the EEC following Britain's application to join, and a means by which the dependent and associated state LDC members could be indirectly represented and their interests protected. An elaborate regional inter-governmental infrastructure was quickly but firmly established, including a Caribbean Development Bank with strong British, Canadian and US help, and capped by provisions for regular CARIFTA Heads of Government summit meetings.

Above all, there was a substantial secretariat based at Georgetown, Its expertise and pressure, and an appreciation by the various political elites of CARIFTA's success, led to moves for a more substantial organisation. The result was the Treaty of Chaguaramas in April 1973 and CARICOM. Besides continuing the former free trade provisions (with due safeguards for the LDCs), prominently featured were plans to co-ordinate economic policies, an equitable sharing of the benefits of trade expansion, the co-ordination of foreign policy and the furtherance of common services.

Optimism was still high at the summit meeting of CARICOM Heads of Government in December 1975 but the onslaught of high energy costs and world recession was already ravaging CARICOM. None thought it possible that the dark post-Federation days of political and economic fragmentation would return, but by 1978 this was starkly apparent. A rebirth of personal jealousies; severe balance of payments problems and internal instability in Jamaica and Guyana; a refusal by these two members to co-operate with oil-rich Trinidad to create a Caribbean bauxite refining industry; LDC demands for ever more preferential treatment: they all contributed to this situation. In 1979 was added the Grenada *coup* by the left-wing JEWEL movement, which served to exacerbate the increasingly deep-seated differences between radical and moderate members. No Heads of Government meeting and only a limited number of ministerial meetings have since taken place and intra-regional trade and co-operation has regressed in the face of newly-installed trade barriers.

There is but one element common to CARICOM and the South Pacific Forum: both are composed of islands. But there similarity ends since not only is the geographical area in the Pacific very much larger but the territories are, by and large, much poorer and smaller than their Caribbean counterparts. Whereas the latter are deprived relative to their nearest point of reference, the USA, many of the isolated atoll states such as Tuvalu (Ellice Islands) and Niue have, and will always have, little. They also have no history of co-operation or sense of common destiny.

The South Pacific Forum was established in 1971 as a reaction to the historic domination of Pacific affairs by the various metropolitan powers. The 1947 South Pacific Commission was essentially nothing more than a colonial club against communism to which the parallel South Pacific Conference, composed of all Pacific territories, was subservient. Frustration, and in particular anger against France and the US for their atomic testing practices and refusal to control fishing, led to demands for a more indigenous organisation with facilities for political debate. Strenuously resisted by France, all attempts to compromise failed until 1974 when, on New Zealand's insistence, the bodies merged. But this was too little, too late due to the emergence of a subregional organisation originally concerned with banana marketing and consisting exclusively of Commonwealth members led by New Zealand. When

Australia joined in 1971 the Forum was formally launched and, by the Apia Agreement, a secretariat established in Suva. From the start it was specifically political with the heads of government in regular meetings, although the economic dimension was planned to predominate. Accordingly, the South Pacific Bureau for Economic Co-operation (SPEC) was established by the Forum in 1973, based also in Suva. Australia and New Zealand contribute one-third each of the annual budget, which has enabled continued co-operation between the members on matters of trade, economic development, transport and tourism, with some success. With this behind it, the Forum came quickly to upstage the much larger Commission. A common Commonwealth link appears to have proved more durable and binding than mere regional proximity. As to its achievements, a little is a lot in the geographical circumstances of the Pacific. Criticisms have been a little unfairly levelled at it by some of the less developed members for concentrating upon the achievement of consensus to the exclusion of action, but the Forum and SPEC are only copying the well-tested Commonwealth convention of flexible consensus rather than collective decision involving voting and the divisive effect of majorities and minorities. In this way the long-term political interests and above all, unity, have been preserved in the South Pacific region.

The Commonwealth Caribbean features once again as a partner with Canada. Together constituting 'the First British Empire',[7] the original initiative was Canadian. Anxious for a recognised middle-power status, it saw in the Caribbean its own 'place in the sun', an economic trading system of its own and a political counterbalance to economic pressures from its US neighbour. Intermittently between the 1870s and 1919 union was proposed but repeated refusal by both planters and popular opinion (backed by the British) in the islands, and a marked racialist campaign pursued by the Canadian media, especially in the Maritime Provinces where settlements of West Indians already existed, led to the pursuit of trade expansion instead.

After the Second World War there was retrenchment and a greater reliance by Canada on its US markets. By the mid-1960s, however, the importance to the West Indians of the Canadian trading links had been considerably enhanced with the withdrawal of Britain from the Caribbean and the threat to preferences and guaranteed market access if Britain were to join the EEC. After much pressure, particularly by the Trinidadian Prime Minister, Eric Williams, the Canadian-Commonwealth Caribbean Conference opened in Canada in 1966. Little of consequence was actually achieved: certainly Canada refused to assume any protective role. Aid and migration quotas were increased and minor shipping and duty concessions made but that did not stop Burnham of Guyana proclaiming 'the birth of a new political bloc'.[8] Continued pressure on Canada led to a further series of negotiations during 1976–9 and even less was achieved. The terms of the eventual agreement stressed industrial co-operation and training programmes but there was a clear warning (aimed particularly at Jamaica and Guyana) that Canadian investment would not be encouraged if stability and 'acceptable' financial safeguards were not forthcoming. However, since the abandonment by Guyana of its socialist experiment and the electoral defeat of the radical Manley administration in Jamaica in 1980, Canadian involvement in their economies has substantially increased, perhaps betraying the not totally disinterested political attitude of Canada, if not a continuing neo-colonialist mentality.

EXCLUSIVE INFORMAL GROUPS

This last category encompasses the activities of Commonwealth states in international fora, notably the UN and its agencies and in the CHOGM itself. In the UN it has taken two forms, either the Commonwealth meeting as a whole or various members gathering to discuss a particular issue or series of related issues. In the early days of the UN the former was prominent, but the practice died out. However, following the establishment of the Secretariat, consultation expanded. Regional caucusing emerged, at first by the African members and Canada, particularly over Rhodesia and the question of mandatory sanctions. On the New International Economic Order, the whole Commonwealth has generally acted *en bloc* but this unity has faltered over the question of Namibia and sanctions against South Africa. Whereas it is normal for abstentions to substitute for positive or negative votes where these would particularly offend Commonwealth partners, the passions aroused by this issue will demand considerable diplomatic effort.[9]

Within the UN Specialised Agencies there has been a similar tradition of consultation, but between the Commonwealth members as a whole. Meetings take place either during conferences or beforehand. Others are less planned, such as consultations before Law of the Sea conferences. Since much of the talent and leadership in these particular conferences come from Commonwealth countries, Commonwealth initiatives are all the more significant. Whatever the form and timing of such consultation, on many occasions Commonwealth meetings within other fora appear in the daily bulletin of conferences together with meetings of other groups, thus adding to the sense of identity.

In the CHOGM, regional caucusing emerged in 1966 over Rhodesia. Although frowned upon and at least initially not accepted as a precedent, it did none the less serve to clarify views and eventually assist in their reconciliation.[10] It has surfaced again from time to time but cannot be regarded as a caucusing system. Rather, a group of leaders may take a lead on an issue to put pressure on a particular member, as occurred with Britain in Singapore over arms sales to the RSA and in Lusaka over Rhodesia.

What can be concluded? While in all the groupings it is ultimately the national interest of the individual participants that is served, it is observable that in non-exclusive groupings, the influence and cohesiveness of Commonwealth signatories depends almost entirely upon the type of grouping, its structure, membership, purposes and priorities. As for exclusive groupings, the fact that a common link exists does not prevent the participants from acting independently in the international political system. Consultation is always acceptable but co-operation reaches only to the point of political acceptability and no more, whatever the particular regional problems and needs. Like most other regional groupings none are on a path to greater political or economic integration. Above all it is the way in which the decisions are reached that demonstrates the Commonwealth connection and this is difficult to evaluate, although its effects are real.

NOTES AND REFERENCES

1. Characterised by Winston Churchill at the 1955 London CHOGM, quoted in N. Mansergh, *The Commonwealth Experience* (London: Oxford University Press, 1969), p. 349.
2. Communiqué of London CHOGM, June 1977, in *A Yearbook of the Commonwealth 1977* (London: HMSO, 1978), p. 44.
3. *Final Communiqué, Meeting of Commonwealth Heads of Government of the Asian and Pacific Region*, Sydney, Australia, 13–16 February 1978 (London: Commonwealth Secretariat, mimeo), p. 2.
4. *Hansard*, vol. 487, col. 388 (25 April 1951).
5. G. Connell-Smith, 'The Organisation of American States' in A. Shlaim (ed.), *International Organisations in World Politics Year Book, 1975* (London: Croom Helm, 1976), p. 219.
6. D. A. Wilson, 'Thailand, Laos and Cambodia', in W. Wilcox *et al.* (eds), *Asia and the International System* (Cambridge, Mass: Winthrop Publishers Inc., 1972), p. 196.

 7. Sir A. Zimmern, *The Third British Empire* (London: Oxford University Press, 1926), pp. 2–3.
 8. *Caribbean Monthly Bulletin* (Puerto Rico), vol. 3, no. 11 (September 1966), p. 4.
 9. Information from interviews with Commonwealth ambassadors to the United Nations, New York, 1976 and 1980.
10. [*Second*] *Report of the Commonwealth Secretary-General* (London: Commonwealth Secretariat, 1968), p. 16.

Part II
Functional Dimensions

4 The Commonwealth Youth Programme and Youth-oriented Activities

L. S. TRACHTENBERG

The Commonwealth Youth Programme (CYP) emerged after several years study, to be endorsed by the Commonwealth Heads of Government Meeting in Ottawa in August 1973.[1] The new Programme was envisaged as one of practical action and a number of easily-definable areas were chosen where it was felt the new programme could make an immediate impact, i.e. youth unemployment and national development. Almost ten years later, the Commonwealth Youth Programme remains a continuing concern but one which has undergone significant changes and, recently, a severe curtailment of its activities. It remains, however, an organisation which has high hopes for the future.

BACKGROUND

The history of official Commonwealth interest in youth goes back to the Heads of Government Meeting in Singapore at which a British discussion paper suggested the field of youth as an area for potential co-operation. The major areas proposed for study were

> the special problem of rural youth, the special problem of urban youth, young social offenders, leisure, the best means of enabling young people to be more involved in the development of their country, the administrative framework at national level which is

55

necessary for this involvement to become a reality, and the formation of creative inter-Commonwealth relations among young people through an extension of existing facilities for youth and young teacher exchanges, school travel tours and students' work schemes within the Commonwealth.

The paper received wide support at the meeting, and the Commonwealth Secretariat was directed to review the document in order to establish priorities for its efforts. The Secretariat chose the problems of out-of-school education and training for young people as its first priority in recognition of the urgent necessity to develop ideas and action in a field of great concern to both developing and developed countries. Youth 'problems' reflected a basic need among young people for increased opportunities and skills through which they could contribute to the improvement of their societies.

Having established its priorities, the Secretariat initiated several lines of action. Special studies were begun on the problems of youth training for development purposes, and reports were produced on vocational and social training of primary school leavers for both the African and Caribbean regions of the Commonwealth. At the request of some governments, the Secretariat began advisory work on youth training and also initiated an exchange scheme for short study visits between developing countries by specialists engaged in out-of-school education and training.

Prior to the Commonwealth youth ministers' meeting in 1973 the Secretariat organised five Commonwealth youth seminars. Each concentrated on a different group of developing countries in the Commonwealth. These meetings produced papers of some significance which suggested that youth problems, especially in the developing countries of the Commonwealth, rarely originated in factors intrinsic to young people. These problems result from developments and changes which are taking place in countries with predominantly youthful populations. Approximately 60 per cent of the total Commonwealth population are 'youths' defined as people between the ages of twelve and twenty-five. While the age range and characteristics denoting 'youth' may vary between and within countries over time, especially in societies undergoing rapid change, there are problems in adopting 'a variety of criteria for ascribing adult status to young people as this could lead to a schizophrenic self-image on the part of young people who, in one situation, might be expected to act as adults and in another might be treated as children'.[2]

Four themes emerged from these assorted studies which encompassed youth-oriented matters of wide and continuing concern. These were:

(1) education and training for young people and those involved with them;
(2) employment;
(3) constructive participation by youth in national development;
(4) the need for effective exchange of information.

The Commonwealth youth ministers meeting in Lusaka in January 1973 had before them proposals for a programme of six functional areas of Commonwealth co-operation on youth-oriented activities. Out of this the ministers created the Commonwealth Youth Programme.

The heart of the proposed new CYP were the six previously-noted project areas:

(1) The Commonwealth Youth Service Awards
(2) The Commonwealth Institute for Applied Research in Social and Economic Development (with particular reference to youth)
(3) The Commonwealth Study Fellowship Fund for Youth Personnel
(4) The Commonwealth Youth Affairs Information Service
(5) The Commonwealth Centre for Advanced Studies in Youth Work
(6) The Commonwealth Bursaries for Youth Personnel

The seventh part of the youth programme was its policy-making arm – the Commonwealth Youth Affairs Council. This was created to allow members to share in the policy-determination and control of the programme. Lastly, the ministers suggested the funding of a small, special staff to handle the programme at the Commonwealth Secretariat, which became the physical embodiment of the CYP. Funding for the new programme was to be based on bi-annual pledges during the meetings of the Commonwealth Youth Affairs Council. The Secretariat suggested, in 1973, that funding for the programme's first three years of operation be set at £1.2 million.

The developed countries' representatives also had a pressing interest in youth questions at a time when, in the late sixties and early seventies, young people and students had become a potent political force capable of tremendous violence and inflicting great damage on a government and its policies. Many of these young people were disenchanted drop-outs from the education and social areas and the feeling seemed to be that this energy and aggression had to find its outlets in a more constructive and socially-beneficial objective. Michael Manley expressed the fundamental goals of the programme when he stated that, 'youth must be regarded as the vanguard in the quest for orderly and stable change'.[3]

THE COMMONWEALTH YOUTH PROGRAMME TODAY

In the early 1980s, although bearing a marked resemblance to its original formulation and holding the same goals, the CYP is a very different organisation. Structural changes in the organisation have been a result of trial and error, as well as rationalisations due to increasing funding difficulties.

Of the six original projects, the Commonwealth Youth Service Awards Scheme was an attempt to recognise and reward efforts by young people engaged in worthwhile projects contributing towards national development. This programme ran reasonably well for its first three years, but eventually collapsed due to poor infrastructures on the national level. After several years of inactivity the CYP is soon to inaugurate the Youth Project Fund, which will provide seed money for potentially viable projects initiated by young people. Priority will be given to team efforts which create jobs for unemployed youth and meet specific community needs. The Commonwealth Institute for Applied Research in Social and Economic Development was never formally created although research of this nature has been carried out under the auspices of the CYP. It was felt that as resources were limited, the emphasis of the programme should go into training, leaving research for universities where, supposedly, resources and staff are available.

The Commonwealth Study Fellowship Fund and the Commonwealth Youth Affairs Information Service still exist, although in a slightly altered state. The Youth Study Fellowships promote short exchange visits by personnel in the youth and development fields. The information service of the programme is one of its most important arms, helping to disseminate information gathered through CYP's growing network of inter-governmental and inter-organisational connections. They also publish a quarterly news bulletin, as well as occasional papers, such as 'Training Courses in the Commonwealth', 'National Youth Co-ordinating Bodies in the Asian-Pacific and Caribbean Regions', and reports of the various meetings which take place every year.

By far the most important changes in the CYP over the last nine years have been in the Commonwealth Centre for Advanced Studies in Youth

Work, combined with the Commonwealth Bursaries for Youth Personnel Scheme, which have evolved into a comprehensive programme of training geared towards regional needs. The concept began in 1973, when Dr Kaunda donated a large piece of land to the CYP for a regional Commonwealth centre to be used as a part of the overall Advanced Studies in Youth Work programme. When the CYP was originally established, the prime movers behind it felt that the paramount need of governments in the youth field was for professional training of youth administrators and field workers who needed to obtain an understanding of the social and economic factors which give rise to the problems facing young people.

By 1974 there were three major regional centres offering a variety of training and skills as well as providing a focal point for Commonwealth interaction and a resource centre of personnel and services for governments. The African centre is in Lusaka (established in 1974), the Caribbean centre in Georgetown (1974), while the Asia-Pacific centre is in India (1975), and to meet the special needs of the South Pacific, a centre was established in 1978 in Fiji. Three of the centres are located on university campuses. The CYP has developed training programmes in youth work at the diploma level at each of the four centres. The diploma courses vary in length and content at each centre but there are common elements in each syllabus, such as sociology, psychology, development economics, social investigation and research, principles and practices of youth work, project and programme planning, and implementation and management skills. Students gain practical experience through a combination of class work and field work, with the latter lasting up to three months in some regions. Since 1975 over 600 graduates have recieved diplomas from these regional centres, and many can now be found in senior government positions responsible for youth affairs. Associated with each regional centre is a programme of bursaries, which allows the CYP to cover the cost of the student who is on the diploma course. These bursaries have taken over from the original Commonwealth bursaries for youth personnel.

Along the same lines, the CYP also runs correspondence courses through its Caribbean centre to cater for those unable to attend full-time courses, as well as training courses on a national level, run in conjunction with the host government. These national training courses focus on such areas as the effects of tourism on young people and questions of youth leadership. Increasingly, the centres are turning to short, intensive, skill-oriented courses, as they seem to provide the greatest advantages and are the most economical to operate.

The seventh element of the Commonwealth youth ministers' original formulation was a Commonwealth Youth Affairs Council which first met in New Delhi in March 1974. This body meets every two years and remains the primary policy-making body of the CYP, although now it has vital inputs from two other organs: the CYP committee of management and the regional advisory boards. The latter provide 'advice' on matters concerning the courses, budgets, research and evaluation for each region of the CYP, while the former oversees the general directions of the operation of the entire CYP. Membership of the management committee is made up of a rotating group of twelve representatives from governments participating in the programme.

The overall policy of the CYP is decided at its office in London, and is based on submissions from these biennial meetings, as well as on specific requests emanating from each region. The CYP, as a whole, is a relatively independent body within the framework of the Commonwealth Secretariat. The London base has had to face the most severe hardship of the entire programme, as funds began being diverted in the late 1970s to the regional centres as a result of increasing decentralisation. The move toward restructuring the programme was formalised in a meeting of the Commonwealth Youth Affairs Council in May 1980, and this led to substantial staff cuts in London, from a peak in 1978/79 of sixteen staff, to only six in 1982.

This decline in staff numbers relates to two serious problems that the CYP, like many organisations, began to encounter in the late 1970s. The first of these was that financial pledges were made once every two years to cover a two year period. Fluctuating exchange rates began to cut deeply into the actual monies available and shortfalls developed. Combined with this was the simple inability of many of the smaller and poorer states to meet their pledges. So, in 1979–80, the proposed budget of £800 000 had to be pruned to £754 000, while actual expenditure was halted at £680 000. It was at this point that the rationalisation and decentralisation of the programme began.

Future budget predictions are much improved and pledges for 1982–83 are expected to top £950 000. Nevertheless, while heads of government agreed in 1980 that the CYP should have £1 million per year available between 1980–82, the 1980–81 budget contributions reached only £750 000 while 1981–82 peaked at £840 000. The projected post–1982 improvement is due to 1985 having been named International Youth Year (IYY) by the United Nations, based on the themes of participation, development, and peace. It is the CYP objective to use this 'run up' to launch new programmes prior to 1985, thus putting pressure on Commonwealth members to keep their pledges generous and payable on time. As the IYY is a United Nations-sponsored programme, Commonwealth members may be more likely to want to play a role in CYP activities which help to promote this 'year of youth'. Certainly the 1982 pledges showed a slight increase and staff at the CYP office in London are predicting an improvement in staffing by the beginning of 1983. There are also plans to increase fundraising activities directed at NGOs and foundations, which it is hoped will increase expendable revenue over the coming years. It is clearly noted in a recent report by the Commonwealth Secretary-General that 'the CYP's resources have not kept pace with inflation. A stable income in real terms at the current level is the minimum necessary to achieve full benefits from the facilities provided by . . . the programme'.[4] One of the major benefits of the IYY to the CYP will be a further expansion in the network of inter-organisational relations. The CYP established a planning group on the IYY which first met in February 1982. It will liaise with the United Nations Advisory Committee (a part of the United Nations Centre for Social Development and Humanitarian Affairs) on the IYY, which itself contains three Commonwealth members (Jamaica, Nigeria and Sri Lanka), who in turn will attend CYP planning meetings on the IYY.

Informal relations between the CYP and governmental organisations vary, but include the OECD (which authorised in 1982 a new programme of work on the employment and unemployment of young people), ESCAP (which runs youth exchange programmes in the regions), the EEC (which has been investigating questions of work-sharing and training schemes for youth), and UNESCO (which established a special fund for youth in 1979). These informal relations, however, usually only involve exchanges of information and publications between the CYP and the IGO. Liaising between the CYP and the United Nations over the IYY is more the exception that the rule.

On the non-governmental level, there is wider scope for relations to develop and some fourteen NGOs particularly involved in youth-oriented activities have 'contacts' with the official Commonwealth. They include:

(1) *The Boys' Brigade* Founded in 1883. Current membership 270 000 in over sixty countries. Involved in information exchanges and programme coordination, especially with regard to the IYY.

(2) *Commonwealth Youth Exchange Council* Founded in 1970 as an

educational charity. A composite of 168 smaller British organisations. Primary objectives are to promote contact between young people in Britain and other Commonwealth countries. Over 1000 exchanges arranged between 1970 and 1980, and in 1982 a special programme entitled 'Project Young Zimbabwe' was launched to promote visits to Zimbabwe by youth development personnel from other Commonwealth Countries.

(3) *Duke of Edinburgh's Awards Scheme*   Launched as a pilot project in 1956, it was officially constituted in 1960, and again reorganised in 1969. The scheme is an attempt to encourage, 'the spirit of voluntary service; self-reliance and perseverence; and the pursuit of hobbies and other leisure activities'. It is active in over forty Commonwealth countries.

(4) *The Girl Guides Association*   Founded in 1909, it helps to coordinate the activities of the Girl Guides in Commonwealth countries. It holds a conference every three years of national Guide leaders of Commonwealth countries.

(5) *Commonwealth Games Federation*   53 national associations make up the Federation, regardless of whether they are states, dependencies, or associated states. The Federation is the main body promoting the four-yearly Commonwealth Games, as well as establishing the rules of conduct and generally encouraging amateur sports throughout the Commonwealth.[5]

Other non-governmental organisations with links with the Commonwealth include COMEX (Commonwealth Expedition), the Girls Brigade International Council, Scouts Association, the International Red Cross (UK), the YMCA/YWCA, Mobility International, and the International Planned Parenthood Federation. There are also hundreds of national and regional organisations which have relations with the Commonwealth and the CYP.

CONCLUSIONS

The CYP, regrettably, is a good example of an IGO whose survival is based on the political and economic realities of its membership. In a CYP news letter article for March 1980, it is noted that

unemployment ... has continued to ravage Commonwealth countries. It has proved deleterious and demeaning, particularly among the
young people of the Commonwealth who constitute the majority of
all unemployed. The ill effects of such conditions can only be
detrimental to young people themselves, their countries and the
international community.[6]

Ironically, the article failed to note that it is these same problems that
prevent the CYP from extending its activities: Commonwealth members, primarily developing countries, are increasingly hard-pressed to
find funds for the purchase of basic necessities, let alone fund
programmes such as CYP. Under these conditions, CYP becomes a
luxury whose activities have to be dispensed with for the sake of other,
more pressing problems within each state. But it is clear that even
operating under a budget smaller than that envisaged by those who
created it, the CYP can be judged to have provided a practical and
valuable contribution in terms of the service rendered.

The CYP, like most youth-oriented activities, does not only benefit
youth. Two meetings sponsored by the CYP of young Commonwealth
leaders, were held in Ocho Rios (Jamaica) in 1977, and Colombo (Sri
Lanka) in 1979, to bring together *young* Commonwealth leaders from all
walks of life to discuss problems of mutual interest and to talk about
strategies for these problems on national, regional, and global levels.
Ironically the majority of the conferees were government ministers and
members of their respective national legislatures. After 1979, no plans
were made for future meetings of this type, as it was implicitly felt that
the basic principles underlying the idea of the meetings had not been
realised and future meetings would be a waste of CYP's limited funds.

One particularly positive aspect of the change the CYP has undergone
is a trend toward regionalism within the framework of the Commonwealth. As the organisation grows in size and complexity, this
regional focus will become increasingly important to the smooth
functioning of Commonwealth activities and it mirrors a trend within
the Commonwealth as a whole.

NOTES AND REFERENCES

1. Special thanks go to Ms J. Morritt of the Commonwealth Youth Programme, without whose help this chapter could not have been written. As

there are no known secondary sources on the CYP, the information provided here comes from the publications of and discussions with officials of the Commonwealth Secretariat.

2. *Commonwealth Youth Ministers' Meeting, Lusaka 1973: Report of the Proceedings* (London 1973), vol. 1, p. 75.

3. Michael Manley, 'Popular Participation' in *Report of the Ocho Rios Meeting of Young Commonwealth Leaders*, Ocho Rios, Jamaica, 4–9 May 1977 (London: Commonwealth Secretariat, 1977), p. 26.

4. [*Eighth*] *Report to Heads of Government by the Commonwealth Secretary-General, April 1979–June 1981* (London: Commonwealth Secretariat, 1981), p. 57.

5. The Commonwealth Secretariat has no practical responsibility for the running of the Commonwealth Games, a role left to the Commonwealth Games Federation. The Secretariat does have a role however, when politics enter into the Games. This consists of information dissemination and quiet diplomacy by the Secretary-General if the situation becomes especially difficult. The Games are increasingly being used for political purposes by the membership, as is sport in general in international relations.

6. Commonwealth Youth Programme News Service, no. 13, March 1980, (London), p. 2.

5 Education

RUTH BUTTERWORTH

INTRODUCTION

The two characteristics of education germane to this study are that it is a personal service and an international commodity. As Empire merged into Commonwealth the personal service aspect of education with its accompanying patron-client relationships declined in importance as an influence relative to the world commodity market aspects of education transactions. In both substance and theory the contemporary Commonwealth attempts to incorporate both. An evaluation of education as a function in the contemporary Commonwealth must begin with the old model and attempt to trace its modifications.

In the Empire and dominions patron-client relationships in education operated at both institutional and personal levels. Education, whether defined as structure, system or process, bears a heavy burden of inheritance, the carriers of which are individuals. The context of any given educational procedure may ostensibly be contained in texts, syllabus and curriculum; the individual input may be distanced from the consumer by the interposition of impersonal communication technology; nevertheless, within any set of environmental constraints, the determinants of structure, system and content lie in the effective relationships of individuals who translate prior experience, perception and prejudice into policy and practice.

The assumption that the Commonwealth's educational inheritance was a direct bequest from the imperial power to the colony meant that variations simply reflected the finances and personnel available in any particular colony. Variations also arose from historico-economic changes within the education system of the imperial power and the coexistence in Britain of the distinctive English and Scottish systems. This view derives from a centre-margin model of empire and the direction of education flows between Britain and the colonies and dominions in the brief heyday of imperialism lends credence to this model. So too does much of the contemporary writing on education for the colonies, both official and advisory, which emphasises the public school ideology of character training, elitism and top-down development. The model does some violence, however, to other factors involved in the quite substantial inter- and intra-continental population movements throughout the era of both Empire and Commonwealth. Moreover, in the twentieth century eager consumers sought education throughout an expanding and diversifying market beyond the bounds of Empire or Commonwealth. There was not one patron but several.

Exchanges around the margin and even outside it had some direct contemporary effects on education. They brought a context of ideas about forms in education and, through personal and institutional contacts, provided a variety of alternative routes through the education world. The earliest colonial educators, the missions, spread beyond the Empire and dominions to include the United States and continental Europe. However, in quantitative terms, exchanges of educators and students around the margin remained insignificant and were in part orchestrated at the metropole.

The North American and Scottish education traditions remained dormant within Empire and Commonwealth until after the Second World War despite the circulation of individual educators and students and despite the fact that systems in the dominions owed as much, if not more, to Scotland and the United States as to England. Yet at some point between 1930 and 1950 in each different region of the Empire education demand came grossly to exceed education supply. Imperial preference and protectionism nevertheless operated to limit effective choice. The reasons must be sought if the current position of education exchange in the contemporary Commonwealth is to be understood.

In the first place, various species of colonial deference infected settlers in the old dominions as well as the colonised peoples of the Empire. An Oxbridge finish for the sons of the Antipodean squattocracy in one direction was balanced by importing sometimes distinctly inferior Oxbridge staff for new universities in the other. In the African colonies the labour market for the educated was dominated by government services; planning for and expenditure on education was limited by narrow projections of demand and both were influenced by the experience of widespread unemployment among the highly educated in India. The connection between occupational opportunities, job status and salary scales, on the one hand, and degree qualifications as laid down in Britain, on the other, served meanwhile to defeat Colonial Office and early African attempts to follow reports such as those from the American Phelps-Stokes Foundation missions of 1920–22.

The Phelps-Stokes missions produced the earliest overall surveys of African education. Composed mainly of American and British missionaries and experts in industrial and agricultural education, the missions' influences were largely Deweyite. Their reference points were the philosophy of the land grant colleges and the work of Booker T. Washington whose methods of practical rural education for American negroes were eulogised. The reports reveal the extent to which literary studies dominated at the expense of industrial and vocational education. They urged that mass education and training of teachers be given priority over the elitist approach of higher education for the few, which British policy provided.

The claims of the colonised for access to the commanding heights of the coloniser's education system was not some psychological adjunct of the colonial condition. It was the product of economic relationships in a period marked by bureaucratisation, emerging specialism and professional protectionism. These trends accelerated markedly as Empire gave way to Commonwealth after 1945. Universities diversified in form and, to an extent, broadened their catchment area for staff and students. But the signposts on the routes to graduate and professional qualifications were made in Britain and import-substitution in the education industry was scarcely begun when the new Commonwealth was established as an entity separate from the British government. Independence removed the artificial depression of demand and removed imperial limitations on variety. At the same time shortages increased and were supplied from non-Commonwealth as well as Commonwealth sources. The routes and sources of supply depended initially upon personal and regional contacts, but were increasingly influenced by ideological cleavage and competition.

The contemporary Commonwealth has assisted with the transformation of the education market through multilateral exchanges within and across geographical regions. Appropriate training is being substituted for single (British practice) standards, with the loss in equivalence minimised by inter-Commonwealth co-operation, facilitated by the Secretariat, between an increasing number of professional associations and non-governmental organisations. The rates of elite exchange have been maintained despite, or perhaps because of, competition from international and non-Commonwealth regional groupings. But does this reflect rather a world phenomenon than a Commonwealth development?

THE INHERITANCE

In the old Commonwealth and Empire modern education systems developed over very different time scales. ·Equally large were the differences in economic resources and environments. Political arrangements, physical distance and economic circumstance dictated differences in the intensity and variety of educational exchange. Nevertheless, it is possible to make some cautious generalisations which may provide a frame within which to assess the adaptations of the last twenty years.

Everywhere in the Commonwealth there developed a mixed economy in education: a partnership, often uneasy, between government and missions, state and church, with a parallel unlicensed education 'streetmarket', often the larger part, inhabited by the entrepreneurs of cram and correspondence. Early dominion as well as colonial education followed the English public examinations. With rare exceptions professional training was established under British rules and with syllabuses laid down in England. The unifying factors throughout Empire and old Commonwealth were provided by the linkages between government service, occupational opportunity, qualification by examination and, above all, by the English language.

English was not, however, the exclusive preserve of the British Empire and dominions. Nor did British examinations preclude entry to non-Commonwealth educational opportunities. Inadequacy of provision throughout the first half of the twentieth century, together with Britain's post-war decision to increase university entrance requirements, directed the attention of Asian and African students towards the United States. The United States offered opportunities and support available only to a selected few in Britain. Since 1918 the British education scene had itself been characterised by increasing levels of Anglo-US elite exchange and co-operation. After 1945 a 'brain drain' from Britain to North America, Australia and New Zealand was evident. An independent and non-aligned India offered education opportunities in the fifties to African students and subsequently became a conduit for new Commonwealth students to Soviet or United States' institutions. The wealthy and the fortunate among the meritorious would still arrive in Britain, but other avenues were opened up by cold war competition.

The inheritance of the contemporary Commonwealth is, then, largely Western and predominantly English in terms of systems and content, characterised by high levels of elite exchange among European sectors, and patron-client relationships centralised on Britain in the African and, to a lesser extent, Caribbean sectors. The Asian sector was already largely self-sufficient, exchanging predominantly at specialist level and dispensing patronage and services outside on its own behalf. The critical mass of graduate, administrative and diplomatic talent in India during the fifties assisted an implosion within the education and assistance agencies of the United Nations which carried new influences into Commonwealth systems in addition to those of cold war competition.

Nevertheless, Cambridge Local and University of London examining boards continued to exercise an influence on post-primary education in the nineteen-sixties and seventies. In the small island states of the Pacific and Caribbean as well as in East and West Africa, Soviet, Scandinavian and US assistants alike taught to the syllabuses developed in Cambridge and London.

INTER-COMMONWEALTH TRANSACTIONS

When the contemporary Commonwealth came into existence, member states had already somewhat diversified their education systems, adapting a variety of models and relying for advice, material support and personnel largely, but by no means exclusively, on Britain. The vast majority of educational transactions, including those between Commonwealth and non-Commonwealth systems, were still, however, conducted from Britain or through British associations and intermediaries. The new Secretariat inherited a raft of associations, bureaux, councils and commissions. A number of these had passed through a confusion of name changes and now faced further crises of identity, resources and direction as Britain moved towards membership of the European Communities.

In association with the Education Division of the Secretariat, five official bodies are concerned wholly or in part with education and training: the Scholarship and Fellowship Plan, the Science Council, the Telecommunications Bureau, the Commonwealth Fund for Technical Co-operation (CFTC) and the Commonwealth Foundation. Under the aegis of these bodies, a variety of educational supports and exchanges have developed involving regional as well as Commonwealth-wide action by or in co-operation with a growing number of unofficial associations. These, in their turn, have both regional and international offshoots and correspondencies not necessarily confined to Commonwealth member states.

The organisations and their educational transactions may be classified in a number of ways. On the organisational side, there are innovative creations such as the Commonwealth Foundation and adaptive bodies such as the CFTC. Educational transactions fall into a number of overlapping categories. They might be classified as programmatic, periodic, developmental or co-operative. Common to both organisational and transactional activity are the characteristics of shoestring budgeting, vulnerability of initiatives to scarcity of appropriate skills and information in participating states, and the attempt to overcome these disadvantages by use of various 'piggyback' devices. The work of the Commonwealth Foundation, the CFTC and the Education Division of the Secretariat illustrates trends in educational exchange in the Commonwealth.

The Commonwealth Foundation

The Commonwealth Foundation's activities have been specifically directed to the reduction of centralisation on Britain by assisting the development of professional associations in countries where professional growth is of recent origin and by supporting increased rates of interchange between associations on a regional as well as a Commonwealth scale. It operates through grants to widen attendance at conferences of professional bodies within the Commonwealth and to increase Commonwealth presence at international conferences. It has also promoted multidisciplinary professional centres in developing countries within the Commonwealth which enable associations with low income to share resources and to build up the strength to increase participation in regional activities.

New developments and demands have resulted in the extension of the foundation's mandate to include assistance to individuals and associations in the areas of culture, information, social welfare and rural development. Its 'Occasional Papers' series, reports of seminars or special reports by individuals, indicate the range of concerns running, for example, from *Social Work Training Needs in East Africa* through *Medical Education in Papua New Guinea* to *Communications and University Teaching with particular reference to the Caribbean.* From the original Commonwealth medical, veterinary, architects and surveyors associations, the Commonwealth Foundation now includes within its purview pharmacists, geographers, librarians, engineers and numerous others. It may be characterised as developmental in focus, and elite exchange in approach.

The great majority of the Commonwealth associations are still based in London due to London's continuing dominance as a centre of communications. The financial support from the Commonwealth Foundation for study visits, seminars and conferences has, however, modified the centralisation on Britain by distributing opportunities for interchange through a developing network. This has involved an equalisation in the flow of information and discussion so that not only problems but also solutions in development are exchanged.

The 'piggyback' concept has been applied in two ways. In terms of development there has been the assistance given by stronger associations to new and smaller national branches on a regional and Commonwealth basis. In a more political context, assistance to poorer associations to attend regional and international non-Commonwealth gatherings has enabled Commonwealth associations and representatives to hold conferences consecutively with those of bodies such as the World Health Organisation. A species of Commonwealth caucus is thereby developing which on specific issues, if not on high policy, may transcend North-South conflicts of interest. The maintenance of systems of elite contact between countries and in and between regions may at the political level assist compromise and adaptation, given that the exchanges are between states of widely differing ideological orientation. Foundation activity meanwhile has certainly assisted the shift in emphasis among professionals away from the single-standard towards more appropriate and multi-faceted assessments. Essentially, however, the process depends upon internal developments and may indeed be inhibited by student exchanges where the balance remains with the North.

Commonwealth Fund for Technical Co-operation

The shift from top-down and single standard has been central to the education and training activities of the CFTC. Whilst the education and training programme has been used to support professional associations which come under the umbrella of the Commonwealth Foundation, the CFTC operates in general at sub-professional and technical levels and its activities are most extensively deployed in African countries which form the poorest and least developed part of the Commonwealth. Its role is that of matchmaker, slotting trainees from one country into courses available in others.

The capacity of Commonwealth organisations such as the CFTC and the Foundation to respond to members' requests in a period of financial stringency is a function of contiguity of the central clearing-houses and the capacity for informal co-operation 'across the corridor'. The mix of official and non-governmental funding provides a flexibility which encourages innovation and cost-effective operations in the field. As the Commonwealth Foundation makes one airline fare serve two purposes, so the CFTC encourages its technical assistance experts to contribute to training programmes in the country of their posting and to recommend and serve as selection conduits for nationals in search of training assistance from outside their own country. Useful, positive, on balance appropriate – the CFTC's report card might please any parent; but an interim assessment must pay attention to the similarity between this and a dozen voluntary agencies and to the small-scale and narrow geographic range of operations compared with international agencies in the same field.

The Education Division

A comparison of CFTC and Foundation operations with those of the Education Division of the Secretariat is instructive in a number of ways. The CFTC and Foundation have distinctive clienteles and identities. They collect and disseminate information and act as facilitators in the effective transfer of personnel. Many of their clients come to them on referral through the Education Division. In official reports of member states, however, the latter seldom figures.

The Education Division grew out of the Commonwealth Education Liaison Unit. The unit had been established under the Commonwealth Education Liaison Committee (CELC), a steering Committee which had operated in London at high commission level since 1959. In the new Commonwealth organisation the CELC itself survived as a 'forum for the consideration of matters of principle arising out of recommendations of Commonwealth education conferences and other topics referred to it by the Secretariat'. The division's most public activity, as with its predecessor, is the organisation of the triennial education conferences and a variety of regional and Commonwealth specialist conferences. It has, in addition, a multifarious set of concerns, as wide as the concerns of education and training for anything everywhere in the world. Seminars, conferences and training courses tend to generate demands for continuing concern by way of research, collation and dissemination. But demands and directives are seldom matched by financial commitments.

The Education Division operates as clearing-house for information and individuals; its 'brokerage' function is exercised between member states and international agencies, and between projects and appropriate funds. It may be seen as a Commonwealth introduction service and as a provider of 'in-fill' for weaker countries with low levels of national resource in skills. Its conferences, seminars and workshops aim at practical results in specific areas and financial constraints concentrate the official mind on the search for multiplier effects.

There is some multiplier effect in conferences, albeit diffuse and unquantifiable, through maintenance of contacts between professionals and the facilitation of the informal dissemination of experience not otherwise easily available. Project evaluation is in short supply, not only because there is a shortage of people with skills for the work, but also because it is politically highly sensitive. Informal contact between practitioners plays some substitute role in this regard. There is, however, ultimately no substitute for evaluation research and the absence of this as an established function of the Education Division reduces the impact of Commonwealth activities.

Commonwealth sources of exchange and assistance are undoubtedly valued and valuable, practical and relatively low cost. The Education Division, however, has so far failed to establish a distinctive presence or contribution for the Commonwealth among a multitude of agencies. Relying as it does on member governments for the dissemination of its communications, it has tended to be merely a file entry, particularly in the larger and more developed education systems. Liaison desks in the education departments of member states are seldom single function, the Commonwealth being linked to international and regional organisations as one among many forms of association.

THE EDUCATION MARKET

Education in the Commonwealth context is both a national and an international commodity and is subject to intense competition. Within the market, Commonwealth organs are variously and simultaneously producer, distributor, banker, contractor and wholesaler. Member states of the Commonwealth may, by the same token, be variously sub-agents, suppliers, customers and also directors of the conglomerate. It is not surprising that the Commonwealth brand image lacks something in clarity of definition.

The absence of the Commonwealth as a 'free-standing' entity on the ground in its member states is evidenced in a number of ways: the varying location of the Commonwealth liaison function; the invisibility of Secretariat publications and reports; the low rate of demand, relative to supply, for education experts on the CFTC books; and the persistence of British and old dominions dominance in the transactions in older schemes like the Commonwealth Scholarship and Fellowship Plan.

Historically, the information divisions and libraries of British High Commissions throughout the Commonwealth have served, with the British Council, as conduits for Commonwealth information and publications. The British output itself is now low. British operations have been redeployed and run down over the past decade. Nowhere is the impact of Britain's entry to the EEC more immediately obvious than in the low priority accorded in its information divisions to Commonwealth affairs. Meanwhile, there has been no compensatory development on the ground from the Secretariat.

At its university apex, from which most formal education content flows, the enduring dominance of the North conflicts with the emergent national concerns of the South. As education becomes a mass production industry, the characteristic Commonwealth transaction of elite, low volume exchange is less able to command attention in the marketplace. The contemporary Commonwealth does not necessarily see itself as in competition with other agencies; it acts, indeed, as agent and partner to many. Nevertheless, the competition in education markets is a reality.

East and West Europe rub shoulders in schools of medicine and engineering in Commonwealth Africa and Asia and what is not national in general syllabuses tends to follow economic vectors. Analysis of the source of qualifications of university staffs in Commonwealth countries shows that Commonwealth degrees are still overwhelmingly dominant. The trend, however, is always changing. On the one hand, there is the strong impetus to grow-your-own staff development schemes which, in Africa and the Caribbean, reflects both the capacity of indigenous institutions to provide a full range of first degrees and the need to cut the costs of expatriate importation, as well as nationalist and developmental concerns. The Asian Commonwealth systems have been for many years self-sustaining and distanced to an extent by greater linguistic diversity and a degree of religious and ethnic exclusiveness. Asian Commonwealth calls upon Commonwealth assistance programmes are virtually restricted to high level expertise, reflecting, among other factors, the operation of an Asian educational sub-system which embraces states other than Commonwealth members.

Education systems in the Commonwealth have developed incrementally and in a context of shortage of skills and resources. It follows that whatever the state may want in content or form for the system, the increments have been functions of the pattern of extant and available personal and institutional linkages. Content and direction, particularly in newly independent polities where there is a relatively small educated elite, flow down from the apex tertiary institution, the university. There is in the university system of the Commonwealth a pattern of diversification away from predominantly British or even exclusively Commonwealth links.

Several movements are discernible:

(1) diversification in sponsorships towards non-Commonwealth universities with subject departments, special research programmes and professional schools being linked to US and, occasionally, East European equivalents and funding;

(2) recent staff appointments in newer systems from among nationals who have their first degree from a university within their own country;

(3) diversification away from Britain as a source of graduate training and postgraduate study;

(4) in the longer-established systems of Asia and Australasia appointments out of indigenous graduate programmes or of returnees from non-Commonwealth as well as Commonwealth systems;

(5) short-term contract expatriate appointments and staff exchanges which may be supported by the British government salary supplementation scheme, but which stem also from US, Soviet, non-aligned and UN support systems;

(6) intra-regional exchanges which are not exclusively between member states.

PROJECTION

In so far as education is an elite activity, it is characterised by professional exchanges across national boundaries which, in the last years of the twentieth century seem likely to follow the current trend. This shows increasing short-term and specialist transactions on a global scale and decreasing incidence of long-term movements other than those associated with displacement of population groups. Formal education is increasingly provided in all but the smallest and poorest states out of national resources, while training and development programmes are similarly reflecting national and regional arrangements. This latter trend away from straight transference of personnel or aid towards mutual assistance and provision of 'resource persons' for self-help programmes is characteristic of the contemporary Commonwealth's transactions. It seems likely, however, that these transactions will increasingly be around the southern part of the North-South divide.

The short-term specialist interchange, which links the anglophone world rather than the Commonwealth, widens the personal networks within the education market. There is a distinctive Commonwealth input to such exchanges, but whilst the networks are naturally more intense in anglophone countries, they could not be said to be distinctively Commonwealth-oriented or sustained by any strong consciousness of a Commonwealth culture. The absence of the Commonwealth from school syllabuses in the past, even in Britain itself for the most part, means that participants in educational exchanges, particularly specialists, must regard the Commonwealth as indifferently one among numerous scheme organisers. The Commonwealth presence within education must increasingly rest upon communication links which are impersonal rather than the product of interpersonal exchange. There are two growth areas in education in the immediate future both of which have been high on the agenda of Commonwealth education conferences in the last five years; the push for universal primary education and the development of the informal sector.

The Commonwealth book development programme has so far been restricted to some technical assistance and training. The characteristic work of the Commonwealth associations in the communications field has been the provision of largely British training and attachment facilities for sound, print and video practitioners. The exchanges have been predominantly South-North and have scarcely begun to respond to the challenge from exponents of a 'New International Information Order'. Accordingly, exchanges in the informal sector will be increasingly along southern, non-aligned and regional axes unless northern members come to terms with the NIIO principles and the Secretariat can increase its output of sound, video and print materials.

The challenge to the Commonwealth's educational and informational organs is to assist in the reversal of the unidirectional flow of information from the industrially advanced to the Third World. In the informal sector in particular, the north must accommodate the south's perception of information as a social and community resource rather than a market commodity, which is at the root of the demand for a new international information order.

The Commonwealth provides an organisational framework for a series of elite exchanges. A programme of academic and professional 'junkets' sustains networks of personal contacts which have been broadened from the old dominions exchange system to one which includes all parts of the former Empire. Commonwealth mechanisms have enabled the maintenance of correspondencies among professions in countries of very different stages of development and with widely varying needs. Commonwealth programmes have provided organisation and finance for mutual assistance and self-help projects among similar and contiguous countries which have lacked depth in established inter-state links. It remains to be seen, however, whether a Commonwealth presence can be established in the impersonal communication systems which will increasingly influence the structure of the education market.

A NOTE ON REGIONAL EXAMINATION COUNCILS[1]

L. S. Trachtenberg

Only two regional examination councils function today; the West African Examination Council and the Caribbean Examination Council. A third, the East African Examination Council, has disintegrated. Most states in the Commonwealth now have their own examination council.

The oldest examination council in the Commonwealth is the West African Examination Council (or WAEC) which is made up of all English-speaking West African states. It has its headquarters in Accra and offices in London as well as in all of those states in which it operates. The WAEC was founded in 1951 to conduct such examinations as would best suit the needs of West Africa. The Commonwealth Development Corporation (CDC) provides funds for the WAEC. The Council not only acts as agent for forty or more examining bodies overseas but it conducts a wide range of examinations of its own. These are examinations for primary schools, middle schools, secondary schools, teacher training colleges, professional, technical and commercial examinations and competitions for admission to the Civil Service. Although the WAEC has been running its own affairs for at least twenty years it has until recently been associated with the Universities of Cambridge and London for the purpose of examinations.

Another functioning examination council today is the Caribbean

Examination Council or, as it is called, the CXC, which is said to be made up of all English-speaking Caribbean states.[2] The CXC is controlled by the individual education ministries of those states which belong to it.

It has been rumoured that a Pacific examination council may be created to set a standard for all of the small states in that region.

Formally, the Commonwealth Secretariat refers to the examination councils as 'autonomous bodies' and claims to have nothing to do with its regional councils or state councils. However, the CFTC has assisted these Councils in the past in such areas as staff training and recruitment and technical assistance and CFTC members when asked, also attend, in an advisory capacity, the meetings of various examination councils. It would appear that the central Commonwealth institutions play no direct role in any of these examination councils and, as is the case with most of the activities of the CFTC, the Commonwealth only becomes involved when specific requests are made of it for technical or specialist assistance. It has no formal relationship with any of these organisations and never interferes without a specific request from the organisation in question.

NOTES AND REFERENCES

1. I would like to thank Mr Apea and Mr Barnor from the Commonwealth Secretariat, and Mr Stephenson, from the University of London Overseas Department, for their assistance in the compilation of this information.
2. A great deal of confusion would appear to exist about the Caribbean Examinations Council, and despite numerous requests to the many high commissions in London, I was unable to obtain firm information on the actual membership of the 'CXC'. It would be reasonable to say that such misinformation (or lack of it) is a probable reflection of the state of affairs of the Caribbean Examinations Council.

FIGURE 5.1 *Commonwealth Organisations concerned with education, training and the professions: functions and headquarters location*

Organisation	Information exchange	Education and training	Professional standards	Headquarters
Official				
CW Foundation		●	●	BRI
CW Scholarship & Fellowship plan		●		BRI
CW Science Council	●	●	●	BRI
CW Secretariat & CFTC	●	●	●	BRI
CW Telecommunications Bureau	●	●	●	BRI
Unofficial				
CW Assocn of Scientific Agric. Socs.	●	●	●	CAN
CW Forestry Inst.	●		●	BRI
CW Veterinary Assocn.	●	●	●	CAN
Royal Agric. Society of the CW	●	●		BRI
CW Arts Cttee	●	●	●	BRI
CW Assocn of Museums		●	●	BRI
CW Philharmonic Orchestra Trust	●	●		BRI
Assocn of CW Universities	●	●	●	BRI
CW Assocn of Science & Maths Educators	●	●	●	BRI
CW Institute, London	●	●		BRI
CW Assocn of Architects	●	●	●	BRI
CW Assocn of Planners	●	●	●	BRI
CW Assocn of Surveying & Land Economy	●	●	●	BRI
CW Human Ecology Council	●	●		BRI
CW Medical Assocn	●			BRI
CW Nurses Federation	●	●		BRI
CW Pharmaceutical Assocn	●	●		BRI
CW Society for the Deaf	●	●	●	BRI
Royal CW Society for the Blind	●	●		BRI
CW Broadcasting Assocn	●	●	●	BRI
CW Journalists Assocn	●	●	●	BRI
CW Library Assocn	●	●	●	JAM
CW Press Union	●	●	●	BRI
League for Exchange of CW Teachers	●	●		BRI
Royal CW Society	●	●		BRI
Victoria League for CW Friendship	●	●		BRI
CW Legal Bureau	●	●	●	NZ
CW Legal Educ. Assocn	●		●	BRI
CW Magistrates' Assocn	●	●	●	BRI
CW Parliamentary Assocn	●	●	●	BRI
CW Engineers Council	●	●	●	BRI
CW Youth Exchange Council	●	●		BRI

SOURCE: *Commonwealth Organisations*, published by the Commonwealth Secretariat in 1979.

FIGURE 5.2 *Commonwealth Scholarships*

The table below shows the number of Scholars holding awards in each awarding country in the year ending 31 March, 1977 (the count was taken in the first term of the academic year beginning in that year). Figures in brackets indicate the number of women award-holders included in the figures immediately preceding the brackets.

SCHOLARSHIPS CAME / **COUNTRIES WHERE AWARDS HELD**

From	Australia	Britain	Canada	Ghana	Hong Kong	India	Jamaica	Malaysia	Malta	New Zealand	Nigeria	Sri Lanka	Trinidad	Total
Antigua		1	1 (1)											2 (1)
Australia		46 (9)	18 (2)		2	2 (1)	1	1		2				72 (12)
Bahamas		1	1 (1)											2 (1)
Bangladesh	6	62 (5)	15 (2)							2				85 (7)
Barbados		3	3											6
Belize		2	2 (1)											4 (1)
Bermuda		2 (1)												2 (1)
Botswana		2	2											4
Britain	16 (4)		25 (5)		1	8 (5)		3		3 (2)	2			58 (16)
British Solomon Is.			1											1
British Virgin Is.														1
Brunei										1				1
Canada	16 (3)	60 (17)		2 (1)	1	3 (2)			1	4 (2)	4 (1)	1 (1)		91 (27)
Cyprus		10 (1)	2						1	1 (1)	1			15 (2)
Dominica														
Falkland Is.														
Fiji	5 (1)	2				4				1				12 (1)
Gambia		4	2 (1)			1					1			8 (1)
Ghana	3	18 (2)	8 (1)			1				1	2			33 (3)
Gibraltar		1	2											3
Gilbert Is.														

COUNTRIES WHE...													Total
Jamaica	2	8 (3)	7 (3)									2		22 (2)
Kenya	2	10	5			5 (1)							22 (2)
Lesotho			2										2 (1)
Malawi	1	9 (2)	1										11 (2)
Malaysia	1 (1)	23 (5)	9			16 (4)					2		51 (10)
Malta	1	5	4										11
Mauritius	2	8 (3)	4			9			1				24 (3)
Montserrat		1	1 (1)										2 (1)
Nauru													
New Hebrides	9 (2)	23 (7)	14										46 (9)
New Zealand	3	62 (8)	16 (1)	1									84 (9)
Nigeria			1		1		1						
Pakistan													6
Papua New Guinea	2		4										28 (2)
Rhodesia	28 (2)	28 (2)											
Saint Helena			1 (1)										1 (1)
Saint Kitts Nevis	1		2 (1)										3 (1)
Saint Lucia	1												1
Saint Vincent													2
Seychelles	2 (1)												18 (1)
Sierra Leone	11 (1)		3	2 (1)		2	1						12 (3)
Singapore	9 (2)		1										44 (6)
Sri Lanka	21 (3)		13 (1)			6 (2)			1	3			2 (1)
Swaziland	1 (1)		1										20
Tanzania	2	9	3			4			2	2			3 (1)
Tonga			1 (1)			2							9 (1)
Trinidad & Tobago			6 (1)			1			1	1			
Tuvalu													
Uganda	1		9			4	1			2		18	
Western Samoa													
Zambia		4 (1)	7							1		11 (1)	
Total	78 (12)	566 (84)	253 (33)	3 (1)	6 (1)	72 (15)	2	6	1	25 (6)	20 (2)	4 (1)	1036 (155)

SOURCE: *Commonwealth Scholarship and Fellowship Plan Annual Report 1977*, Commonwealth Secretariat.

FIGURE 5.3 Commonwealth Students in Britain 1965–6 and 1976–7

	Universities and Further Education		Inns of Court		Hospitals				Industry		Business and Professional		Government	
					Nurse training		Other							
	1965–6	1976–7	1965–6	1976–7	1965–6	1976–7	1965–6	1976–7	1965–6	1976–7	1965–6	1976–7	1965–6	1976–7
Australia	555	820	1	9	62	130		10		29		18		3
Bangladesh	n.a.	683		2		11		1		5		30		5
Botswana	10	65			2	3						8		
Canada	831	1077	4	3	193	157		18		13		5		
Ghana	1228	764	23	15	543	391		34		15		1		16
India	2650	1742	170	17	227	228		38		52		80		10
Malaysia	1432	1958	440	179	845	3087		212		32		41		4
Malawi	112	288	23		56	13		7		3		4		17
New Zealand	248	250	1		26	30		5		6		5		
Nigeria	4260	5574	124	4	1011	237		27		19		17		3
Sri Lanka	650	2656	21	1	420	467		61		11		4		11
Tanzania	810	739	5		227	66		4		5		26		7
Trinidad and Tobago	498	347	112	6	1831	577		70		1		4		
Jamaica	460	321	141	10	3129	844		28		3		2		5
Kenya	1326	1698	17	2	399	136		25		12		18		5

SOURCES: *The Commonwealth Office Yearbook 1968, Yearbook of the Commonwealth 1978.*

6 The Arts: an Emerging Dimension

A. J. R. GROOM

The arts in the Commonwealth are extraordinary in many senses, yet they are the one major area of human endeavour which stands largely unorganised and fearsomely neglected in the Commonwealth. In the past no formal organisation was deemed to be necessary. In the context of the old dominions artistic life was essentially an extension, with local variations, of British artistic activity. The establishment institutions were equipped and ready for such a role and generally they performed it efficiently. However, it was never very important, since the arts themselves were not thought of as central in British life.

However, culture in a more general sense was part of the equipment of a colonial power. It was not just a question of bringing 'order', 'justice', 'good government', science and technology, and, of course, trade and Christianity to a disorderly and heathen world; there was also that all-encompassing ingredient that knitted these together in the colonial package – civilisation and a commanding culture. But in so far as the colonies were concerned these were encapsulated more by the varying nostrums of the Christian churches, scientific discovery and a penchant for efficient administration than by artistic endeavour. The British, moreover, remained largely impervious to the cultures within which they found themselves. With the exception of India, indigenous culture was either ignored or suppressed as tiresome, primitive, indecent or dangerous, whereupon it had either to be harnessed to British administrative purposes through indirect rule or undermined. But great civilisations do not vanish by imperial fiat, especially when they form the very fabric of social, economic, political and religious life. What use, then, was made of indigenous and British culture by the non-Western colonised peoples?

83

Faced with the colonial power's (and now the developed world's) economic, military, political and scientific prowess framed in an assertion of cultural superiority, the reaction of the indigenous people was often one of extreme nationalism and, at the same time, of 'cultural cringe'. This has given rise to what Rex Nettleford has called, in the West Indian context,

the unending paradox: we hanker after the fruits of metropolitan technology and economic prowess while we reject metropolitan cultural dominance by asserting a collective identity rooted in our own historical heritage ... But how do we ... get the world to understand that the 'universal' goods of scientific and technological development must be made to work within the framework of political and cultural experience specific to this or that people?[1]

This suggests the need for a 'new international cultural order'.[2] In Nettleford's view, 'the newly "independent" nations [are] really in control of very little beyond their creativity, their intellect and imagination'.[3] In this sense little is new since cultural expression was a survival skill and a statement of personal and group identity with political overtones in colonial times. In Africa there is likewise a tremendous hunger for cultural identity, and culture was in colonial times, and is now, a vehicle of self-expression with political implications and content. It was for good reason that British colonial administrators saw it as a threat.

In the Commonwealth setting the importance of the English language in these developments is obvious – especially in the Caribbean. It is through the medium of English that international communication is made, even in cultural matters where there is an 'international' language such as music. Yet English was also the language of colonialism, and no language is an independent vehicle, for it entraps its users in a system of thought, processes and values that reflect those of its dominant users. Thus it could become, as Nettleford suggests, a 'potential "instrument of domination" '[4] and a possible means of driving people into an 'institutionalised cultural marginality'.[5] Thus, while English can be the medium for the business of Commonwealth co-operation in the arts, Nettleford argues that it can only do so if Third World members ensure that they are not thereby 'being relegated to a subordinate position in a hierarchical conception of international culture'.[6]

Many developing Commonwealth countries have now been independent long enough for their governments to decide upon a cultural policy, both internally and internationally. Cultural matters were not the immediate concern of post-independence governments. Furthermore, there was precious little inheritance by way of organisation, infrastructure and policy when the colonial power withdrew. Yet the arts were thriving as an organic part of daily life, especially in the villages, and the nationalism of post-independence governments led them back to culture as did the need for an education policy. In addition, definitions of development largely in economic terms began to prove unsuccessful and unsatisfactory, which led to a re-evaluation of development with an increased awareness of and importance being given to social and cultural factors. Cultural policy therefore assumed a greater relevance, but in a domestic context. Culture, after all, has indigenous roots even if it has international facets. Thus, apart from the unofficial transnational ties in Western artistic activity among the former dominions and Britain, and ties between communities which shared the cultures of the Indian sub-continent on a similar basis, there was little by way of pan-Commonwealth arts which reflected the new Commonwealth. Only in the last five years has such a movement begun to emerge. This has necessitated action by governments in the developing countries, since few local organisations exist because the arts are part of the daily life of the people who frequently have neither the expertise, the resources, nor the will to act internationally unaided. Commonwealth arts at these levels are only just emerging, usually in the form of isolated ventures associated with a festival rather than as an integral part of a cultural policy. The Commonwealth Arts Organisation represents a desire to change this.[7]

Festivals illustrate the need for a Commonwealth arts organisation. Festivals are 'occasions': they give artists something to strive for, they aggregate and disseminate information, they provide stimulus and satisfaction and they bring together the best, the bizarre and the out-of-the-ordinary. When they end an intense psycho-social community collapses, or at least becomes latent. Communications, particularly between Third World participants, are difficult to sustain. The public drifts away and politicians feel they have done their duty. But festivals are showpieces, stimulants, focal points. The arts, however, require sustained support and practice: they require organisation, the more so in their international dimension. The prize is great: it is nothing less than the enrichment of world civilisation through example and cross-fertilisation. The Commonwealth is not the world, but it is blessed with equitable working methods, legitimacy, relevance for practical tasks and diversity. In the arts it lacks the organisation to facilitate the undoubted desire to communicate, to exchange, to explore and to share some of mankind's richest and most cherished activities. The attempts to endow the Commonwealth with an arts organisation have been faltering, but they are coming to fruition. Art and artists are notoriously difficult to organise, but an organisation is necessary not just for the arts, artists and the public, but for the Commonwealth itself and its governments and peoples.

The British Empire sometimes brought participants from its farthest reaches to celebrations in London. The Commonwealth Arts Festival held in Britain in 1965 pointed towards the contemporary Commonwealth. But Commonwealth arts remained dormant for a decade until a festival of 'Commonwealth Folk' was organised in Malta in 1975.[8] On this occasion there was a significant follow-up in the founding of the Commonwealth Arts Association (CAA) in January 1976 under the leadership of John McKenzie, who had played a major role in Malta. The CAA operates on a minimal organisational basis and is privately financed, but it has an active programme of events, for the most part in Britain and Europe, and it has established a lively journal *Art Links* as a Commonwealth arts review.

The successful artistic activities of the Edmonton Commonwealth Games were a milestone in the development of an organisational framework for Commonwealth arts. Seen by a quarter of a million people, the artists also performed for and with each other in what was undoubtedly 'a brilliantly successful mingling of cultures which added a special magic to the splendid traditional spirit of the Games'.[9] The arts festival was an essentially co-operative venture in contrast to the necessarily competitive element of the Games. Its success was such that a two-day seminar was immediately organised on the future development of Commonwealth arts with the participation of some of the artists performing in the Carnival. This eventually gave rise to a Conference in London in January 1980, which resulted in the founding of a Commonwealth Arts Organisation (CAO).

After a sticky start financially and organisationally, the CAO is responding as best as it can to an obvious felt need for a Commonwealth arts organisation – a need felt most by those who despite a strong commitment do not have the resources available to make it work. The questions of finance and of governmental or non-governmental status are thus closely linked, since intergovernmental status is likely to untie the purse-strings of the developed members of the Commonwealth on the usual basis of contributions to official Commonwealth activities, or at least to create a momentum for voluntary contributions by governments. However, the CAO has won recognition through its role as sponsor and organiser of the Arts Festival associated with the Brisbane Commonwealth Games.

At the Melbourne CHOGM Jamaica proposed that the CAO be established as a Commonwealth intergovernmental organisation. This matter was discussed by the Committee of the whole, which recognised the value to Commonwealth relations of strengthening cultural ties between the peoples of the Commonwealth, but in view of the financial implications for Commonwealth governments the matter was referred to the review group which is considering the priorities and objectives for the Secretariat in the 1980s. Those governments who are major potential financial contributors to intergovernmental activities are wary about incurring further financial obligations. There is also confusion due to seemingly overlapping organisations such as the Commonwealth Institute, the Commonwealth Foundation, and Commonwealth bodies dealing with specific aspects of the arts. Other governments are lukewarm since they are not sure what the CAO would do besides organise festivals. Would it organise a data bank and get involved in education and training? Would it become a politicised body on such issues as 'restitution' of works of art? Would it merely be an umbrella organisation through which particular arts' bodies around the Commonwealth would be engaged to undertake particular functions and promote Commonwealth arts? Would it act as the co-ordinating body for Commonwealth arts councils? However, a successful festival in Brisbane gives the CAO salience and, despite the curious foot-dragging of the Secretariat on cultural questions, the matter is on the agenda, and the CAO has the support of most governments, including that of India, the next CHOGM host, where the fate of the CAO as an intergovernmental organisation will be decided.

Finance is but a means, and in the end it is artists who are important. But artists are frequently not amenable to the niceties of bureaucratic practice: they are individualistic and headstrong, seeking after ideals and little apt to make compromises and to come to terms with reality. Indeed, they often view their role as that of changing, perhaps even overthrowing, the existing situation. Their propensity to let the best be the enemy of the good is well-known. Moreover, the second-rate frequently compensate for their lack of talent by emphasising their 'artistic conscience' and the 'right to freedom' no matter what the cost and to whom. There can be little surprise then that the relationship of artists to arts organisations is not always easy. While the CAA is run by and for artists and is rigorously non-governmental, it is not pan-

Commonwealth. There is thus room for an organisation such as the CAO to bring in those official bodies which are so important in the Third World and to develop and sustain a long-term developmental programme for Commonwealth arts. This necessarily involves arts administrators, but not to the exclusion of the artists themselves.

The arts and politics are intertwined but not always in a happy manner. Both are a reflection of experience, a statement and promotion of values and ideals and a vehicle of expression. To a large degree they are in the same business only with different means. In Western countries politics has anaesthetised the arts by putting them in separate compartments outside the mainstream of daily living. They are supported well enough for them to survive, and be beholden to the hand that feeds them, but not sufficiently to give them a threatening independence. In Third World countries the arts are being offered a partnership in a national development programme, but only a junior partnership to a strong-willed and sometimes autocratic 'political' senior partner. Clashes between the partners are, not surprisingly, from time to time stridently evident. The balance between politician, administrator and artist is not easy to achieve but it is one that is a necessary condition for a successful CAO.

The CAO has adopted a geographical region and a country mode of organisation, but do the arts flourish along geographical and state lines? An alternative form of organisation, followed by the Association of Commonwealth Universities and the Commonwealth Association of Museums, would make the CAO an umbrella organisation for bodies for each of the arts and, within each of the arts, membership would be by individual unit without reference to geography or nationality. Such an organisation would be more clearly non-governmental, and artist-dominated, but it would have financial and organisational difficulties. By using state structures the CAO hopes to gain financial support, while at the same time incorporating artists.

Although interest in Commonwealth arts on a pan-Commonwealth basis has recently been centred upon the CAO it is not the only body to be active on a pan-Commonwealth basis. Both the Commonwealth and Gulbenkian Foundations have a significant role. The Commonwealth Foundation's mandate was extended at the Lusaka CHOGM to include cultural questions. The prime function of the Foundation in the cultural area is that of pump-priming and, in particular, to help Third World arts in a Commonwealth context. The Foundation has supported several festivals including those at Edmonton and Brisbane, as well as *Art Links* and *ad hoc* projects. It hopes to give Commonwealth arts sustained, if modest, structural support.

The Gulbenkian Foundation recognises Commonwealth arts in an internal administrative grouping in the Foundation and numerous Commonwealth arts projects have been given practical support. Not least of these has been the meetings of Arts Councils' representatives from Commonwealth countries. The first meeting was at the University of Kent in 1979. These discussions were continued at Montreal in 1981 with a wider participation from the Third World, which was reflected in the ideas and experiences that formed the basis of discussion.[10] A further meeting is planned to be held in Nigeria and organised by the CAO on the theme of Third World cultural preoccupations and, in particular, how the Third World protects cultural traditions against twentieth-century intrusions from the West. To say the least, it should prove interesting.

Commonwealth arts councils, the CAO, the CAA are not the only manifestation of new artistic developments on a pan-Commonwealth basis. A Commonwealth Film and Television Institute, to be based in Cyprus, was welcomed in principle by the Lusaka CHOGM but it looks as though it will not get off the ground for financial reasons, the overlap of television with the Commonwealth Broadcasting Association and the general parlous state of cinema in most Commonwealth countries.[11]

The Commonwealth Association of Museums (CAM) has also made a slow start. It was set up in 1976 for the purposes of mutual training, the promotion of interchange and the provision of additional facilities on a regional basis. This association has the backing of the Commonwealth Foundation and the older Commonwealth countries are the moving force, although the Caribbean members are becoming more active. The African countries have their own pan-African organisation and it is the policy of the Commonwealth body to support this pan-African organisation. The association would like to establish a training scheme, but it is handicapped by lack of finance. However, it has a potential role in a major moral, political, artistic and technical problem in the cultural domain. The problem is exemplified by the tortured title of a UNESCO Committee – Intergovernmental Committee for Promoting the Return of Cultural Property to its Countries of Origin or its Restitution in Case of illicit Appropriation.[12] It is not at all difficult to generate a fearsome debate on this issue but such debates lead to few helpful practical outcomes. It is perhaps here that Ramphal's axiom that while the Commonwealth cannot negotiate for the world it can help the world to negotiate is appropriate. For if the Commonwealth, in the shape of the CAM and the CAO, cannot broach this issue in a meaningful manner it is unlikely that the world will be able to do so.

Several principles suggest themselves, the first of which is fundamental: do not look to the past for it cannot be altered and it will not repeat itself and to do so will lead to endless and destructive recrimination; rather, look in practical terms at the problem now, and ways in which it can be resolved in the future. Recognise that there are clear local needs: these needs include, as a minimum, that indigenous cultures should have direct and continuous access locally to the range, diversity and high points of their cultural flowering. To deny such access is tantamount to a denial of their identity. This implies that local provision must be such as to take proper care of cultural resources which may in turn call for technical assistance in the form of training and capital investment for housing cultural manifestations. The CAO and the CAM could be the organisations through which such resources are furnished where they are insufficient locally, perhaps financed, in part, with Commonwealth Foundation funds. But if local needs are to be recognised, so are world needs. Culture is a particular reflection of a universal phenomenon – the relationship of man and his environment – and there is a legitimate need to see what others have made of it. Yet the problem arises from the current inbalance between museums in developed countries stuffed with the treasures of the world and, in some cases, the complete absence of such treasures in their indigenous setting. Training and capital will overcome some difficulties but there are also political and legal problems. Ownership only becomes an acute problem with political overtones when it is an obstacle to access. Perhaps there is a need therefore for a Commonwealth heritage trust to establish and monitor technical standards and facilitate exchanges. If Ghana wanted to display Ashanti artefacts presently at Sandhurst the authorities would approach the Trust that would establish and monitor the standards for the loan (perhaps 'permanent') and Sandhurst would make the loan to the Trust under agreed conditions. This buffer–facilitator role butressed by training programmes and capital resources might put on a functional basis what threatens to become a divisive political issue. It would be an impressive achievement if the Commonwealth could show the way.

The Association for Commonwealth Literature and Language Studies (ACLALS) was founded in 1964 to encourage the reading and study of writing in English outside Britain and the USA. Such writing has flourished in many Commonwealth countries, particularly since independence. ACLALS is a pragmatic organisation and an active one. It is pragmatic because, whether or not there is such a thing as a Commonwealth culture, there is a literature in English in Commonwealth countries and the association exists to promote it. There are many university courses on Commonwealth literature and a *Journal of Commonwealth Literature*, so a considerable potential membership exists. Membership is from all parts of the Commonwealth and meetings are held not only regionally but also Commonwealth-wide. The fifth such triennial conference was held in Fiji in January 1980 with support from the Commonwealth Foundation. An unusual feature is that the administrative committee's base rotates around the Commonwealth. It is encouraging to note that Third World participation is strong and that the association has a practitioner-university mode of functional organisation rather than a bureaucratic state-centric one.

At the Melbourne CHOGM the Commonwealth Institute in London received explicit and deserved recognition for its excellent work. It has had a hand in many of the positive developments described earlier. Moreover, it has moved with the times and, although Britain provided the site and still bears the main financial responsibility, the institute is a pan-Commonwealth body which is clearly reflected in its board of governors and its activities. It works closely with the Commonwealth Secretariat and also with UNESCO while keeping in touch with both national and international agencies. It is firmly committed to the notion of pan-Commonwealth arts in a pan-Commonwealth way. There is, however, only one such institute and its duplication in other parts of the Commonwealth in a co-ordinated way would be a welcome development.

ACLALS, the Commonwealth Institute and other bodies are typical examples of the unofficial Commonwealth at work: pragmatic, task-oriented, open and participatory. The relationship of such bodies to the Secretariat and the official Commonwealth is a difficult one, not least in the arts. The unofficial Commonwealth has in general been given the cold shoulder by the Secretariat and Commonwealth governments despite a strong recommendation that a NGO desk should be established in the Secretariat.[13]

Perhaps governments are frightened of the arts. Culture is an autonomous force which can sometimes be harnessed for a national liberation struggle or kept in the developed world's tarnished cage by official patronage, but ultimately it is its own master. In some countries it is of the people and in others it is led by a dangerously intelligent, often attractive and above all independent elite. Was it Plato who suggested that artists, being potentially dangerous animals, should be fed, garlanded and sent on to the next city or, in contemporary terms, to the next Commonwealth Games or festival? Culture is about the commonality and the diversity of man's experience. The spiritual source is the same but the setting of each culture is different. Some governments are frightened of such independence, interdependence and diversity. Thus, while Commonwealth arts flourish in some informal networks, while the desire to establish new networks is strongly manifest, governments may well be relieved that the organisation of the arts on a pan-Commonwealth basis is but in its infancy.

NOTES AND REFERENCES

1. R. M. Nettleford, *Cultural Action and Social Change* (Ottawa: International Development Research Centre, 1979), pp. x–xi.
2. Ibid., p. 173. See also *Le Monde*, 22 September 1981 in which a similar call was made in the context of a major meeting of thirty-nine delegations attending the first Conference of Ministers of Culture of Francophone Countries held in Benin in September 1981.
3. R. M. Nettleford, speech reported in *Caribbean Life and Times*, Vol. I (1980), no. 4, p. 19.
4. Ibid.
5. R. M. Nettleford, speech to the Commonwealth Arts Conference, London, January 1980.
6. R. M. Nettleford, speech in *Caribbean Life and Times*, Vol. I (1980), no. 4.
7. In the course of preparing this chapter an attempt was made to generate data on existing Commonwealth ties in the arts by means of a questionnaire. This largely failed since those respondents who had little or nothing to report did so and those who potentially had a great deal to report did not have the information available. Thus any formal analysis would have been hopelessly skewed and pointless. However, the responses to the questionnaires and the information in the very useful series of country cultural political studies sponsored by UNESCO do give the possibility of an impressionistic *tour d'horizon* of Commonwealth arts at the present stage. See A. J. R. Groom in *Round Table*, April 1983.
8. See Commonwealth Youth Programme: 'Commonwealth Folk', Malta 1975, report of a seminar 22 March–5 April 1975. Sponsored by the Ministry of Education and Culture Malta, Commonwealth Secretariat, Commonwealth Institute.
9. The Commonwealth Day Message of the Queen, 1979.
10. See a summary of the Conference Report in *Art Links*, Autumn 1981.
11. See Ansan Ng: 'Should the Commonwealth take this CFTI idea seriously?' *Commonwealth*, April/May 1981 and Angela Martin: 'A tale of two cinemas', *Art Links*, Autumn 1981.
12. For a discussion of these issues see Peter Freedman: 'Third World Nations press for return of national treasures', *Commonwealth*, June/July, 1981 and his 'Whose art is it anyway?', *Art Links*, Autumn 1981.

13. See *From Governments to Grassroots*. Report of advisory committee on relationships between official and unofficial Commonwealth (London: Commonwealth Secretariat, 1978).

7 Science and Technology: the Commonwealth Dimension

KAYE TURNER

Soon after taking office in 1976 the present Commonwealth Secretary-General expressed concern that the Commonwealth scientific effort as a whole had been inadequate in relation to the basic needs arising from poverty and deprivation (of people in the Commonwealth).[1] In particular he urged the need for a low-cost but innovative programme directed towards neglected grass-roots problems. Mr Ramphal argued that the scientific facilities and skills to mount such an effort in carefully selected areas existed within the Commonwealth and the appropriate scientific agencies and institutions – especially those in developing countries – needed to be brought into more fruitful contact with each other in order to make more effective use of technological information which already existed. The thrust of the Secretariat's future programme would be to stimulate a greater awareness of basic rural problems, and create improved linkages between these problems and the scientific effort, both national and co-operative.[2]

The body charged with the implementation of this new Commonwealth effort in science and technology was the official conduit of scientific collaboration in the contemporary Commonwealth, the Commonwealth Science Council (CSC), a body which, for all practical purposes, functions as the science division of the Commonwealth Secretariat,[3] but with a separate policy-making and funding apparatus.

However, scientific collaboration in the Commonwealth predates the formation of the Commonwealth Secretariat in 1965. The institutional bases of future co-operation were laid as early as 1929, with the founding of the Imperial Agricultural Bureaux, and with the establishment of the

British Commonwealth Scientific Conference, which concentrated mainly on agricultural research, in 1936. As the Commonwealth Secretary-General noted in his 1979 report to Commonwealth heads of government: 'In those early days [co-operation between Commonwealth countries in science and technology] consisted mainly in collaboration and exchange of research results between the scientifically more advanced countries, and these bilateral links are maintained as strongly as ever.'[4] Indeed, such bilateral links have expanded with the Commonwealth. The 'scientifically more advanced countries' have become today's major Commonwealth donor countries, promoting Commonwealth science as part of their bilateral aid programmes. Some Commonwealth developing countries are also donors. India, for example, contributes to economic co-operation (including scientific co-operation) among developing countries, by reserving (for this purpose) five per cent of the United Nations Development Programme (UNDP) assistance it receives.

The successful collaboration of Commonwealth scientists during the 1939–45 war gave tremendous impetus to Commonwealth scientific co-operation. In 1943 the Royal Society published a report recommending the establishment of peacetime machinery for permanent scientific liaison and in 1946 the British Commonwealth Scientific Conference established a standing committee – the forerunner of today's CSC – to act as a liaison body between Commonwealth national scientific research organisations.[5]

Closer collaboration and co-operation were discussed at a series of meetings in the 1950s, and in 1958 the standing committee became the British Commonwealth Scientific Committee.

SCIENCE AND TECHNOLOGY IN THE MODERN COMMONWEALTH

The first significant change in the nature of Commonwealth scientific co-operation did not occur until the 1960s, when the rapid attainment of independence by former British colonies led to the growth of the Commonwealth association. In 1964, in line with the evolution of the Commonwealth, the word 'British' was dropped from the title of the Commonwealth Scientific Committee, the membership of which grew steadily in tandem with that of the Commonwealth as a whole. In 1965, when the Commonwealth Secretariat was established, the CSC remained separate from it. The proposals by Commonwealth prime ministers for the formation of a secretariat had not contained any specific reference to collaboration between Commonwealth countries in the field of scientific research. It was the CSC itself which wrote to the new Commonwealth Secretary-General late in 1965, suggesting that collaboration between the official scientific organisations of Commonwealth countries should be strengthened, and that the recently established review committee on intra-Commonwealth organisations should consider the activities of the CSC. In 1968, in line with that Committee's recommendations, the Secretary of the CSC became Science Adviser to the Commonwealth Secretary-General.

The significant changes in the nature of Commonwealth scientific co-operation during the 1960s received their expression in policy terms at a meeting of the CSC in Ghana in 1966. The CSC took on as a priority task the provision of information and advice on science and technology to Commonwealth developing countries, as well as the task of assisting Commonwealth donor countries to determine the size and target of their scientific and technological aid to developing countries.

These remained the main roles of the CSC until the mid-1970s when

the focus of concern of the CSC . . . shifted sharply . . . It was accepted then that the Council should engage in an expanded programme of applied science and technology, and that the aim of this programme should be to help meet the basic needs of the most disadvantaged people in the Commonwealth, principally those in rural areas.[6]

The major thrust of the CSC programme now became the alleviation of poverty, and the CSC's programme goals were tied in with those of the call by developing countries for a new international economic order. Regional co-operation was emphasised and

the broad primary role of the Commonwealth effort in the fields of science and technology [was] seen to be to meet the needs of the developing member countries by assisting them to build up their own scientific strengths and to achieve recognised national capabilities in the use and management of science and technology for economic and social development.[7]

This policy direction was endorsed by Commonwealth Heads of Government at their meeting in Kingston, Jamaica in 1975. The Commonwealth Scientific Committee also emerged in its contemporary guise from that meeting, as the Commonwealth Science Council.

THE CSC – MEMBERSHIP, STRUCTURE AND ROLE

Thirty-two Commonwealth countries are now formal members of the CSC: those which are not are the smaller, recently-independent countries and some 'mini-states' unable to sustain a multiplicity of international memberships and obligations. Lack of formal CSC membership does not preclude any Commonwealth country from participating in CSC programmes or from receiving information, and so small Commonwealth states can enjoy some of the benefits of CSC membership, without incurring its burdens.

The CSC meets every two years to review the state of science in the Commonwealth, to examine progress in the programmes, and to formulate policy guide-lines. These full Council meetings are attended by the heads of national science councils, or similar bodies. An executive committee, elected from the CSC's membership, and representative of the different regions of the Commonwealth, meets approximately once every eight months, to give more detailed supervision to the CSC's work. Today, this work is in applied science and technology, to meet the basic development needs of Commonwealth member countries.

> While the promotion of pure and basic research remains of importance the emphasis in CSC/Secretariat programmes is shifting toward the promotion of smaller-scale, locally-based technologies which make optimal use of limited available resources – particularly at the rural community level – and which enhance the capacity of local communities to achieve a larger measure of self-reliance.[8]

The CSC sponsors studies in the fields of science and technology and promotes the exchange of science and technology information and personnel among Commonwealth countries. It encourages member countries to collaborate on specific science and technology projects. If individual member countries request it to do so, it attempts to locate funding and expert advisers. It has also carried out a number of exploratory studies and projects in response to specific requests, in such fields as research management and administration, metrication, energy storage, local building and housing materials, road corrugations, natural disaster preparedness, selection criteria for technology choices, remote sensing, the impact of tropical dams, and scientific and technical information processing. The CSC also develops and maintains contacts with and among professional organisations and institutions of science and technology in member countries. The CSC Secretary offers scientific and technical advice to the Commonwealth Secretary-General, and his mandate covers a wider span than that of the CSC. Approximately one-third of his time is spent on CSC business; the rest in advising other Secretariat divisions, particularly the CFTC, and briefing the Secretary-General on matters relating to science and technology. Because such activities require a constant exchange of information with governments, research institutes and international organisations, he is well-placed to monitor world trends in science and technology, and his knowledge can, in turn, contribute to the long-term planning of CSC activities.

CO-ORDINATED RESEARCH AND DEVELOPMENT PROGRAMME

The main thrust of the CSC's work is its co-ordinated research and development programme, concentrated in five broad sectors: alternative energy, rural technology, natural products, metrology and quality control, and mineral resources and geology. There are eight operational regional collaborative programmes designed to implement the co-ordinated research and development programme through surveys, discussions, workshops, training programmes and the exchange of information and technical assistance or advice. Within the eight programmes, approximately sixty specific projects among those iden-tified are being advanced by the means described above. The CSC holds about twenty-five technical meetings a year, involving national parti-cipants, as well as over 300 government-appointed regional and national co-ordinators.

The CSC recognises that '... the capacity within the division to manage an expanded science programme is ... clearly limited'.[9] However it also believes that

> these limitations can be turned to good account by making close collaboration with other Secretariat divisions a necessity, and by prompting the CSC to build a structure for its research and development programme upon regional committees which pursue action programmes in sectors identified as being of high priority in that region.[10]

The CSC itself sets broad policy guide-lines and programme themes at its biennial meetings. The executive council, meeting more frequently, reviews specific initiatives in each policy area and prepares budget submissions. Regional programmes are devised, made up of inter-related projects identified by a group of professionals from the member countries concerned. The CSC has extended this project identification mechanism to cover also the monitoring and evaluation of all its projects, relying on the contributions of professionals in the countries involved as national co-ordinators and members of regional steering committees. Each programme is co-ordinated regionally, by a person provided by a member country, at the CSC's request, to act as a regional programme co-ordinator. This co-ordinator is assisted by a steering committee made up of representatives from participating countries within the region, which may include non-Commonwealth countries. Nor is the national dimension neglected – on each *project*, every participating country is invited to nominate a professional to provide national co-ordination. And, as with programmes, each *project* also has a regional co-ordinator, provided by one participating country (and almost always their national co-ordinator for that project). Every eighteen months to two years, a regional group meets to review the progress of the programme concerned, and the executive committee and the CSC also review all programmes at their regular meetings.

In the words of the Secretary-General to Heads of Government in 1979:

The first role of the CSC, then, has become that of a priming group that, through regional group meetings, creates the environment for working scientists to identify the scientific problems of development within a region and to collaborate on their solution; it also has a further role in disseminating their findings and in encouraging the application of these findings. By these means a smaller budget has a multiplying effect; the forming of regional project groups develops the internal capabilities of member countries to use science and tech-nology for their economic and social development, and the co-ordinated programme helps to avoid duplication and to share resources.[11]

EXAMPLES OF COMMONWEALTH SCIENCE PROGRAMMES

(1) An Alternative Energy Programme

This programme originated in a CSC seminar held in December 1976 on alternative energy resources and their potential in rural development. A follow-up project group meeting in September 1977 proposed ten projects, concentrating especially on the use of solar, wind and bio-gas energy at village level. A four-country steering committee, now chaired by Jamaica, has supervised implementation. This committee met in February 1979 for the first time, sixteen months after the project group meeting, and again in June 1980 to review the whole programme.

(2)   A Rural Technology Programme

The rural technology programme grew out of a workshop to discuss appropriate technologies and energy requirements for rural industries, and their social, environmental and institutional implications, held in Dacca in January 1978, with participants from six countries in the Asia/Pacific region, as well as Mauritius, Seychelles, Guyana and Cyprus. The Secretariat's Food Production and Rural Development Division was also involved, since its concern lies with the improvement of the means of food production, processing, storage and marketing. The Dacca workshop originally proposed fifty-seven projects, and twenty of these were later identified by the five-country steering committee for priority work. Twelve countries participate in the Asia/Pacific rural technology programme. The project which has attracted the widest participation and attention is one in the management of water hyacinth, a fast-growing weed that plagues tropical waterways, but which also has potential for biogas generation, fodder, fertiliser and pulp and paper manufacture.[12]

(3)   Metrology and Quality Control

A survey conducted by the CSC on standards organisations in the Commonwealth showed that, while the importance of standards was generally recognised, several countries could not afford to develop their own national metrology systems. (Measurement standards and specification standards are essential for the industrial development of a country.) In April 1979 a project group meeting in Trinidad planned a metrology and quality control programme for the Caribbean. Trinidad and Tobago co-ordinated a project on testing measurements for accurate use in industry. Guyana is responsible for the development of a Caribbean information system on measurement standards and quality control. Barbados, which is responsible for training, made plans for a basic regional course on standardisation and metrology, which took place in September 1980, jointly run by the CSC and the International Standards Organisation, and funded by the CFTC.

(4) A Natural Products Programme

This presently involves Caribbean countries only. A meeting of specialists in Guyana in 1978 strongly recommended regional meetings in the Caribbean on schemes to utilise natural products for local industries – whether medicinal plants, algae, forest products, or waste material from agro-based industries. A natural products programme was set up in April 1979 made up of projects under several broad headings including: the identification and use of medicinal plants; the production and marketing of essential oils; and the use of marine products for human and animal foods, fertilisers, building, handicrafts and other industries. The steering committee met in Jamaica in early 1980, to decide on priorities, work out the details of chosen projects, and discuss funding and country involvement. The eleventh CSC, meeting in Nairobi in September 1980, decided, on Tanzania's suggestion, to start a new natural products programme in Africa similar to that in the Caribbean.

(5) A Mineral Resources and Geology Programme

This was carried out by the Commonwealth Geological Liaison office (CGLO) which has provided an information service on new developments in geology and mineral resources for member countries since 1951. Today the programme is managed within the consolidated CSC budget, but is guided separately under the auspices of the Commonwealth Committee on Mineral Resources and Geology (CCMRG), made up of the heads of geological services in member countries. A London management committee, including the Chairman of the CCMRG, the scientific representatives of the Australian, Canadian, Indian and New Zealand High Commissions in London, as well as the Science Adviser, meets frequently and oversees policies and activities. The CGLO produces a periodic newsletter, organises regional workshops and seminars, reports on geological meetings, provides information on geology and mineral resources, and establishes contacts between geologists in the Commonwealth.

FINANCE

In 1979–80, Britain was the largest contributor to the CSC (£48 253), followed by Canada (£32 168), Australia (£32 168), India (£16 084) and New Zealand (£16 084). The other members of the CSC contributed slightly over one per cent each to the budget. All new members make a nominal contribution of £100, in accordance with CSC practice, in the first two years of membership. The CSC's regular budget covers administrative costs and some limited operational costs. Programme financing is sought substantially from the CFTC through the Commonwealth Secretariat, other funding sources are increasingly available through shared costs and joint meetings. The CFTC is not the statutory funding agency of the CSC, but assesses the project financing requests in the same way as other Secretariat functional divisions. The Commonwealth Secretariat contributes an amount to cover the costs of the CSC's Secretary and Deputy Secretary, and one supporting staff member.

RELATIONS WITH OTHER COMMONWEALTH ORGANISATIONS

Science and technology co-operation and collaboration in the Commonwealth is also promoted through a number of organisations apart from the Commonwealth Secretariat, both official and unofficial. Their role is not, in itself, central to an understanding of the Commonwealth as an international institution. However, an understanding of their relationship with the Secretariat, of the flow of information and co-operation between them, does contribute to an understanding of the Commonwealth Secretariat as 'the single umbrella under which the official Commonwealth views all science matters in its purview.'[13] Among Commonwealth organisations, the Commonwealth Agricultural Bureaux, made up of four institutes and ten bureaux, is very significant. Twenty-four countries sit on its governing executive committee; it has over 400 staff, and aims to provide a world information service for agricultural scientists and other professional workers in the same and allied fields, a biological control service, and a pest and disease identification service. Each institute and bureau is concerned with its own branch of agricultural science and acts as a clearing-house for the collection, collation and dissemination of information of value to research workers. Information is published in twenty-four main abstract journals, with a circulation of 30 000 in 150 countries, as well as in seventeen journals on specialised subjects. Annotated bibliographies, books, maps and monographs are also published. All but one of the bureaux (the Commonwealth Institute of Biological Control in Trinidad) are British-based.[14]

There are many unofficial Commonwealth organisations in the field of science and technology. They range from professional organisations such as the Commonwealth Engineers Council and the Commonwealth Association of Science and Mathematics Educators, to the Commonwealth Forestry Institute (teaching and research in forestry), the Commonwealth Association of Scientific Agricultural Societies (which aims to strengthen the application of scientific agricultural practices in Commonwealth countries), and the Royal Agricultural Society of the Commonwealth.

A professional organisation such as the Commonwealth Engineers Council (CEC) provides an important focus for professional engineering opinion in the Commonwealth. As all Commonwealth countries with an established engineering institution are members, it represents more than a quarter of a million Commonwealth engineers. The CEC aims to advance engineering science, and has been instrumental in establishing a Commonwealth board on engineering education and training. This board aims to help all Commonwealth countries to develop their engineering capability. The CEC's main emphasis is on education, and an important part of its programme is the attempt to establish parity of engineering qualification standards within the Commonwealth. It holds regular regional conferences, and a biennial pan-Commonwealth conference. it disseminates information to its members, and is able to arrange expert assistance in response to requests.

Many unofficial Commonwealth organisations in the field of science and technology share this characteristic of promoting the exchange of information and technical assistance and advice among their members. The Intermediate Technology Development Group (ITDG), for example, a private non-profit registered charity based in England, uses voluntary panels of experts to prepare specifications of equipment, teaching manuals and technical reports, and promotes new research and development in universities, technical colleges and professional associations. It aims to develop and promote technologies to assist developing countries to make the best use of their productive resources, both technically and in terms of policy-making. The ITDG is active throughout the Commonwealth, working through individuals as well as local, national and international institutions.

THE CSC AND OTHER INTERNATIONAL GOVERNMENTAL ORGANISATIONS

The Commonwealth Secretariat has entered into agreements or memoranda of understanding with a number of international agencies for the purposes of co-operation and mutual information. In a world of proliferating international agencies, some instruments that at least recognise the need for co-operation and communication seem desirable. Between 1979 and 1980, the Secretariat agreed articles of co-operation with, among others, Agence de Coopération Culturelle et Technique, UNIDO, UNESCO, HABITAT and UNEP. The Science Council, acting as a division of the Secretariat, has argued strongly for co-operation.

The role of the Commonwealth at the UN Conference on Science and Technology for Development (UNCSTD, August 1979) was not as prominent or as formalised as that of the Commonwealth in some other international fora. Commonwealth finance ministers, for example, now meet regularly before IMF and World Bank meetings, as do Commonwealth health ministers before World Health Assemblies. UNCSTD, however, was a unique, and not a regular, conference, and science enjoys a less secure rating in the ministerial ranks of national governments. The CSC none the less devoted a considerable amount of time to preparations for UNCSTD, and the exercise served as a very useful 'focus for the setting of priorities and action programmes for the Commonwealth . . .'[15] Similar detailed preparations, providing a likewise useful focus for Commonwealth policy-making and programmes, were made for the UN Conference on New and Renewable Energy Sources held in Nairobi, Kenya in August 1981.

CSC AND THE FUTURE

Seven major areas were highlighted by Commonwealth developing countries as areas of concern in the field of science and technology during their preparation for UNCSTD. They were anxious to alleviate the problems of the 'brain drain', as well as to increase the numbers of trained staff at every level. They emphasised the need for more and improved education and training, especially the provision of regional centres and scholarships. Information exchange was a matter of prime importance, and funds were needed to provide such things as libraries, staff and publishing capital. A greatly increased research and development capacity, based on indigenous technology and local resources, was required. Many countries pointed out the high proportion of science and technology manpower and money devoted to defence and military research and development in industrialised countries, and expressed a strong desire for more research and development resources in the developed world to be devoted to development problems.[16] Funding was required, especially for training and study tours, to alleviate serious shortages of foreign exchange. Transfer of technology was vital, including financing an actual mechanism for technology transfers, and the training of people to act as selectors. The special difficulties of small states, a major concern of the Commonwealth, were also emphasised, and at the eleventh CSC meeting in Nairobi in September 1980, the CSC decided to pay '. . . special attention in the 1980s to ways of increasing the participation of small island states in CSC programmes, despite their present lack of science infrastructure and their shortage of skilled human resources'.[17]

Budgetary constraints, prompted by economic conditions in member countries and by the expressed belief of Commonwealth heads of government that the Commonwealth Secretariat should not grow significantly beyond its present staff levels, will ensure that the CSC's operations remain modest in international terms. The account of the present CSC programme given in this chapter shows that the reality of that programme is modest indeed – not, it should be emphasised, in terms of the work accomplished by individuals, but in terms of the needs of Commonwealth developing countries and of the means made available to satisfy those needs. In real terms, the CSC is involved in only sixty projects throughout the Commonwealth, some of these really the initial *phases* of projects, such as preparatory evaluative studies. Even in these sixty projects, CSC involvement consists largely of roles as an initiator and a co-ordinator. The role of the CSC, with its limited funds and staffing, must be seen, in the final analysis, as useful but essentially peripheral in the overall tasks of development.

NOTES AND REFERENCES

1. The author would like to acknowledge the considerable help received from Christian de Laet and Colin Beavington of the Commonwealth Science Council. However the author alone is responsible for this chapter.
2. *Report of the Commonwealth Secretary-General, 1977*, p. 54. (London: Commonwealth Secretariat.)
3. In 1977 the Secretary-General advised heads of government that 'the

Commonwealth Science Council has expressed the view that the Council be fully integrated with the Secretariat, as the nucleus of a Science division. This matter is being actively pursued, and a Memorandum of Understanding between the CSC and the Secretariat is now being finalised' (*Secretary-General's Report, 1977*, p. 54). The integration was completed in 1979.

4. *Secretary-General's Report, 1979*, p. 44.

5. It should be noted that national institutional arrangements for science and technology in Commonwealth countries vary considerably. (So do views on science policy – some countries do not believe in a centralised policy, others have no science and technology policy at all.) National arrangements may take the form of advisory bodies to Cabinet (e.g. Barbados). They may be co-ordinating bodies (e.g. Guyana, Ghana, Kenya); or they may be responsible for a combination of functions in science and technology such as advising, co-ordinating and planning (e.g. Bangladesh, India). In a few Commonwealth countries (e.g. Ghana, Guyana) central science and technology bodies also have a funding capacity. Some Commonwealth countries do not have either a central agency or any statutory machine to co-ordinate science and technology (e.g. Sierra Leone, Mauritius). Most and technology policy planning and research in Commonwealth countries is done by a variety of bodies: government departments, central agencies, public corporations, industry, universities.

6. *Secretary-General's Report, 1979*, p. 44.

7. From a CSC proposal made to the Commonwealth Heads of Government, meeting in Kingston, Jamaica, April/May 1975.

8. From a CSC note to Commonwealth Heads of Government, meeting in Lusaka, Zambia, August 1979.

9. *Secretary-General's Report, 1979*, p. 44.

10. Ibid.

11. Ibid.

12. *Commonwealth Currents*, October 1980. (Published monthly by the Commonwealth Secretariat, Marlborough House, London.)

13. The Secretary of the CSC, in a personal interview, November 1980.

14. It should be emphasised that the work of the CSC is entirely devoted to civil, non-military fields. There is a quite separate Commonwealth Defence Science Organisation, founded in 1946, of which fourteen Commonwealth countries are members. It aims to promote the advancement of defence science throughout the Commonwealth. Nor is the development of nuclear energy within the ambit of the CSC – such co-operative programmes as exist in Commonwealth countries are the product of bilateral links, the most significant being those of Canada and India.

15. *Secretary-General's Report, 1979*, p. 47.

16. The United States is responsible for 70 per cent of the world's research and development expenditures, the other developed market economies for 28 per cent, and the developing countries for only 2. (These figures exclude the centrally planned economies.) Of the R & D expenditure of the OECD countries, 51 per cent is spent on atomic, space and defence research, 26 per cent on economic research, 22 per cent on fundamental and welfare research, and 1.0 per cent on the specific problems of developing countries. (From: 'Science and technology for development – proposals for the second development decade,' UN, 1970.)

17. *Commonwealth Currents*, October 1980.

8 Commonwealth Co-operation in the Field of Health

JOHN MARTIN

International co-operation in the field of health dates from 1851 when the first International Sanitary Conference was held in Paris. The driving force in this and subsequent conferences until the outbreak of the First World War was the desire to control the spread of serious epidemics of cholera, plague and yellow fever which killed scores of thousands of Europeans. Co-operation was restricted to European nations and later the American republics.

Between the World Wars the League of Nations was established and within it the health organisation of the League. This brought the numbers of international health organisations to three, the others being Office Internationale d'Hygiène Publique (OIHP) in Europe, established in 1907, and the Pan American Health Organisation (PAHO) established in 1902. It was not until 1946 that a single universal health organisation, the World Health Organisation (WHO), was established, although its governing body, the World Health Assembly, did not meet until 1948.[1]

The main role of WHO is 'to encourage and assist governments in fulfilling their responsibilities for the health of their peoples and in securing the active participation of the public.'[2] Collaboration in the promotion of good health is in marked contrast to that earlier collaboration confined to control of the spread of major diseases.

In the field of health, the political influence of emergent nations has been felt, as it has in general in international relations, contributing to the movement towards a preventative and promotive approach, with the aim of good health for all, not just a privileged few. Recently this has

107

been expressed in the primary health care approach which stresses that health is an essential component of overall socio-economic development and that achievement of good health is a matter of just resource allocation, not merely of scientific progress.

HEALTH AND THE COMMONWEALTH SECRETARIAT

Modern Commonwealth involvement in the health field began soon after the establishment of the Secretariat with the first Health Ministers' conference, which was held in Edinburgh in 1965. Subsequently these conferences have taken place triennially, in Uganda, Mauritius, Sri Lanka, New Zealand and Tanzania.

Initially the absence of a health section in the Secretariat was a hindrance to conference organisation and the follow-up of conference recommendations. This was overcome in 1969 by the establishment of the office of the Medical Adviser to the Secretary-General which subsequently became the Medical Division in 1979.

The twin objectives of the Medical Division have stemmed from an acceptance of the importance of good health in economic and social development: to share experience and knowledge as a means of raising health standards and the encouragement of regional co-operation to spread resources and reduce costs in areas such as training and procurement of drugs and equipment and to relate to local conditions.[3]

The division has been guided by the decisions and recommendations of the triennial conferences. Its main tasks are as follows:

(1) Organisation of the Health Ministers' conference every three years;
(2) Follow-up and implementation of decisions and recommendations made by Health Ministers' conferences;
(3) Organisation of a one day meeting of health ministers and country representatives annually in Geneva immediately prior to the World Health Assembly;
(4) Promotion of regional co-operation;
(5) Special projects such as the organisation of seminars on issues of particular interest.[4]

In carrying out these tasks the Medical Division uses three main methods: the convening of meetings and seminars; the dissemination of information and opinions from member governments; and the commissioning of short-term consultancies to research particular issues and report to the Health Ministers' conference. The following examples from 1979/80 will serve to illustrate the division's annual work programme:

(1) A study on health education for Commonwealth youth was completed and distributed to governments, and the curriculum proposed was introduced into the training courses at the three regional centres of the Commonwealth Youth Programme in Guyana, India and Zambia.

(2) A consultant health planner, financed by CFTC, carried out assignments for governments in Botswana, Lesotho, Swaziland and Malaysia.

(3) The first two regional courses for medical technicians at the Swaziland College of Technology were completed.

(4) Two medical-legal workshops, in collaboration with the Legal Division, were held in Barbados and Malawi and a meeting of experts in London discussed problems of small island states and recommended ways of tackling their problems.

Regional Co-operation

The Commonwealth Secretariat supports three regional secretariats: the West African health secretariat set up in Lagos, Nigeria in 1972; the secretariat for East, Central and Southern Africa (including Mauritius and Seychelles) established in Arusha, Tanzania in 1974; and the longer established health section of the Caribbean Community Secretariat in Georgetown, Guyana. The West African association has since developed into the five member West African Health Community established by treaty in October 1978 with a membership comprising The Gambia, Ghana, Liberia, Nigeria and Sierra Leone. Although Liberia is not a Commonwealth member she has been a full member since 1974.[5]

At Health Ministers' conferences in 1965, 1968[6] and 1971, recommendations about regional co-operation have been made, about the machinery to develop and sustain such co-operation by utilising existing organisations, and more specifically about medical-paramedical training and repair of equipment.[7] In practice the regional secretariats function in similar ways. Each is headed by a doctor with a small administrative and secretariat staff. In each region health ministers meet annually to decide on policies and activities. In the Caribbean and West Africa there are annual meetings for permanent secretaries and chief medical officers. In the East, Central and Southern Africa region there is an advisory Committee of four country representatives appointed by the regional Health Ministers' conference, which supervises the activities of the secretariat and prepares the regional budget. It meets twice yearly. Similarly in West Africa there is a finance and general purposes committee to supervise the secretariat's activities. As examples of activities supported by the regions during 1979/80 there were health management courses in Accra and Arusha, a workshop in Arusha for senior officers on health management training, and workshops on control of particular diseases, for example, a meeting on regional cholera control in Lusaka, Zambia.[8]

COMMONWEALTH FUND FOR TECHNICAL CO-OPERATION (CFTC)

Support by CFTC for activities carried out by the Medical Division and the regional secretariats is considerable. It funds a health planning consultant in each region. In the East, Central and Southern African region it provides an expert to run the medical engineering course in Swaziland; and it sponsors a joint study with the Medical Division on bulk drug purchase. All three regional secretariats receive support for their activities and for some staff salaries, the latter only as an interim measure – for example, the two regional offices in Arusha ceased to be directly employed by CFTC at the end of June 1980.[9]

COMMONWEALTH FOUNDATION

The Commonwealth Foundation, although an independent mainly government-financed body, co-operates with the Medical Division to encourage interchanges between Commonwealth organisations and individuals, for example, the recent introduction of a scheme to enable senior medical students to spend an elective period working in Commonwealth countries other than their own.

Other Funding

The Medical Division is funded from the annual budget

Secretariat, together with some support from CFTC. With a medically-qualified director, assistant director and secretarial staff the total resources of the division are strictly limited. However the 1980 Health Ministers' conference approved the recruitment of a second doctor to join the staff and increase its capacity accordingly.

The secretariats of West Africa and of East, Central and Southern Africa are financed mainly from agreed contributions of member countries, calculated on the bases of population and national income. The activities of the Caribbean secretariat receive major assistance from several sources besides CFTC, including UNICEF, in food and nutrition, and the Pan American Health Organisation (PAHO), in maternal and child health and epidemiological surveillance.

THE COMMONWEALTH SECRETARIAT AND WHO

The World Health Organisation (WHO), a specialised agency of the United Nations has as its objective 'the attainment by all peoples of the highest possible level of health.'[10] The organisation divides its activities into sections: development of comprehensive health services; health manpower development; disease prevention and control; promotion of environmental health; promotion and development of biomedical and health services research; and programme development and support. In addition there are activities concerning health regulations as well as co-ordination with other agencies.

WHO holds the World Health Assembly annually and the Commonwealth Secretariat is usually represented by the Medical Adviser. WHO is an organisation which operates on a far vaster scale than the Commonwealth Secretariat can hope to do. The total WHO budget for 1978–79 was US $354 330 000 out of which US $146 million was allocated for headquarters, global and interregional activities.[11] These figures contrast markedly with the budget for the Commonwealth Secretariat *as a whole* which was £2 453 200 over the same period, with CFTC contributing a further £9 millions approximately.[12] It is clear that in terms of capacity the health activities of the Commonwealth Secretariat and WHO cannot be usefully compared. However, as an organisation the Commonwealth has considerable potential for influencing WHO policies and programmes since 36 out of a total WHO membership of 155 are also Commonwealth members, that is almost one quarter.[13]

Commonwealth health ministers and their delegations meet each year in Geneva immediately prior to the World Health Assembly to exchange views on agenda items and, if possible, agree on a common approach to the most important issues. However, the meeting lasts for only one day and thus discussion is restricted, even more so since there is also a review of follow-up by the Medical Division of recommendations made at the triennial Health Ministers' conference. This takes the form of a written report presented by the Director of the Medical Division and subsequent discussion and appraisal by countries' representatives.

THE UNOFFICIAL COMMONWEALTH

No review of Commonwealth health activities would be complete without mention of the important work carried out by organisations not formally linked with the Secretariat. These are divided into two groups, those carrying out charitable medical work in poor Commonwealth countries and those representing professional groups.

In the first category there are four organisations. The oldest is LEPRA (British Leprosy Relief Association) established in 1924. Based in Britain, it operates mainly in Africa and India. Its activities include leprosy research, prevention and cure of leprosy and training of local health personnel.[14] The Royal Commonwealth Society for the Blind was founded in England in 1950. It is governed by a council representing seventeen Commonwealth countries and has regional offices in Asia, Africa and the Caribbean. The Society sponsors the world's largest programme of sight restoration through eye examinations and operations. As an example, during 1978 some 140 000 blind people had their sight restored and another 23 500 had operations to prevent imminent blindness.[15] The Commonwealth Society for the Deaf was founded in 1959 to promote education, health and welfare of the deaf and partially-hearing throughout the Commonwealth. It supports training of teachers of the deaf as well as research into prevention of deafness. An example is a research project at the University of Ibadan, Nigeria, on deafness in children as a result of prenatal maternal rubella. It has also organised regional seminars on problems of deafness for doctors, teachers and social workers, funded by the Commonwealth Foundation.[16] Operation Eyesight International, based in Canada, funds eye hospitals, mobile eye units and eye camps mainly in Africa and India. Founded in 1963 it has a membership of around 5000 in Canada, Australia, New Zealand, India, Britain and the USA.[17]

Pan-Commonwealth organisations for health professionals are three in number: the Commonwealth Medical Association, the Commonwealth Pharmaceutical Association and the Commonwealth Nurses Federation founded in 1962, 1971 and 1973 respectively. Each exists to promote the interests of their professions, to maintain high professional standards and to promote close links and the exchange of information between members. The Commonwealth Medical Association submits papers on occasion for consideration by the Commonwealth Health Ministers' meetings and has observer status at the World Health Assembly. Sharing an office building with the association is the Commonwealth and International Medical Advisory Bureau. Founded in 1948 the Bureau is maintained by the British Medical Association to assist foreign doctors to visit Britain for further study and experience.[18]

THE COMMONWEALTH – FORCE FOR PROGRESS?

Comparison with WHO immediately reveals the very limited resources available for Commonwealth health activities. Nevertheless this in itself does not justify criticism. After all, Commonwealth members represent almost one quarter of WHO membership and thus share the resources of that organisation. As has already been said, Commonwealth members seek to influence WHO policies, but effect is limited by the short time for consultation.

Within the Commonwealth itself the common heritage of language and systems of education and administration have had a particularly strong influence in the health field. In many countries professional qualifications in medicine and nursing have been accepted as equal. This has contributed to the maintenance of high standards of practice in medical care through the sharing of undergraduate training facilities and the provision of postgraduate training for professionals from developing countries by institutions in the developed countries. However there has also been a very damaging side effect of this professional equality. This has been the alarming flow of medical personnel from developing to developed countries – the 'brain drain' – especially rapid during the late 1960s and early 1970s, for example from the Indian subcontinent to Britain.

The problem was first raised at the 1971 Commonwealth Health Ministers' conference in Mauritius and has appeared on the agenda of every subsequent conference. The Commonwealth Secretariat commissioned a study of the brain drain presented in 1977 in New Zealand. Subsequent discussions resulted in agreement at the 1980 conference in

Arusha, Tanzania, on the need to expand postgraduate education in developing countries, for temporary registration only for postgraduate students in developed countries, and the development of medical curricula more relevant to the needs of individual countries. In addition, some individual member governments have taken action. Examples are the curb on postgraduate study in Britain introduced by India and the curb on employment of foreign doctors in Britain through the introduction of a compulsory examination. Thus it is intended that personnel trained at high cost will remain in their own countries.

The emergence of the developing countries as a strong political force has had a strong and positive influence on Commonwealth health affairs. In the 1965 and 1968 Ministers' conferences it was accepted that the way to bring about improvement in health was to train more doctors and paramedical personnel through the improvement of existing 'centres of excellence'. This concept was challenged at the 1971 conference which called for an examination of the health needs and priorities of developing countries. This marked the beginning of a re-examination of the conventional medical approach to meeting health needs. The conference subsequently called for improved training in health planning and management, a prominent position for health in overall national planning and a shift of emphasis from curative to preventive measures in health care.

Subsequent conferences up to and including 1980 have continued this trend with discussions including allocation of scarce resources, the needs of rural areas, food and nutrition, community participation in health care and family health. Such discussions are much more relevant to the needs of the vast majority of the people of the Commonwealth who suffer from malnutrition and preventable diseases and whose governments have very limited resources with which to provide health care.

The aim of the Commonwealth Secretariat is to share experience and knowledge as a means of raising health standards. The reports of the Health Ministers' conferences show that sharing of knowledge and experience is regularly achieved. However that does not imply an automatic improvement in health standards. What is needed is an evaluation of the actions taken by member governments following the triennial conferences and not merely examination of the activities of the Secretariat with its meagre resources.

NOTES AND REFERENCES

1. *Introducing WHO* (Geneva: WHO, 1976).
2. Ibid.
3. *Report of the Commonwealth Secretary General, 1979* (London: Commonwealth Secretariat).
4. *Medical Division Work Programme 1980–81* (London: Commonwealth Secretariat).
5. *Report of the Commonwealth Secretary General, 1979* (London: Commonwealth Secretariat).
6. *Report of the Commonwealth Secretary General, 1968* (London: Commonwealth Secretariat).
7. *Report of the Commonwealth Secretary General, 1971* (London: Commonwealth Secretariat).
8. *Medical Division Work Programme 1980–81* (London: Commonwealth Secretariat).
9. Ibid.
10. *Introducing WHO* (Geneva: WHO, 1976).
11. *WHO Budget 1978–79* (Geneva: WHO).
12. *Report of the Commonwealth Secretary General, 1979* (London: Commonwealth Secretariat).
13. *Biennial Report of the Director-General 1978–79* (Geneva: WHO).
14. *Report for Commonwealth Heads of Government Meeting, 1980* (London: Commonwealth Secretariat).
15. *Annual Report 1978–79* (Royal Commonwealth Society for the Blind, England).
16. Publicity pamphlet, Commonwealth Society for the Deaf (undated).
17. *Report for Commonwealth Heads of Government Meeting, 1980* (London: Commonwealth Secretariat).
18. Ibid.

9 Military Ties

WILLIAM GUTTERIDGE

Military co-operation between the self-governing members of the Commonwealth has, since the Second World War, never been a matter of comprehensive multilateral action. There has been no pretence or semblance of such a relationship. Commonwealth Prime Ministers' Conferences in the 1950s from time to time debated the international situation but the outcome was always diplomatic, political or economic rather than military. As Empire progressively became Commonwealth, with members achieving fully independent status, the titles, but not the function, of certain British military institutions were slow to reflect the changes. The Chief of the Imperial General Staff (CIGS) retained his title until after the effective imperial structure had disappeared, and eventually the Imperial Defence College became the Royal College of Defence Studies, attracting to its prestigious courses senior officers, civil servants and diplomats from a far wider range of apparently friendly countries than ever before. Even such institutions in their heyday were essentially Anglocentric, even British national, in terms of their management and control.

The old Committee of Imperial Defence never re-emerged in the post-war period. Commonwealth defence ceased to be conceived on a global basis. Throughout the 1950s and early 1960s a British military liaison team in the Commonwealth Relations Office in London, co-ordinated training and military assistance to the newly-independent African and Asian armies. Even here the sensitivities of the emergent states on issues relating to their stability and security demanded confidentiality which could only be achieved through bilateral arrangements. If, for example, they wanted their officers trained at junior or more senior staff level, they dealt directly with the state which they felt could best satisfy their needs or was most convenient. Initially and naturally Britain dominated this scene. Substantial foundations for new army officer corps were laid in

116

the 1950s by the education and training in Britain of relatively large numbers of young men from Ghana, Nigeria, Malaysia, Sri Lanka, and, initially even Burma. Anxiety to ring the changes and reduce dependence soon involved Canada, Australia, New Zealand, Pakistan and India. By the time the pull of historic relationships was waning, and the locale and source of military aid began to be sought in, for instance, Israel and the Soviet bloc, an important foundation for more informal and incidental future Commonwealth co-operation existed. The extent and nature of these ties are still a matter of debate and need to be seen in the context of other developments.

It was not only the sensitivities inherent in post-colonial independence but practical considerations on the part of all parties which quickly reduced operational Commonwealth military co-operation to a range of largely bilateral agreements. As early as 1946 the annual British Defence White Paper envisaged a series of sometimes overlapping, regional member alliances. The participation of particular nations of the Commonwealth would, it was accurately predicted, become largely a matter of geography and local strategic perceptions.

None of the newer members of the Commonwealth in Africa or Asia in fact joined later any of the treaty systems established in the first ten years of the cold war. The one possibility, raised in the Anglo-South African agreement of 1955, of a new organisation either free-standing or conceivably relating Africa and parts of the Middle East in some way to NATO disappeared when South Africa left the Commonwealth in 1961. The short-lived British-Nigerian defence agreement, cancelled after only fifteen months in 1962, never had any potential for expansion into a regional grouping even though there were then still some traces of the original Accra-based West African common structure. These abortive arrangements demonstrated that intra-Commonwealth relationships were now incidental to a network of agreements of which Washington was the effective centre and not London.

The concept of Commonwealth defence had depended on the ability of one strong member with a global capability going to the aid of others. Even if Britain had remained relatively strong, her ability actually to get assistance to Australia or New Zealand, for example, was put in doubt by the tenuous substitute of staging rights and island bases for the largely unquestioned imperial lines of communication.

It was, however, more the sustained shift in the emphasis of British defence policy and provision than regional agreements and perspectives, which spelt the end of Commonwealth defence. Nor, in spite of the expanded regional roles of Australia, Canada or even India, was any replacement focus likely to emerge. The British nuclear force, her commitment to NATO and to the provision of forces in West Germany, and the related withdrawal from bases east of Suez, provided the clearest indicators to other Commonwealth members. The retreat from Aden simply set the seal on a process firmly established much earlier, long before the last cursory reference in the British annual review of policy to Commonwealth defence, which occurred in the 1959 Defence White Paper. Any pretensions of a comprehensive approach even to the Middle East had been abandoned after the Suez fiasco.

The Commonwealth Prime Ministers' meeting of 1964 followed by the creation of the Commonwealth Secretariat in June 1965 effectively ended the residual instrumentality of military co-operation via White-hall. There apparently no longer exists any means of appraising or reviewing the Commonwealth connection in these terms. Within the Secretariat at Marlborough House only the section concerned with constitutional matters has the slenderest of official interest in military questions. The Foreign and Commonwealth Office appears to have neither the means nor the motivation to look at the question in any comprehensive Commonwealth fashion. Only fragmented knowledge exists and is safeguarded mainly to avoid diplomatic embarrassment to a partner in a bilateral arrangement by revealing the nature or scale of that agreement. The Ministry of Defence is naturally and pragmatically interested only in the operational, intelligence and similar co-ordinatory characteristics of any relationship, without particular regard for the Commonwealth dimension. Linking of arms sales with training facilities would put Saudi Arabia or Zaire, for example, on a similar or higher plane than a Commonwealth country for this purpose, according to advantage in the individual case.

In general the extent of co-operation in really sensitive areas such as intelligence and counter-subversion – and almost all defence matters are sensitive – depends on undeclared political factors. Eastern bloc connections are one obvious determinant of the level of mutual confidence. But several other elements lead to a tiered system. A deterioration in the security situation in Southern Africa might well enhance the tendency to discrimination between member countries on the basis of the North-South divide.

The extent of the disintegration of the Commonwealth relationship should not, however, be overstated. There remains across at least twenty countries a professional military culture with Commonwealth over-tones. While joint strategic planning may no longer be even a possibility, consultation and exchange of personnel and information do help to link the more enthusiastic members of the Commonwealth militarily. The centre of this 'system' is still primarily Britain, its focus is the training of Commonwealth officers, which in its turn clearly encourages some development of joint training programmes and perhaps political sympathy, economic co-operation and trade.

The education and training provided are at several levels. Though Commonwealth officer cadets no longer attend the Royal Military Academy Sandhurst on the 1950s scale, several countries have maintained a sporadic connection with it since then. Kenya and some of the smaller African countries like Malawi have in recent years made considerable use of this facility; so have new island states in the Caribbean. This has also been true of senior officer education: the Royal Naval Engineering College of Manadon has attracted Malaysians and Nigerians and the West African connection of Ghana and Nigeria with the Royal Military College of Science at Shrivenham has continued. In the last year or two, however, attempts to assess and charge true cost-related fees have become a deterrent. This, like the original ceiling of places for overseas students at, for instance, RMA Sandhurst in the 1950s and early 1960s, reflects a lack of government enthusiasm in Britain for cementing ties through trans-national professional peer groups – or a shortsighted view of the financial balance of advantage.

Probably the most successful connections have been at staff college level. The army staff colleges, usually for captains or majors, in Britain, Canada, Australia, India, and at one stage Pakistan, have helped to create an informal Commonwealth military brotherhood, not only socially but by their common approach to operational and organisational problems. In so far as strategic and tactical doctrine is held in common it is inculcated by this means. This, as well as immediate political considerations, has often influenced the purchase of arms and equipment, so that an element of standardisation, albeit very erratic, remains.

Fifteen years ago there were about seven hundred officers from Commonwealth countries attending British training establishments simultaneously. This number has steadily decreased, but even in 1981 it was still significant. What has necessarily been reduced far more dramatically is the number of officers and NCOs from Britain, Canada, and other Commonwealth countries with well-developed armed forces, serving with or training the newer armed forces. The policy of integrating the guerrilla armies with elements of the old Rhodesian security forces in Zimbabwe has revived temporarily in a unique form a once well-established practice. Perhaps the most important contemporary example of this kind of co-operation is the return, since 1976, of British officers to Nigeria, to assist with teaching and with the development of the Defence Services college in Kaduna. A parallel enterprise starting from scratch has been carried out over much the same period at Dacca in Bangladesh. Tanzania has recently considered reapproaching Britain for advanced military training after a long period of often frustrating experience elsewhere. Notably the African countries of the Commonwealth have recurrently looked to Britain and Canada for assistance, since Ghanaian independence when first the British and then the Canadians provided training at the military academy at Teshie. Language, combined with cognate systems of education up to university level, are in the military as well as other spheres the most important elements inducing Commonwealth co-operation.

Thus it is perhaps not surprising that virtually all Commonwealth countries continue to use the British system of staff, duties, command and organisation. This is in spite of the attraction for Australia and especially for Canada of the United States' system which has itself been totally reconstructed once and modified several times since the war. New weapons systems and especially new battlefield concepts are forcing radical changes on the defence forces of the more advanced countries.

In spite of common training links, factors exist which militate against any large-scale standardisation of equipment cost, allied to distance from the source of supply and reliability of lines of communication in times of crisis. Shopping around for equipment has become normal practice in a buyers' market (and to some extent provenance of equipment influences its use). However, it is worth noting that in the first decade after independence France by direct insistence successfully linked military aid to most of her former colonies in Africa to the purchase of French equipment, while Britain was less effective in this respect.

There have nevertheless been a large number of arms transactions between Commonwealth countries which have reinforced the connection and encouraged continuing dependence. India, for example, has purchased 'combat' aircraft from Britain including, at an early stage, the Gnat. Kenya has acquired Vickers Mk III tanks with transporters and Hawk jets. Zambia in 1978 was supplied with Rapier and Tiger Cat missiles. A British frigate was sold to Malaysia in 1976 and two patrol boats went to Tanzania in 1975. Nigeria bought corvettes in 1978. Australia's interest in the defence of Malaysia has led to channelling of equipment and spares in that direction; Canada has supplied Buffalo transporters to Zambia. In general these bilateral arrangements indicate the Commonwealth as a fall-back source of supply, especially when commitment elsewhere, for instance to the Soviet Union, is seen as politically embarrassing. Sales usually carry with them training facilities.

In general, however, the increasing sophistication of preparations for war and of the intended means of deterring it have in the last twenty years engendered a military 'gap' comparable with that existing economically between developed and developing countries. Hence the more advanced and industrialised of Commonwealth countries with their advanced technologies will have little that is appropriate to offer to the less developed. If the Commonwealth connection, however, were to remain at all buoyant in other respects then it is possible that those countries which are towards the middle of the spectrum of sophistication might link the extremes, thus becoming more significant internationally and in the Commonwealth. The attitude, for example, of India towards the Commonwealth relationship could regain an enhanced importance: India has not only very large armed forces – her army is currently, at about 800 000 men, third in the world after China and the Soviet Union and ahead of the United States – but is in every sense developing and has a long established indigenous arms industry dating from the period of British rule.

The picture with regard to formal ties of a military nature between the countries of the Commonwealth at large is then in some respects negative. Such structural links as exist are largely symbolic, even though there may be for individual states a small practical advantage in perpetuating longstanding administrative arrangements. Of the institutionalised arrangements the Commonwealth Committee on Defence (Operational Clothing and Combat Equipment), originally located in 1946 in the British Ministry of Supply, reflects most clearly the continuing character of the Commonwealth relationship. The initiative to establish it came in the first place from India. It has twenty-eight full members and three associate members, only one of which, the USA, is from outside the Commonwealth. Its triennial conferences have been held in India, Britain, Canada, Australia, Kenya, and most recently in Ghana in 1978. A further meeting was scheduled for Malaysia in 1981. It does not deal with arms and ammunition but with all other categories of military equipment. Information, research and development, the exchange of scientific and technical staff and testing are the main fields of activity. Standing sub-committees are concerned with human factors, materials testing and quality control, and research and development organisation for developing countries. Continuity is maintained by a secretariat working with the committees in between conferences. It is parallel to, but independent of, the Commonwealth Defence Science Organisation also founded in 1946 which has an executive staff of three and fourteen member Commonwealth countries. Their chief defence scientists constitute an executive committee. The purpose is to promote the advancement of defence science throughout the Commonwealth. Recently the main areas of activity have been in military and civilian food research through a food study group, and corrosion research through the corrosion cell based in India. There has been some co-operative research.

Both these official organisations are located in the British Ministry of Defence and not in the Commonwealth Secretariat. There are one or two unofficial bodies of a quite different character. The Commonwealth War Graves Commission has its own distinctive function and its membership is restricted to Australia, Britain, Canada, India, New Zealand and South Africa, reflecting the participation of the so-called 'old' Commonwealth in the two World Wars, though its activities are now spread over 145 countries. More closely reflecting professional ties is the British Commonwealth Ex-Services League embracing forty-five member ex-service organisations in forty-three Commonwealth countries. Though on the face of it more sentimental than practical, the function of aiding member organisations in their concern for the welfare of ex-servicemen amounted effectively to twenty-seven projects in twenty countries in 1976–7 and triennial conferences are held.

Such committees reflect the essential nature of current Commonwealth military ties. It is, therefore, inevitable that the main impact of these ties on events is circumstantial, intangible and difficult to assess. There are, however, potent affinities, especially in military ethics and procedures, sometimes even in crisis circumstances. For example, the work of UN peacekeeping forces has often been facilitated by the easy co-operation of Commonwealth contingents. This was first seen in the Congo in 1960, when Ghanaian, Nigerian, Malaysian and Indian units with smaller contingents from, for example, Sierra Leone were involved. Even where Commonwealth participation has been less extensive the influence of British Commonwealth practices relating to military aid to the civil power has often been apparent. The dovetailing into peacekeeping operations of Scandinavian, Irish and even Austrian forces has ironically been affected by these practices, most sharply typified by the Ghanaian demonstration of techniques of riot control to Irish and Swedish contingents in the Congo in 1960. On several occasions since the aftermath of Suez, common staff procedures of the Canadian and Indian armed forces have encouraged speed and effiency.

The role of Commonwealth contingents in UN peacekeeping forces has been significant of the characteristic professional tradition. Ghanaian troops in both Sinai and the Lebanon, and Nigerians in the Lebanon have played an important role. The possibility of specifically Commonwealth forces in Commonwealth situations has from time to time been considered; most notably in Rhodesia where the Nigerian government would have liked to participate as a symbol of their emergence as the leading African state. There had also at an early stage been talk of an Indian Commander. In the event a Commonwealth monitoring force, 1300 strong, supervised the concentration of guerrilla forces at assembly points before and during the 1980 election that followed the Lancaster House agreement. Half the force was provided by Britain and the remainder by Australia, Fiji, Kenya and New Zealand.

From time to time during the prolonged negotiations on a UN supervised election and a demilitarised zone in Namibia, the possibility of a supervisory force from Commonwealth sources has arisen with Britain, Canada, Nigeria, Kenya and India the most likely participants.

The willingness of Commonwealth members to help each other has not seriously been tested since the Chinese attack on India in 1962. Direct operational aid such as that mounted by Britain at the request of Kenya, Uganda and Tanzania in January 1964 to deal with army mutinies has not become a regular feature of Commonwealth relations. The military connections of Commonwealth countries within the framework of regional agreements have remained firm. British troops sometimes train in Canada. Australian links with Singapore and Malaysia have been maintained, as well as New Zealand's with Fiji and other South Pacific islands. Outside such agreements, Britain still has a special military relationship with Kenya, providing equipment, training and general support: at different times in the last six years engineer squadrons have assisted with road building and community aid, stocks of arms and ammunition have been built up in the face of the threat from Amin's Uganda, and Vickers Mark II tanks and transporters are being supplied.

Commonwealth military co-operation in practice, whatever the historical and cultural ties, is now, as it was perhaps even fifteen years ago, still of real value within the framework of an international system which needs a range of instruments for the maintenance of peace and stability. The channels of communication have been maintained at a sufficient level for a relatively speedy response to be possible in the face of emergencies arising from international terrorism, subversion, local aggression or even natural disaster. There may be occasional threats to British or Commonwealth interests, if they can be defined, but it is today much more likely that Commonwealth members will deploy their undoubted ability to co-operate militarily on behalf of the UN or of a regional grouping of responsible countries with which they happen to be connected.

10 Law of the Commonwealth

ALFRED M. KAMANDA

The most important factor in Commonwealth relations is the principle of Commonwealth consultation and co-operation which has given birth to what is generally known as the *inter se* doctrine of the Commonwealth association.[1] Accordingly the member states of the Commonwealth do not consider each other as foreign countries. Nevertheless, membership of the Commonwealth association does not necessarily affect the primary legal capacities and personality of member states any more than does membership of an international organisation, and indeed, has less effect than membership of some organisations, for example, the EEC, which has a slight federal element, albeit on a treaty basis. The emphasis is on a community of states in which the absence of a rigid legal basis of association is compensated by the bonds of common origin,[2] colonial experience and solidarity of mutual interests. It follows that Commonwealth relations, which if subsisting between any of the independent member states of the association and foreign countries would be regarded as international relations governed by international law, are flexibly conducted on the basis of the regular and effective machinery of consultation and exchange of information. In 1946 the Commonwealth Prime Ministers' Meeting put on record their conviction that the existing methods were 'preferable to any existing arbitral machinery' which 'would not facilitate, and might even hamper, the combination of autonomy and unity which is characteristic of the Commonwealth and is one of their great achievements'.[3]

CHANNELS FOR COMMONWEALTH CO-OPERATION

Beyond the Commonwealth Secretariat, the Commonwealth has relatively little political machinery and the Commonwealth's most important institution for formal exchange of views, the Commonwealth Heads of Government Meeting (CHOGM), has no executive authority. Conference resolutions have no legal effect until adopted by the individual countries, and the CHOGM is therefore a means of consultation rather than a formal organ for reaching decisions. But because of the basic willingness of Commonwealth countries to work together, conference decisions actually have more influence than might be supposed.

The Crown is the great symbol of the unity of the Commonwealth. This fact is given dramatic expression through the visits of the Queen to various parts of the Commonwealth and by her formal presence recognised by all members, as 'Head of the Commonwealth'. In addition, as Queen of many members, she provides a bond of unity whose force should not be underestimated. There are other institutions through which intra-Commonwealth relations are carried on. Exchange of information and consultation between Commonwealth countries is in fact a continuous process and the Secretariat plays a major role in this. Commonwealth countries' diplomatic representatives with each other are high commissioners who act in the same capacity as ambassadors, except that contact with the government to which they are accredited is often more informal and more continuous than is true of the representatives of foreign countries. Commonwealth countries often consult together in the context of other international organisations.

CO-OPERATION IN TERMS OF LAW

The designation 'Commonwealth Law' does not mean that there is a supranational legal order or system throughout the Commonwealth. On the contrary, the Commonwealth tradition recognises the various legal systems and traditions which member states have inherited or adapted to suit their individual needs regarding constitutional development. Within the territorial jurisdiction of each member state there has developed a separate, largely indigenous legal tradition (organisation of courts and legal practitioners, a body of principles, rules of precepts, and a body of knowledge and thinking about law) in the sense of having grown and developed naturally within the territory concerned, rather than having been imposed by colonial rule from without; yet it is not narrowly parochial, having strong historical affinities with the common law and equity of England. Sometimes a specific area of English law was adopted by reference; sometimes a whole area of common law was codified and enacted by a colonial legislature. But the most common form of reception of English law was by a general reception statute, which existed in almost every English-speaking Commonwealth country. That statute, of which Hong Kong's may be taken as an archetype, usually appeared either as local legislation or in the order-in-council establishing the colony or protectorate.

The Hong Kong Supreme Court Ordinance of 1950 contained the following clause establishing the basic law:

> Such of the laws of England as existed when the Colony obtained a local legislature, that is to say, on the 5th day of April, 1843, shall be in force in the Colony, except so far as the said laws are inapplicable to the local circumstances of the Colony or of its inhabitants, and except so far as they have been modified by laws passed by the said legislature (The Supreme Court Ordinance (Rev. Laws 1950, c. 4, S. 5)).

The extent to which, in consequence of this provision, Chinese customary law applies, is discussed in the report dated February 1953, of a committee on Chinese law and custom in Hong Kong. The view of the committee was that, apart from cases where Chinese law and custom are expressly preserved by local enactments, they are in force in the colony only where English law is inapplicable to the local circumstances of the colony or its inhabitants; and that it would probably be essential to show that the application of English law would lead to injustice, oppression or at all events to some fundamentally inequitable result. The Hong Kong courts have held that the inapplicability or otherwise of English law is to be determined in the light of circumstances as they existed on 5 April 1843; and that the Chinese customary law to be applied is that which obtained at the time when the colony was ceded.[4] In general, while Chinese law and customs are given effect in questions of family relations and inheritance, English law governs succession to immovable property. In any proceedings with respect to land in the New Territories, however, the courts have power to recognise and enforce Chinese customs (*New Territories Ordinance* (Rev. Laws 1950, c. 97), s. 17).

OTHER SYSTEMS OF LAW WITHIN THE COMMONWEALTH

There are several Commonwealth countries in which, though the common law of England has had its influence,[5] elements of other legal systems of modern continental Europe were preserved as the principal ingredients of their modern development. For example, the civil law of Quebec is broadly based on French law – notably the custom of Paris (a legal system reduced to writing in 1510, revised in 1580 and declared in 1663 to be the law of Canada), the French Codes, and French Ordinances if registered in Canada.[6] Quebec's rules, however, are by no means always identical with those observed by the French courts. English law has had its influence, particularly on the criminal law, which was accepted from the outset when French Canada became British territory, and commercial law, from which Quebec statutes have borrowed much. The result of these changes and reintroductions was that the courts in Quebec applied a mixture of French and English law. It will therefore be correct to say that the civil law of Quebec has a closer association with the Franco-German school of legal thought referred to as the 'Roman' or the 'continental' school of thought, which, like the Anglo-American school, has also spread its influence to large areas of the world far removed from its original home in Europe.

Every system[7] has at least some features affiliating it, more or less strongly, to one or several of four principal groups, namely

(1)   the common law in England on a stipulated date;
(2)   the civil law in continental Europe;
(3)   laws of Spanish and Portuguese origin; and
(4)   Roman-Dutch law – the Roman-Dutch law of the Netherlands – introduced in the Republic of South Africa by the Dutch East India Company which continued in operation after the takeover of the Cape of Good Hope by the British.

It should be remembered, however, that the four principal groups, all of which are characterised by features of European origin, do not account for all of the features in all the legal systems in the member states. Thus in the Asian and African Commonwealth states, there are a number of legal systems which, although in some way connected with one or two of the principal groups, retain certain elements of non-European origin. This is particularly true of (though not limited to) the Islamic member states of the Commonwealth. The penetration of these (non-European) systems in many parts of the Commonwealth has produced mixed systems which elude easy classification.

During the colonial period the British rulers usually adhered to the policy that in matters of family law, marital property, succession upon death, and related questions of land tenure, the personal law of the individuals involved should be applied. Islamic law – the influence of which has been considerable not only in the near East and in South Asia, but also in large parts of Africa – Hindu law, and other non-European systems, thus continued to be of great importance throughout the Commonwealth in so far as the personal relations and property interests of the indigenous populations were concerned. Nevertheless, even in these matters, common law influences made themselves felt because disputes were often decided by British judges, the Privy Council acting as court of last resort. As a rule these judges were empowered by statute or ordinance to interpret – and sometimes even to correct or reject – the parties' personal law in the light of the court's notions of 'justice, equity and good conscience'.[8] In other fields of law, relating especially to contracts, commercial law, procedure and evidence, the common law tended to displace the non-European systems either entirely or to a very large extent. Sometimes, when they acquired a territory originally colonised by another European power, the British retained the legal system previously established, i.e. a system, the European component of which was derived from the civil law, rather than the common law. As we have noted above, examples are Roman-Dutch Law in South Africa, Sri Lanka, and Zimbabwe, and French law in Quebec, Mauritius and the Seychelles.[9]

The strong influence of the common law in the Asian and African parts of the Commonwealth, though originally imported during a period of occupation or colonisation, has generally persisted after the end of that period. It appears, indeed, that upon gaining independence most of the former colonial territories, tending to modernise their law in the interest of economic development, jettison some of the customary and religious elements and strengthen the Western-influenced components of their legal systems. An example is India's abolition of the caste system and its ambitious attempt to modernise and 'codify' the customary law pertaining to family relations and family property. One of the important objectives of this legislation was to get rid of archaic restrictions upon the alienability of real property.[10] There are remnants of civil law influence in those small parts of India that were formerly Portuguese or French. It does not seem, however, that these civil law pockets have substantially affected the overall legal development of independent India.

The newly-independent Commonwealth countries invariably face fundamental problems of constitutional law. Almost all of them have adopted written constitutions. The draftsmen of these documents and the judges interpreting them are usually familiar, not only with British traditions, but also with at least some aspects of American constitutional law. More often than not they have to choose between (somewhat conflicting) British and American approaches on these matters, thus strengthening the basic common law orientation or knowledge of their public law, whether their preference in the particular case be for Dicey or for Wendell Holmes. The Nigerian constitution, for example, although essentially of a British constitutional and administrative origin, as had been laid down earlier by Luggard, in many ways shows a very strong American influence, especially in its judicial organisation and its constitutional and administrative law.

The common law of the Commonwealth has worked also upon the uncodified civil law systems within the Commonwealth, for example in the Republic of South Africa, Sri Lanka, Guyana and Scotland. The substantive private law of the Netherlands was codified in 1838. In those overseas territories, however, which the Dutch had lost prior to 1838 (including the former Dutch possessions in South Africa, Sri Lanka and Guyana), these nineteenth-century Dutch codes were never introduced; to the extent that the new sovereign retained the prior law in those territories, it was preserved in the form of uncodified Roman-Dutch law. In Guyana the three Dutch settlements later united as British Guiana. After cession in 1814, the then-existing systems of law (i.e. Roman–Dutch law) was retained for over a century; but in 1916, after the commencement of the British administration, the Civil Law of British Guiana Ordinance abrogated most of the Roman-Dutch law, except that relating to real property and intestate succession.[11] Scots law retains much of its original character, particularly in the traditional fields of marriage, property and inheritance; but centralised legislative and judicial control, combined with the economic integration of the United Kingdom, have had the effect of anglicising many facets both of substance and procedure. English influence has been particularly marked in those areas in which Roman law was defective and failed to provide adequate solutions, for example in agency and trust situations. Along with English rules of substantive law, some common law notions of *stare decisis* seem to have infiltrated into Scots law, a development regretted by some Scots lawyers.[12]

In Zimbabwe (Southern Rhodesia) the law has been influenced to a considerable extent by the common law: but it seems to have preserved its basic Roman-Dutch character from the days when the territory was administered after the practice in the Republic of South Africa. Unlike Scots law, the law of Zimbabwe is no longer subject to legislative and judicial controls exercised in the United Kingdom or ruled after the manner of South Africa[13] and this fact, coupled with political senti-ments, may assure the survival of the interesting Roman-Dutch system for the visible future. The notorious system of racial legislation in the Republic of South Africa is not inherited from traditional Roman-Dutch or common law sources.

The foregoing examination clearly supports the view that there is no supra-national 'Commonwealth law' with a plenary faculty to compel obedience upon the member states of the Commonwealth. In other words there are no supra-national legal rules regulating the intra-Commonwealth conduct of the member states, which are definite and susceptible of being brought together into a systematic whole by a logical arrangement. What is probably referred to as Commonwealth Law (for want of a better term) involves the traditional constitutional principles of the unity and indivisibility of the Crown and the formal allegiance owed to it by its subjects throughout the Commonwealth. Though directed outwards, to securing the political unity of the Commonwealth in its international relations, these principles and precedents were essentially constitutional conventions of the former British Empire. They differ from the distinct and varied territorial legal systems presently obtaining as regards jurisdiction and competence.

We have already suggested, however, that the absence of such a supra-national legal system is compensated by the bonds of common colonial experience, common law tradition and solidarity of interests. It is also admitted that the member states have separate legal systems; but there is always a desire to keep the other members of the Commonwealth fully informed of new developments in the field of law. These consultations are reinforced by frequent meetings of the Commonwealth law minis-ters, in different Commonwealth capitals, from time to time. These informal and intimate meetings afford the opportunity of free and frank interchanges of views on legal problems at the highest ministerial level and also help to solve differences of opinion. But above all, they eliminate mutual misgivings and suspicions on particular aspects in the field of law. It must be reiterated that the full international personality of the member states of the Commonwealth is not inconsistent with the fact that their relations *inter se* are not, in some respects, primarily international in character. They are *sui generis* in the sense that they are relationships which, if subsisting between any member state and foreign countries, or between foreign countries, would be regarded as in-ternational relations governed by international law. Take for example, the justiciability of Commonwealth disputes by the International Court of Justice. In the absence of other special provisions, compulsory jurisdiction of the court rests upon acceptance by the parties of Article 36(a) of the Statute of the Court – the so-called *optional clause*. Of immediate interest to our discussion is the reservation of disputes with any other member of the Commonwealth which originates in the declarations ratified by the United Kingdom and the Commonwealth states in 1930. In 1955 the declarations to the optional clauses of Australia, Canada, India, New Zealand, Pakistan, South Africa and the United Kingdom included reservations of disputes with other members of the Commonwealth. It is true that in recent years, as the justification for this Commonwealth reservation has been questioned, changes in practice have occurred. Pakistan is no longer a party to the Commonwealth reservation and, like South Africa, is no longer a member of the Commonwealth. But Canada, the Gambia, India, Kenya, Malawi, Malta, Mauritius and Nigeria have each incorporated the Commonwealth reservation in their declarations to the court. Indeed, certain member states of the Commonwealth retain the Commonwealth reservation albeit with differences of wording. For example, the declaration of India which reserves 'disputes with the government of any state which is or has been a member of the Commonwealth of Nations'. The adoption of this formulation followed Pakistan's leaving the Commonwealth. In the previous declaration of 14 September 1959, the reservation covered 'disputes with the government of any State which, on the date of the Declaration, is a member of the Commonwealth of Nations'. It follows that, in accepting the obligations of the 'optional clause' of the Statute of the International Court of Justice, the members of the Commonwealth are free to reserve reciprocally from its operation disputes which might arise among the member states of the Commonwealth.[14] The continued adoption of the Commonwealth reservation, even by republican governments within the Commonwealth, can be explained by the growing admission that it is an *inter se* policy to settle Commonwealth disputes by some other method.

THE JUDICIAL COMMITTEE OF THE PRIVY COUNCIL

If there is any decline in the acceptability of a Commonwealth legal institution it is in that of the Judicial Committee of the Privy Council which had served as an appeal court for cases from courts in various parts of the Commonwealth outside the United Kingdom itself. But though its jurisdiction is very different from that of the House of Lords, its personnel is almost identical because, at the time when the Law Lords were created as salaried life peers, it was decided that they could carry the bulk of work in both courts. Moreover, whoever else participates in the judicial work of the House of Lords is almost always a privy counsellor and thus entitled to be a member of the Judicial Committee of the Privy Council. The only difference in the membership of the two bodies is caused by the practice of giving a few places on the Judicial Committee to Commonwealth judges, particularly when a case affecting a particular area is under consideration.

Most of the independent member states of the Commonwealth have limited or abolished the right of appeal to the Judicial Committee of the Privy Council, but it still serves as the final court of appeal for Commonwealth territories which have not acquired full rights of independence. The right of appeal in criminal cases was abolished in the Dominion of Canada in 1933 and in civil matters in 1949 by legislation enacted locally. Appeal had been abolished in the case of South Africa and Ireland in 1933 (before either had left the Commonwealth), by India in 1949 and Pakistan in 1950 and in 1968 from the High Court of Australia where the right had been restricted by the constitution of 1900. The republican members of the Commonwealth, in Africa, for example, Ghana, Nigeria and Uganda have all abolished the right of appeal, though appeals pending at the time of independence were retained. Appeals to the Privy Council from Cyprus were abolished by the Cyprus Act 1960 on Cyprus becoming independent. Appeals from Sierra Leone, Singapore, Zambia, Zimbabwe have been abolished. Even under the Statute of Westminster 1931 there is no uniformity of practice among the members of the Commonwealth with regard to the place of the Privy Council after independence of the territory concerned. But what anomalies remain are due to individual choice. They could be changed at any moment if the country concerned wished to do so.

Since the House of Lords is the final authority for declaring English law, and where a case involves only principles of English law, which admittedly are part of the law of a specific Commonwealth member state, and there are no relevant differentiating local circumstances, the House of Lords must be regarded as finally declaring the law. It may be possible, then, to regard the Judicial Committee as in a formal sense a Commonwealth tribunal, which sits in effect as the final court of the country from which the particular appeal comes, applying the law of that country, including English law, as finally declared by the House of Lords, in so far as it is part of it. Given this, and given the power which every Commonwealth member has to modify or abolish appeals to the

Judicial Committee, in so far as provision for them still exists, there appears to be little justification for holding that it restricts the judicial autonomy of Commonwealth countries.

COMMONWEALTH SECRETARIAT'S ACTIVITIES IN THE LEGAL FIELD

Recently, through its research and consultative machinery, the Commonwealth Secretariat in London embarked upon keeping the member states generally informed on all aspects of legal developments including special developments in the fields of extradition, reciprocal enforcement of judgements and orders, and intra-Commonwealth judicial assistance. Through the auspices of the Secretariat, Commonwealth law ministers have succeeded in harnessing their collective experience for the benefit of individual members, by the exchange of proposals and legislation, training legal draftsmen, and the use of the services of experts for specific assignments on the training programme and giving advice wherever needed within the Commonwealth. The main impetus to this legal co-operation derives from decisions and guidance at biennial meetings of Commonwealth law ministers.

Through its three-monthly publication, the *Commonwealth Law Bulletin* (circulated widely among law reform commissions, parliamentary and other libraries, individual parliamentarians, law faculties of the Commonwealth, individual academics, Commonwealth legal periodicals, and members of the practising profession) the Commonwealth Secretariat is able to keep member countries aware of legal developments in other parts of the Commonwealth so that, in developing their own distinctive legal systems and in drafting legislation in an age of rapid change, they can benefit to the maximum from the experience of others. The *Bulletin* has thus renewed and reinforced one of the most tangible of Commonwealth links of the law in the Commonwealth, namely, the common law which has the value of a common legal heritage among member countries and has helped to place them in a unique position to profit.

To alleviate the severe shortage of skilled legal draftsmen in the newly-independent Commonwealth member states and speed up the implementation of essential legislative programmes in such countries, the Secretariat has engaged in the search for available draftsmen for service with those governments (either on a long-term or a short-term basis) in order to cope with urgently-needed legislation. The long-term service of such highly-skilled draftsmen helps governments to develop their own drafting resources through effective training programmes. In earlier regional courses in the Caribbean, Africa and Asia, some ninety officers from thirty Commonwealth countries benefited through a solid foundation in the basic principles, techniques and practice of drafting legislation, especially on matters such as constitutional law and specialised legislation on economic and social development. The Secretariat assisted the Government of Zambia with the launching of the Zambian Institute of Legislative Drafting by providing its first Principal, and by the extension of training awards to officers from other Commonwealth countries selected to attend the institute. *A Manual on Legislative Drafting* designed to facilitate training and help inexperienced draftsmen was commissioned and has already been distributed throughout the Commonwealth. In 1975 the legal division of the Secretariat organised a seminar as part of a continuing evaluation of the training programme.

The Commonwealth Legal Education Association (the secretary of which is the director of the Secretariat's legal division) has achieved the aims for which it was established in 1972. With a generous grant from the Commonwealth Foundation the association succeeded in compiling a list of 155 Commonwealth schools of law for the benefit of academic staff and public authorities. The Secretariat has also successfully compiled a bibliography of official publications, monographs and periodical articles on legislative and other legal drafting, and on the interpretation of statutes, which has been widely circulated and adopted by members of the Commonwealth.

The inclusion of legal expertise in the multidisciplinary technical assistance group established under the Commonwealth Fund for Technical Co-operation (CFTC) has proved invaluable. The realisation of appropriate returns from the exploitation of a member country's natural resources often requires the combined expertise which a multidisciplinary team of advisers can provide, particularly when the government concerned has to deal with powerful multinational corporations. It has been possible for the Secretariat to assist Commonwealth governments in connection with the exploitation of oil and geothermal energy, copper, diamonds and other minerals, both by providing draft legislation and other legal instruments and in the negotiation of agreements. A recent example of this type of activity was the assistance of the Secretariat with the successful renegotiation by Papua New

Guinea of arrangements relating to a copper mine which, although the most profitable in the region, was providing inadequate returns to the government.

The Secretariat has been able to use CFTC resources to respond to requests from Commonwealth governments for assistance in many other specialised areas of the law. It has been able to do this either by employing the legal expertise of the CFTC team of experts at headquarters or through the co-operation of member governments in finding persons with the relevant experience. Legal advisers or draftsmen have been provided for both short and long-term projects concerned, for example, with succession to treaties and other international rights and obligations, merchant shipping legislation, the establishment of law reform commissions, law revision and consolidation, and taxation and other fiscal matters.

CO-ORDINATION WITH OTHER COMMONWEALTH ORGANISATIONS ON LAW

A feature of Commonwealth co-operation in legal matters is the overlap of the Secretariat's legal functions with those of other legal organisations within the Commonwealth, for example the overlap with the Commonwealth Legal Advisory Service which had been set up earlier in 1962 by the British Institute of International and Comparative Law. Like the legal division of the Secretariat, which came into being seven years later, the Commonwealth Legal Advisory Service has provided experts and information needed by member governments. It was originally financed by the British Institute, then by the British government, then by a number of Commonwealth governments. Senior officers of both organisations have agreed to co-ordinate so as to avoid duplication of projects. There are several other bodies engaged in particular aspects of co-operation in legal matters:

(1) The *Commonwealth Legal Education Association* noted above, which was established in 1981 as a result of discussions at a Commonwealth law conference in New Delhi. The object of this organisation is to promote legal education and research through contacts, exchanges and collaboration generally.

(2) The *Commonwealth Legal Bureau*, formed in 1969, with the object of encouraging strong, viable organisations of lawyers in countries where none exist – mostly the developing countries. It meets annually in different parts of the Commonwealth.

(3) The *Commonwealth Magistrates' Association*, established in 1970 with a membership which comprises the national associations of magistrates in thirty-nine Commonwealth countries. It is governed by a general assembly, consisting of representatives of each member country, which meets once every four years. Management is by a council comprising officers and twelve members representing all six regions of the Commonwealth, and by two executive staff. The aim of this organisation is to improve standards in the administration of justice by promoting training, disseminating information and fostering contacts between the members of the judiciary within the Commonwealth. It convenes pan-Commonwealth conferences and regional seminars, sometimes in collaboration with other bodies. It publishes the *Commonwealth Judicial Journal*, twice yearly.

CONCLUSION

It may well be asked: Why does the Commonwealth hold together? The Commonwealth as such has neither a constitution nor a supra-national legal system. The machinery it has evolved for consultation and co-operation does not bind individual member states to a particular course of action. The link of a common crown is no longer shared and was hardly enough to determine policy. It may also be asked, in the light of the frequency with which its member states oppose each other at international conferences, whether the Commonwealth has any real value. That it is not an exclusive group is demonstrated by the defence arrangements between some member states of the Commonwealth and third states. Why then, does the Commonwealth continue to exist and what is its significance?

The very lack of exclusiveness is itself a source of strength to the Commonwealth since it does not prevent a country from pursuing individual policies that are conducive to its particular interests. On the other hand, membership entails legal and other rights and privileges and, of course, informal obligations which are known to members themselves, and, even though, as a matter of jurisprudence, one may admit that those rights and privileges hardly crystallise into a supra-national 'Commonwealth Law' with the capacity to compel obedience, they are none the less within the lawyer's province.

Ultimately, most of the special aims of the Commonwealth could be fulfilled more satisfactorily by a strong United Nations. But in the meantime the Commonwealth is a group which is particularly interested in the problems of its own members. For this reason it may be expected to continue providing mutual advantages on its traditional basis of loose, flexible arrangements, through which co-operation in pursuit of common purposes can be facilitated.

NOTES AND REFERENCES

1. See: James Fawcett, *The British Commonwealth in International Law* (London: Stevens & Sons, 1963), pp. 144–94; Marjorie Millace Whiteman, *Digest of International Law*, 15 vols. (Washington, D.C.: Department of State Publications, 1963–73), 1 (1963): pp. 476–544.
2. Historically the legal order of Commonwealth countries has been derived from legislation of the United Kingdom, either by the Crown in Parliament, in the form of statutes and subordinate legislation, or by the Crown in Council, in the form of prerogative or statutory orders. The transfer of the power first of internal self-government, and then of conducting external relations, has been effected for Commonwealth members by United Kingdom legislation in the first place.
3. See also United Kingdom, Parliament, *Parliamentary Debates* (Lords, 5th series), 153 (1948): 1154–8; Heather Harvey, *Consultation and Co-operation in the Commonwealth* (London: Oxford University Press, 1952). As to the results of the Commonwealth Conference of 1949, see Ivor Jennings, 'The Commonwealth Conference of 1949', in *British Yearbook of International Law, 1948*, vol. 25 (London: Oxford University Press, 1949), pp. 414–20.
4. These decisions have been criticised – see E. S. Haydon, 'The Choice of Chinese Customary Law in Hong Kong', *International and Comparative Law Quarterly*, 11 (1962): pp. 231–50.
5. See symposium on 'The Migration of the Common Law', *Law Quarterly Review*, 76 (1960): pp. 41–77.
6. Jean-Gabriel Castel, *The Civil Law System in the Province of Quebec* (Toronto: Butterworths, 1962), p. 15.
7. For a detailed and comprehensive study, see Kenneth Roberts-Wray, *Commonwealth and Colonial Law* (London: Stevens & Sons, 1966).
8. Rudolf B. Schlesinger (ed.), *Formation of Contracts – A Study of the Common Core of Legal Systems*, 2 vols. (Dobbs Ferry, NY: Oceana Publications, 1968), 1: 281–93; J. N. Anderson (ed.), *Family Law in Asia and Africa* (London: George Allen and Unwin, 1968).
9. See above.
10. See the instructive discussion by J. D. Derrett, 'Statutory Amendments of the Personal Law of Hindus since Indian Independence', *American Journal of Comparative Law*, 7 (1958): pp. 380–93.
11. M. C. Dalton, 'The Passing of Roman-Dutch Law in British Guiana', *South African Law Journal*, 36 (1919): pp. 4–17; J. Hazard, 'Guyana's Alternative to Socialist and Capitalist Legal Models', *American Journal of Comparative Law*, 16 (1968): pp. 507–23.
12. T. B. Smith, 'English Influences on the Law of Scotland', *American Journal*

of Comparative Law, 3 (1954): pp. 522–42; T. M. Cooper, 'The Common Law and the Civil Law – A Scot's View', *Harvard Law Review*, 63 (Nov. 1949–June 1950): pp. 468–75.

13. Appeals from Zimbabwe (Rhodesia) to the Privy Council were abolished long ago; even before the declaration of the Unilateral Declaration of Independence by Ian Smith.

14. R. Y. Jennings, 'The Commonwealth and International Law', in *British Yearbook of International Law, 1953*, vol. 30 (1954), p. 326.

11 The Residual Legatee: Economic Co-operation in the Contemporary Commonwealth

ARTHUR KILGORE AND JAMES MAYALL

Of all international institutions the Commonwealth is notoriously the most difficult to classify. This is as true of its economic as of its more overtly political activities. Where many studies of international economic organisation are concerned with integration, a study of the Commonwealth must necessarily concern itself with a process of disintegration – the dismantling of the British Empire – and with the creation of an institutional framework to manage and reflect this process. However useful its members find the contemporary Commonwealth it is no longer the centre of their universe, or the repository of their major international hopes.

It is not difficult, in broad outline, to account for this metamorphosis. After 1918 the world economy was transformed and the political, legal and institutional superstructure of the Empire inevitably reflected the change in the general economic environment. Challenged by other powers, particularly by the United States, for the economic leadership of the world it gradually became clear that the Empire was an 'unnatural' economic grouping which lacked the bonds of geographical proximity or cultural and social homogeneity which would enable it to survive Britain's decline.

The imperial economic structure was also under pressure from within. After the First World War it was increasingly argued that Britain's economic greatness was an imperial rather than merely a British achievement. The dominions were now endowed with a dignity derived from their own sense of sovereignty and a heightened consciousness of their own role in bolstering the Empire and Britain's position at the head of it.[1] This led them to put pressure on Britain in the 1920s for the formal recognition of their independent status and simultaneously to demand greater influence over the Empire's economic affairs.[2]

The political transformation of the Empire thus ran parallel to Britain's retreat from economic primacy. On 31 September 1931, a few months before the Statute of Westminster was passed through the British parliament, formally defining the independent political status of the dominions as freely associated members of the British Commonwealth of Nations, Britain abandoned the gold standard.[3] By severing the link with gold the British government initiated the long descent of sterling from its position as a 'top currency' to its present status as a 'negotiated currency': that is, one that maintains its international importance by means of economic and political inducements offered to its users.[4] It is, of course, only with hindsight that the abandonment of the gold standard can be seen as an historical watershed. In 1931 the Empire was not perceived to be crumbling and the Commonwealth was never intended to preside over its disintegration. On the contrary, it was hoped by most, if not all, member governments that the Commonwealth would provide a new framework – the Empire, so to say, reconstituted on the basis of voluntarism – within which its members would be able to co-operate under British leadership more closely than ever.

Britain's position at the head of the new Commonwealth was accepted by the other members as 'natural'. Thus the administrative machinery of the Commonwealth remained part of the British government and when Britain abandoned the gold standard there was still sufficient confidence in her as an economic power, source of investment, supplier of industrial goods and market for exports to convince the dominions to co-ordinate their monetary policies and peg their currencies to sterling.[5]

The forces that were dismantling the Empire, however, also worked against the stability of the original Commonwealth system. Since Britain, unlike France, can no longer be regarded as the centre of its former empire the question arises as to who leads the modern Commonwealth and for what purpose? Does it remain, as its critics insist, an emaciated version of the original neo-imperial design? Or have the changes in form over the years, and in particular the establishment of a permanent multinational secretariat also signalled a change in the nature of the organisation? It is with these questions that this chapter is concerned. We begin by tracing briefly the history of the economic relations of the Commonwealth to identify the major factors that have shaped its current organisation. In the second part we then examine the structure of the modern Commonwealth (together with the programme produced by the Secretariat) in order to assess its economic importance, both for its member states and as an international organisation in the broader international economic system.

THE MAKING AND BREAKING OF THE COMMONWEALTH ECONOMIC SYSTEM

Many writers, when searching for a rationale to explain the survival of the Commonwealth, stress the truism that no country would belong to it if it were not in its interest.[6] Certainly, in 1931 few doubted that there were tangible benefits to be derived from membership. The question was how far it was possible to co-ordinate economic policy to promote the interests of the whole. The dominions, for example, sought economic benefits to complement the independent political status they had already achieved. They wanted to be consulted on economic policy; more particularly they wanted guaranteed preferential access to the British market and unrestricted capital and investment flows from Britain. They were not, of course, wholly successful in achieving these aims; nevertheless the shock of the world-wide depression helped their cause. During the 1930s the 'sterling bloc', comprised of those countries that pegged their currencies to sterling in the aftermath of Britain's float against gold, and the Commonwealth system of trade preferences were established. There was also a growth of Commonwealth economic consultation as the member countries sought to bolster their national economic defences through a limited form of multilateralism.

Monetary policy was not a subject on which initially the British government was anxious to consult with Commonwealth or other sterling governments. Indeed it was reluctant to recommend to any country that it join the bloc for fear of the corresponding responsibility that would devolve upon Britain for the stability of the system.[7] Britain relied instead on the past strength of sterling as a top currency, the economic links established prior to 1931, and simply on British power, to convince other countries to follow the British on monetary matters. Two cases may serve to illustrate the methods adopted by the British government to keep the Commonwealth in line. In December 1931 in

Australia the Commonwealth Bank had assumed responsibility for managing the exchange rate which was fixed at £1.25 Australian to £1.00 sterling.[8] But by July 1932 it seemed doubtful that Australia had enough sterling to continue operations at this rate. The alternative to devaluation was to secure a drawing credit from the Bank of England to cover any demands on Australia's reserves. The Bank readily granted a drawing credit of £3 million.[9] Similar credits (of £5 million) to shore up Australia's reserves were arranged in 1936 and 1937. None was actually drawn down but their availability was sufficient to cement one of the key operating principles of the sterling bloc – the maintenance of stable sterling exchange rates.[10]

In the case of India, the British Raj was given no choice.[11] Soon after Britain abandoned the gold standard, the Viceroy's finance member, Sir George Schuster, expressed the desire to peg the rupee directly to gold rather than the pound. Indeed, India had been trying to devalue the rupee against sterling (or alternatively obtain credit to support the existing rate established in 1927) since the government was required to finance its own deficit. The rigid exchange rate was reckoned by Schuster to be the source of bitter anti-British feeling in India, particularly among Congress party members and Indian millowners. The reply from the India Office in London was uncompromising – the rupee would have to be linked to sterling or to nothing.

In such ways Britain held the sterling bloc together until 1939 – using inducements or coercion only when it was deemed necessary to secure the continued participation of a Commonwealth country. At the 1932 Imperial Economic Conference in Ottawa, Britain forestalled the proponents of the internationalisation of sterling management by announcing instead a policy of cheap money, low interest rates and easy credit.[12] This policy was to be reiterated on several occasions during the following years to placate Commonwealth governments which were disaffected by the lack of consultation.

Despite signs of internal strain within the Commonwealth and the appearance of external constraints on Britain's effective management of the sterling area, members of the bloc were generally persuaded that Britain would strengthen her economic position through the sterling area. In 1939, with the outbreak of war, the sterling bloc became the sterling area. Britain initiated exchange controls to prevent the draining of her reserves, which were desperately needed to fund the war effort. For those countries that joined the sterling area and erected exchange controls, Britain promised not to restrict the flow of capital. Furthermore, all the gold and monetary reserves of the sterling area were pooled in London. This monetary union was to bind the Commonwealth countries together in a system that after the war was both too restricting for comfort and too expensive to leave.

As with the sterling bloc, the imperial preference system was introduced against the background of worldwide depression, escalating protectionism and strong pressure from the dominions. At the Ottawa Imperial Economic Conference in 1932 Britain finally broke with her traditional policy of free trade and instituted a series of bilateral trade agreements, following closely on the Import Duties Act of 1932, which placed a ten per cent '*ad valorem* duty' on all but a few essential imports into Britain and allowed for retaliatory duties of up to 100 per cent.

By raising tariff barriers on non-Commonwealth goods, Commonwealth countries attempted to establish a stable trading community amongst themselves. The evidence suggests that the preference system had a marginal effect. In 1932, the year of its introduction, Commonwealth goods represented about 35 per cent of total British imports.[13] This was a six per cent increase over 1929. By 1936, the Commonwealth was the origin of a little over 39 per cent of Britain's imports. Since this was a period of general trade contraction, the increasing Commonwealth share of British imports shows only that Commonwealth exporters were more successful in preserving their traditional market than other exporters. But despite the hopes of the participants, preferences did not create trade. When in the late 1930s world trade began to expand once more the significance of intra-Commonwealth trade declined. The problem appears to have been that the demand for Commonwealth imports in Britain, to whose market the economic fortunes of other Commonwealth countries were tied, was relatively inelastic. For example, during the 1930s, three-quarters or more of New Zealand's annual exports went to Britain;[14] but in those years when the value of New Zealand's exports shrank a greater percentage of her exports went to Britain, while in those years during which the value of imports was on the increase, the percentage going to Britain decreased.

Not surprisingly, since it was openly discriminatory, the imperial preference system was never universally popular. The United States government, in particular, viewed preferences as a diversionary tactic, used by Britain to frighten off her competitors in Commonwealth markets. Even within the Commonwealth, some countries had little to gain from the system. In 1935 India withdrew from the preference system; Canada negotiated new trade agreements with the United States, reflecting the inescapable pull of the US economy,[15] and Australia maintained her trade levels throughout the depression by establishing strong trading links with Japan, an economy that was a-typically expanding at a time of general and widespread contraction.[16]

As with sterling, so with trade; Britain attempted to keep the Commonwealth in line wherever she could. After Australia had greatly increased her exports of wool to Japan during the early 1930s in return for increased imports of Japanese textiles, Britain became concerned that her own textile industry would be displaced by the Japanese in the Australian market. Pressure was brought to bear, and in the middle of negotiating a trade agreement with Japan during 1935, Australia suddenly did an about-turn and announced steps to curtail Japanese textile imports.[17] Britain also refused to abandon agricultural protection, despite the dependence of most of the Commonwealth on agricultural exports.[18]

The policies adopted by the Commonwealth during the 1930s reveal the interest Britain had in preserving the relations of Empire where possible. Ian Drummond calculates what he refers to as the 'gross yield on the sterling bloc' for 1938 and concludes that when the cost of maintaining the sterling balances is subtracted from the return on investment in the sterling bloc, Britain made £26 million or 0.5 per cent of GNP.[19] Britain's foreign investments had long been a key component of her economic strength but in the 1930s overseas investment declined as a percentage of total new investment.[20] Still, the Commonwealth component of overseas investment grew, particularly in raw materials, for which the return to British investors was exceeded only by that from shipping.[21] Add to this the consideration that preferences directed trade toward Britain from Commonwealth countries and we are able to see how the two most important Commonwealth economic programmes of the 1930s served to reinforce the transnational links that had been established under the empire, and to create further transnational links.

In the long run, however, the Commonwealth economic system was doomed. That it lasted as long as it did – its final demise being postponed until 1975 when the remaining preferences were dissolved in the Lomé Convention between the EEC and forty-six African, Pacific and Caribbean countries (ACP) and the trade agreements negotiated between the EEC and the Asian Commonwealth countries – was largely a consequence of the Second World War, which led to closer monetary co-operation (the sterling area arrangements) and in the trade field to a shift from preferences to bulk purchase arrangements, thus deepening the ties between Britain and certain Commonwealth commodity producers. During the war the 'rules' of the international economy were suspended. In order to support the war effort Britain was offered lines of credit on a 'buy now, pay later' basis. Thus not only did the United States rule out finance as a limiting factor under the lend-lease agreement but in the operation of sterling balances Britain built up obligations in return for the goods and services she received during the war.[22]

Both lines of credit were to weaken the Commonwealth system. Throughout the war the United States demanded that Britain take steps to restore convertibility of sterling, to eliminate exchange controls and to dismantle imperial preferences. And immediately after the war convertibility was disastrously made a condition of the loan which the United States negotiated with Britain in 1946.[23] Initially, a strong body of opinion in Britain and the Commonwealth rejected the idea of United States' leadership and favoured a strengthened Commonwealth system as an alternative.[24] Such Commonwealth common feeling did not, however, survive long beyond the peace: indeed, many of those in Britain who had favoured the Commonwealth solution to Britain's economic problems came to regard holders of large sterling balances as potentially subversive of Britain's own economic recovery, while in the face of the undisputed supremacy of the United States and the magnetic attraction of its economy, it was felt in the Commonwealth, particularly in the Indian subcontinent, that they had attached themselves to a falling star.

The final demise of the sterling area lies beyond the scope of this chapter. It struggled on through the 1950s and 1960s, increasingly perceived in Britain as an unwelcome constraint on domestic economic policy, and by its other members as an unnecessary restraint on their sovereignty. After the international monetary crisis of 1971, it withered quietly away, unmourned by Britain and the Commonwealth alike.

Commonwealth trade also underwent a transformation during the 1950s, as Commonwealth trade with non-Commonwealth countries expanded far more rapidly than intra-Commonwealth trade, while Britain directed more trade to Europe.[25] Moreover, the Conservative government announced in 1952 the termination of the bulk purchase arrangements, and returned responsibility for trade in those commodities to the private sector (with the notable exception of the Commonwealth Sugar Agreement).[26] Finally, the creation of the Bretton Woods Institutions and the General Agreements on Tariffs and Trade (GATT) undermined the Commonwealth system. The International Monetary Fund embodied the principle of convertibility, and the GATT, by freezing preferences and providing for liberalisation through a generalised reduction of tariffs, progressively reduced the margin of preference enjoyed by Commonwealth.

Those that were to suffer from this 'withering away' of the old Commonwealth system were, not surprisingly, the weakest members. The old dominions complained (indeed stridently at the time of Britain's first application to join the EEC) but came to terms.[27] So did the successor states of British India, which had always had an ambiguous relation to the British economy. It was different for the developing states in Africa, the Caribbean and the islands dotted across the Pacific, whose modern economic activities were generally an exotic import of the colonial period, which had little to offer in trade liberalisation negotiations based on reciprocity and whose governments looked to the Commonwealth for help with their plans for economic diversification and development. Although they often felt ties of sentiment less strongly than the old dominions and were unwilling to contemplate any Commonwealth infringement on their economic sovereignty, they still needed to capitalise on those ties and to transform the Commonwealth, not into an economic subsystem within the world economy, but into a service organisation, of more limited and more strictly utilitarian design. It is to this latest metamorphosis that we now turn.

THE SERVICE COMMONWEALTH

The foundation of the Secretariat in 1965 symbolised an important change in the economic structure of the Commonwealth. Paradoxically, the creation of a new international bureaucracy was to mean less, not more, policy co-ordination. In economic matters the new Commonwealth was to act as a forum for discussion and the clarification of viewpoints, and as a bridge of sorts between the rich and poor states in the so-called North-South dialogue.

Once Britain had abandoned the Commonwealth as the cornerstone of her policies for economic and political revival, the Commonwealth was in turn deprived of strong national leadership. What emerged in its place was a personal leadership based on the office of the Secretary-General. Since this means that Commonwealth goals and programmes are largely defined by the Secretary-General, the effectiveness of the organisation will greatly depend on the strength of personality of the incumbent. What he can achieve is inevitably quite limited – no Secretary-General can pursue programmes which the richer members, that is Britain, Canada and Australia, are unwilling to finance – although just where the limits lie on any particular issue can only be determined through the forceful and deliberate exertion of his will and the skill of his diplomacy. The importance of personal leadership emerges clearly from a comparison of the programmes of the Secretariat during the reign of the two Secretaries-General to date.

Arnold Smith, the first Secretary-General, was primarily concerned with establishing the political identity of the new, 'trimmed down', multinational Commonwealth. Although the Agreed Memorandum setting up the Commonwealth Secretariat specified that there was to be only one Deputy Secretary-General (DSG), who was to be 'responsible for economic matters', with the possibility of a second to be created some time in the future when the general progress of the Secretariat could be measured, Smith almost immediately created a second DSG for political affairs.[28] In addition, he engaged energetically in skirmishes with national bureaucrats – particularly those of the Commonwealth Relations' Office – to establish the multilateral/supranational character of the fledgling Secretariat.[29] Where economic issues were concerned, he was more patient. At the 1966 Commonwealth Heads of Governments' Meeting (CHOGM), he pressed for a limited programme of multilateral technical assistance which would be funded by richer Commonwealth members but would draw on the technical expertise and training available in developing Commonwealth countries. It was not until 1971 that his proposals came to fruition with the creation of the Commonwealth Fund for Technical Co-operation (CFTC).[30]

By contrast, Smith's successor, Shridath Ramphal, has placed great emphasis on the economic role of the Commonwealth in the attempt to secure a new international economic order. This has meant putting the Commonwealth at the service of a much broader movement of Third World revisionist states. For example, he was a Commissioner on the Independent Commission for Development Issues (The Brandt Commission), and also a key adviser on the format for the summit which was held in Cancun, Mexico, in November 1981 to discuss, *inter alia*, the recommendations of the Brandt Report. Within the Group of 77, the Commonwealth often seems to be the mouthpiece for those members which belong to both groups, and which are thus able to exploit their access to a more exclusive group of developed countries than is possible within the UNCTAD as a whole.

How is this function performed? Before attempting to answer this question, it may be helpful to describe the institutional structure of the Secretariat as it relates to its economic activities. It is headed by the office of the Secretary-General. Below the office of the Secretary-General there are a number of divisions. Two of these have a central role in the economic activities of the Secretariat. The Economic Affairs Division is charged with the conduct of most of the Secretariat's economic activities; it takes the initiative in arranging consultations on important economic issues and is responsible for servicing the annual meetings of Commonwealth finance ministers. It also conducts its own research, services the specialist groups and committees set up by the Commonwealth to study specific problems and takes the lead in the Secretariat's informational activities in the economic field.

The other division concerned with economic affairs is the Export Market Development Division. This provides services to Commonwealth developing countries for the promotion of their primary and secondary exports. It engages in informational activities such as market surveys and practical programmes such as 'buyer-seller meets'.

In what follows we discuss the activities of the Commonwealth under three broad headings: practical programmes, informational activities and residual relations. First, a word of explanation about these categories. By practical programmes we mean those activities undertaken by the Secretariat that effect a transfer of resources from the developed Commonwealth members to developing ones through the multilateral internationalised administration of the Commonwealth Secretariat. The most important among these programmes is the CFTC which consumes a larger proportion of Secretariat funds than any other Commonwealth activity. On the whole, however, practical programmes do not involve substantial transfers. Faced by financial constraints, the Secretariat has placed considerable emphasis on informational activities. These involve the collation and dissemination of information and the commissioning of research for distribution to Commonwealth governments on issues either of interest to specific countries or generally. The Secretariat also sponsors seminars and meetings whose primary function is information. Residual relations are those Commonwealth economic ties that derive from the past rather than from the promotional work of the Secretariat. As well as transnational relations which continue to lock Commonwealth countries together, they include British bilateral aid allotments which remain heavily skewed toward Commonwealth countries.

Practical Economic Programmes

The bulk of the Commonwealth's activities under this heading are concentrated under the aegis of the CFTC. The fund is financed by voluntary donations from Commonwealth countries separate from the assessed contributions each gives to the budget of the Secretariat. The CFTC was established in 1971 after the Singapore CHOGM and has an administration which is separate from but overlaps with that of the Secretariat. It operates primarily as a development fund which finances and administers four programmes. These are a general technical assistance programme, the function of which is to create a pool of technical and managerial expertise for countries in need; an education and training programme, which sponsors Commonwealth nationals from developing countries on educational and vocational training mostly in other developing countries; an in-house technical assistance group (TAG), which provides advice on the legal, economic and policy aspects of the development of natural resources (including negotiation with transnational enterprises),[40] on constitutional matters and which also advises on the initiation and maintenance of national statistical series; and finally, since 1980, an industrial development unit (IDU), which provides advice and assistance for industrial diversification schemes.

When the CFTC was established in 1971 the voluntary contributions pledged at the Singapore CHOGM totalled £400 000. By 1980 the budget had grown to £10.8 million. This does not mean however that CFTC has enjoyed uninterrupted growth in its funding and activities or that it can necessarily be expected to continue expanding at a rapid rate. The peak year was 1978/79 when the budget totalled £11.3 million. The following year there was a drop of nearly £2 million which has still not been retrieved. In real terms the reduction meant that in 1979/80 the number of experts funded by CFTC dropped from 300 to 226 and the number of people trained under the educational and training programme was nearly halved from 2200 to 1300. Although there was an increase in CFTC funding for 1980/81 there was also a further reduction of experts and trainees.[31]

This 'crisis of funding' was discussed by Commonwealth finance ministers at their annual meeting in Malta in 1979 after which, to quote their final communiqué, they urged their governments to 'urgently re-examine the degree to which they could contribute to meeting the immediate need of the CFTC' and requested the Secretary-General to 'put forward for consideration of governments, proposals to afford greater stability to the Fund's operations'.[32] A working party was appointed to study the possibilities for stabilising the methods of financing CFTC. Its recommendations were subsequently endorsed by the Melbourne CHOGM in 1981. They included an agreement to restore the capacity (that is to say, the funding in real terms) of CFTC to its 1978/79 level by 1983/84, and a blueprint for three year forward planning. Thus the best that can be said is that CFTC will have stagnated during the five years from 1979/80 to 1983/84.

The decline in commitments to CFTC is symptomatic of the relative lack of importance of the Commonwealth as a conduit for economic assistance, at least in the eyes of certain of its richest members. There are a number of indicators that can be used to establish this point. Contributions to the Secretariat budget are assessed according to economic indicators such as GNP and population. The major Commonwealth countries tend to disburse funds to CFTC in roughly the same proportion – that is a country that is assessed 'x' percentage of the Secretariat budget will contribute an equal percentage of CFTC's funds. There are however some notable exceptions. Britain and Australia accounted for 30 and 9.93 per cent of the Secretariat budget in 1980/81 and pledged 32 and 9.38 per cent of CFTC respectively. But Canada, which was assessed 17.81 per cent of the Secretariat budget pledged 38.74 per cent of the CFTC budget; Nigeria, the fourth largest contributor to CFTC, volunteered 8.3 per cent of the budget in 1980/81 compared with a mere 1.5 per cent of the Secretariat budget,[33] and Australia, in the wake of the Melbourne CHOGM, significantly increased its contribution for the future. Canada's generosity can be traced to the long-standing Canadian tendency to use the Commonwealth to promote a specifically Canadian identity in international relations as a counterweight to United States influence on Canada itself, and to Prime Minister Trudeau's decision to align Canada with Southern interests in the North–South dialogue at the heart of which is an appeal to shift more responsibility for economic transfers to multilateral agencies. Similarly for Nigeria, the CFTC is a relatively cheap way of demonstrating active sympathy for the multilateralisation of aid and of claiming a position of influence in the 'developing' Commonwealth.

By contrast Britain's relative lack of enthusiasm for CFTC can be explained by reference to the official criteria for the disbursal of aid. In February 1980, these were described by Neil Marten, Minister for Overseas Development: 'We believe that it is right at the present time to give greater weight in the allocation of our aid to political, industrial and commercial considerations alongside our basic developmental objectives.' In other words since British aid is designed to promote political and commercial interests it follows that it must remain largely bilateral.[34] In 1980/81 Britain contributed £3 million to CFTC, a mere 0.35 per cent of the total British aid allocation for that year. If we take aid to Afghan refugees as an illustration of politically motivated aid, then over the two years since the Soviet Union established its military presence there, more British aid has been directed to Afghan refugees than to CFTC.

As a means of protecting British commercial interests CFTC has little to recommend it. In a memorandum to the Development Assistance Committee of the OECD in 1981, Britain reiterated that its bilateral aid (which accounts for 73 per cent of the total) remains 'tied to the procurement of British goods and services'.[35] Thus, for example, during October 1980 alone British industry was reported to have received £19.9 million from contracts arising out of the British aid programme.[36] The British have also sought to persuade the multilateral agencies to direct a greater proportion of contracts arising from their activities to Britain. CFTC is a programme for training and advice so that it offers little immediate relief to British commercial interests. Furthermore, CFTC is committed to the principle of technical co-operation among developing countries (TCDC) and to date has drawn 62 per cent of its technical experts and advisers from developing countries.

Clearly Britain does not view CFTC as a significant instrument of its own aid policy. Indeed, it tells us something about the character of the new Commonwealth that it has evolved a programme for the transfer of resources that is run on principles other than those on which British aid policy is currently based. The emphasis on TCDC can be interpreted as a conscious effort to loosen the transnational ties of dependency between the traditional metropole and the developing Commonwealth countries. Moreover, The New Industrial Development Unit of CFTC is unlikely to be greeted with much enthusiasm in Britain at a time when fear of rising industrial exports from developing countries is present in all developed countries. Goodwill will no doubt protect the British contribution at its present level. Any expansion of CFTC activities, however, will depend on the willingness of Britain to surrender control over a greater portion of its aid, or on the willingness of other developed Commonwealth countries to take on an increasing share of the cost. Neither of these alternatives seems very likely in the immediate future. The impact of CFTC programmes on the numerous small and island developing countries in the Commonwealth, however, will continue to be significant and their value to these communities is very probably underestimated in a largely statistical analysis.

Another practical programme consists of the 'buyer-seller meets' which are generally organised by the Export Market Development Division of the Secretariat. The division provides technical assistance to countries that need help in establishing overseas markets. 'Buyer-seller meets' have been held in Japan for Indian exporters, in Dubai for Bangladeshi exporters, in Cologne and London for Kenyan exporters and in New York and Copenhagen for Sri Lankan exporters. They are generally preceded by studies of the potential market and the problems faced by would-be exporters to the market (such as product adaptation to meet the requirements of demand and regulations in the importing countries).

The Secretariat claims dramatic success for this part of its work. In one celebrated case, the meet in New York in May 1978 which was organised at the cost of $300 000 to put Sri Lankan exporters in contact with the American market, approximately $2 million worth of orders were placed in the first instance, a figure which had apparently grown to $6.27 million by 1980.[37] As with the CFTC, such activities depart from the traditional pattern of Commonwealth economic relations by promoting and directing trade to markets outside the Commonwealth itself. Indeed it appears that one function of the contemporary Commonwealth is to reduce the dependency that was the central feature of the imperial period when Britain was the core market, or at least to diversify it. Even from the British point of view market diversification may not be unwelcome, since export promotion in rich non-Commonwealth markets can act as a safety valve by redirecting manufactured exports such as textiles away from the UK, thus lessening external pressure for access to the British market and internal pressure for protection from competitive imports. Concentration on export diversification also reveals the Secretariat's own bias in favour of export-led growth, a strategy which has been widely canvassed in the North-South debate, for example in the Brandt Report.

Informational Activities

Two linked trends are notable in the informational activities of the Commonwealth since the founding of the Secretariat. There has been a decline in Commonwealth-specific economic information, for example the preparation of statistical series concentrating on economic interactions among Commonwealth countries. The second trend is in the emphasis now placed on global economic issues – particularly problems relating to the integration of the Third World into the world economy.

An example of the first trend is the discontinuation of *Commonwealth*

Trade, a statistical review of both intra-Commonwealth and extra-Commonwealth trade patterns. Until 1966 this series was maintained by the Commonwealth Economic Committee (CEC). In 1966 the Secretariat absorbed CEC and took over responsibility for its publication, which continued until 1973. There are several reasons why the publication of Commonwealth-specific trade information was discarded. Britain's entry into the EEC signed the death warrant of the Commonwealth preference system as well as of the sterling area. At the same time the developing Commonwealth countries realigned their own economic policies by joining the Associated African States and Madagascar (AASM) to form the ACP (African, Caribbean and Pacific States) in an effort to obtain favourable treatment from the enlarged EEC. The discontinuation of *Commonwealth Trade* may therefore be seen as a symbol of the declining importance of Commonwealth economic relations for most of its members.

Examples of the second trend are the workshops, seminars and reports on subjects that are of economic significance to Commonwealth countries, which are currently organised by the Secretariat. The Food Production and Rural Development, Science and Technology and Export Market Development Divisions as well as the CFTC have all been involved in informational activities of this sort. The work of the Economic Affairs Division also illustrates the change of emphasis. This division publishes regular statistical and informational series on a range of commodities (meat and dairy products; hides and skins; tobacco; and wool), and undertakes economic studies commissioned by outside organisations such as the ACP. It is the reports on global economic issues commissioned by the Secretariat, however, that best exemplify the switch in emphasis from Commonwealth-specific information to Third World problems in the global economy. These reports are not attempts to co-ordinate Commonwealth policy but represent the Secretariat's contribution to the North-South debate.

Since 1974 three reports have been published on different aspects of the Third World campaign for a new international economic order. The first was commissioned at the Kingston CHOGM in May 1975 after the Sixth Special Session of the United Nations General Assembly had adopted a resolution calling for a 'New International Economic Order'. The report, commonly referred to as the McIntyre Report, after Alistair McIntyre, Chairman of the expert group which produced it, finally appeared in March 1977 under the title, *Towards a New International Economic Order*. The group was requested to 'draw up ... a comprehensive and interrelated programme of practical measures directed at closing the gap between the rich and the poor countries'. Two interim reports were issued to coincide with the UN Seventh Special Session in September 1975 and UNCTAD IV in Nairobi. The second interim report was published in March 1976, several months prior to the Nairobi conference, although it was not discussed by the Commonwealth itself until after the UNCTAD conference. In September 1976, however, Commonwealth finance ministers endorsed the report at their annual meeting in Hong Kong 'without necessarily committing their governments to every aspect', a *caveat* which made it clear that the report was not a statement of collective Commonwealth policy. Individual countries were left to their own judgement as to the importance of the report in framing their own policy in UNCTAD and elsewhere.

The McIntyre Report was followed by the Campbell Report on the Common Fund. It was commissioned at the London CHOGM in 1977 and published in September of that year. Its origins lay in the adoption at UNCTAD IV of Resolution 93 (IV) on the Integrated Programme for Commodities (IPC), which envisaged the creation of a Common Fund to promote the establishment of new international commodity agreements and to strengthen existing ones. The UNCTAD resolution called for the implementation of the IPC within two years with negotiations on the Common Fund itself to begin in 1977. From the start the IPC threatened to deepen the conflict between the industrial and developing countries. Since the Commonwealth included members of both camps, and since some of the richer members such as Australia were producers as well as consumers of commodities, as were some of the poorer countries such as India, the dispute seemed ripe for Commonwealth mediation. Lord Campbell's terms of reference were:

to examine the issues which need to be addressed in further work in UNCTAD and ... inform Commonwealth leaders on the range of objectives and purposes for which the Common Fund might be used, its method of operation and the measures to be adopted to help developing countries which are net importers of the commodities concerned, with a view to facilitating greater progress at the UNCTAD Conference in November.[38]

It cannot be claimed that the report overcame the fundamental scepticism of many industrial countries about the feasibility of the scheme and the philosophy of market intervention on which it was based. But it undoubtedly helped to resolve the diplomatic *impasse*. After the Commonwealth ministerial meeting on the Common Fund in

1978, the finance ministers noted that the meeting had 'clarified aspects of the dialogue' and perhaps given some additional momentum to the delayed negotiations that were scheduled to resume in November of that year. By the 1979 CHOGM in Lusaka the heads of government were able to review the debate on the IPC and note 'with satisfaction the contribution made by the Commonwealth in helping to bring about a convergence of positions on the Common Fund'.

Although the Campbell Report was not an attempt to co-ordinate policy among Commonwealth countries, it demonstrates the way in which the Secretariat can attempt to influence the policies of member states on a particular issue. The usual *caveat* was contained in the Secretary-General's foreword to the report, stating that it did not 'commit Commonwealth governments, either collectively or separately'. However, the authors did go beyond their terms of reference by suggesting 'specific courses of action', thereby attempting to give Commonwealth governments a push in a direction favourable to the Fund. In the end agreement was reached on the creation of a Common Fund and no doubt the Secretariat can claim some of the credit. The significance of the achievement – by early 1982 only twenty countries had ratified the agreement – is more questionable.

The third major report was commissioned at the Lusaka CHOGM in 1979 'to investigate and report on the factors inhibiting structural change and a sustained improvement in economic growth in both developed and developing countries'. A group of experts was set up under the chairmanship of Professor Heinz Arndt from Australia. Their report, entitled *The World Economic Crisis: A Commonwealth Perspective*, was prepared as a background document for Commonwealth delegates to the 11th Special Session of the UN General Assembly in September 1980, and was subsequently included in the documentation for the Session as a whole.

In addition to commissioning special reports, the Secretariat itself increasingly services the developing Commonwealth by providing background briefings on North-South concerns. Thus, for example, the Economic Affairs Division prepared studies on food security and on world food policy for consideration by Commonwealth food and agriculture ministers when they met prior to the biennial FAO Council meetings in 1979, 1981 and 1983. The Secretariat also co-operates with other international organisations such as the World Bank and the ACP. With the World Bank it has developed a division of labour on the problem of establishing processing industries in countries where at present only the raw material is exported: under this scheme the

Secretariat is investigating four commodities and the Bank two. In collaboration with the ACP the Secretariat has organised seminars for officials from African countries on the problems of economic adjustment.[39]

One final aspect of the Secretariat's information work deserves note. This is the special emphasis which is increasingly placed on small and island countries which now account for more than half the membership of the Commonwealth. In the communiqué issued after the Lusaka CHOGM in 1979 the Secretary-General was requested 'to pursue the programme of action recommended for the Secretariat' on the problems of island developing and other specially disadvantaged countries.[40] Their needs were also supposed to have priority in decisions on aid allocation, although this is no doubt a more difficult goal to achieve since it is likely to conflict with the perceived commercial and political interests of the major Commonwealth aid donors. On the information side, however, the Secretariat devotes considerable resources to these countries. Since the Lusaka meeting it has produced a draft manual on project-evaluation for small economies, convened a meeting of development economists in June 1981 to discuss problems of small economies, and compiled statistics and social indicators for countries with populations of less than 1 million. The Secretariat also publishes a bulletin on 'discussions and decisions at major meetings on international organisations in the economic field', aimed at those countries that do not maintain representation or cannot afford to monitor such functions. On at least one occasion the Secretariat has acted for a single 'specially disadvantaged' country by preparing a study for the government of St Lucia on the marketing of bananas from the Windward Islands.

It is arguably in this area that the contemporary Commonwealth has its greatest potential impact. Because Commonwealth data is often collected with the problems of small economies primarily in mind, it is likely to have greater relevance for economic decision-makers in these countries than in others. Moreover, since most small economies have very limited resources to commit to research on their own behalf they rely heavily on the reports and series compiled by the Commonwealth Secretariat in international economic negotiations. And since as a class of states they rely on the same information, they will inevitably tend to view international economic issues in roughly similar terms.

Too much, however, should not be claimed for the Commonwealth connection. Regardless of their common institutional viewpoint the small and island countries will always remain vulnerable to pressure from OPEC or from the larger developing countries on particular issues.

But while the Secretariat cannot finally proof the weaker states against such pressure it may indirectly be able to strengthen a collective economic defence by the diffusion of ideas.

Residual Transnational and Intergovernmental Ties

There are a number of links which have their origins in the relationships established prior to the founding of the Secretariat, that continue to characterise the economic relations of the new Commonwealth.

The pattern of British bilateral aid disbursements is perhaps the most striking example of the past living on in the present in this way. While the Overseas Development Administration prides itself on its concentration of aid to countries classified by the UN as least developed, it is significant that in 1979 seven and in 1980 eight of the top ten recipients of British bilateral aid were Commonwealth countries. The concentration is even more marked if a one-time and currently aspiring member, Pakistan, is included. This pattern emerged after the Second World War when the British aid programme was developed in the context of de-colonisation. British aid was initially conceived as an economic stimulant to former colonies entering into the world economy as independent actors, and of course, as a way of maintaining British economic influence.[41] Despite new criteria for aid allocation, such as 'those most in need' (i.e. the least developed) the continuing obligations arising from what was initially a deliberate Commonwealth system mean that glaring anomalies survive. Botswana, for example, received more aid from Britain than all of the non-Commonwealth least developed countries in Africa put together except Sudan, which had itself been a British dependency although outside the Empire.[42] There is nothing surprising about such anomalies: the pattern of French aid similarly pays respect to the colonial past, but it indicates the resilience of Commonwealth ties despite changes in the world economy.

Other residual ties remained deeply-woven into the international economic system below the level of formal intergovernmental relations. For example, investment patterns initiated during the colonial period, and sustained by deliberate policy during the Commonwealth period prior to 1965, have sometimes not only refused to 'wither away' in response to changes in the world economy but have been reinforced. The extensive operation of British transnational enterprises whose activities are concentrated in the Commonwealth such as RTZ in Papua New Guinea, Australia and parts of Africa or Unilever in Nigeria are testimony to this process.

A third variant consists of private transnational relationships established under the old Commonwealth which have been deliberately maintained, against the trend, by intergovernmental co-operation. Take the case of the Caribbean banana producers who had traditionally and successfully looked to Britain to counter the monopolistic power of the United Fruit Company.[43] By the time the Secretariat was set up in 1965 the pattern of dependence of Jamaican banana producers on the British market had been firmly established by a combination of public and private actions. Jamaica is the largest exporter of bananas in the Caribbean Commonwealth, although other Commonwealth countries rely wholly on Britain as a market for their bananas and have developed ties in a manner similar to Jamaica. Dominica, St Lucia, St Vincent and Grenada, where the production of bananas occupies a more predominant position in the total economy than in Jamaica, are linked to the British market through the operations of the Geest Organisation.

The ties between all these producers and Britain were again threatened in 1973 when Britain acceded to the Treaty of Rome. The rules of free circulation in the EEC meant that bananas from non-traditional suppliers could be re-exported into Britain from the Continent. However, at the insistence of the British government and the West Indian producers, this possibility was countered by the 'banana protocol' in the Lomé Convention (Protocol no. 6 in Lomé I, Protocol no. 4 in Lomé II). The protocol states that 'no ACP State will be placed, as regards access to its traditional markets and its advantages in those markets, in a less favourable situation than in the past or at present'. This has for the time being ensured continuity of the traditional links between Commonwealth banana producers and the UK market, by alleviating the possibility that non-Commonwealth producers, particularly the highly competitive Central and Latin American producers, will slip in by the back door.

As with bananas, so with sugar. The special relationship established between Britain and developing Commonwealth sugar producers under the Commonwealth Sugar Agreement was largely preserved by the special arrangements for sugar negotiated, admittedly not without difficulty, in the Lomé Convention.[44]

How should these survivals from the imperial economy be viewed? Do not such arrangements merely perpetuate the deeply resented grip of dependence against which the Secretariat, in its role as spokesman for the poorer Commonwealth, has set its face? After all, it may be argued that the Commonwealth producers of raw materials who were previously exploited by multinational companies and tied to the British market are still exploited, usually by the same companies and sub-ordinated now to the EEC as well as to British interests. The provisions of the Lomé Convention are more effective in preserving the EEC's sources of raw materials than in providing access to European markets for ACP manufacturers or encouraging rapid industrial development in ACP countries.[45] Worse still, by creating a special interest group in the Third World, whose interests and economies are tied to Europe, the EEC/ACP relationship preserves, the modern idiom barely concealing the sinister intent, the old imperial tactic of divide and rule. Any success that the ACP countries have in protecting the meagre benefits they have gained under the Lomé Convention will be at the expense of Third World solidarity in the broader negotiations concerned with restructuring the world economy.

In the debate about North–South relations this is a familiar and sobering line of argument. However, several qualifications must be entered. While the Lomé Convention may do little to shift developing Commonwealth countries from their position as raw material suppliers in the world economy, it provides them at the very least with an opportunity to diversify their dependence: the African, Caribbean and Pacific Commonwealth countries now have greater access to the other European markets. Moreover, contrary to the charge that Lomé constitutes a potentially disruptive element in the Group of 77, the evidence suggests that the Convention has enabled a group of disparate developing countries to work more closely together than might have been expected. The Commonwealth role is important here. The key obstacle to ACP solidarity at the beginning of the negotiations with the EEC was a conflict over whether or not to maintain the principle of trade reciprocity in any new agreement. In the end, however, it was the Commonwealth view that prevailed: the new agreement was to be based on the contrary principle, namely non-reciprocity as the basis for economic relations between industrial and developing countries.

The essential justification for this change was to promote industrial development and self-reliance. All developing Commonwealth countries feared the destructive effects of opening their fragile economies and embryonic industries to European competition. For the Caribbean Commonwealth this fear had other dimensions. One was the danger of having their preferential treatment in the US and Canadian markets withdrawn in retaliation for allowing European competition to their Caribbean interests.[46] Another was that European competition would be likely to undermine CARICOM's efforts at economic integration: if European industries captured the markets of the less developed

Caribbean countries this would hit, for example, Jamaica and Guyana whose own industrial expansion was geared to the wider Caribbean market.[47]

But if on one level residual Commonwealth links actually contributed to consolidating a wider Third World alliance, it remains true that in other areas they imposed constraints on co-operation within the Third World. Just as the idea of a West Indian Federation was impracticable because, as a result of their history, Commonwealth Caribbean countries were linked to Britain but not to one another, so too were Eric Williams' proposals for a Caribbean-wide economic community dashed on the rocks of reconciling the British, French, Dutch and American colonial legacies of the various countries of the Caribbean.[48] Thus CARICOM finds itself today having to overcome its historic Commonwealth entanglements in order to consolidate even the limited integration to which it aspires. Inherited institutions of language, administration and education also inevitably limit the options for future co-operation. The same point could be made about the now defunct East African Community, and even more about the Economic Community of West African States, an organisation which links French and English-speaking Africa, but which has still to demonstrate that it can make a major contribution to the re-structuring of the regional economy.

CONCLUSION

How finally are we to assess the value of the contemporary Commonwealth to its members? As with most legacies the one over which the Secretariat now presides has positive and negative entailments. In this chapter we have attempted to draw the balance by concentrating first on the rise and fall of the Commonwealth economic system and secondly on the ways in which the Secretariat has serviced the residual Commonwealth, particularly its weaker members, by responding modestly but positively to such opportunities for co-operation as are offered by the post-imperial world.

In the last analysis the Commonwealth had no alternative but to conform to changes in the structure of the world economy. Economic forces set loose in the world after the First World War eventually destroyed the Anglocentric Commonwealth as it was originally conceived. The rise to economic primacy of the United States, decolonisation and the reorientation of Britain itself towards Europe all forced the Commonwealth to adapt in order to survive. The Commonwealth Secretariat was the child of this process. The new environment, which is the product of these and other changes, today sets the parameters of intra-Commonwealth co-operation while at the same time shaping the concerns that preoccupy the current Secretariat. Foremost amongst these concerns is the structural inequity of a world which is perceived as divided into a rich north and a poor south.

But as always the old world lives on in the new. 'De-linking' has been much talked about but little practised as a strategy for dealing with global injustice. In this chapter we have noted the transnational ties that are the residue of the imperial system. It is ironic to contemplate that these historical links provide the continuity which supports a multinational organisation whose main activities are directed at breaking ties of dependence and combating underdevelopment through greater self-reliance in the Third World. These links, in other words, create the perceived mutual interests that underlie the 'service' Commonwealth in its efforts to secure new foundations on which to base North-South relations.

While one may safely predict that the Commonwealth will never again be a major influence on the structuring of the international system, it is more difficult to speculate sensibly on the future course, or extent, of Commonwealth economic co-operation. As we have seen much depends on the central position of the Secretary-General in defining a role for the organisation. This dependence on a personality rather than on institutional power or tradition should not be overstated. The wider concerns emphasised by the Ramphal Secretariat have complemented – and in some instances enhanced – not eliminated the functional intra-Commonwealth co-operation that was the product of Arnold Smith's reign. The members themselves also seem unlikely to forgo altogether the opportunities for co-operation across the North-South divide that the Commonwealth offers. Nevertheless the functions that the Commonwealth assumes in the future will ultimately depend on the ability of the Secretary-General of the day to construct programmes which reflect the realities of the world's economy, minimise the conflicts of interest and perception and maximise the commonality between its developed and developing members.

NOTES AND REFERENCES

1. The subsidised flow of surplus labour to the dominions was encouraged by the Empire Settlement Act. See W. David McIntyre, *The Commonwealth of*

Nations: Origins and Impact 1869–1971 (Minneapolis: University of Minnesota Press, 1977), pp. 318–21.

2. Nicholas Mansergh, *Survey of British Commonwealth Affairs: Problems of External Policy, 1931–39* (London: Oxford University Press for the RIIA, 1952) pp. 9–33.

3. The best account of the period after Britain abandoned the gold standard in 1931 is Ian Drummond, *The Floating Pound and the Sterling Area, 1931–1939* (Cambridge: Cambridge University Press, 1981).

4. Susan Strange, 'Sterling and British Policy: A Political View', *International Affairs*, 47, pp. 306–7. Strange devises a taxonomy of currency categories that takes into account both political and economic factors surrounding the use of currencies.

5. McIntyre, *Commonwealth of Nations*, pp. 321–2.

6. Two such arguments are to be found in Guy Arnold, *Economic Co-operation in the Commonwealth* (Oxford: Pergamon Press, 1967); and Derek Ingram, *The Imperfect Commonwealth* (London: Rex Collins, 1977).

7. Drummond, *Floating Pound and Sterling Area*, p. 9.

8. Ibid., pp. 9–10 and 101–16.

9. Ibid., p. 11.

10. Philip Bell, *The Sterling Area in the Postwar World* (Oxford: Clarendon Press, 1956), pp. 3–17. Bell notes the importance of stable exchange rates in both the pre-World War II sterling bloc and the post-World War II sterling area.

11. Drummond, *Floating Pound and Sterling Area*, pp. 29–51.

12. Ibid., p. 22–6. Among the proponents of internationalised management of sterling was J. M. Keynes, who circulated a paper to that effect in 1931.

13. Nicholas Mansergh, *The Commonwealth Experience* (London: Weidenfeld & Nicolson, 1969), p. 245.

14. Figures derived from Mansergh, *Survey*, 1931–39, p. 181.

15. Arnold, *Economic Co-operation*, p. 15.

16. Mansergh, *Survey*, 1931–39, pp. 150–4.

17. Ibid., p. 153. Britain relaxed protection of agricultural goods by allowing products from Australia easier access as a *quid pro quo*.

18. D. J. Morgan, *The Official History of Colonial Development*, 5 vols, *The Origins of British Aid Policy, 1924–45*, vol. I (London: Macmillan, 1980).

19. Drummond, *Floating Pound and Sterling Area*, pp. 258–9.

20. RIIA, *The Problem of International Investment* (Oxford: Oxford University Press for the RIIA, 1937) p. 134.

21. Ibid., p. 160.

22. Judd Polk, *Sterling: Its Meaning in World Finance* (New York: Harper Brothers, for the Council on Foreign Relations, 1956), pp. 42–54.

23. For a full account of the Anglo–American discussions at the time see Richard Gardner, *Sterling–Dollar Diplomacy in Current Perspective*, new expanded edition (New York: Columbia University Press, 1980).

24. See Nicholas Mansergh, *Documents and Speeches on British Commonwealth Affairs, 1931–1952*, 2 vols (London: Oxford University Press for the RIIA, 1953), vol. I, pp. 562–85; and *Survey of British Commonwealth Affairs: Problems of Wartime Co-operation and Post-War Change, 1939–1952* (London: Oxford University Press, 1958), pp. 164–89; and Gardner, *Sterling–Dollar Diplomacy*, pp. 110–61.

25. Commonwealth Economic Committee, *Commonwealth Trade, 1950–1957* (London: HMSO, 1959); Commonwealth Economic Committee, *Commonwealth Trade with the United States, 1948–1957* (London: HMSO, 1959).
26. For a discussion of the formulation and operation of the Commonwealth Sugar Agreement see Michael Moynagh, 'The Negotiation of the Commonwealth Sugar Agreement, 1949–1951', *Journal of Commonwealth and Comparative Politics*, 15 (1977): 170–90; and Vincent A. Mahler, 'Britain, the European Community and the Developing Commonwealth: Dependence, Interdependence and the Political Economy of Sugar', *International Organization*, 35 (1981), 467–92.
27. An account of economic relations in the Commonwealth up to the founding of the Secretariat can be found in J. D. B. Miller, *Survey of Commonwealth Affairs: Problems of Expansion and Attrition, 1953–1969* (London: Oxford University Press for the RIIA, 1974), chapters 12, 13 and 20.
28. Arnold Smith (with Clyde Sanger), *Stitches in Time: The Commonwealth in World Politics* (London: Andre Deutsch, 1981), p. 45. In Smith's memoirs chapters are generally delineated by political events to which the major portion of the book is devoted.
29. Ibid., pp. 40–3.
30. Ibid., pp. 106–29. There was an interim programme begun in 1967 that was of a more bilateral nature but none the less did help prepare the ground for securing approval of CFTC in 1971.
31. Commonwealth Secretary-General, *Report of the Commonwealth Secretary-General, 1981* (London: Commonwealth Secretariat, 1981) pp. 70–8.
32. Commonwealth Finance Ministers' Final Communiqué, Valetta, Malta, 26–27 September, 1979.
33. Figures computed from statistical table in *Report of the Commonwealth Secretary-General, 1981*, p. 94.
34. Overseas Development Administration (ODA), Press Release, 20 February 1980.
35. ODA and FCO 'United Kingdom Memorandum to the Development Assistance Committee of the Organisation for Economic Co-operation and Development, 1981', September 1981.
36. ODA, Press Release, 3 December 1980.
37. *Commonwealth Currents*, October 1981, p. 7; also *Report of the Commonwealth Secretary-General, 1981*, p. 44.
38. Report of the Commonwealth Technical Group, *The Common Fund*, (London: Commonwealth Secretariat, 1977), p. 7.
39. *Report of the Commonwealth Secretary-General, 1981*, pp. 36–7.
40. Commonwealth Heads of Government, Lusaka Communiqué, August 1979.
41. Miller, *Survey 1953–1969*, pp. 296–300.
42. ODA, *British Development Co-operation With the Least Developed and Poorest Countries* (London: HMSO, 1981), p. 18.
43. Banana Company of Jamaica, *History of Jamaican Banana Industry*, September 1981.

44. 'Lomé Dossier' reprinted from *The Courier*, no. 31, special issue, pp. 73–4. This was Protocol no. 3 of the Lomé Convention.
45. Coverage of both the Lomé Convention and the role of Commonwealth countries in the ACP is given in Allen Frey-Wouters, *The European Community and the Third World: The Lomé Convention and its Impact* (New York: Praeger, 1980).
46. Ibid., pp. 31–3.
47. For discussion of the problems of Caribbean integration in relation to Britain and the EEC see Anthony Payne, *The Politics of the Caribbean Community, 1961–1979* (Manchester: Manchester University Press, 1980); and W. A. Axline, *Caribbean Integration: the Politics of Regionalism* (London: Frances Pinter, 1979).
48. Payne, *Politics of Caribbean*, pp. 211–17.

12 By Way of Comparison: French Relations with Former Colonies

R. J. HARRISON

The Commonwealth is a unique post-imperial phenomenon. France's relations with her former colonies, nevertheless, do present some points of comparison, helping to establish what is unique and, alternatively, what is simply part of a basic and virtually inescapable relationship, modified by the colonial legacy, between advanced and developing societies. The French comparison beckons far more obviously than that which might be made with other former colonial powers; but the French experience is, itself, in many ways unique, and to examine it with the British experience as a model, searching, structure by structure, for parallels and divergencies would distort and mislead. What follows, therefore, after a brief and necessary historical excursion, is an examination of the post-colonial period within the very broad comparative framework of cultural, economic, security and political relationships.

COLONIAL SETTLEMENT AND COLONIAL POLICY

The absence of sovereign territories of predominantly French settlement overseas is the most obvious of socio-economic differences between the Commonwealth and the former French Empire. Just as important, however, is the legacy of a different colonial policy.

For France, there are no 'old dominions' settled by Europeans as almost virgin territories, rapidly becoming independent, and harbouring generations later a residual nostalgia for the 'old country'. Quebec has had no distinctive place, until recently, as an object of French politics, nor have important *direct* cultural or economic linkages existed.[1] Other French colonies have always had substantial 'native' populations, and where European settlement was relatively heavy, the settlers were nevertheless a minority and in no hurry to sever their links with France and the security and protection of its administration and forces. Even at home the French political tradition was to maintain centralised government, minimising local responsibility.

Although as early as 1794 all men in the colonies were first granted citizenship and later there were several attempts to grant representation in central metropolitan institutions, nothing in the practice of French colonial rule compensated for the absence of an established formula for developing political independence. While the Empire was centrally administered in theory, power tended in fact, to be localised, but not in a way to promote or facilitate responsible indigenous government. The only long-term, significant conception of colonial development was that of assimilation – namely, the attainment of French citizenship by individuals in native populations, or in sufficiently advanced areas, the collective achievement of metropolitan status, subject to the regular pattern of prefectoral administration, as in France itself.[2] It was a conception which was little appreciated. Citizenship was not widely sought even among those whose education entitled them to it. It involved too complete a break with indigenous society and its institutions. The aspirations of native populations for independence, therefore, when they were aroused, could not easily be accommodated. No formula, such as that gradually worked out in the British Empire, and eventually enunciated in the Statute of Westminster, was available to the French.[3]

Consequently, important parts of the French colonial Empire were emancipated only as a result of a bloody war of independence. There was the war of repression in Tunisia in 1952 and the *ratissage* in Morocco in 1955. Indo-China and Algeria, both areas of considerable French settlement, were relinquished only after a particularly violent struggle which has had a lasting effect on relations with France. Kenya and Zimbabwe are the best points of comparison with the British Empire, but, even where violence has played a part, the undoubted prospect of eventual independence through stages of political responsibility has mitigated the struggle in the British case.

CONSEQUENCES OF THE EMANCIPATION PROCESS

The different circumstances in which colonies won their independence from France have affected subsequent relations. General de Gaulle's willingness to accept the inevitability of colonial emancipation, and his ability to impose this on France, averted violent struggles for independence during the Fifth Republic. However, those that had taken place earlier still affect the situation. Franco-Algerian relations have been particularly strained, and the internal consequences of Algerian independence have been profound for both countries. Before it could be achieved, the independence issue destroyed the Fourth Republic and provided the conditions which led to the foundation of the new, more stable Fifth Republic. Algeria had been the most heavily settled of French territories, governed as an integral part of France. Since independence it has lost most of its French population and the repatriation continues still.

Southern France has had to absorb a very large part of the exodus. There has been some benefit stemming from the entrepreneurship of the repatriates but the most important effect has been the exacerbation of unemployment in the area. For its part, Algeria has nationalised French firms without prior agreement on compensation, cancelled a large part of its financial debt to France, assumed control of its oil in 1971 (the critical element in French oil supplies) and generally tried to eliminate all vestiges of its former dependent status. It has not been discouraged in this by the closure of the French market to its former main export – wine – which worsened relations between the two countries. Algeria nevertheless continued to benefit from French aid while de Gaulle was in office and benefits also from the remittances of Algerian workers in France, of whom there are some three-quarters of a million. It has, however, been deprived of its former elite. For example, ninety per cent of teachers at the high school level were formerly French, most of whom have gone, not to be adequately replaced. Thus, socio-economic problems are the consequences rather than the causes of political relations.

Different, though equally violent, conditions at the time of emancipation have determined relations with Indo-China. After the humiliating defeat at Dien Bien Phu the French presence was, in effect, replaced by an American one. De Gaulle disassociated France from the United States' effort of containment which followed in Vietnam, seeing the war very clearly, as in Algeria, as one which could not be won, and recommending honourable withdrawal. Subsequently the area has been so unsettled that no definable political relationship has emerged with

France. Virtually all other links were dissolved during the long period of war and of American presence after 1954.

Elsewhere, where the transition to independence was relatively peaceful, close relations have tended to persist, including many aspects of the dependent status of the colonial era. In cultural and economic terms the colonial legacy is striking.

CULTURAL RELATIONS – 'LA FRANCOPHONIE'

French culture has a profound influence throughout the former Empire. Even in Algeria, despite political differences and notwithstanding the 'arabisation' policy, it remains strong, and a factor in relations with France. There, more people now write and speak French in the native population than before independence. French is obligatory in schools. In primary schools the languages of instruction are equally French and Arabic, as they are also in Morocco. In secondary schools, throughout North Africa, French is the main language of instruction, and in general the language of the elite. All official documents are in both French and Arabic. Outside North Africa, *la francophonie* prevails. Because of the multiplicity of native languages in the former colonies, French is the official language and the natural language in common, as English is in many Commonwealth multilingual states.

Any summary assessment of the effects of the cultural legacy on relations between France and her former colonies must be in terms of the importance of *la francophonie*. The link between language and cultural, economic and political relationships is complex and hard to demonstrate in detail. That the spread of languages has historically been linked in practice with imperial venture is clear. Imperial languages fostered the perception of a distinction between 'modern' superior ideas and ways and the inferior traditional culture, established a distinction between the language of command, of administration, of business, new technology and science, education, and written theoretical knowledge, and the language of the ruled, the labourer and of folklore. The immediate convenience of the ruling elite rather than any clear conception of the costs and benefits of the process have dictated it. The costs have been difficult to count or even to perceive.

Contemporary France has a relatively high degree of sensitivity to, and awareness of, the problems of linguistic dominance. France's strength of purpose for defence of the international status of the language finds conceptual and organisational expression in *la fran-*

cophonie. Viatte has defined it as an international cultural community united through its use of the French language.[4] Others have argued the benefits of economic exchange and transfer of technology which are boosted through ease of communication. The proposition that language is also an instrument of colonialism or neo-colonialism has not deterred Senegal's former President Senghor from his efforts to provide an organisational framework for *la francophonie* though it does partially explain the arabisation policy in Algeria and the refusal of certain states to participate in the Cultural and Technical Co-operation Agency of French-speaking countries set up in 1970.

The Agency was the fruit of two conferences in 1969 and 1970 which discussed a suggestion made in 1964 by Senghor. He saw the language as a mode of thought and action: a certain way of setting out problems and resolving them, and one, furthermore, which, in a symbiotic relationship with another culture, could benefit both. These ideas were taken up by President Bourguiba of Tunisia in 1965 and by President Diori Hamani of Niger. Membership of the Agency is wider than the former French Empire (including some Commonwealth members) although the Agency is located in Paris and France provides 45 per cent of the budget.

The Agency has an evident symbiotic importance, although it is limited in its functional scope to cultural and technical co-operation. It meets every two years. It is not, in any case, the only organisational expression of *la francophonie*. There is an Association of French and Partially French Universities, AUPLF, which includes thirty participant countries, a French–African Ministers of Education Conference, meeting twice a year and, at the highest level, the summit meetings between French–African heads of state (including the former Belgian and British French-speaking colonies) and the French president. The summit met first in 1973 and then, annually, since 1975. The analogy with Commonwealth institutions has not escaped the participants and the Dakar summit in 1977 did advance the idea of a '*Commonwealth à la française*.'[5]

In spite of the lofty sentiments used by Senghor and others, the dominance of French, on which *la francophonie* depends, creates problems for the former colonies, particularly in education. The system of education everywhere is directly copied from the French system as it was prior to the reforms which have taken place in France since 1960. The organisation of schools and the competitive hierarchy is the same. In principle education is free, universal and obligatory, though in the countryside this cannot be ensured and children who have no French – the language of instruction – cannot take advantage of the opportunity when it is available. In Algeria and Morocco something like 80 per cent of children do receive some education, but the figures are very much smaller for the Central African states.

The general use of French as the language of instruction, and the exclusion of African languages from the curriculum, has been strongly criticised. The school is seen as an alien institution which divorces the child from the indigenous environment for no good purpose. The percentage of those finishing primary school is rarely higher than 40 per cent and the number who complete secondary school education with the *baccalaureat* is invariably less than 5 per cent of those who had once started primary school. The majority are said to leave school frustrated; the knowledge acquired tends to be of little practical use; minds are often turned to mere mimicry; even knowledge of language is little advanced and most soon revert to illiteracy.[6]

French is essentially the legacy bequeathed to an urban elite as are other aspects of the cultural, language-linked heritage which are without reference points in native languages and values. All these countries have universities but admission to the highest positions in teaching, industry, commerce and the like generally depends upon having a diploma from a French institution or from the United States, even though the same training at an equivalent standard may be available in the home country. In spite of existing relations with France the position in this respect is the same in Algeria. There are at present some 20 000 students in Algeria, but there are 9000 more in Europe. Of Moroccans, at least half of all students are studying in France or the United States.

The mass media in the former colonies depend to a very large extent on material of French or dubbed American origin, particularly television, although a good deal of radio is in Arabic in North Africa and the music is also Arabian. But above all, French language dominance would seem to be one of the key factors in the maintenance of a particularly close and basically dominance-dependence relationship between France and her ex-colonies. It is an inviting gateway for the French investor and trader. The slightly beleaguered aspect of the language internationally fosters a sense of solidarity and separate common interest which the more pervasive English does not provide. This is exploited by France to further a special relationship of political co-operation, educational linkages, technological transfer, commerce, financial services and military assistance of a peculiarly French dimension of the core-periphery relationship between the advanced industrial societies of the North and the developing states of the South.

INSTITUTIONAL FACTORS

Neither *liberté, egalité et fraternité,* nor the equally important French tradition of *étatisme,* has had much influence on the working of institutions in the former colonies. Movements of independence were typified by a stress on national unity and charismatic leadership. The Fifth Republican presidential constitution was easily modified to give these characteristics direct expression. The presidency combined the dignity of head of state with real political power and was the obvious model office for the leader of the dominant political movement in a newly-independent state. Assemblies, where they were retained, had mainly symbolic roles. Parties could be absorbed within a single organisation of national unity or allowed a separate but co-operating existence. Administration, central and local, remained modelled on France, a direct inheritance of the colonial administrative pattern with departments and prefects (retained in effect even by Algeria). Representative interest group activity could be allowed to exist but in a limited, corporatist mode. During the colonial era, socio-professional organisations, including trade unions, were formed by French residents, linked to the unions in France. These have declined in number over the past two decades and in some states altogether disappeared. Where they do still exist, their role is an intermediary one between government and rank and file. Consequently there are no remaining links between the French unions and those in the former colonies. Democracy in any real sense has succumbed virtually everywhere to authoritarianism. Only Senegal and Morocco still have a residual opposition and a press free to criticise, though the facade is preserved elsewhere.

This has not necessarily made for strong efficient government, but rather in some cases to the development of irresponsible tyrannies later to be overthrown in a costly upheaval. It has meant policies pursued without benefit of free advice or criticism to the point of economic difficulty or near disaster. It has meant, for France, suffering a certain amount of international discredit through association with disreputable regimes which have looked to France for support, but also a continued special place in resource exploitation and the local market. Inefficient autocracies have negotiated with the highly sophisticated state machinery or the business bureaucracy of France, with predictable consequences. The centralised autocracy has also made possible a special, covert relationship between France and the effective heads of government in the former colonies. While formal relations are conducted by the Foreign Ministry, Defence, or the Ministry of Co-operation, the more important informal contacts with heads of state were handled until 1974 by a Secretariat for African and Malagasy Affairs responsible to the president, within the Elysée. During de Gaulle's presidency, and then, after a brief interruption under Pompidou, the secretariat was headed by Jacques Foccart. He had a very close relationship with the president since he was also his advisor on secret service matters. It would be difficult to exaggerate this single influence on African politics and on the French position in Africa. The independent, anti-colonial stance assumed in public by some African governments for local consumption, contrasted with the co-operation and understanding achieved privately with France, through the presidency and Foccart's secretariat. Foccart's reign ended with the advent to power of Giscard d'Estaing, and French overseas territories became one of the functional divisions of the general secretariat of the presidency, but the close personal relationship with individual heads of African autocracies has remained a factor in Franco–African relations, although Mitterrand is putting it on a new footing.

ECONOMIC RELATIONS

It is in the economic sphere that core-periphery relations between advanced industrial societies like France and the less developed countries are most apparent and clearly defined. The general position is that growth per capita in the developed 'core' countries is faster than in the underdeveloped periphery, so that the poverty gap is growing.

Within countries peripheral regions are dependent on the centre for regional aid programmes and policies to favour industrial investment and resource exploitation. Aid programmes play a similar role in international politics. Acceptance of economic assistance, however,

gives donor states a major, sometimes decisive, voice in the recipients' investment decisions, which in turn directly affect all aspects of domestic relations . . . Since most aid flows are tied to purchases from the donor state, less-developed countries also find aid commitments to be an important constraint on their choice of major trading partners among advanced industrial states.[7]

Aid is also, in many cases, contingent on favourable conditions for foreign investment – such as low taxes and no costly welfare programmes. Sometimes this is quite formal and explicit, rather than just a matter of practice. In the case of France and her former colonies, aid is subject to bilateral and multilateral treaty provision, and like donor–recipient relations in general is affected by conceptions of the economic and political interest of the donor country as well as altruistic and responsible developmental goals. France is, in a sense, more open about such conceptions than other Western donors. Whereas other countries discriminate among a large number of recipients by varying the amount of aid given, France allocates aid to a limited number of countries: these are former colonies and other low income countries which trade with France.[8]

French aid, as a percentage of GNP, was higher than that of any other OECD country during the 1960s but fell in the 1970s behind Scandinavia and the Netherlands.[9] Development aid creates a greater degree of dependence when it is in the form of loans rather than outright gifts, since repayment grows, reducing the net value of new aid. Most French aid is in the form of grants. The French aid figures, however, include aid to the overseas departments and territories – Guadeloupe, Martinique, Reunion and French Polynesia. These are legally part of France, with departmental status and full representation in the French parliament. The 'aid' allocated to them reflects their status as regions of France and is, therefore, massive in comparison with even the most favoured of the ex-colonies. It accounted in 1975 for 39 per cent of the total of French overseas development aid:[10] of the seventeen Development Assistance Committee members of OECD, Australia, Austria, the USA and France were the countries who, in 1975, devoted the lowest share of their aid to the least developed countries.

Trade is another dimension of dependence. Typically, a Third World state trades a very small range of exports, often primary products in competition with neighbouring countries. They tend to be destined for a specific market – one of the advanced industrial societies, often the former colonial power. For the peripheral Third World country, the export market is the vital one, the internal market for all products being very weak. The country for whom the product is destined, however, usually has a wide range of exports and markets. Another problem is that the price of primary products tends to fluctuate more than that of industrial goods so that primary producers like to make long-term purchasing agreements with importers to ensure stability and in return grant favoured or monopoly access to their market.

Trade between France and her colonies has not been as directly and swiftly sensitive to politics as has aid. Aid is frequently a signal of support or commitment by a donor country to the recipient. The statistics suggest that gross trade, in the French case, is an important factor in determining whether such a commitment will be made, and aid given. Gross trade is affected favourably by commitment but the latter is not a vital determinant. France retains a trade ascendancy, though it is declining, over most of her former Empire, particularly as supplier, rather than customer. Thus, Algeria, over half of whose exports were going to the United States by 1977, with Germany her second-best market (over 14 per cent), nevertheless bought more from France (12.7 per cent) than from any other single country. Imports consisted mainly of capital goods. Everywhere throughout the former colonies for which UN trade figures are published there has been some decline in the French share of trade. The colonies have diversified their export markets. Imports from France still constitute the largest share of their markets, though this share is declining. Between 1961 and 1974 it fell from 74.9 per cent overall to 45.4 per cent.[11]

Another dimension of dependence is capital – very much tied up in practice with the operations of foreign companies. Commercial or profit-seeking capital avoids ventures where productivity and consumption are low. Typically, in the peripheral countries it seeks out the profitable export sector of the economy. Where foreign capital and investment are concerned it must be recognised that a proportionate part of the profits of any enterprise will be repatriated to the core country from which the investment came. However, a surprising amount of the capital for the operations of big foreign firms is raised in the host countries. The little indigenous private capital is attracted to the export market and to the big, overseas established firms which are a 'good risk'. It is not, therefore, available for home-controlled enterprise. Where a country does determinedly try to undertake, in part, its own controlled development it must rely on loans from overseas, thus adding the burden of interest payments to that of profit repatriation. These cancel out quite a large part of aid and development assistance programmes. Indebtedness makes for dependence. It is one of the incentives, for example, for the ex-colonial powers, whose banks and financial institutions generally have gone on functioning in the territory, to accede to requests for military assistance, bolstering-up existing elites. This helps to guarantee debt repayment although it is another aspect of dependence.

French investment has tended to follow political relations and stable domestic conditions. It is very much reduced in Algeria, it remains substantial in Guinea, where France retains a 10 per cent holding in the bauxite mining consortium FRIA, but, again, because of the political situation, it has stopped in Madagascar. On the other hand, the Ivory

Coast and Gabon have been major attractions for French investors – a kind of El Dorado, with petrol, rubber and diamonds. Taking the former colonies as a whole, more than 50 per cent of all industrial investment is French, and gross investment is increasing. The major business corporations in the private sector have national titles but are usually French owned and run affiliates.

In a sense the colonial relationship persists and develops, but two categories may be distinguished: those states which have remained in the franc zone and those which have left it. The latter, Algeria and other 'socialist' states like Guinea, Mali, Madagascar and Mauretania, as well as Indo-China, have had until recently very few ties with the French banking system. For the other African states the currency is the franc CFA which has maintained a stable relationship with the French franc. In these states the banking system is centred on Paris and the operating banks are mostly French. There are national central banks but their role is limited. The French banks are an important agency for the retention of France's ascendancy of business influence in the former colonies. Furthermore, the operational rules of the two zones into which the CFA is divided give France a formal role in the monetary and fiscal policy of member countries.

The African Financial Community (or CFA) has its origins in the franc zone of the colonial era. With independence, two central banks of issue – the Bank of Central African States (BEAC) and the Central Bank of West African States (BCEAO) – were created, serving the two zones of the CFA: the western zone comprising the Ivory Coast, Benin, Upper Volta, Niger, Senegal and Togo; and the central zone comprising Cameroon, the Central African Republic, Congo, Gabon and Tchad. Each zone has a customs union and the CFA franc is the common currency of both zones. Only a letter in the serial number of notes serves to differentiate between the issues in use in different member countries, and notes and coins are, in any case, legal tender throughout each zone. Member countries pool their reserves, which are held in the two central banks, and channel any IMF operations through them. The bulk of exchange reserves are deposited with the French Treasury which, by treaty with France, provides an unlimited guarantee of the money issue. The treaties also specify what measures are to be taken if a zone should go into debit and how the parity with the French franc is to be maintained. The limits of borrowing by member countries from the central banks are subject to well defined limitations. Credit may be extended to national treasuries up to 20 per cent of the budget receipts of that country for the previous financial year. Each category of credit, short-term or medium-term, has a separate ceiling. The expansion of credit is thus designed to keep pace with the growth of the economy in each country. The system, in this respect, does limit the potential for internal government-financed development and increases the reliance on importation of foreign capital for development. On the other hand, the stability afforded by the system may constitute an attraction to foreign investment – though this effect cannot clearly be demonstrated.[12] Senegal, Ivory Coast, Togo, Gabon and Cameroon have borrowed extensively on the Euromarket and have also obtained bilateral credits and suppliers credits. Gabon borrowed heavily also from its own domestic commercial banks, bringing itself to debit with the rest of the CFA in the process, and limits have subsequently been imposed on domestic commercial bank lending to governments.

A ministerial council on which each country is represented makes grand decisions of policy for each of the zones as a whole. France is represented on the board of directors of each of the central banks. This system of monetary discipline allows some local autonomy, but France, in return for the guarantees it offers, has considerable influence over the controlling institutions. It is significant, nevertheless, that Guinea, Mali and Mauretania, which opted out of the franc zone, have sought to link up with it again after having experienced economic difficulties. Mali was readmitted in 1967 and Mauretania in 1978 after only four years outside. Guinea has re-established indirect links after some twenty years and has been admitted to the Association of African Central Banks and the West African Clearing House system. It signed the Lomé Convention in 1975 and has joined ECOWAS.

Guinea remains the only African state to have chosen and held to a policy of dissolution of ties with the former colonial power. Under Sekou Touré, president since 1958, it has pursued a 'socialist' policy through a single party – the Democratic Party of Guinea (PDG). The country has rich agricultural, mineral and energy resources which were barely developed during the colonial period – a source of strongly expressed dissatisfaction among national leaders. When Guinea rejected Community status, French administrative and teaching personnel withdrew from Guinea as did most French enterprise, and all technical, economic and financial aid was stopped. An emigrée bourgeoisie in France, Senegal and the Ivory Coast has provided a continuing opposition to the regime, allegedly financed by Foccart's Secretariat for African and Malagasy Affairs until its abolition in 1974.

Eastern bloc countries were the first to provide assistance after 1968, but Sekou Touré has managed to preserve a balance between both blocs and both have invested, particularly in the mining industry. Investments have been on the basis of conventions intended to serve Guinean interests – generally by conceding to Guinea a larger share of the profits than its share of ownership. Soviet and Eastern bloc assistance has proved less effective than aid from Western sources and Touré has himself openly criticised the Soviet role in recent years. The closer Western orientation of Guinea was marked by the visit of President Giscard d'Estaing in 1978, signal also of *rapprochement* with France. Dependence on France, where it is the price that has to be paid for French commitment, has been seen to have compensating economic benefits.

Yet another source of dependence between core and periphery is the technology and skills gap. Research and development expenditure are minimal in the Third World countries. Payments for the import of technology in the form of patents, licences, trade marks, management and service fees are approximately 15 per cent of export earnings in 1980 for the developing countries. With technology come foreign nationals for its operation and maintenance. The business of trying to *educate* one's own nationals to manage and operate modern technology is yet another dimension of dependence. They have to be trained and educated abroad or, if at home, by foreign nationals. Tertiary education is done abroad, and though some countries (Algeria for instance) have good universities, the foreign-trained are preferred for the highest jobs: the language inheritance inevitably means that those trained in France are most numerous.

A consequent dimension of dependence in core-periphery relations is the movement of people. The migration of labour toward core areas and the flow of entrepreneurial, managerial and technologically-skilled settlers and tourists in the opposite direction are, it is clear, consequences of the asymmetries under discussion, but they too are causal, helping to perpetuate the pattern and adding to dependence. Emigrant remittances, capital transfer by returning migrants, the inhibition of peripheral development because of induced skilled labour scarcity, are all products of migration. The need to meet, on the other hand, the expectations of settlers and tourists and retain their goodwill, the influence of their life-styles (and of returning migrants) are other aspects of dependence.

Immigration from former colonies (other than the overseas departments) has now been stopped by France. There are, nevertheless, still in France well over half a million Algerians, about 300 000 Moroccans and half as many Tunisians. The black African states of the Sahel have been a source of controlled and clandestine immigration. Of the overseas departments, the biggest influx has been from Martinique and Guadaloupe. The migrants have tended to take inferior or dirty jobs, congregating in the Paris area and thereby giving rise to the usual problems and tensions which have occasionally affected relations. Street violence against Algerians, for example, has been one of the factors inhibiting the development of 'normal' relations and delaying formal agreements on orderly repatriation of Algerians desired by France. The more general problem of immigration, representing approximately 8 per cent of the work force, generally unskilled, first to be unemployed, increasingly radicalised (a fact which also worries some of the governments of countries of origin),[13] remains unsolved.

The three countries of heaviest *French* immigration since the traumatic break with Algeria and, before that, Indo-China are now the Ivory Coast, Senegal and Gabon. In these states there are now twice as many French settlers as there were on independence. In other former colonies the trend is similar. Overseas departments like Martinique, Guadeloupe, Reunion and Tahiti also have important European minorities but since all the inhabitants are French citizens figures are not available. The majority are *métis*, of mixed blood. The more emphatic orientations toward development since independence, opening up opportunities, and, perhaps to some extent, the sense that it would be easier to extract concessions from the post-colonial government than from the colonial administration, are probable explanations of the growth of European settlement. The fact, too, that there are no sovereign lands of French majority settlement, as counter-attractions, must also be taken into account in explaining this phenomenon.

TREATY ARRANGEMENTS AND SECURITY LINKS

To the extent that relations between France and the former colonies are actually formalised in treaties or agreements, the most important are bilateral. Apart from the period of short-lived French Community from 1958–60, there have been no multilateral ties which may be compared with those existing in the Commonwealth, excepting in certain functional areas, like air transport (Air Afrique) and monetary regulation (CFA). The Lomé Convention is a notable multilateral agreement but it is wider than the former Empire, as is the language Agency.

Lomé in 1975 was a renegotiation, with British accession to the EEC, of the former Yaoundé Convention. The latter was a product of French pressure to maintain its relations with former African colonies within the context of its own membership of a customs union. In spite of the accession of former British colonies, the arrangements still have a strongly French imprint. France not only remains the principal supplier and importer from the African, Caribbean and Pacific states adhering to the convention, but has actually increased its relative share in comparison with other EEC members. Currently, however, technologically sophisticated industry, encouraged by state policies, is becoming more important in the total industrial complex in France, reducing the influence of the traditional industries, which have been most active in the ACP countries and have constituted a French Africa lobby in Brussels in the shape of the *Association Internationale pour le Dévéloppement Economique et l'Aide Technique.* A general trend away from investment and preferential trade in ACP countries may be expected. France for this reason is likely to have fewer differences with Germany, the UK, and the Netherlands, who have shown some reluctance to go on subsidising the French ex-colonial relationship. One other important framework for continuous multilateral contact is that provided by the UN. Although France does not participate in the work of the Decolonisation Committee, its liaison with the francophone delegations is close and the permanent French delegation normally includes a specialist on post-colonial questions.

However, the advantage of bilaterialism for France since independence has been that problems and crises in relations with any one, do not immediately involve all other ex-colonies. New leaders sometimes regard the relationship with France as disguised colonialism and profess an alternative, but these have been passing phases and the web of formal treaty lines, centred on France, with less important lateral linkages, remains strong. The bilateral agreements which exist with all the former colonies except Guinea, Madagascar and, until the recent accords, Algeria, vary considerably from country to country but they tend to cover foreign policy consultation, access to raw materials and strategic products, common monetary policy within the CFA, trade preferences, aid and technical assistance. In most cases they also cover defence, often including agreement on French bases and recognising a French military presence, an important indication that a state accepts itself as being within a French sphere of influence. Defence treaties, arms sales, military assistance and a French military presence are valued as a contribution to internal stability, reassurance for prospective foreign investors, a deterrence against intervention by neighbouring states, and a barrier to the extension of Soviet interest. The French have maintained a considerable military capability in Africa available for immediate use there. Nor have they been reticent in its use, often with *éclat*.

French military influence in the former colonies, however, cannot be described solely in terms of military presence and engagements. Military training and arms supplies are other important aspects. In addition to local forces being trained by French cadres, some 1600 trainees from seventeen states were in France in 1977.[14] A Mission of Military Co-operation is established in each country attached to the Ministry of Co-operation and in liaison with the ministries of Defence and Foreign Affairs. Immediately following independence the task of the mission was to create a national gendarmerie and army, lightly equipped by France. Since then, France has continued to give equipment to the ex-colonies and is also a major supplier commercially. In Africa as a whole, to which the Soviet Union supplies more than half of all arms, France is the second major supplier. The principal recipients of French arms, apart from Libya (which takes almost half the total of all arms supplied to African states by all suppliers) and South Africa (which has trouble obtaining arms from other sources), are the former colonies, including Algeria. The largest ex-colonial recipient of French arms in 1978 was Morocco.[15]

France's relations with her former colonies are in the core-periphery pattern – the pattern which obtains also within the Commonwealth and between the Netherlands and Belgium and their former colonies and overall between the advanced societies and the Third World. France has been direct and open in its efforts to maintain influence since the dissolution of empire, concentrating on its former colonies in its Third World relationships. It has involved itself in their internal politics and economics to preserve friendly regimes and a favourable economic climate for itself. But equally, it has adapted itself, in most cases, to changes in regimes, with a perhaps typically French scepticism about whether change can ever be, in politics at least, more than superficial.

It may be that these are the qualities which have allowed France, in comparison with Britain and other advanced societies, to retain a relatively high place in the esteem of the Third World. French actions are comprehensible in terms of French interests, whether in selling arms to South Africa, or sustaining and then helping to oust Bokassa, or keeping a foothold in Congo–Brazzaville at the height of its flirtation with the Soviet Union, or supplying arms to Biafra during the Nigerian civil war. There are no moral judgements, no patronising messianic ideologies, no sense of the white man's burden, and hence there is virtually no condescension in the relationship. France's historic '*mission civilisatrice*' is directed impartially toward all other countries, not just the Third World.

There is, however, it must finally be admitted, an element of the inexplicable and irrational about France's relations with her former colonies, and even more about the interest shown by Rwanda, Burundi, Zaire, Guinea–Bissau, Cape Verde, Mozambique, Somalia, and Sierra Leone and Liberia, from time to time, in becoming part of the family. As Tamar Golan has put it, there is 'A certain mystery: how can France do everything it does in Africa – and get away with it?'[16]

NOTES AND REFERENCES

1. Since 1977, initiatives taken by Quebec have led to co-operation, exchange of visits between premiers, cultural exchanges, joint economic, technical and scientific projects between French and Quebec firms, and proposals for further linkages. As yet, however, the new relationship is embryonic.
   See *The Times*, 17 December 1980, 'France adopts policy of "non-indifference" on Quebec Question'.
2. The fact that indigenous populations in the French colonies were small and that, with the exception of a few 'far-flung outposts', the French Empire was restricted in geographical scope, gave some prima-facie credibility to this conception.
3. This comparison, applying to general conceptions and legal formulae, does not mean that there was anything like so clear a difference in colonial practice. It was a difference that became important at the time of colonial emancipation.
4. In his *La francophonie* (Paris: Larousse, 1969).
5. Frank Tenaille, *Les 56 Afriques*, vol. 2 (Paris: Maspero, 1979) p. 196.
6. S. K. Panter-Brick, in W. H. Morris-Jones (ed.) *Decolonisation and After* (London: Frank Cass, 1980), pp. 342–3.
7. David H. Blake and R. S. Walters *The politics of global economic relations* (N.J.: Prentice-Hall, 1976) p. 138.
8. See R. D. McKinlay and R. Little, 'The French Aid Relationship', *Development and Change*, vol. 9 (1978).
9. 59 per cent in 1980. *The World Bank*, *World Development Report, 1980* (New York: OUP, p. 140).
10. OECD, Development Co-operation *1976 Review* (Paris, 1976) p. 90.
11. *UN Yearbook of International Trade Statistics* and *UN Statistical Yearbook*.
12. Frank Tenaille, *Les 56 Afriques*, vol. 2, p. 236 argues that it has not been an additional attraction but it has led to development contrary to that preferred by governments.
13. Ibid., p. 238.
14. Ibid., p. 192.
15. US Arms Control and Disarmament Agency, *World Military Expenditures and Arms Transfers, 1969–1978* (Washington, 1980) p. 161.
16. Golan's article with this title appears in *African Affairs*, vol. 80, 318, January 1981, pp. 3–11.

Part III
High Politics

13 Continuity without Consensus: the Commonwealth Heads of Government Meetings, 1971—81

MICHAEL O'NEILL

'Did you perceive, He did solicit you in free contempt,
When he did need your loves . . . ?'

Coriolanus, William Shakespeare

INTRODUCTION: THE TRANSITION TO THE 'THIRD PHASE'

The Commonwealth Heads of Government Meetings (CHOGM) has passed in fairly rapid succession through several stages. From being a kind of imperial cabinet of white members whose empathy and common origins made broad agreement possible, it became a more diverse and thereby contentious forum, spanning the racial, ideological and developmental divisions of the post-colonial world. In this second phase the Commonwealth found it difficult to agree on a satisfactory common denominator to guide its deliberations and, at certain junctures, its future was in some doubt. However, it weathered those traumatic moments. Chastened by the experience on all sides, it willingly entered a new period of compromise far removed from both the outdated hegemonic assumptions of the established white members and the equally unworkable multilateral ambitions of some of the new radical

185

intake. The outcome of this process was, in fact, not ultimately destructive, and prepared the membership for the challenges yet to come.

The turning point came in the sixties, although there were moments of regression into tense confrontation in the new decade too. Nevertheless, these crises – which are an unavoidable 'occupational hazard' of any diplomacy conducted on such a wide scale – were less fraught with the bitterness and rigidity of the earlier period. By and large, the Commonwealth Heads of Government Meeting had entered a new phase of adjustment which guaranteeed its survival.[1] As the heads of government embarked on another decade of meetings the prevailing mood was, far from disenchantment or foreboding, one of realism. The trend in the six meetings under discussion was broadly one of acceptance by the political leaders of what they could most fruitfully deal with to mutual advantage, as well as what was outside their province. This new *modus operandi* was not immediately evident and its discovery was a gradual process of accommodation that ran throughout all of these conferences. Above all, it was characterised by a new mood of pragmatism that was even in evidence at stormy sessions like those at Singapore in 1971.

Jaundiced or less practised commentators saw this as merely a continuation of the uncompromising decade just past. In fact, although the heads of government had yet to agree to procedural arrangements which would minimise the temptation to adopt a narrow or self-centred approach to issues, there were already some encouraging signs, even at Singapore, both of an awareness of the problem and of the need to overcome such rigidity if meetings were to retain credibility and remain useful. Notwithstanding the intensity of the issue at stake, therefore, the atmosphere of pragmatism informing the debate at Singapore augured well for the future. Thereafter, the resolve of even the most militant participants to accept such organisational changes as would minimise the meetings' tendency to formalised and strident exchanges emphasised the extent to which the Commonwealth had absorbed its experiences and responded positively, to ensure continuity of what, without exception, they regarded as a valuable forum.

By and large this accommodation reflected the changes which had already occurred in the Commonwealth's 'second phase', initiated by India's entry in 1949. The Commonwealth then became less a white man's club and increasingly – with the onset of rapid decolonisation after 1957 – a post-colonial relationship, with Britain adopting the central hub position in relation to the newly-independent rim. There were, however, widely divergent interpretations of this symbiotic relationship, not least from the African members who adopted a self-conscious, often aggressive racial perspective which soon made deep inroads into any sense of natural harmony or collective interest, of the sort which had prevailed before the Second World War. Britain, for its part, continued to define it in a way little removed from the first or inter-war phase. According to this unrealistic rendering, the Commonwealth could somehow remain a grand, post-imperial cabinet under British guidance. It would thus retain something of the cohesion in in-ternational politics which, under the British aegis, would prove capable of wielding an authority in the world equivalent to that of the two emergent and populous 'super powers'.

There were good reasons why the Commonwealth had this appeal as an imperial surrogate. Quite simply it continued to fill an important gap in the imagination of British policy-makers, helping to ease the painful decline from 'Great power' status. Epstein captured the magnitude of this transition, and something of its problems, when he observed that 'no nation has ever so successfully surrendered so much in so short a time as has Britain since 1945'. Regardless of the self-congratulation which surrounded this almost bloodless and often amicable transfer of power, there were bound to be reverberations. In particular, there were problems of mental assimilation to the resulting vacuum: 'the accom-modation to massive imperial withdrawal, even if graciously accom-plished, [does not] appear as impressive as the policies that had previously established Britain's leadership and Empire'.[2]

This was hardly an overstatement. In the early period of decol-onisation, the notion of a continuing trusteeship to provide precisely this sense of missing purpose figured prominently in the Commonwealth policies of both major British parties.[3] There were, however, also early signs of a break in this bipartisanship. The Conservatives appeared more readily to adapt to the inevitable strictures imposed by changing circumstances. Occupying the crucible of office for thirteen unbroken years, they had already begun to set aside the inappropriate notions which had guided post-war policy, before they lost power in 1964.

Meanwhile Labour, admittedly from the relatively distorting role of Opposition, had continued to assume an idealised but equally unre-alistic mantle of Commonwealth 'leadership'. It retained a vision – if not without some hint of *realpolitik* – that an active Commonwealth role would boost Britain's depleted international prestige. Predictably, the early attempts by the incoming Labour administration in 1964 to use the rapidly expanding Commonwealth Heads of Government Meeting as a springboard for positive action came to grief on the active hostility of the new members to any hint of continued British leadership.

For some purposes, the other members were quite willing to accept a paramount British role, but certainly not on Britain's terms. The quarrels of the sixties were essentially, therefore, about an appropriate post-colonial relationship. The outcome was predictable enough. Faced with a Commonwealth which was less compliant than British politicians had anticipated, even the Labour Party began to revise its assessment in its search for a foreign policy appropriate to Britain's altered world status. Confronted by the unseemly prospect of a new membership which made unreasonable demands, couched often in the uncomfortable guise of moral outrage, British policy-makers began to put the Commonwealth under more critical scrutiny than ever before. Under a government of either party, Britain proved unwilling to display unlimited patience in the face of pressure and even abuse, or to allow British policy to be treated to special scrutiny. Moreover, Britain was not prepared to accept a role in which it was expected to contribute more than it received. It made clear that it wanted membership on the same, limited and utilitarian terms as the others.

To comprehend fully these changes of approach towards the Commonwealth – which in turn did much to influence the transition in Commonwealth attitudes – we need to appreciate the reorientation that was under way in Britain's general view of its international commitments.[4] Under the press of events, the various strands of establishment opinion were taking on a new bellicosity, fully prepared to put what they saw as chimeras to the strict test of relevance. As one influential British commentator put it,

> the fact is that [Britain] no longer has any liberal feelings of guilt about its behaviour and its legacy as a colonial power. Quite the reverse; it is now demanding a greater sense of realism among Commonwealth governments, both in their words and their actions, as the price of Britain's continued interest in the Commonwealth at all. This is not a country clinging to a pseudo-imperial link at all costs any more.[5]

This change of gear was apparent throughout mainstream British opinion by 1970 but was especially noticeable in the Conservative Party. Deprived of the old and cherished leadership role, with its shades of a self-indulgent Disraelian paternalism, something of the Conservatives' affection for the Commonwealth died. The moderate pragmatists who determined its policy were agreed that, though they accepted a qualified Commonwealth role, the organisation must play a much reduced part in a revamped external policy. There was more to this reassessment than purely pique. British opinion generally was preoccupied with domestic economic problems. In the ensuing debate about how best to maximise Britain's shrinking opportunities, the regional solution loomed largest. By coincidence, the new decade saw the return of a Conservative government in Britain, led by Edward Heath, who personified this new mood. His uncompromising belief in the necessity of a European role promised only to increase the momentum for a more self-centred British external policy than even Labour had been groping towards by the end of its term. Moreover, this reorientation was likely to be less ambivalent for the Conservatives who, possessed of a more pragmatic tradition, were less reluctant to abandon awkward ideological luggage if they believed the facts failed to fit it.

The new conditional attitude in Whitehall presented a considerable threat to the Commonwealth's long-term viability, given the extent of Britain's contribution. As this dramatic reassessment of national priorities threatened the central position Britain had traditionally allocated to the Commonwealth, it was left to the other members – fully aware that they could not arrest its momentum – to ensure that something was at least salvaged from an arrangement which, on their terms, continued to be highly useful. Anything less than a positive response would have been disastrous. This was the task successfully accomplished by the Heads of Government Meetings in the seventies. In this latest series of meetings a new degree of consensus was achieved as the members revealed a willingness to accept the minimalist rather than maximalist concept of membership, which was clearly the most that was on offer from any British government.[6]

The need now was to refashion the CHOGM into an effective medium of exchange, communication and, where possible, of co-operation. By 1981 this task was completed and the Commonwealth firmly embarked on its new course, with the biennial Heads of Government Meeting providing a regular testament of its maturity and relevance.

THE HIATUS AT SINGAPORE, 1971

The process of adaptation to these stresses, begun so reassuringly at the 1969 CHOGM, faltered momentarily at Singapore in 1971. It seemed to some commentators that the Commonwealth had reverted to old habits. In fact, the circumstances surrounding this conference were always likely to put the fragile consensus achieved in 1969 under pressure. While that meeting had elicited the will to survive, it had not found a suitable procedural framework to help minimise the tendencies inherent in all international meetings to overformal and even ritualised deliberations. Without such a code of conduct it was unrealistic to expect that the harmony established at one conference could necessarily be carried over to another. This was especially so in an organisation where two years could see dramatic political changes within member states and in the international situation which it was the CHOGM's task to review.

This was precisely what precipitated the trouble at Singapore. A new British Conservative government, bent on pursuing what it saw as its own clear vision of national interests, had decided to sell arms to South Africa as part of a revitalised strategic commitment to containing Soviet naval activity in the Indian Ocean.[7] Apartheid and a growing fear of South African continental expansionism gave such deep offence to most of the Afro–Asian Commonwealth that the decision was bound to disturb the uneasy compromise secured in 1969. Although superficially similar to the Rhodesia issue, it was much more central to the Commonwealth's minimum *raison d'être*. Most members felt that discussion of the issue did not contravene the now accepted rule of non-interference in members' domestic affairs. The special emotive connotations of this issue raised it above any mere objection to a policy decision.

For race-consciousness lay at the very root of any post-colonial relationship. However benign or liberal the imperial tenure which prefaced it, race remained a highly sensitive aspect of a fundamentally one-sided 'common' past, about which the subject races continued to feel ambivalent.[8] The Commonwealth, although it had grown beyond its origins in many respects, was no exception to this. It was, after all, an institutionalised reminder that its members had once been in a position of social and political subservience. Inevitably, the continuing emotive potential of this legacy enhanced the tension when anything touching on racial matters came up for discussion. The centrality of the issue guaranteed that it would never be far away from their deliberations. If there has been a recurring theme since the important transitional period of the early sixties, race issues have provided it. In fact, conferences have taken on a watchdog function in this area. Here, more than on any other issue, members feel entitled to comment and to seek to persuade.

This view, which drew a fine but tangible line between the extant principle of non-interference and the modern Commonwealth's over-whelming sensitivity on racial matters, was at the root of Afro–Asian lobbying at Singapore. The subtle distinction was expressed by the otherwise impeccably moderate Botswanan President, Sir Seretse Khama, who argued that

> in general, there is a tendency for governments when faced with moral issues, to take refuge in diplomatically correct formulae about non-interference in the affairs of sovereign states. But Southern Africa has not troubled the world's conscience for so long simply because there is a vocal group of African states which keeps it before men's minds. The problems of Southern Africa remain a matter for world concern because of the peculiar nature of the oppression and injustice involved which are, to a greater or lesser extent, based on race.[9]

Thus far this ethic has been implicit. The Commonwealth had escaped any formal codification of its underlying common principles, which reflected the difficulty of adequately synthesising the diverse opinions about its legitimate scope and purpose. Even so, it was felt that there was a broad, underlying consensus that any, even minimal, concept of membership would include the tenet of racial equality. The fact that now a leading member could contemplate arming the world's pre-eminent racialist regime threw this assumption into doubt and provoked some members to consider the possibility of framing a more overt statement of the essential basic principles of membership.

The outcome of this campaign did not undermine the established equilibrium. Although it started a trend which cropped up periodically throughout the decade, the result was always similar. The Declaration of Commonwealth Principles eventually agreed was little more than a highly generalised reification of the already accepted axiom of racial tolerance which had been the norm since 1949, without which the organisation would have long since perished. In fact, this statement of intent – which every member felt able to endorse – came close to formalising the implicit understanding that had emerged between Britain and its critics over Rhodesia. Wilson's recognition of the African preoccupation with racial matters had persuaded him to allow some tactical flexibility on the principle of absolute non-interference in, at least Britain's, internal affairs. This was a finely calculated concession to keep intact an organisation still regarded as useful to Britain. According to this estimation, the Commonwealth was worth maintaining as a useful bridge to an increasingly important cross-section of international society, whose problems and future development could not be matters of indifference.[10]

It followed from this pragmatic assessment (although it was informed by more positive sentiments too) that it remained important to retain Commonwealth goodwill, or to at least avoid unduly alienating the Afro–Asian members.[11] This did not imply, by any means, Britain always taking the line of least resistance or surrendering control of its own policies. The Labour leader had firmly established these as the working rules of CHOGM's by 1969. Tolerance of some limited intervention by other members on issues such as Rhodesia, which were Britain's sovereign concern but were, realistically, also of central importance to other members, was incorporated into this flexible British approach.

The new Conservative prime minister's equally cautious approach to the general issues of arms, and the call for a Declaration of Principles which flowed from it, was informed by similar prudent considerations. In spite of his known lack of enthusiasm for the Commonwealth, it contrived to offer a useful insight into the wider world. Although Heath's enthusiasm for it was dimmed, he certainly did not want to carry what would probably still have been a heavy political stigma in Britain – that of being the premier who presided over the Commonwealth's demise. He managed, therefore, to combine the same judicious flexibility with the firm resistance to unwarranted intrusions into his policy prerogatives that had characterised Britain's even-handed approach to Commonwealth militancy since 1965. As such, he sustained the conventional view: that the only obligation on any member was to talk about difference, by taking advantage of the opportunities for consultation, without any compulsion to endorse either specific or collectively-binding objectives.

The extent of Britain's success in reaffirming these premises was clearly apparent, even amidst the turbulence at Singapore. The fact that the rule was already firmly assimilated was evident in the approach of most of Britain's harshest critics.[12] They showed great care not to alienate Britain and took their cue in this from Nyerere's altogether modest attempt simply to answer Britain's case for arms sales in a way that, on the most critical interpretation, merely hedged members' absolute sovereignty with quite reasonable preconditions. He suggested, for instance, that it was incumbent on all members not to pursue policies which threatened another's basic interests, without at least giving proper consideration to alternatives. Even his further argument, that this was a more requisite obligation on Britain because it was most able by its sovereign decisions to affect other members, conformed with the established conservative formula.[13] Indeed, his emphasis on the continuing preponderance of British policies as matters of legitimate concern to other members was more flattering than threatening, and helps to explain something of their continuing preoccupation with British affairs at their successive meetings.

This was certainly a more candid exposition of the 'Third World' view than might have been expected. It was an unlikely admission nevertheless, because it involved a tenuous allusion to the now quaint notion of imperial trusteeship which had hardly in the past commended itself to African nationalists. The fact of this frankness was no less significant than its timing. Such an overture (for its tone was certainly closest to that of an appeal) would have been impossible at earlier conferences. In the first place it would have been too soon after independence, when members were looking for every opportunity to stress their own sovereignty. For precisely such reasons, Nyerere himself had once publicly repudiated a successful British military intervention, invited by him to Tanganyika, after it had saved his regime from a *coup*. Secondly, the British government was then still mesmerised with an image of Commonwealth leadership over and above even a role of *primus inter pares*.

For these reasons it would have been inopportune to remind either side of this evolving and highly sensitive Commonwealth relationship of Britain's continuing centrality, although the fact of it was implicit in the very tone and focus of successive CHOGMs. Now, perhaps, it seemed reasonable to do so. For one thing, the new British government was more preoccupied than even its predecessor with a narrower regional role and certainly less guilt-ridden about the colonial past. In addition, the deteriorating economic position of the developing countries enhanced more than ever the value of a strong residual link – a benefaction that grew in appeal as its prospect receded with the likelihood of a less sympathetic Britain-in-Europe.[14]

Nyerere's dictum was both anticipatory and retrospective. While it helped to set the guide-lines that prevailed in discussions over other contentious issues throughout this decade, it was also firmly based on a well tried formula which had already been found necessary to keep previous meetings from breaking down when they tackled divisive issues. It was immediately apparent that the same degree of caution would have to be applied on this issue as well. On the other hand, there was cause for optimism too. The early discussions showed that many states did not regard the issue as anything like as clear cut as the two

extreme positions. The ground in between was filled by statesmen from
some West African countries, and from India, Ceylon, Malaysia and
Canada. This provided a balm; their contributions to the debate injected
a sense of proportion which undoubtedly had a constructive impact on
the protagonists and contributed to the amicable solution recommended
in Nyerere's careful precept.

Consequently, this medley of views softened the edges of confrontation and enabled the meeting to resort more easily to the
mediatory technique which had been used to resolve differences in the
past. The Canadian prime minister, building on his country's legacy of
goodwill with the developing members, inherited from Lester Pearson,
was able to act as an effective arbiter. His solution – following Nyerere's
judicious recommendations – stressed both that it was a duty of any
member to take fully into account the effects of unilateral decisions on
other members, thus reinforcing the established recipe of such consultations, while at the same time acknowledging that participants
unquestionably retained the right to define their own strategic interests.[15]

In essence, this reaffirmed the practice which had characterised
CHOGM diplomacy throughout the post-colonial period. Indeed, the
impasse at Singapore was alleviated by the same enterprising mixture of
personal initiatives, compromise, verbal gymnastics and intimate discussion, conducted in an atmosphere of easily communicated sincerity
which had been amongst the most positive aspects of Heads of
Government Meetings since the post-independence expansion, when the
Rhodesia issue was so often defused at the eleventh hour. Above all, this
exercise of mutual accommodation was informed by the same over-
whelming desire on all sides to maintain the Commonwealth intact. The
Third World members, in particular, were checked by the fear of
straining the Commonwealth's fabric too far. Accordingly, they
couched their appeal to Britain in pragmatic terms; arguing that arming
South Africa could stimulate a race war which, in turn, might well
attract the malevolent Soviet interest in the area which the arms sales
were supposedly designed to prevent.

The CHOGM's chairman, Lee Kuan Yew expressed another, more
obvious moderating facet of this endemic pragmatism: the reassertion of
his timely reminder in 1969 that the costs of alienating British goodwill
and jeopardising important functional benefits, was perhaps less
apposite here; it was already accepted by the developing members. Most
of them had also drawn the obvious conclusion from this, that with
Britain in its present mood the essence of a continuing working

relationship had to be the *quid pro quo* Lee felt it incumbent on him to underline as his keynote for the meeting. He had warned that membership 'cannot be just on the basis of a donor and donee relationship; because if you are members just because you want gifts-in-aid and expertise, then you have got to give something in return.'[16] This equipoise between cost and benefit had been a consistent theme not only in Singapore's approach to the Commonwealth but in relations in general between small and more powerful states. It was the essence of the logic of non-alignment too, and therefore deeply rooted in the collective imagination of Third World states. Moreover, it had a wider application than merely to economic or commercial matters, however important these functional considerations were bound to be. In this instance, it impinged on the strategic calculations of key African delegations.[17] Botswana, Lesotho and particularly the Nigerians – concerned lest they be called upon to fill the breach if Britain turned from its traditional balancing role *vis-à-vis* South Africa – all sensed the danger in pushing the issue too far.

Even those Africans most critical of Britain's decision showed a surprising degree of constraint. Significantly, while soundings were taken about reviving the African caucus, there was no concerted plan for confronting Britain, nor anything like the same degree of organised disruption at plenary sessions.[18] While the tone of the public debates was strident, such postures are, of course, an inevitable by-product of international relations at all levels. In stark contrast, the informal, private session was more than usually supplicatory and notable for its moderation and sense of compromise. Here the members had agreed not merely to differ but, in the time-honoured way, to consider the problem dispassionately and from every angle by setting up an eight member Commonwealth Committee. This may have been something of a euphemistic device for clothing discord with a veneer of agreement but it had represented an honourable outcome in the circumstances, with all sides able to claim some advantage. However, this *modus vivendi* was spoilt immediately by the one plenary session of the week which concentrated on the arms issue. The signs that a new sense of moderation had settled over the conference, even when dealing with the most emotive issues, was marred by a reversion to the vituperative set speeches which were currency earlier.

In part, this was an attempt by members to balance their political accounts. It was the more disconcerting, however, because these often acrimonious exchanges were somewhat stage-managed. Inevitably perhaps, media attention focused on the negative rather than positive attitudes.[19] The private sessions, however, where the leaders sat without officials, seemed to point in the right direction. They offered a positive example to those who were concerned to strike a reasonable balance between pursuing differences of opinion and the need for accepting that some of these were irresolvable. It showed, not incidentally, the CHOGMs' flair for creative diplomatic initiative, as well as illustrating the sort of useful, frank exchanges which make them at their best, amongst the most constructive of international gatherings and, as such, a valuable diplomatic asset to their participants.

Of course, the disparity between the public and private debate was a local difficulty which needed to be ironed out if such continuing contacts were to be properly beneficial in future. On the other hand, it was unrealistic to expect to remove this element altogether. To appreciate this, the problem has to be put in its proper perspective. The turbulence at Singapore was less an uncontrolled outbreak of malevolence than a resort to a ritual common in international diplomacy. It illustrated the potential for capitalising on domestic or regional linkages in any international organisation. In this regard Commonwealth members are as prone as participants in any other international arena to play to domestic or regional audiences.[20] The Commonwealth Heads of Government Meetings, after all, have always been seen as an opportunity for members to pursue their broader political objectives. Where the gap in members' outlooks was wide, so the temptation has increased to capitalise on the propaganda opportunity offered by a highly-publicised event. This tendency to posturing – what commentators have come misleadingly to call 'UN-ism' – is an occupational hazard in all gatherings of this breadth. It was still an irritant to some participants who believed that the ephemeral 'local' gains were far outweighed by the losses in understanding and goodwill. More important, it also increased their resolve to find ways of curtailing such diversions at future meetings.

Above all, this episode served to confirm the essentially limited concept of membership. Acceptance of the status quo was nowhere better illustrated than in the outcome of Kaunda's attempt to secure a more rigorous framework for membership. His original draft, which sought to bind members in their relations with racist regimes, received less support in practice than in principle. The prevailing mood of caution was amply illustrated by the reservations of Milton Obote, one of Britain's most prominent critics, who maintained that

the Commonwealth should not be forced into a state of disintegration and illwill because of the interests of the racist regime in South Africa. It is not in the interests of the international community that this very important association of nations should break up or that its members be deliberately forced out of membership.[21]

Faced with this general disinclination to threaten the Commonwealth by pushing it beyond its limited potential for agreement on specific and binding principles Kaunda, too, subscribed to a much-diluted resolution more in line with the 'non-interference' norm.[22] The outcome of Singapore was, therefore, by no means wholly negative or regressive. As well as revealing its intrinsic weaknesses, the Commonwealth also showed that it possessed positive assets too. Perhaps most important for the future, it revealed a will to survive.

It was essentially because of the continuing need for such an organisation that the group of leaders who had expressed a 'middle range' opinion – which had acted energetically as a mediating influence at Singapore – decided to mobilise and secure agreement on more decisive procedural changes.

A REVISED IMPETUS FOR REFORM: THE AFTERMATH OF SINGAPORE

There was a widespread reappraisal of the procedures and expectations of Conference diplomacy in the Commonwealth after Singapore, even though the meeting had been far from a débâcle. In some respects there, the heads of government had built on earlier foundations. However, the lapses into less constructive behaviour strengthened the demand for a more deliberate reform of CHOGM practices, with a view to enhancing the informal diplomacy which had been a more positive outcome.

It was encouraging too, that the Commonwealth was not divided into entrenched and opposing camps on this issue. Indeed, it was a strange paradox, lost in the overt confrontation on one issue, that the Africans were far from disenchanted with the idea of easy-going informality which used to characterise the meetings. In fact, they were disillusioned, if anything, with the extent to which this had been overtaken by some of the recent changes which they had helped to engineer: for instance, some expressed disappointment with the outcome of removing CHOGMs, as permanent fixtures, from London. In their concern to erase the overtones of the periodic 'return' to the imperial metropolis they had failed, in part, to comprehend the attitude underlying Britain's easy acquiescence to this reform. Britain, in fact, was more than willing to jettison this onus of responsibility for the same reason it had welcomed the establishment of a secretariat to service conferences and manage interim business. For the rotation of meetings was seen in London as indispensable to withdrawing from the burdensome role of being the Commonwealth's focal point. It freed Britain to concentrate on the urgent task of redirecting its external policy. The Secretariat had filled the organisational vacuum admirably. Yet the Africans, as they revealed more than once at Singapore, were less pleased with the negative connotations of these changes. Even though this venue was the outcome of reforms deliberately undertaken to democratise the Commonwealth, they clearly missed some of the advantages accruing from a London location.

For one thing, rotation encouraged the mood that the Commonwealth was genuinely multipolar rather than an Anglo–African axis. While this was acceptable in principle, it threatened their overriding concern to concentrate discussion on the issues most important to them. Instead they were now likely to face a host chairman who, as with Lee, favoured greater coverage of other regional issues. In a real sense, too, such leaders would always feel more free to pursue this wider-ranging approach than British chairmen at London conferences had managed to do. A further decisive blow to the old sense of familiarity was the absence, in occasional host capitals, of the extensive and established channels of informal communication for which London is still famous. Whereas conflicts had certainly arisen during past meetings, by the same token, an appropriate and experienced framework for defusing them had been readily to hand. In Singapore, however, many African delegations felt disorientated. This sense of dislocation was as unavoidable as it was temporary, and not too much should be made of it. It was a short-term price for the more permanent benefits to be gained from emphasising, wherever possible, the diplomatic parity of the members of the modern Commonwealth.

There was, however, an unforeseen bonus from this sense of unrest. It persuaded even the more intransigent Africans of the need to look closely at the CHOGM, with a view to bolstering informality and regaining something of the lost sense of purpose. Other members expressed different concerns, but which led to the same end. Some were alarmed that unrestrained vitriolics would lead to the fragmentation of a forum which offered some hope of bridging important international divisions. A more selective, but equally understandable version of this viewpoint was the fear that Britain might become so alienated as to forgo exercising its influence on behalf of members seeking a favourable commercial arrangement with the EEC.[23]

There was a broad consensus, too, on the sort of changes needed. The importance of maximising the potential for constructive discussion had been undermined by the general trend towards formalism. In particular, the sheer size of the gatherings and the consequent clash of interests could quickly ensure that a mood of negotiation settled over them. This was likely to be especially the case if they got 'bogged-down' on any divisive issue which afforded clearly entrenched positions, as the Rhodesia and South African items illustrated. An attendant consequence of this development was the resort to set speeches, delivered as monologues on fixed 'negotiating positions', as some members tried to reach agreements which were already well beyond the conferences' scope. This contrasted sharply with the more relaxed and conversational exchanges of the past. Even the confidentiality of the new, supposedly informal, private sessions at Singapore had been eroded by heavily slanted press leaks.

Most of these developments annoyed a cross-section of new and established members alike. Many saw meetings as prone to irrelevant and lengthy diversions which simply wasted the opportunity for more constructive discussion and consultation. A senior Indian diplomat, for instance, had pertinently warned after Singapore against turning the CHOGM into a scaled-down United Nations, as follows:

> We find most of our time involved in long debates, procedural wrangling and heated arguments about joint communiqués and the like. I would respectfully suggest that we should shed these formalised conventional modes of thought and behaviour and make the Commonwealth into an association where discussion can be held in an informal, friendly and fraternal manner as between friends [and] equals.[24]

Given that these deep reservations were shared by the Secretariat[25] and the next host chairman, Pierre Trudeau, some consideration of practical reforms was bound to figure in the usual informal consultations which preceded the meetings. Trudeau was quite prepared to take the lead. A newcomer in 1969, he had witnessed the tail end of a turbulent series of CHOGMs and come away, on his own admission, distinctly unimpressed.[26] A number of more positive influences soon caused him to revise this premature judgement and he developed a definite enthusiasm for the Commonwealth.[27] For one thing, he began to establish close personal links with prominent colleagues such as Kaunda, Nyerere and Mrs Gandhi, which emphasised the Commonwealth's rare breadth and opportunity. In addition, there were Canada's close regional ties with the Caribbean.[28]

More revealing, however, is the effect of structural influences which make Canada's consistent commitment to the Commonwealth under all shades of Government an important object lesson in the mechanics of the organisation's continuing appeal to medium or small powers, short of independent, international leverage. Canada had long been in the van of positive thinking about the Commonwealth during every stage of its evolution. As a medium power whose geopolitical setting placed it under the shadow of an assertive regional 'superpower', Canada had sought to cultivate balancing relationships which would give it some degree of independent influence, or at least widen its window on the world.[29] Its primary aim had been to avoid becoming a more dependent satellite: hence its active role in the Commonwealth. Canada's contribution to conflict-solving here has undoubtedly been influenced by considerations of self-interest, not least to maintain this valuable dimension of its external policy as a going concern. This was far from the sole motivation. Canada's closeness to the developing Commonwealth did induce a genuine understanding and sympathy for the special problems of the developing countries, which has given Canada's external policy a decidedly liberal outlook. It has been an unstinting contributor to the various Commonwealth schemes for functional assistance.[30]

To this extent, Trudeau undoubtedly inherited the perspective of his predecessor, Lester Pearson, transmitted through the administrative environment in which foreign policy attitudes are formulated and perpetuated. It is more difficult to judge whether Trudeau's positive intervention after Singapore 'saved' the Commonwealth from disintegration. It was certainly crucial in carrying many other similarly placed leaders with him on the need for specific reforms to increase the scope for harmony rather than conflict. He helped, therefore, to galvanise a new mood of determination which has stood successive CHOGMs in good stead.

On the other hand, there has been no shortage of leading Commonwealth figures during this decade who have made a similar contribution to the collective well-being. Trudeau certainly began the process by endorsing Lee Kuan Yew's successful 'holding operation' at Singapore.[31] Michael Manley took up the challenge at Kingston and also exerted himself to avoid disruption on the difficult issue cf Third World development.[32] Even Nyerere and Kaunda, perpetrators of a more muscular brand of Commonwealth diplomacy, caught the rising mood of accommodation and helped cement the 1977 Conference's united stance on condemning outrages in Amin's Uganda. Both leaders also assisted in securing the first real breakthrough on Rhodesia, at Lusaka in 1979. Neither should we ignore the continuing, benign influence of Harold Wilson (who became elevated to the unlikely role of elder statesman in 1975) and the equally constructive contribution of later British leaders like Callaghan and Thatcher.

A sense of harmony was further enhanced by the rediscovery of the Commonwealth by two other former dominions, Australia and New Zealand, who had shared a salutory experience as a result of British singlemindedness during the campaign to enter the EEC. These countries, too, came to see advantages in maintaining this link but in a way that differed markedly from their earlier, narrow conception of membership. The 'Menzies View', which best summarises this, had amounted to a limited and outdated British–Dominion concept of the Commonwealth.[33] Subsequent Antipodean leaders accepted that this was archaic and less than useful to them. They saw instead that while the British link was less beneficial in itself, the Commonwealth provided an important route of access to other states by means of an organisation whose comprehensive network of international relations placed it at the intersection of a valuable range of important alliances and organisations to which even indirect access was important.[34]

In short, the Commonwealth increased the scope for influence and exchanges with some of the major arteries of international communication. No less relevant to this assessment, the Commonwealth's value was increased by its inclusion of important 'bridge-builders' from other regions – not least Asia and the Pacific[35] – whose interests overlapped those of Canberra or Wellington. Taken together, this multilateral web of communication and exchange opened up access to and potential influence upon many areas of international politics.[36] The Antipodeans shared this realistic assessment with most other members and this positive outlook goes some considerable way to explaining their readiness to embrace the reforms on offer at Ottawa.

THE 'OTTAWA SPIRIT': THE HEADS OF GOVERNMENT MEETING, 1973

Trudeau harnessed this tide of opinion and used his growing influence to turn this meeting into one of the most constructive in the modern series.

By adopting some new procedures it undoubtedly laid a positive foundation for the future.[37] The formal plenary sessions were cut to two – at the beginning and end of the conference. The interim, executive sessions were restricted to leaders and a few officials, which helped to recapture something of past intimacy by encouraging a freer range of debate and comment.[38] This, in turn, facilitated mutual understanding and even compromise. A further useful innovation in this vein, which became a regular fixture thereafter, was to decamp the leaders away from the still fairly structured conference milieu to a weekend retreat where the emphasis was on personalised discussions, informal working parties or merely conversations on matters of mutual interest, unencumbered by agenda or protocol. In succeeding years the 'weekend retreat' secured some notable successes in mediating members' differences on key issues, including Rhodesia.

Finally, Ottawa saw the introduction of an ingenious agenda item on 'comparative techniques of government'. In a less spectacular way, the discussion of shared technical or administrative problems helped restore something of the sense of common purpose which racial policy or other obvious differences between members tend to obscure. This innovation, which made its greatest impact at Kingston when Wilson addressed himself to it, enabled leaders in confidentiality, to drop their public guard and explore their mutual difficulties as heads of government.[39] They were able, if briefly, to escape from national interests and candidly exchange views and advice on such topics as rational policy-making and implementation, political communication, administrative reform and the effective maintenance of stable, integrated policies.[40]

As a result of these innovations, the tenor of the meetings was noticeably improved. Their value is underwritten when they are set beside the more familiar recurring themes which provide modern CHOGMs with their inevitable parameters. For example, while it ranged over the usual panorama of international issues, this meeting, too, followed the now established pattern of focusing on a small number of topics for special scrutiny. It also trod familiar ground in its debate on yet another proposal for a binding Commonwealth Declaration – this time aimed at condemning recent French nuclear tests in the Pacific. Both residues from the past might have quickened the mood of disillusionment had these reforms not dulled the susceptibility to conflict and brought to the fore the determination to affirm the Conference's continuing relevance and value.

This was confirmed by events. Members gave a new prominence to an issue of much wider concern than any merely regional or sectional interest. Discussions on the deteriorating terms of trade for developing countries was opportune as Britain had just entered the EEC with some of the transitional terms of the Community's future trade with its former colonies still undecided.[41] The ensuing debate on the practical outcome of such negotiations gave this discussion a sense of precision sometimes missing on more emotive subjects. As such, it showed realistically what these meetings could expect to achieve.[42]

The new maturity was most evident when the meeting touched on issues which had been divisive in the past. Those supporting a precise declaration on nuclear tests got no further than their predecessors. Instead, the conference only endorsed another diluted and highly-generalised statement, so open-ended that there was no question of sovereignty being compromised.[43] Such proposals for a collective stance on a controversial issue, which not so long since would have seriously affronted the limited view of membership, were now put firmly into perspective. They were treated as periodic but highly manageable rituals.

This new climate was sustained on Rhodesia. All members, even Britain, now accepted its inclusion as unavoidable so long as it remained unresolved on the ground. The most contentious problem remained that it had been from the start – the role of force. Although here, too, there was a subtle shift in the African position. Instead of demanding British military intervention, they asked for recognition of the legitimate role of the Zimbabwean nationalist guerrilla armies. For its part, Britain remained adamant that the solution must be peaceful. Although there was a brief recurrence of African anger, the generally more relaxed atmosphere helped to defuse the tension. At Ottawa the Africans, already cognisant of the strategic reality of an armed struggle, were content to leave Britain with its illusions of a purely negotiated solution, in full expectation that the war would sooner or later take its inevitable toll. The Communiqué performed its now accepted function of acknowledging these fundamental differences without any obligation to reconcile them. This new, balanced approach – of accepting the inevitability of sometimes deep-seated disagreement – helped to replace the former strident and aggressive mood of negotiation, with one of realistic bargaining, communication and, above all, mutual education. The growing concern to understand the other side of the argument rather than solely putting one's own case was illustrated most clearly in the debates on trade. This issue provided the middle conferences of the decade with a core theme, giving them a sense of constructive continuity, regardless of the limited outcome.

The urgency of the economic problems facing the new states contrasted vividly with their spokesmen's generally moderate approach, even where discussion uncovered the deep gap in actual economic interests between the industrialised and non-industrial members. The latter had, by and large, suffered disproportionately from the recent general down-turn in world economic trends. Rising inflation in industrial countries had worsened the developing countries' terms of trade. The increase in the cost of their imported manufactures was not off-set by a compensatory rise in the price for their raw material or other primary products such as food exports. These still remained largely under the influence of the industrialised countries, who could manipulate the commodities markets to their own advantage.[44] By using synthetics or other substitutes, by bulk purchasing when prices fell and storing, or simply by hard bargaining in situations where, as at the Kennedy Round, GATT or UNCTAD negotiations, they possessed the more favourable cards.[45]

The problem was made more urgent because Britain's entry into the EEC threatened to cut off the established Commonwealth trading preferences instituted ironically at the first Ottawa Imperial Conference in 1933.[46] However, the 1973 Heads of Government Meeting did not get bogged-down in vacuous rhetoric or intransigent positions. India, as staunch a defender of non-alignment as any state, set the tone by couching its case for a serious review of the issue in terms of an appeal rather than a condemnation. Swaran Singh, in his call for a positive Commonwealth approach to the EEC on commodity prices, reminded Britain of its continuing responsibilities in this area as he saw it; whilst stressing India's acceptance of the fact that no other member could do anything to enforce them. 'We would like to make a special plea to the United Kingdom to lend its support to this proposal and to take steps with the Community to ensure an expeditious examination and solution of the trading problems of the Commonwealth.'[47] A cynical assessment might suggest that this was merely a shrewd response to a weak bargaining position where inflexibility offered little advantage. Certainly, an appreciation of their continuing dependence on British good favour in mediating on their behalf with the EEC, probably did tone down these debates.

There were also more positive indications of an awareness on all sides of the mutual benefits of ameliorating this problem. The threat of international economic chaos and ensuing political instability helped to concentrate the minds of an impressive cross-section of leaders and increased their recognition of the benefits of putting world trade on a more equitable footing.[48] The keynote of this concordance was set by a general acceptance of British sincerity. Both of its major political parties continued to justify British membership of the EEC on the grounds that it was less a retreat from an outward-looking policy than a means of more surely playing an effective international role, by opening up an insular continental bloc to wider influences.[49] The Commonwealth had taken Heath at face value when he said in 1971 that 'I have not worked to try and bring about a wider European unity in order to take a lot of little Englanders into a mini Europe'.[50]

There were, of course, here, as at Kingston, more militant Third World voices who sought more than amelioration and wanted nothing less than a wholesale reordering of the ground rules of the international economy. While they approached the issue less as supplicants than as an exercise reminiscent of large-scale wage bargaining, they too were aware that the real levers of economic power lay outside the Commonwealth.[51] Accordingly, they acted with restraint, convinced by the more moderate mood which prevailed, aware that, at best, the Commonwealth could rehearse arguments and possibly uncover practical, if partial, remedies which might be passed on for consideration to these more determinative fora.[52] On this issue too, therefore, these meetings ran true to contemporary form, emphasising the Commonwealth's continuing value as a constructive medium of education and communication.

CONSOLIDATION AT KINGSTON, 1975

The Commonwealth approached the Kingston Heads of Government Meeting in a more optimistic frame of mind than any previous conference in the modern series. The transition from a somewhat self-conscious residual relationship, in which Britain remained the main focus of attention and criticism, was not entirely completed. Yet a prevailing sense of realism was clearly visible now in its deliberations. Members on all sides were coming to accept the limitations of membership and sought to maximise whatever benefits were available from it.[53] They recognised that there were still opportunities through the Commonwealth network for diplomatic and functional exchanges which were not so readily available to them in any other forum. The Commonwealth helped, as Arnold Smith often pointed out, to keep open contacts between nations that might otherwise remain closed.[54] The Secretary-General summarised the fundamental change in outlook which had occurred, in his final report before retiring. The organisation had, he acknowledged, successfully restructured its image 'to get it seen for what it is, an effective multilateral instrument available to all its members to help them shape the future'.[55]

The relevance of this perspective was seen in the 1975 CHOGM's return to the issues of trade and development, given added impetus by a new British Labour government's determination to review EEC membership. Economic issues were bound to be of central importance in an organisation dominated numerically by poorer countries. Moreover, the uncertainty expressed at Ottawa had been increased by a further deterioration in their economic position. Since 1973 the total deficit of the non-oil exporting developing countries had quadrupled to almost forty thousand million dollars per annum, triggered by the steep rise in world oil prices. This increased the prospect of indefinite arrears, dragging back any independent growth potential in their economies by reducing employment prospects and adding to their already large debt cycle by increasing borrowing.

While the CHOGM was in some ways better equipped to review these issues, informally if not dispassionately, it suffered from the same constraints as the other international fora which had already examined them, without getting much beyond highly generalised statements of intent. The problem was apparent at Kingston from the outset, but it was neither peculiar to the Commonwealth nor of its own making. There was clearly a genuine and undisputed concern with the plight of the developing countries, not least because of a pragmatic recognition – emphasised by the British Foreign Office's detailed review of the problem – that severe economic imbalance was bad for world trade generally as well as threatening political stability, with ramifications for world peace. Nevertheless, even in this harmonious climate, narrow preoccupations with national interests remained an enduring consideration. Certainly, no leader of an industrial country could expect to survive politically any undertaking to reduce his people's living standards on arguments as seemingly nebulous as long-term self-interest or moral equity.[56]

The Kingston meeting was therefore no exception to this continuing and fundamental division of interest which had afflicted all of the international fora broaching this controversial subject. Beneath its expressions of concern, Britain's delegation took the predictable position of any industrial consumer of raw materials faced with rising production costs and balance of payments difficulties. It offered concessions which barely touched the root problem. Indeed, Wilson's much publicised proposals for alleviating the trading strain on the developing countries reflected, in some degree, his overriding domestic preoccupation with inflation. After all, in a situation of worldwide economic uncertainty, the developed countries, too, were bound to see advantages in securing commodity agreements which allowed for more predictable pricing arrangements.[57]

It was revealing, therefore, that Wilson's proposals broadly followed the line adopted at the Lomé Convention signed by the EEC and the developing countries.[58] Some of his suggestions were marginally helpful to commodity producers, such as his recommendations for improving communication on the forward supply and demand for commodities and for establishing a framework for stabilising export earnings from commodities.[59] By and large, however, these proposals were seen to offer more apparent benefits to the industrial consumers. The broad drift of his proposed general agreement on commodities, for example, adhered to the conservative commercial remedy of fixing price ranges by individual commodity and amounted to a suggestion to maintain market prices within a negotiated range favourable to the industrial 'establishment'. His proposal of clearer rules for defining the circumstances under which import and export restrictions could be applied to commodities were also designed to facilitate an orderly conduct of trade.

The spokesmen for the developing Commonwealth were not slow to respond to this marginal trimming of the economic status quo and formulated more far-reaching proposals of their own to secure what they ambitiously called 'The New World Economic Order'. They, too, represented an entrenched position whose locus lay outside the Commonwealth in, for example, specialist lobbies such as the UNCTAD Board at Geneva, which had already made its own comprehensive proposals for reforms. The developing Commonwealth therefore endorsed Michael Manley's parallel proposal of a commodity stabilisation and indexing scheme to link prices to the rate of Western inflation, which would have helped shift the terms of trade back towards the primary producers.[60]

This recurrence of the familiar Anglo–Third World dichotomy might once have provoked bitter confrontation. By 1975 the scope for mutual understanding, which had already become currency in CHOGMs, was brought to bear on this issue too. Its essence was pragmatism: the majority of developing members acknowledged the intrinsic and particular weakness of their negotiating position on this issue, not merely in the Commonwealth but also in the wider fora which would determine its practical outcome. Even members sympathetic to a firmer stance, such as Nigeria, were undoubtedly influenced by the need to retain a favourable British response when it renegotiated its terms of entry with the EEC. Consequently, they saw little value in alienating a potential advocate in these more decisive arenas, even if only modest concessions were on offer.[61]

Most developing members were so heavily dependent on commodity exports that they were prepared to accept tangible if less than satisfactory proposals for single commodity agreements,[62] just as those concerned had been glad to endorse the Sugar Agreement which had formed part of the package accompanying Britain's original entry in 1971.[63] Manley himself emphasised their limited bargaining power when he quipped that 'we would not hold back commodity agreements because we had not agreed to restructure the IMF.[64] The continuing sense of dependence implied by this was underlined by members' unsolicited declaration of support for the British government's recommendation to its electorate to vote for continued EEC membership in the forthcoming referendum. This overriding concern to secure some immediate amelioration persuaded a majority of the developing Commonwealth to avoid the more acerbic stance of militants such as Guyana and Mauritius, who demanded nothing less than a fundamental redistribution of wealth towards the poorer nations.[65] It was left to the conference to undertake a cosmetic exercise which bridged this gap with some semblance of accord. This essentially limited undertaking (to establish a committee to assess the contrasting approaches) made little inroad into the fundamental problem.

There were few illusions, however, that the well-tried formula of adopting the most limited option, had triumphed once again. This feeling was only reinforced when this committee's report was discussed at the London CHOGM of 1977. The issue was debated with precisely the same limited outcome. While the gist of the report backed the radical perspective on development and put forward far reaching proposals – such as the establishment of a permanent international fund to encourage development investment in new energy resources, to be funded by the oil and industrial states, a reduction of import restrictions on Third World products, the discounting of debts and fundamental changes in the international financing system – Britain approached these findings with its customary reticence.[67] It made only modest concessions, such as increasing its contribution to the admittedly useful Commonwealth Fund for Technical Co-operation established at Singapore. More significantly, the 1977 CHOGM reiterated the stalemate on the core problems by establishing yet another working party to examine the feasibility of one of the original committee's less revolutionary recommendations, for a common fund to assist in establishing world commodity prices.

Regardless of these perfunctory achievements, the prevailing view at both conferences was one of a sense of relief that members could still part amicably after discussing such a sensitive issue. Many of the 'old hands' endorsed Wilson's opinion that Kingston was 'by far the best of the five' conferences he had attended.[68] To some extent this was because Rhodesia was no longer the divisive issue it had been. Rhodesia – indeed African issues generally – continued to crop up with regularity. In this sense, the seventies confirmed the trend of an 'African Commonwealth', although the CHOGM proved more versatile and issues of even peripheral interest – such as Cyprus – were able to receive an airing with more alacrity than in the past.[69] This, in turn, strengthened the general climate of relevance.

The continuing predominance of Africa was probably greater than it need have been, because of India's distinctly subdued approach. The Commonwealth's most populous member, its decisive intervention would have effectively redressed the balance of discussion which tended to give the meetings a rather lopsided look. Instead, India had continued to adopt a more diffident approach, for which there are several possible explanations. For one thing, its leaders were undoubtedly aware of a legacy of suspicion surrounding its role in the Third World. Like China, it is a populous and resourceful state with a comparatively sophisticated infrastructure. These assets immediately place it in a different league amongst developing countries[70] and to a degree put it in a more isolated position even in the Third World.[71] India had also aroused some resentment from its activities in the non-aligned movement.[72] This diplomatic liability was compounded by hostility, in parts of the African Commonwealth, to what was perceived as a less than forthright Indian endorsement of their independence struggles.[73] In a sense, then, India had been obliged to carry over its non-aligned stance to the Commonwealth too.

From its own perspective, these experiences had strengthened the strong utilitarian disposition which had always informed India's approach to international commitments. On the other side of the equation, India always refused to behave hastily when other members' policies gave offence. Instead, it allotted the Commonwealth a less central position in its external policy in a way that paralleled Britain's own downgrading of the organisation since 1960. The Commonwealth was accordingly seen as useful to India but not determining. In this way India managed to cope with the prospect of a reduced British contribution as well as the CHOGMs' continuous preoccupation with African issues.[74] To a large extent this is because the Commonwealth is less politically serviceable to India than it is as a source of functional assistance and favourable commercial arrangements. By the same token, its leaders were well aware that these mainly technical issues could be pursued just as well by bilateral negotiations or through the available nexus of specialised or regional conferences and organisations in which India has more readily taken an active part.[75] These considerations have led to a relegation in the importance attached to Heads of Government Meetings, signified by only an intermittent attendance by Indian premiers after 1965. This diminished commitment was alluded to by an Indian diplomat, who suggested that the Commonwealth's political functions were more directly useful to the less powerful members, providing them with a useful forum in which to cut a diplomatic dash and vent their frustrations. Whereas India had 'matured as a nation [so that] we do not expect any miracles from the Commonwealth'.[76]

Whatever the reasons, India's self-imposed back seat approach helped to distort the proceedings at CHOGMs. Moreover, it was not until the 1981 meeting, after the new round of itinerant conferences had already visited less central Commonwealth venues, that India showed any inclination to temper this lukewarm approach and put itself forward as the host of a full-scale Heads of Government gathering, having first tested the water with a Regional Heads of Government meeting in 1980.

FAMILIARITY WITHOUT CONTEMPT: LONDON, 1977

The 1977 CHOGM returned to familiar ground in more ways than one. It was once more dominated by African issues. Two of them, however – the search for an appropriate response to widely-publicised carnage in Uganda and for acceptable common guidelines to deter sporting links with South Africa – had a wider application. Both redirected attention to the Commonwealth's continuing fascination with attempts to formalise something of a substantive code of membership.

The rapid movement of events in central Africa also determined that Rhodesia would again move centre stage. However, the tolerance revealed in previous conference discussions of this topic enabled it to be broached without rancour. The final element of *déjà vu* was added by the CHOGM's return to London. Yet these similarities with the past were more superficial than the facts might suggest. For one thing they have to be set against some noticeable changes. London, for instance, was chosen solely as a mark of respect for a popular Head of the Commonwealth in her silver jubilee year.

The extent of the changes in mood, style and expectation in the Commonwealth were amply illustrated by the contrast in conferences during the twenty-five years span.[77] At the first Heads of Government Meeting of the Queen's reign there were only nine prime ministers most of whom were from the old dominions. By 1977 there were thirty-five participants whose approach underlined the sea change from an upgraded imperial cabinet, into a diverse and often fragmented organisation, which typified the intricate post-imperial diplomatic milieu. As such, it brought together representatives of many other, more decisive and cohesive international bodies that help to compose the fabric of modern international relations, such as the OAU, the EEC, OPEC, the OAS, UNCTAD and so on. This Commonwealth matrix has been appropriately styled by one commentator, the 'Clapham Junction' of international diplomacy.[78] It is precisely this internal complexity that makes agreement on details difficult and often impossible. At the same time, this range of contacts provides one of the best reasons for membership. It offers an ideal opportunity for communicating and sometimes removing the sorts of obstacles to understanding which, if left unresolved, can so easily block the arteries of international politics, with potentially disastrous consequences. Again on the positive side, goodwill engendered in its more relaxed environment can sometimes be carried over to these other gatherings.[79]

Some leaders were ambivalent about the choice of London, not because they feared any longer a British imperial hegemony but precisely because they valued the open exchanges of opinion and did not wish to see these inhibited by undue concern with etiquette. Any suggestion that the meeting would be turned into merely another celebratory event was precluded by Britain's decision to indicate its strong disapproval of events in Uganda. In a lengthy diplomatic preamble, Callaghan advised Amin he was unwelcome, proposing that Uganda's delegation be led by someone else.[80] This suggestion of interference caused concern in some African delegations, but the Ugandan issue presented them with a more disturbing predicament. For so long the advocates of moralistic campaigns to implement universal, ethical standards, the existence of a black regime on their own continent whose inhumanity was indisputable,[81] yet led by a man who had recently been President of the OAU, faced them with an excruciating dilemma.[82] Then there was the added embarrassment that any condemnation of this regime might elicit equally unfavourable comparisons with other African (including Commonwealth) regimes which had strayed from the liberalism predicated in the Westminster model of government.

Yet this was the corollary of precisely the sort of formal declaration constantly sought by radical members.[83] In any association where member states subscribe to different political principles, the looser the framework of commonly enunciated ideals, the less the chance of dislocation. To apply a universal code of humanitarianism as a condition of membership invites its application across the board to all human relationships rather than merely racial ones.[84] This can open a Pandora's box of recrimination and accusation, as no state anywhere can stand up to a strict measurement against the noblest standards of conduct. In these circumstances, even slight inconsistencies or transgressions could turn CHOGMs into rather sterile 'war crimes' tribunals. This was the attendant risk of documents such as the 1971 Singapore Declaration, yet that was now on record and while loosely defined (precisely because most members had anticipated these risks) it could not be ignored in the circumstances of Uganda. To its credit, the meeting emphasised its new maturity by dealing with Uganda in a way that suggested it was an exceptional matter. They were ably assisted to this end by the new Secretary-General, Sonny Ramphal, who shrewdly anticipated these problems and included a rubric in his first report which pre-empted any disruption of the delicate balance between common principles and political self-determination. He maintained, as follows, that while there was 'a long and necessary tradition' of non-interference in members' internal affairs,

> how to strike the balance of political judgment between the two extremes of declamation and silence is sometimes difficult, but it would be entirely illusory to believe that such a judgment could or indeed should, be avoided altogether. There will be times when one member or another will provoke the wrath of others' beyond the limits of silence. Any other relationship would be so sterile as to be effete.[85]

As a result of this prudent guidance, the CHOGM was able to add another useful precedent to a growing list, by criticising the internal policies of a member without compromising either the Commonwealth's essentially conservative ethos or touching the sensitive racial nerve. The complete acceptance of this precise yet subtle yardstick also enabled it to avoid trouble when the Africans raised the question of New Zealand's sporting links with South Africa. This issue was important, both in terms of the abstract principle involved, but also because it threatened to disrupt the forthcoming Commonwealth Games.[86]

In a way, however, the stark contrast with what was at stake over Uganda, showed it to be well capable of amicable resolution. Hence, the weekend retreat at Gleneagles was able to produce an agreed form of words that offended nobody, reinforcing the general opposition to apartheid, whilst necessarily avoiding any strict or binding code that would have challenged the more fundamental axiom of sovereignty, by which each government retains the inalienable right to decide the limits of its powers over its citizens.[87] But the underlying issue remained unresolved. For Gleneagles was open to different interpretations and New Zealand's singular approach to this led to further, acrimonious debate at the 1981 Melbourne Conference.

These issues illustrated, nevertheless, something of the modern Commonwealth's perplexing admixture of assets and limitations. The meeting convened one of its special private sessions so that the delicate issue could be discussed candidly. For in matters touching on race, the Commonwealth does not possess the advantages of a racially homogeneous body such as the OAU. Of course, that organisation is no better placed for securing hard agreement (indeed, the intensity of territorial rivalry can be enhanced in such regional gatherings),[88] but the absence of any sense of the 'colonial mentality', with its lingering sense of 'inferiority', which invariably remains in a post-imperial relationship, places fewer prohibitions on discussions. On the whole, this is because members are less inclined to be on the defensive. This legacy makes Commonwealth meetings difficult places to raise issues that sometimes ought to be discussed; not least, the conflicts between members – such as in South Asia, which led to Pakistan quitting the organisation – or equally debilitating internecine wars. The Commonwealth's helplessness in these internal crises offers an uncomfortable reminder of this unfortunate but inevitable lacuna.

Yet the informality of these conferences gave them a degree of flexibility which was useful in minimising potentially disruptive controversies in some areas, and did ease the discussions on Rhodesia.[89] A sober acceptance that events there were rapidly moving to a conclusion beyond the control of any Commonwealth government, allowed for the first time, and certainly in marked contrast to the entrenched mood of the sixties, a more open debate.[90] Both sides of the argument seemed prepared to acknowledge the real constraints operating on the other,

even if important differences of emphasis remained.[91] Notably, Britai
conceded, if reluctantly, that the guerrilla forces 'might' have to fight o
while negotiations continued. Whereas the representatives of th
African 'front line' states were prepared to tentatively endorse the ne
Anglo–American initiative, in exchange for limited tactical con
cessions.[92]

THE MODERN COMMONWEALTH COMES HOME TO ROOST: LUSAKA, 1979

The final CHOGM of the decade was the culmination of the process o
adjustment which has been the keynote of the modern series. Above all
it illustrated the Commonwealth's capability for positive accomplish
ment, once a balance of mutual interests could be mobilised behin
broadly acceptable proposals. The achievement was even greater in thi
instance because it occurred on the issue which had seen the mos
consistent resistance to negotiation in previous conferences and had als
provided the impediment on which a more ambitious multilatera
concept had faltered.

The prospects did not seem propitious. A Conservative governmen
generally held to be right-wing in outlook, had recently returned t
power in Britain. It seemed unlikely that it would be amenable t
changes in policies already initiated by its predecessors, which ha
resulted in elections in Zimbabwe–Rhodesia regarded as unrepresen
tative by African opinion.[93] Pessimists, however, who anticipated
return to acrimony, proved wide of the mark.[94] In an atmosphere o
flexibility and realism, Britain agreed to the 'front-line' Commonwealt
states' request for fresh elections, a constitutional conference in
corporating all the internal parties, and acknowledgement of a monitor
ing role for the Commonwealth in the transition to self-government.[9]

While this represented a breakthrough on the issue *per se*, none of thi
compromised the central premise of Commonwealth discussions o
Rhodesia since UDI – that it remained unequivocally a Britis
prerogative. Instead, these concessions signified a new pragmatism i
Britain's response to the Commonwealth Meeting.[96] The incomin
government balanced these relatively small concessions against th
wider considerations of the protracted guerrilla war on the ground
Weighed against the prospect of racial bitterness and the insiduou
threat of the Soviet bloc profiting from unabated instability in centra
Africa, the opportunity of harnessing the active support of influentia

African Commonwealth leaders, who could help to deliver the compliance of the nationalists, accorded well with Britain's long term perspective on this problem.

There is some evidence to suggest that these calculations were already in the British premier's mind when she arrived in Lusaka. Certainly, she was fully apprised of Britain's diminishing options and needed little persuasion to accept what was on offer at the meeting. It would be over cynical, however, to discount the impact of the meeting itself in clarifying the scope for compromise on both sides. It is significant that the breakthrough came, as so often before, during the informal weekend 'rest period', when a small group of interested members set up by Kaunda and Ramphal,[97] recaptured through their seminar technique, the atmosphere of easy-going sincerity which elicited mutual agreement.

The importance of this accomplishment on the substantive issue, should not overshadow the wider import of this thoroughly amiable exchange. For by removing the major albatross from around the Commonwealth's neck – and in a way that reaffirmed the CHOGM's *métier* for mutually profitable consultations – it helped to secure more firmly the organisation's foundations for the forseeable future.[98]

INTO THE EIGHTIES: MELBOURNE POSTSCRIPT, 1981

The CHOGM at Melbourne emphasised the extent to which the Commonwealth had settled into a more tolerant acceptance of the limits, as well as the possibilities, attendant upon a gathering of such size and diversity. Not that they could afford to be complacent; for there were the inevitable moments of drama aroused again by the persistance of the race issue in one of its many guises. Yet there were encouraging signs from this disturbance too. The manner in which this conflict developed showed that the stark confrontation between new, highly-sensitive members and the more phlegmatic 'establishment' had subsided. In fact, on the evidence available from Melbourne, only one member on either side of that emotive 'divide' now seems to be marching out of step; and, even then, probably less out of respect for an inviolable 'principle' than for what looks like a narrow political expedience.

Certainly, the Africans continued to show concern at any hint of compromise with racialism, which encouraged them to raise the issue of New Zealand's continuing sporting links with South Africa, amounting, they believed, to a flouting of the Gleneagles Agreement. Judged against past disagreements, however this issue fell far short of crisis proportions.

The New Zealand premier, Mr Muldoon, was given a respectful hearing when he defended his looser interpretation of that purposely non-binding compromise. With these points on the record, the conference, well aware of other, more urgent and far-reaching issues, followed its now customary procedure for resolving an *impasse*. It was prepared simply to re-endorse that earlier, usefully ambiguous agreement. This artful solution was marred, however, when, with at least one eye on his domestic electoral fortunes, Muldoon reverted to threats and gratuitous insults, totally alien to the abiding spirit of constructive exchanges and compromises which had become the CHOGM's hallmark in recent years. Of course, any international gathering offers a tempting platform to those spoiling for a fight. It is a necessary precondition of constructive diplomacy anywhere, that participants exercise a modicum of self-control and good manners. It has been one of the Commonwealth's most striking achievements that most members have readily absorbed this crucial lesson in the recent past.

Accordingly, no other member rose to Muldoon's bait and the various incidents over the week reflected badly on him rather than on the meeting *per se*. The stark contrast between his outbursts and the prevailing atmosphere of serious-minded debate on important issues of common interest, did the Commonwealth more good than harm. It showed, above all how far the members have progressed towards creating a refined and beneficial working environment. It was certainly noticeable that this incident failed to develop into one of the 'old style' confrontations. The prevailing mood was one of commonsense. The Africans made their points forcibly but without past rancour, clearly realising from experience that there was nothing to be gained by being sidetracked from concentrating on the more pressing matters which the meeting had begun to dwell upon in the seventies. In particular, Melbourne underlined once again the Commonwealth's serious concern with the various threats posed by deep-rooted global pressures. This consensus gave the conference a sense of perspective and, as such, confirmed the positive developments of recent CHOGMs, illustrating just how far the Commonwealth had travelled along the road of conciliation and constructive diplomacy during that time.

The Melbourne Meeting emphasised, therefore, what was already a widely-acknowledged truth; that the modern Commonwealth is now sufficiently accomplished to be able to take even fairly serious and potentially divisive issues in its stride and to discuss them in a climate of openness and maturity. In this enlightened vein, Melbourne broached – with a refreshing frankness as well as with a surprising degree of accord, given the range of interests represented – the effects of recent changes in the international balance of power as well as the increasingly urgent problem of world economic disparities. This issue was especially pertinent in view of the impending latest round of North–South summitry scheduled for Cancún in Mexico.

In this, as on the other matters of 'high politics' that Commonwealth Meetings broach, the membership have now assimilated the limited scope for achievement open to them. They accept that nothing, as such, can be solved; that, at best, they can perform the, albeit, still valuable task of rehearsing arguments, of clearing away some of the more unproductive ground, the better to facilitate fruitful discussion around workable compromises and proposals that these wider fora might conceivably consider. It follows from this that they accept, in performing this function, an additional important responsibility; that of advertising the fact that there still exists an intent or will amongst an important cross-section of the community of nations to solve these critical problems at all. Hence their general statement on underdevelopment – the Melbourne Declaration – was intended to be a clarion call to those statesmen about to meet at Cancún, more capable of effecting real reforms than themselves.

It was here that the Melbourne CHOGM illustrated – to those sceptics who resisted the obvious conclusion that the Commonwealth had fashioned for itself a useful international role and who interpreted any expression of unanimity as merely platitudinous – that the Commonwealth is alive and functioning purposefully. Above all, it has shown admirable resilience in shaking off any hint of a demeaning patronage – real or self-induced – that made its role as a bridge between the new and established members in the immediate post-colonial phase so fraught with tension and awkwardness. It now provides, demonstrably, a much more effective link between the new world and the old and, in present circumstances, it hardly needs stressing that it is, as such, more than ever a necessary dimension of international relations.

CONCLUSION: THE COMMONWEALTH DISCOVERS POSITIVISM

The Commonwealth Heads of Government Meetings of the seventies took up and refined the mood of realism and understanding that was already becoming apparent in 1969. After a brief regression at Singapore, the Commonwealth, by implementing judicious reforms, quickly galvanised itself to minimise its more negative tendencies and build on its assets. In this sensible equation, contentious issues were not avoided, and to have tried to exclude them from the agenda would only have diminished the meetings' importance and utility. Nevertheless, all the members finally accepted that mutual tolerance of conflicting viewpoints was the minimum condition for survival. Equally important, the meetings found ways of coping with dissension in a manner that minimised the chance of acrimonious confrontations.[99]

A major key to this greatly-improved climate lay in the conscious decision to maximise informality and to improve the quality of exchanges at the expense of the climate of summitry which had once threatened to reduce CHOGMs to the status of scaled-down UN sessions. There were periodic lapses, but the broad trend was sustained throughout this decade, strengthening a sense of recognition of the meetings' enduring value. This in itself was no small achievement in a decade when international affairs became even more prone to rancour and uncertainty, as the North–South dialogue failed to alleviate the rising frustration of the developing countries with their economic plight, and the social problems consequent on this.

It was here that the value of the Commonwealth Heads of Government Meeting was most evident. For, paradoxically, their lack of effective resources and influence enhanced the developing Commonwealth's awareness of the opportunities – however circumscribed – offered by such an essentially amenable arena. The meetings, in response to this mood, became less a negative opportunity for venting wrath on the former colonial power and certainly less attractive (because unprofitable) as a means of forcing the pace on controversial issues. Neither could it operate as an agency for collective or binding decision-making. These prohibitions – which had been much less apparent in the previous decade – clearly circumscribed the scope of meetings in the seventies, only to signify better where it could play a more fruitful role. The meetings now existed to furnish a useful opportunity to persuade, to advertise, to bargain, to explain, and, even occasionally, to censure. Above all, they provided a platform for the expression of diverse, specialised and frequently irreconcilable interests and opinions which did not necessarily (or indeed, often) imply common action. They offered instead the valuable opportunity for a modicum of quiet influence and communication at first hand, even if this could not always be enshrined in some formal manifesto or overt, binding commitment. As much as anything, these exchanges had an important educative value. They were, in addition, more likely to be constructive because they were rooted in a residue of sentiment, friendship and mutual respect bred of the close, informal contacts which the meetings encouraged. This proved a useful asset in overcoming their periodic differences.[100]

This decade, then, is best seen as one of consolidation: of putting Commonwealth diplomacy on a surer footing by making sensible adaptations and compromises and above all, by accepting that, like any other international organisation, it had intrinsic limitations. This was the task the heads of government set themselves at Singapore, when it seemed that the discordancy reminiscent of the previous decade threatened to obliterate the encouraging signs of equilibrium revealed in 1969. The success of this undertaking can be seen from the events of subsequent meetings. The gist of the realistic formula established then was aptly captured in the assessment of one leading source of political comment which had observed that,

> the Commonwealth association was not created for decision making, but rather as a forum for pooling experiences and arguing viewpoints as a result of which attitudes mutually change and a consensus or accommodation emerges, that sometimes makes possible a concerted Commonwealth policy in other international bodies.[101]

This appraisal of the Commonwealth as a vital bridge to international understanding is a succinct distillation of the scope of the modern Heads of Government Meetings and provides a fitting conclusion to a study of the latest, momentous decade in the Commonwealth's continuing evolution.

NOTES AND REFERENCES

1. Editorial, 'After Ottawa', *Round Table*, October 1973, p. 417.
2. L. Epstein, 'British Foreign Policy', in R. Macridis (ed.), *Foreign Policy in World Politics* (Hemel Hempstead: Prentice-Hall, 1967) pp. 29–30.
3. For a testament of Conservative enthusiasm at this time, see Duncan Sandys, *The Modern Commonwealth* (London: HMSO, 1962).
4. S. Young, 'UK Foreign Policy in a new context?' *World Today*, October 1971, pp. 434–5.
5. The *Economist*, 11 January 1969.
6. For a more detailed discussion of these problems of adjustment, see James Eayrs, *Minutes of the Sixties* (Toronto: Macmillan of Canada, 1968), pp. 188–97.
7. Editorial, 'The price of those arms', The *Economist*, 9 January 1971, pp. 11–13.

8. The potency of this issue is amply revealed in the writings of Africa's most articulate political scientist. Thus, Ali Mazrui has maintained that 'the black man . . . has simply been the most humiliated' of the racial specimens of the world.

   The black races have historically been looked down upon more universally than almost any other race . . . Black humiliation both within Africa itself, and in the Diaspora, has been a major feature of the contemporary world. (A. Mazrui, *Africa's International Relations: The Diplomacy of Dependency and Change* (London: Heinemann) p. 215.)

9. Quoted in *The Times*, 21 January 1971.

10. Although attitudes to the Commonwealth in Britain had demonstrably changed, there was still a general acceptance that it had some useful part to play in the world. This was the case even in the Conservative Party. See in this vein the speech by Sir Alec Douglas-Home to the Conservative Commonwealth Council in April 1964. *Guardian*, 4 May 1964.

11. This *realpolitik* view was widely canvassed in influential sections of British opinion during this Conference. See, for instance, 'Odium without advantage', editorial, *The Times*, 13 January 1971.

12. See editorial, 'Mule in the China Shop' *New Statesman*, 15 January 1971.

13. *The Times*, 16 January 1971; Nyerere elaborated his views in an article, 'Arming Apartheid', in *The Times*, 16 January 1971, where he firmly stated that 'membership of the Commonwealth does not limit a nations right to act in its own interests. This has not been the issue, and is not going to be the issue between Britain and Tanzania or any other Commonwealth country'.

14. The widespread concern of the developing Commonwealth to maximise whatever benefits still accrued from membership, at this precarious transitional 'moment', is conveyed by a number of specialist contributors to a special edition of the *Round Table* which examined the likely impact and results of British–Commonwealth–EEC relations. They were D. Kumar, 'The New Community and the Developing Commonwealth: Problems of Trade and Aid', *Round Table*, October 1971, pp. 475–84; Sisir Gupta, 'Commonwealth South Asia and the Enlarged Community: the continued value of the Commonwealth link', *ibid.*, pp. 507–10; and R. Lewis, 'Commonwealth Africa and the Enlarged Community: political, cultural and economic Impact', *ibid.*, pp. 515–21.

15. *The Times*, 13 January 1971.

16. Quoted in *The Times*, 8 January 1971.

17 'Around the rugged rock', article in *The Economist*, 16 January 1971, p. 27.

18. Ibid., 14 January 1971.

19. The *Economist*, 23 January 1971, p. 25.

20. For a theoretical appraisal of the relationship between the 'internal' and 'external' components of international negotiations, see Gilbert Winham, 'Practitioners view of International Negotiations', in *World Politics*, vol. 32, no. 1, October 1979, especially pp. 116–19.

21. *The Times*, 18 January 1971.

22. Any suggestion of compulsion was removed from the final draft. How best to treat with racist regimes was left unambiguously to the judgement of individual members; quoted in *The Times*, 23 January 1971.

23. 'Any other business', article in The *Economist*, 9 January, 1971, p. 13.

24. Mr R. N. Mirdha, Minister of State for Home Affairs, quoted in *The Times*, 23 January 1971.

25. Arnold Smith maintained that over formality has made all the difference between a useful exchange of views and occasionally bitter confrontation. *The Times*, 2 June 1971.

26. This led to some premature judgements about the likely redirection of Canada's external policy under Trudeau. See, in particular, Bruce Thordasson, *Trudeau and Foreign Policy* (Toronto: Oxford University Press, 1972).

27. 'Harder to laugh', article in *The Economist*, 16 January 1971, p. 28.

28. P. Dobell, *Canada's Search for New Roles: Foreign Policy in the Trudeau Era* (London: Oxford University Press, 1972).

29. Pierre E. Trudeau, 'The Commonwealth After Ottawa', *Round Table*, January 1974, p. 37.

30. *The Times*, 8 June 1977.

31. See 'The Year of the Commonwealth', M. Mortimer, *The Spectator*, 30 January 1971, p. 155.

32. The impact of the Caribbean Commonwealth was bound to be offset by its lack of large, populous or otherwise powerful states. Even so, its impact on successive Conferences since 1965 has been out of all proportion to its power resources or place in the international hierachy of 'sensitive' or strategic locations. Its contribution, if not influence, grew as the meetings focused more attention on economic issues, to which their experience as 'plantation' economics was of direct relevance.

33. The 'classic' statement of this perspective is found in 'A Critical Examination of the Modern Commonwealth', Chapter 9 of Sir Robert Menzies' memoirs, *Afternoon Light* (Harmondsworth: Penguin, 1967).

34. A. Macleod, 'The New Foreign Policy in Australia and New Zealand', in *Round Table*, July 1974, especially pp. 296–7.

35. P. Darby, 'Australia's Changing perspective of the World', in *World Today*, March 1973, pp. 119–25.

36. There is an excellent conceptual appraisal of this impetus in a *Round Table* editorial written at the time. While it acknowledged that the Commonwealth was a community in the sense, of 'being rooted in a natural historical growth', it also recognised that this retrospective link was just as capable of breeding discontinuity as harmony. For the wider it grew, the more diluted the shared values which must exist to sustain any meaningful sense of community. In spite of this, the editorial believed that the Commonwealth had found a new relevance on a surer foundation than a nebulous, common (or for that matter, contentious) past. For

> if the community is to be sustained there must be a continuous engagement of interests and wills on the institutional plane: the habits of functional co-operation must be extended and developed, and the governments and peoples of the Commonwealth must be encouraged to see in their association a future as well as a past, a source of benefits as well as obligations. (Editorial, 'After Ottawa', *Round Table*, October 1973, pp. 418–19.)

This reassessment was precisely what was in train at Ottawa.

37. Editorial, 'Continuity Restored', *The Times*, 13 August 1973.

38. This prohibition freed many officials from sitting in conference and allowed them to work in committees which applied considerable energy to the practical task of improving functional co-operation; for instance, in youth exchange and training projects. See *The Economist*, 11 August 1973, p. 28.

39. *The Times*, 7 May 1975.

40. *The Times*, 30 July 1973.

41. S. Henig, 'A foreign policy for Europe', Socialist Commentary, May 1972, pp. 14, 19.

42. Significantly, the preliminary negotiations to create a new associate agreement between the EEC and a large number of developing countries, had begun just prior to the Commonwealth Meeting, in Brussels, *The Economist*, 28 July 1973, pp. 52–4.

43. *The Times*, 11 August 1973.

44. T. Josling and S. Harris, 'The Revolution in World Commodity prices: A problem for the Commonwealth', in *Round Table*, April 1974, pp. 187–202.

45. R. Cooper, 'Tariff issues and the third world', in *World Today*, September 1971, pp. 401–10.
    For a more conceptual approach to this important problem – which suggests that there were important cleavages within the 'Third World' itself, further weakening their bargaining position, see D. Smyth, 'The Global Economy and the Third World: coalition or cleavage?', in *World Politics*, vol. 29, No. 4, July 1977, pp. 584–603.

46. *The Economist*, 11 August 1973, p. 72.

47. India's Secretary for External Affairs and delegation leader at Ottawa, quoted in *The Times*, 7 August 1973.

48. Editorial, 'Commonwealth and Common Market', *Spectator*, 18 August 1973, p. 203.

49. John Pinder, 'British interests in an enlarged European community', *World Today*, October 1971, p. 430.

50. *The Times*, 16 January 1971.

51. *The Economist*, 8 September 1973, pp. 57, 61.

52. The new Secretary General put this well in his 1979 Report when he noted that while 'the Commonwealth cannot negotiate for the world . . . it can help the world to negotiate'. *Report of the Commonwealth Secretary-General, 1979* (Commonwealth Secretariat, 1979), p. 6.

53. *The Economist*, 3 May 1975, pp. 60–1.

54. *Report of the Commonwealth Secretary General, 1973* (Commonwealth Secretariat, 1973), especially pp. xi–xii.

55. *Report of the Commonwealth Secretary-General, 1975* (Commonwealth Secretariat, 1975).

56. See G. Martin, 'The British Labour Movement and the Third World', *Socialist Commentary*, October 1978, pp. 14–17.

57. *The Economist*, 10 May 1975, p. 97.

58. *The Times*, 28 April 1975.

59. *The Times*, 2 May 1975.

60. See Michael Manley's discussion of this problem, 'Parallels of Equity: New Horizons in Economic Co-operation', *Round Table*, October 1975, pp. 335–47.

61. Editorial, 'Britain and Lomé', in *West Africa*, 5 May 1975, p. 498.

62. 'Commonwealth and the Commodities', article in *West Africa*, 28 April 1975, p. 483.

63.| *The Economist*, 11 August 1973, p. 49; ibid., 22 September 1973, p. 70.

64. *The Times*, 8 May 1975.

65. *The Times*, 3 May 1975.

66. *The Economist*, 18 June 1977, p. 76.

67. See John Hatch's critical estimation, 'Twenty Five Years of the Commonwealth', *New Statesman*, 3 June 1977, pp. 734–5.

68. *The Times*, 7 May 1975.

69. See 'Commonwealth Afloat', *West Africa*, 20 August 1973, p. 1145.

70. The extent of this difference is amply illustrated by Ashok Kapur, 'Nuclear Weapons and Indian Foreign policy: a perspective', in *World Today*, September 1971, pp. 379–89.

71. A. G. Noorani, 'India and Asian Security', *World Today*, March 1970, pp. 110–17.

72. See the highly informed articles by G. H. Jansen; in *The Statesman* (Calcutta), 5 April 1970; and 'Geopolitical Alignment of the Nonaligned', ibid., 21 April 1970.

73. Anirudha Gupta, 'A Note on Indian Attitudes to Africa', *African Affairs*, April 1970.

74. *Hindustan Times*, 19 June 1965.

75. India had been particularly active in the Commonwealth Regional Heads of Government Meetings of the Asian and Pacific members. At the Sydney meeting in 1978 it agreed to stage the next meeting at New Delhi.

76. *The Times*, 8 May 1975.

77. Editorial, 'Commonwealth Quest; from a faith in symbols to a commitment to practical action, *Round Table*, April 1977, pp. 111–119.

78. Roy Lewis, 'Now is the time to break silence', *The Times*, 8 June 1977.

79. 'A Quiet Conference': interview with S. Ramphal, *Round Table*, October 1977, pp. 314–24.

80. *The Times*, 1 June 1977.

81. This was highlighted by the timely revelations of Henry Kyemba, Uganda's former Minister of Health, when he disclosed the barbaric circumstances surrounding the death of Mrs Dora Bloch, one of the hostages held by Palestinian terrorists with Amin's connivance at Entebbe Airport, as well as other equally horrific episodes. *The Sunday Times*, 5 June 1977.

82. *The Economist*, 4 June 1977, p. 14.

83. See the discussion of these inconsistencies in the editorial, 'The Question of Commonwealth values; What does the Commonwealth have in common?', *Round Table*, October 1974, pp. 359–67.

84. *The Economist*, 23 January 1971, p. 14.

85. *Report of the Commonwealth Secretary-General, 1977* (Commonwealth Secretariat, 1977).

86. *The Times*, 15 June 1977.

87. *The Commonwealth Heads of Government Meeting 1977: The London Communiqué* (The Commonwealth Secretariat, 1977).

88. 'Stresses and Strains in OAU', *West Africa*, 30 May 1977, p. 1022.

89. Editorial, 'Commonwealth of compromises', *West Africa*, 20 June 1977, p. 1186.

90. *The Times*, 8 June 1977.
91. Ibid., 11 June 1977.
92. Ibid., 10 June 1977.
93. P. Cosgrave, 'Two Ladies in Lusaka', *Spectator*, 4 August 1979, p. 6.
94. *The Economist*, 7 July 1979, p. 78.
95. Editorial, 'All Zimbabwe's Friends', *The Economist*, 11 August 1979.
96. Ibid., 4 August 1979, pp. 38–9.
97. *Daily Telegraph*, 6 August 1979.
98. *West Africa*, 13 August 1979, p. 1448.
99. S. Ramphal, 'Reflections on Lusaka', text of his speech to the Royal Institute of International Affairs, 21 September 1979, pp. 5–6.
100. Pierre Elliott Trudeau, 'The Commonwealth after Ottawa', *Round Table*, January, 1974, p. 38.
101. Editorial, 'Commonwealth Compromises', *The Times*, 16 June 1977.

14 Conflict Management in the Commonwealth

C. R. MITCHELL

The successful transfer of political power in Zimbabwe and the Commonwealth Observer Mission for the Ugandan elections have rekindled interest in the Commonwealth as an institution for handling conflicts both within and between its members. This is not a new idea since it was part of the rhetoric and reality of the British Commonwealth. The idea was downgraded in the new Commonwealth but the pendulum is swinging back to envisage a conflict-handling role for both the Secretariat and the Heads of Government Meetings (CHOGMs). The Secretary-General has extolled the Commonwealth's evolution of '... some rather special approaches to dialogue ...' and suggested that such innovations in techniques of conference management could be applied more widely in the search for solutions to global problems.[1]

The nature of a conflict-managing role and the Commonwealth's potential therein raises several broad questions. Why should the Commonwealth, as an intergovernmental organisation, have any kind of conflict-management role? What functions might the Commonwealth fulfil in managing conflict, and what is meant by 'the Commonwealth' in this context? What are the necessary conditions for the Commonwealth to adopt such a role? What has been the Commonwealth's record to date as a conflict-manager? What are the prospects for a future conflict-management role, particularly in the light of the lessons of the Zimbabwe settlement?

THE COMMONWEALTH AS AN INTERGOVERNMENTAL ORGANISATION

It is not obvious that the Commonwealth should possess a conflict-handling function, despite long-standing claims regarding ease of dialogue and mutual understanding among Commonwealth leaders. Conflict-management is the highest of 'high politics' and even international organisations specifically charged with it often undertake it reluctantly or not at all. Historically a Commonwealth role in managing conflict has been ambivalent.[2] Two important norms were established early in the 1950s: there should be no discussion of the internal problems of members at Commonwealth conferences and discussion of inter-member disputes could only take place with the express consent of the members involved. This did not prohibit informal discussions of Commonwealth problems at such conferences, but the norms did inhibit the formulation of any Commonwealth consensus and the launching of formal Commonwealth initiatives to handle disputes. Indian Prime Minister Shastri was able to assert these entrenched norms at the 1965 Commonwealth Conference when fighting had already occurred in the Rann of Kutch and the situation in Kashmir was tense.[3]

Yet the establishment of the Commonwealth Secretariat helped to revitalise a Commonwealth role in managing conflicts among members. In his first report Secretary-General Arnold Smith emphasised that the more severe international stresses then 'the greater the need for bridge-building institutions and associations to try to resolve them'.[4] Similar sentiments were expressed in his last report in 1975, when he argued that the Commonwealth's 'ready-made machinery and experience can contribute to diminishing political tensions of concern to member countries . . .'[5] However, conflict-management was *not* one of the roles assigned to the Commonwealth in the Declaration of Commonwealth Principles agreed at Singapore in January 1971 and to some degree this ambivalence has remained.

Yet intergovernmental organisations such as the Commonwealth may have some inherent advantages as conflict-managers over, for instance, regional political organisations, due to their heterogenous nature. The Commonwealth 'club' usually has members that share norms and sympathies with the adversaries, and yet are genuinely uninvolved in the outcome of the dispute in question because of their distance from it. They can act as contacts, 'honest brokers', a pressure-group for compromises, or as a general intermediary, and they possess an access to the conflicting parties not open to governments outside the Commonwealth.

Furthermore, the very heterogeneity of the Commonwealth enhances its potential as a conflict-manager through overlapping membership with other blocs, alignments and regional or local organisations. The network of contacts set up by the current membership of the Commonwealth not merely crosses '... the lines of geography, race and wealth ...',[6] but also puts the Commonwealth in close and constant contact with nearly all other important regional and ideological groupings. The extent to which this might be used fruitfully to extend the Commonwealth's conflict-management role remains problematical and partly dependent upon the claims of regional organisations to operate exclusively in that role. However, the potential remains to be exploited, should appropriate opportunities arise.

THE COMMONWEALTH AND THE 'CONFLICT-MANAGEMENT' ROLE

How suited is the Commonwealth as an intergovernmental organisation to carry out all or any of the varied functions of a conflict-manager?[7] The Commonwealth is not a unitary actor and so different bodies or groupings may act in particular cases. Nevertheless, there are four key levels of Commonwealth interaction at which conflict-management processes might either originate or be implemented: these are CHOGMs, the Secretariat, informal networks of Commonwealth leaders particularly concerned about a problem who decide to act in concert using a Commonwealth identity, and the *ad hoc* special committees or conferences set up or called to deal with a particular problem as it arises. It is possible that CHOGRMs may play a regional conflict-management role on a similar basis to the 'good neighbour' arguments used by more conventional regional organisations.[8]

CHOGMs are the best opportunity for the development of a unified Commonwealth initiative in any relevant dispute and for the marshalling of Commonwealth opinion behind a particular line of action. Such occasions provide an unusual opportunity for informal discussion and exchange of ideas, for persuasion of other leaders and for the development of plans and proposals among both the parties who might be directly involved in a dispute, and those who might be intimately connected with some conflict-management or intermediary initiative.

The present Secretary-General has recently referred to the development of a 'Commonwealth capacity to do business together' which is made possible by discussion 'among a relatively small group of political leaders',[9] and CHOGMs are usually characterised by an uncommon degree of informality and an easy working atmosphere. The Commonwealth may, indeed, have evolved a 'rather special approach to dialogue', as the Secretary-General claims, and developed a process conducive to agreement rather than to confrontation even on high political matters of conflict-management.

Yet the Commonwealth suffers in many ways from the disadvantages of senior government representatives meeting only periodically and discontinuously. The biennial nature of the Commonwealth Heads of Government Meeting can make for long gaps between the development of agreed Commonwealth initiatives, the adoption of fresh Commonwealth stances on international issues or the construction of a full Commonwealth consensus to underpin some effort at conflict-management. To some degree this can be overcome by the development of *ad hoc* networks of a few key Commonwealth leaders that has become a feature of interaction within the Commonwealth, and the use of committees set up to monitor one particular issue in the range of high political matters confronting the organisation.

In part this has been offset by the development since 1965 of an active and initiative-taking Secretariat, whose activities have been spearheaded by two very different but equally vigorous Secretaries-General. In 1965, for example, the newly appointed Secretary-General seized the opportunity to become involved in the conflict between Singapore and Malaysia over Singapore's withdrawal from the Federation and subsequent application to become a full member of the Commonwealth. This action was one of his first on taking office. Again, Commonwealth strategies in the Nigerian civil war were very much initiated and carried through by Arnold Smith, with the support of the British government and other Commonwealth leaders. Mr Ramphal's role in both the achievement of the Zimbabwe settlement and in the dispute between Tanzania and Uganda have been well documented and discussed. Thus, the execution of policies of conflict-management (and, frequently, the initiative for their being undertaken) has, since 1965, come more and more to rest with the Secretariat. The Secretary-General's role now resembles that of an active UN Secretary-General, rather than that of a passive functionary arranging biennial conferences and otherwise servicing the organisation in a purely administrative capacity.

Both Secretaries-General (as well as other Commonwealth leaders such as President Obote, General Ankrah and President Nyerere) have acted as intermediaries in disputes that have reached the stage of overt coercion and violence, as go-betweens, convenors of exploratory dialogues and negotiation meetings, contact points, sources of compromise suggestions and settlement proposals, and the conveyers of subtle pressures from the Commonwealth at large towards the continuation of dialogues, the avoidance of extreme moves from which retreat is impossible, and the playing down of tensions and hostilities that might hinder a settlement. In a major sense, the fact that the Commonwealth currently appears on the verge of developing a major conflict-management role for itself is, to a large degree, a function of the expansion of tasks undertaken by the Secretariat over the past fifteen years, and the carving out of an independent role for its chief executive.

The activities of informal groups of Commonwealth leaders, who either seek to operate within an existing Commonwealth consensus to do something about a situation they regard as dangerous but amenable to influence, or who seek first to create such a consensus and then operate within it, are also important. A recent example of this vital second process in operation were the activities of Mr Manley, Mr Fraser and the Canadian Prime Minister, Mr Clark (supported by Mr Ramphal) in the period leading up to a Lusaka Conference which threatened to become an occasion for a final explosive confrontation over Zimbabwe. Such cases help to emphasise the importance of informal coalitions of Commonwealth leaders, both for the maintenance of Commonwealth unity overall and for the launching of Commonwealth initiatives in conflict-management.

A further means of direct involvement is through post-agreement conflict-management. Commonwealth observers have monitored elections in Uganda and reported on their relative degree of freedom from corruption, intimidation and sharp practice. A Commonwealth mission observed the fairness of the referendum on Gibraltar's future. A Commonwealth military force monitored the ceasefire in Zimbabwe following the Lancaster House agreement. Again, the subsequent Zimbabwean elections were supervised by a Commonwealth observer team. From this list it can be seen that the potential for Commonwealth involvement in post-agreement conflict-management exists, even though the record to date is a sparse one.

Finally, conflict-management activity from 'the Commonwealth' may emanate from *ad hoc* or special conferences or committees set up by the Heads of Government Meeting to deal with specific issues of concern to the Commonwealth. An early example of this was the abortive

Commonwealth conference on the Kashmir problem held in 1951, but more recently there was the special conference held in Lagos immediately following the Rhodesian UDI, and the committees set up to monitor the problems of independence for Belize and the conflict on Cyprus. In the last case, the record shows that such bodies can play a useful role, even when the major conflict-management initiative is being carried by the UN or any other regional intergovernmental body. The committee on Cyprus has succeeded in making some contribution to the exchange of views between Greek and Turkish Cypriot leaders, to the encouragement of inter-communal talks on the island, and to the support of the UN in its intermediary role. The fact that such a function can be carried out by a Commonwealth committee, in spite of the previous presence of the UN, and also the close connection between the parties on the island and external patrons, neither of whom are members of the Commonwealth, does suggest that such continuing committees can fulfil a conflict-management function on behalf of the Commonwealth as a whole, and that more might be made of this particular process.

NECESSARY CONDITIONS FOR CONFLICT MANAGEMENT

For any intergovernmental political organisation to operate as a conflict-manager certain basic conditions have to be favourable. These can be subsumed under the headings of *consensus* and *legitimacy* (which is not the same as legality). In the Commonwealth consensus on any problem arising for the membership is arrived at in a variety of ways. Initially, it often results from the process of continuous consultation of an informal nature so characteristic of the Commonwealth. More officially, however, a consensus is usually enunciated at formal conferences, after further informal contacts. A third means of solidifying a Commonwealth consensus has developed into a recognisable Commonwealth pattern of behaviour over the last fifteen years, and this is the establishment of an *ad hoc* body to implement the consensus and to try to ensure that Commonwealth members in general, and particularly those more directly concerned with the problem, do not stray too far from the line agreed at the main Conference. Subsequent CHOGMs receive reports from these 'issue-specific' committees and reinforce Commonwealth commitment to the previously agreed line of policy. The committee on Cyprus, on Belize, and the Commonwealth Committee established much earlier to oversee the implementation of sanctions policy against Rhodesia during the period of UDI, are important examples.

It seems obvious that any intergovernmental organisation can develop a variety of types of consensus about how it should react to conflicts between its own members or outsiders. In some cases the consensus consciously arrived at may be to stand neutral and do nothing, as in the case of the Commonwealth's stance on the civil war in Pakistan (to be distinguished from the case where no consensus emerges, so that the organisation is paralysed and helpless). After this basic choice, many options arise, but from a conflict-management perspective a simple two category classification makes an important distinction between:

(1) A consensus to allow the parties in conflict themselves to discover a solution to the dispute but to assist them to do this by deploying as wide a range of conflict-management techniques as are available and appropriate. This could be termed a *neutral consensus*.

(2) A consensus that a particular outcome is preferable to others and that the organisation should use its resources and influence to achieve that outcome, irrespective of the objectives of one of the adversaries directly involved in the conflict, in other words, a *partisan consensus*.

Both types of consensus appear difficult to achieve and maintain, but the latter the more so especially in a heterogenous grouping such as the Commonwealth. Heterogeneity may indeed breed paralysis through lack of consensus. Yet Rhodesia demonstrates that a partisan consensus can be achieved and maintained, if painfully, over a very long period. Moreover, the Commonwealth was even prepared to aid a non-Commonwealth member, Mozambique, once it began to apply pressure to a party in an intra-Commonwealth conflict against whom the whole of the Commonwealth had agreed to act.[10]

However, actions based upon a partisan consensus, no matter how irregularly achieved, resemble intervention rather than mediation, with the organisation itself becoming a party to the conflict. For a genuine conflict-management role to be carried through it is important that the members of the organisation be prepared to accept the principle of helping the parties to arrive at their own satisfactory solution, peacefully and through negotiation – a more attractive and certainly less costly role than that of indirect participant in the conflict. It postpones the necessity for choosing sides, and enables governments and organisations to achieve credit for playing the honest broker. It is often an easier matter than deciding which side to support and convincing others to accept that choice. Situations as unambiguous as the white Rhodesian declaration of independence seldom arise. Hence the record of Commonwealth high political activity has tended towards the assumption of a conflict-management role, based upon the concept of the Commonwealth acting as an honest broker; a concensus that peace through negotiation is preferable to peace through conquest; and a desire to minimise friction within the membership while not neglecting to support members in their conflicts with non-members of the Commonwealth.[11]

Once a neutral consensus has been achieved the parties in the conflict need convincing that the organisation can actually help to manage the conflict successfully, that its activities will not prove to be partisan (whatever its impartial intentions) and that the proffered intermediary help is something more than well-meaning meddling in a situation only half-understood by outsiders. The offer of help to find a solution must be *legitimate*, by being acceptable to the parties in the conflict. The extent to which the Commonwealth has an advantage in this respect over other organisations varies according to the nature of the dispute in question. Obviously, in inter-member conflicts other Commonwealth governments as well as the Secretariat can justifiably claim a legitimate and friendly concern and interest, and thus gain an initial access to the parties in conflict.[12] Such an advantage does not arise in the case of Commonwealth initiatives in conflicts involving non-Commonwealth members, which helps to explain the lack of action in such disputes. In a similar fashion, constraints exist in disputes between members and non-members, where the Commonwealth is hardly likely to be perceived as an impartial body. Finally, even Commonwealth members are likely to rebuff offers of intermediary activity in cases where the dispute is a domestic one.

Despite these differences, the rules of thumb for successful conflict-management still apply to Commonwealth initiatives, once these have been agreed and launched. All intermediaries must be perceived as skilled and *impartial*. However, for all intergovernmental organisations a concerned interest in the conflict rather than the complete disinterest sometimes advocated in textbooks appears more realistic and appropriate. Once again, the often denigrated statements about the gradual building-up of a network of informal and personal Commonwealth contacts, about the existence of contacts and relationships cutting across entrenched lines of demarcation, and about the overall 'familial' nature of the Commonwealth may have their greatest relevance in creating a built-in legitimacy for Commonwealth efforts at conflict-management among its members.

THE COMMONWEALTH AS CONFLICT-MANAGER

To what conclusions does the historical record of conflict-management by the Commonwealth point? It may be that the Commonwealth developed a capacity for conflict-handling less because of the rhetoric of Commonwealth ties and common background than in spite of a marked reluctance of many (especially new) members of the organisation to fulfil that rhetoric. However, a major impetus for expanding the Commonwealth's conflict-handling role has arisen from the Secretariat, particularly in the early years of Arnold Smith's incumbency, when there was an active search for a positive role rather than becoming either an adjunct of the FCO or a mere set of administrative functionaries.

Conflict-managers can be faced with five different types of conflict:

(1) Conflicts between governments who are not members of the international organisation in question but in which the organisation has some interest, even if this is only the general 'social' interest of containing a conflict and preventing it becoming more disruptive, dangerous or destabilising ('*Outsider v. Outsider*' conflicts).

(2) Conflicts between a member of the organisation and an outside government or governments ('*Member v. Outsider*').

(3) Conflicts, either bilateral or multilateral, between governments which are members of the organisation in question. Traditional theory in such disputes holds that common membership of the organisation should exercise a restraining influence on conflict behaviour and that other members of the organisation, or the organisation itself, should be able to act in some manner to ameliorate the dispute ('*Member v. Member*').

(4) Conflicts that take place within members of the organisation and which are conventionally regarded as forming part of the 'domestic affairs' of that member, a fact which usually renders them – particularly in the view of the government in question – immune from external interference and intermediary action ('*Intra-Member*').

(5) Conflicts that involve both member governments and some (usually intense) intra-member conflict which has become internationalised by the process of drawing in various outside patrons of incumbents, insurgents or both (*'Transnational'*).[13]

For example:

	Structure	Type	Commonwealth
(1)	Outsider–Outsider	International	N. Vietnam + NLF v. S. Vietnam + USA
(2)	Member–Outsider	International	Belize v. Guatemala UK v. Argentina (Falkland Islands)
(3)	Member–Member	International	Indo-Pakistan War 1965
(4)	Intra–Member	Domestic	Nigerian Civil War
(5)	Member/Outsider –Intra-Member	Transnational	Uganda v. Anti-Amin Ugandans + Tanzania

FIGURE 14.1   *Types of 'manageable' conflict*

Since 1965 the Commonwealth has confronted examples of all five types of conflict, and its record offers an indication of its potential in a conflict-management role. However, the performance of any conflict-manager has to be assessed in the context of all the conflicts it could have tried to resolve, rather than merely taking note of those cases where an organisation chose to take some action.

This principle is, however, hardly applicable as far as the first type of conflict is concerned, since their number is legion. Commonwealth ventures into this type of conflict have been rare and arose from the temporary enthusiasm of the Labour government in Britain in the mid 1960s, and particularly from Mr Wilson's belief that he could use the Commonwealth as a base for playing a larger role in international politics as in the ill-fated Vietnam peace mission. Since that experience, the idea of the Commonwealth as an organisation that could act in a conflict-management role on a global basis has very rapidly been downgraded, and the organisation's conflict-management activities confined to disputes involving Commonwealth members or direct Commonwealth interests.[14]

In disputes between a member and an outsider inter-governmental organisations tend either to remain inactive because peacemaking initiatives may be rejected by the outsider, or to adopt the stance of the member and support that government diplomatically and, sometimes, materially. The Commonwealth usually supports members against outsiders. Commonwealth support for Malaysia and the United Kingdom during 'confrontation' with Indonesia was firmly in evidence, while similar attitudes were broadly maintained over the dispute between Spain and the United Kingdom over Gibraltar (although a few Commonwealth delegates voted for a UN resolution in 1969 calling for Britain to return the territory to Spain). In the latter case the Commonwealth helped to legitimise British Policy by supplying obser-ver teams for the referendum on the future of Gibraltar held in September 1967. In much the same way, Commonwealth attitudes towards the independence of Belize and the Guatemalan claim to that territory were firmly against any compromise with the non-Commonwealth party. At the Kingston CHOGM a declaration of 'full support for the aspirations of the people of Belize' was made, and a ministerial committee on Belize was established with the task of rendering 'all practicable assistance to the parties concerned in finding early and effective arrangements for the independence of Belize in accordance with the [UN] Charter'.[15] However, in spite of the committee's emphasis on ensuring that its activities should 'enhance the prospect of a satisfactory negotiated settlement between Britain and Guatemala',[16] in no way could the Commonwealth role in this matter be regarded as other than partisan – an example of supportive intervention rather than honest brokerage. The role of the Belize committee was plainly seen as 'sharpening international focus on the plight of the people of Belize' and 'mobilising greater awareness of the principles and rights at stake'.[17] The Commonwealth committee obviously did play a part in the problem, but it was a part designed to ensure that the Commonwealth's clients in the matter achieved their ends successfully, while their adversaries in Guatemala were frustrated. Most recently Britain received significant support in the Falklands War, politically, diplomati-cally and, in effect, militarily, although this was not done collectively and formally through Commonwealth institutions but in a variety of ways in various fora. Nevertheless, Britain could, in essence, count on the Commonwealth for support.

The bilateral 'Member v. Member' type of dispute presents a rather different problem and raises the opportunity of acting either in a partisan or an intermediary role. Like most organisations, the Commonwealth reacts to inter-member conflicts with a mixture of alarm and concern, and usually perceives its role as one of ameliorating the conflict rather than taking sides. For one thing, a firmly partisan stance runs the risk of losing a member and of splitting and damaging the organisation. On the other hand, an active intermediary role is one which, among other effects, avoids the necessity for taking sides and provides some generally acceptable activity for the organisation itself and for member governments. It is with this category of conflicts that the Commonwealth has been most concerned. The long drawn-out confrontation which has sometimes erupted into open violence between India and Pakistan (before the latter left the Commonwealth) gives abundant examples of the two things which are essential if any conflict-managing role is to be successfully played out; a consensus about desirable action within the organisation and acceptance of that action as desirable and legitimate by the parties involved in the conflict. The importance of such preliminary conditions being 'right' for successful conflict-management is indicated by other 'Member v. Member' conflicts within the Commonwealth and the lack of any really successful Commonwealth initiative in managing such conflicts. For example, the bitter dispute between the Ugandan regime of Idi Amin and the Tanzanian Government ended with the abortive Ugandan invasion of northern Tanzania and the resulting Tanzanian counter-invasion of Uganda culminating in the overthrow of Amin, rather than any compromise settlement managed by the Commonwealth Secretariat, CHOGM or informal consortium of African Commonwealth leaders. It is true that the Secretary-General, Mr Smith, launched a mediation initiative in September 1971, but the only public Commonwealth action resulting from the open invasion of Tanzania was a call by Mr Ramphal for withdrawal of Ugandan troops and an end of the violations of Tanzania's frontiers.

The difficulties for Commonwealth agents in fulfilling a conflict-management role in inter-member disputes are even greater in efforts to ameliorate domestic conflict within members, whether these be relatively straightforward secessionist movements and civil wars or more complex cases of intra-national conflict in which outsiders (perhaps including other Commonwealth members) have become actively involved. Both types of conflict are notoriously difficult to affect, mainly because of the protective wall built around the problem by the political incumbents on grounds of domestic jurisdiction and the doctrine of non-interference in the internal affairs of other countries. (This latter argument remains particularly powerful, as political incumbents often fear that they may be the next victims of any breach of the principle.)

Such types of conflict have proved the most difficult and sensitive for the Commonwealth to handle. There are many examples of intra-member and transnational conflicts where the Commonwealth has taken no initiative at all, as in Northern Ireland, and also of similar conflicts where a Commonwealth initiative has been largely abortive. For example, Commonwealth leaders were reluctant to become directly involved in the communal conflict on Cyprus. The Secretary-General's report of 1975 mentioned it only as a relief and refugee problem. It was not until the Kingston CHOGM that a Commonwealth Committee on Cyprus was set up, and the comments in the 1977 Secretary-General's report make it clear that the committee defined its role as very much secondary to, and supportive of the activities of the UN, although the Secretary-General continued to be active as a go-between and a goodwill visit was made to both Greek and Turkish areas of the island in May 1977. Beyond that, however, the Commonwealth role has more recently consisted merely of keeping closely in touch with the UN Secretary-General, and observing the slow progress of the inter-communal talks on the island.

The two Commonwealth cases that perhaps best illustrate the difficulties of any organisation dealing with a conflict within one of its members are the Nigerian civil war, and the successful secession of East Pakistan and its emergence, with Indian help, as the independent state of Bangladesh. In this long drawn-out and complex transnational conflict, which contained elements of the India-Pakistan confrontation which had previously proved impervious to Commonwealth initiative, the best that could be managed by the Commonwealth Secretary-General was a concerned and supportive stance as events moved towards a catastrophe; an attempt by other Commonwealth governments to maintain a neutral posture once the conflict had reached open repression, violence and warfare; and an effort to initiate a programme of relief, rehabilitation and development in the region once the actual fighting had ceased. Even such an impartial approach to the dispute by the Commonwealth as a whole proved abortive. Not only was the organisation unable to ameliorate the conflict and avoid extreme repression and violence but, ultimately, the unity of the organisation was lost when Pakistan withdrew over a single member's decision to recognise Bangladesh. Arguments underlining the lack of any multilateral Commonwealth Action and the refusal of members to take sides during the war were ignored by the Pakistan government, as was the

Secretary-General's point that for Pakistan to sever Commonwealth links because she disagreed with the decision of one member 'showed a basic misconception of the nature of the association'.[18] In this case, conflict management had never begun and a neutral policy had, to a degree, backfired.

With the Nigerian civil war, Commonwealth action was more vigorous yet again the effect was, at best, peripheral. The main initiatives were taken informally by the Commonwealth Secretary-General. As early as October 1967 contacts were established in London between Biafran agents and representatives of the Federal Government and subsequently the Commonwealth Secretary-General wrote to the Federal Government's Commissioner for External Affairs inviting the Nigerians to begin talks with the Secretariat to discover whether any basis for direct Federal-Biafran talks existed. Meetings took place in London during January 1968, but appeared to promise little, as the Federal Government representatives were firm to the point of intransigence over issues crucial to involving Biafrans in direct negotiations, particularly over the matter of a prior ceasefire. The Federal Government delegation, for its part, returned to Lagos firmly convinced that there was no prospect at all for any really meaningful negotiations with the Biafrans, a conviction that remained in some Federal Government circles for the remainder of the civil war.[19] Hence rumours of another attempt to mediate by the Commonwealth Secretariat in February 1968, when Mr Smith visited Lagos for the Commonwealth Education Conference, appear no more than newspaper speculation and were rapidly denied by the Commonwealth Secretariat.

In spite of this initial failure to make any progress with an intermediary initiative, the Secretary-General again tried to mediate in May 1968, this time with firm encouragement from the British Government and some public commitment to talk from both parties in Nigeria. Informal discussions occurred in the Secretary-General's London flat, to settle an agenda to form the basis for later substantive discussions to be held in a Commonwealth capital – subsequently agreed to be Kampala. The difficulties of obtaining any agreement on even such relatively straightforward agenda items as a chairman for the conference indicated clearly the low probability of substantive success at Kampala. When the conference finally convened under the joint auspices of the Commonwealth Secretariat and the Ugandan government, it resembled a confrontation rather than a peace conference. Both sides were unwilling to compromise or make concessions, in spite of all the efforts of the Secretary-General and President Obote to salvage something from the talks. In the end, it was the Biafran delegation who first withdrew from the conference, but this action merely signalled what had been apparent from the start of the peacemaking process – that neither side was willing to make any concessions that the other would regard as a reasonable basis for a settlement.

From the collapse of the Kampala Conference, any major role as an intermediary eluded the Commonwealth Secretariat and, indeed, the Commonwealth as a whole. Efforts to revive the peacemaking process by the British government failed to have any real effect on the war, an almost inevitable concomitant of the Labour administration's public commitment to the Federal Government. Eventually, attempts to bring about a negotiated settlement of the conflict moved back into the African arena with the activation of the OAU Consultative Committee under the chairmanship of the Ethiopian Emperor and with this return to a regional forum any chance of a major role for the Commonwealth effectively vanished. This is not to say that the OAU committee was any more successful in arranging either direct negotiations or successful compromises than their predecessors had been. However, the change does underline one of the difficulties for a non-regional organisation such as the Commonwealth, in acting as a conflict-manager, namely that it will often be in competition for this role with regional political organisations. Frequently, these organisations will have the advantages of prior involvement, greater legitimacy in the eyes of the conflict parties, no involvement with major Western powers as members and (often) a prior claim on the loyalties of their members who also happen to be part of the Commonwealth. These obstacles must, therefore, be added to those which already make it structurally difficult for the Commonwealth to undertake a peacemaking role in intra-member or transnational conflicts.

THE ZIMBABWE CASE: A MODEL FOR THE FUTURE?

Viewed overall, the record of the Commonwealth as a conflict-manager is a rather mixed one, with a few successes, rather more failures and a number of cases where the Commonwealth has been unable to get to the first stage of launching some initiative, wither because of an acknowledged lack of intra-organisational consensus or because the parties have made it plain that no approach would succeed. But have the prospects changed radically as a result of the undoubted success of the Zimbabwe settlement and the Commonwealth's role in helping to bring this about?

Can the Zimbabwe case offer a new model for Commonwealth conflict management? The new model might start with the development of a consensus in the organisation, the adoption of an intermediary role, the supply of impartial observer and monitoring services and, finally, the less tangible, but equally important, provision of international legitimacy for an eventual settlement.

There are a number of elements in the Zimbabwean settlement that are not merely unique to that situation, but which throw doubt on whether it can be regarded as a case of impartial conflict-management at all. Nevertheless, all of the Commonwealth agencies discussed above played an important role in the overall process. An informal group of Commonwealth leaders worked to prepare both a Commonwealth position on the internal settlement and a process by which this imperfect handing over of political 'power' could be replaced by a genuine transfer to Zimbabwean nationalists. The Lusaka CHOGM provided the occasion for bringing the UK government into a modified consensus. Commonwealth leaders from Africa played a significant role in convincing the Patriotic Front leaders of the importance of a positive reception for the new British initiative, and were active in supportive roles during the Lancaster House Conference. Commonwealth resources were made available as observing, legitimising and reassuring agents for the carrying through of a ceasefire, an interim pre-election period and the election itself. Throughout the entire process the role of the Secretary-General as planner, co-ordinator, and one man pressure-group was vital. Surely this case represents the Commonwealth as conflict-manager in a way no other conflict can possibly do?

All of this is true, and in a paradoxical way the Zimbabwe settlement shows the potentialities of the Commonwealth in undertaking a wide variety of conflict-management functions with considerable success. However, the role of conflict-manager calls normally for the intermediary to be impartial, non-partisan and disinterested in the eventual outcome of the dispute. In this regard, the whole point about the eventual settlement of the Zimbabwean conflict is that it was eventually initiated by third parties who were thoroughly committed to one particular range of outcomes (with a minimum set of circumstances deemed to be satisfactory) and against the solution that was being pursued by one of the parties, the white-dominated regime in Salisbury. Thus Commonwealth action in this case was indeed based upon a consensus, but it was clearly and publicly a partisan consensus. A compromise settlement which did not meet the minimum conditions generally accepted by Commonwealth members (i.e. genuine majority rule) was regarded as an unsatisfactory solution and hence rejected.

The Commonwealth role in helping to arrange a final settlement was really a matter of arranging a surrender on suitably painless terms and in such a way as to allay the worst fears of those surrendering. This basic fact underlay Commonwealth support for a period of return to British rule and the provision of observers and ceasefire monitors. Conflict-management functions became a realistic possibility once a negotiated settlement *of which the Commonwealth could approve* had (admittedly with Commonwealth help) been achieved under British auspices. The two crucial points seem to be that throughout the entire final process, Commonwealth agencies were acting to achieve a solution which fulfilled the objectives of one side and frustrated those of another; and that all of the Commonwealth's peacemaking and peacekeeping activities were designed to smooth the way to just such a solution rather than to leave the nature of that solution solely to the parties.

It is in this sense that the Zimbabwe settlement needs to be treated with caution as a model for future Commonwealth conflict management. For a start, the achievement of a consensus about the nature of a desirable outcome in Zimbabwe was extremely fragile, a fragility that indicates the difficulty likely to attend the achievement of any operating consensus for future situations. Next, the achievement of such an operating consensus will make it difficult for the Commonwealth to fulfil any conflict-management functions, as such a partisan consensus will destroy Commonwealth legitimacy in the eyes of the party against whom the consensus is directed. Finally, even if this latter party is eventually driven into a situation where intermediary services are seen as helpful in arranging an easy and possibly less damaging surrender-settlement, it seems likely that other international organisations will be approached before a Commonwealth which has made its antipathies clear and constant. It was only the 'pariah' nature of the Salisbury regime that, when the time came to seek some not too damaging solution, forced it into the arms of the British and the Commonwealth as the least hostile of all available alternatives.

We end, therefore, with a paradox. The Zimbabwe settlement has significantly revived public debate about the Commonwealth's potential as a conflict-manager, yet it can be argued that similar situations are likely to be rare in future and that it provides an inappropriate model for future conflict-management activities. A more likely result of the revitalisation of the Commonwealth as a conflict-manager is that the organisation will find itself trying to organise a neutral consensus among its members to undertake disinterested legitimacy and usefulness as an intermediary; and grappling with all those intractable problems of being a conflict-manager that bedevil intergovernmental organisations. This is not to say that the Commonwealth will make no contribution to the management of dangerous conflicts or the maintenance of peace in the future. Any increase in this form of activity is to be welcomed and can justifiably be regarded as an end in itself. It is, however, to say that the success of such a contribution will be as mixed as it has been in the past and that future success should not be measured against the undoubted triumph of the achievement of a solution in Zimbabwe. To do so would be to use an inappropriate standard of measurement.

NOTES AND REFERENCES

1. See 'Conflict Resolution in the Eighties; The Need for Innovation' address to the Swedish Development Association by Mr Shridath Ramphal, 14 October 1980, p. 1.
2. Pakistan appealed for Commonwealth mediation in the Kashmir dispute in 1947, and even at this early stage in the development of the post-war Commonwealth the Indian Government argued strongly that the Commonwealth should not interfere in the 'domestic' affairs of its members.
3. *The Hindu*, 16 May 1965. Ironically it was Indian and Pakistani presence at the conference that enabled a British mediation initiative to proceed and a draft agreement worked out – although the delegations never met face-to-face to discuss the problem.
4. [*First*] *Report of the Secretary-General to Heads of Government* (London, 1966) pp. 3–4.
5. [*Fifth*] *Report of the Secretary-General to Heads of Government* (London, 1975) p. 3.
6. The argument is implied in Mr Ramphal's introduction to his first report as Secretary-General (London, 1977; p. 1).
7. This conception of 'stages' in the development of a conflict, and changes in accompanying conflict management techniques, is dealt with fully in my *The Structure of International Conflict* (London: Macmillan, 1981) chaps 3 and 11.
8. A sign of possible future directions for CHOGRM's efforts at regional conflict management was the initiative, launched at New Delhi, for a major conference to be called to discuss the defusing of superpower tensions in the region, with particular regard to the problems of Afghanistan and the Indian Ocean. The proposal was for a conference to be held on the general problems of the region to include not merely regional governments, but also those of the USA and USSR.
9. 'Conflict Resolution in the Eighties; The Need for Innovation', address by the Commonwealth Secretary-General to the Swedish Development Institute, 14 October 1980.
    Details of the Commonwealth approach, as applied to the Lusaka meeting

include the practice that 'Presidents and Prime Ministers met in a room reduced to make it intimate, not enlarged to make it grand – at no time with more than two delegation members with each of them. We have found from experience the need to provide a conference environment that encourages conversation not address. We use a room without a podium. No one stands to speak and while there is often an order of speakers as they catch the chairman's eye, spontaneous intervention is encouraged as an aid to lively dialogue' pp. 2–3.

10. Note the establishment of the Commonwealth Fund for Mozambique.

11. Disputes between Commonwealth members and outsiders are, of course, cases where it is much easier to construct a partisan consensus. Commonwealth governments tend to stick together against 'outsiders' such as Argentina, Guatemala or Venezuela, and in an earlier period against the CPR in its dispute with India.

12. As the Secretary-General notes in his very first report to heads of government 'the right of access to Heads of Government given to the Secretary-General in the Agreed Memorandum is, perhaps, the best guarantee of his role as servant of the Commonwealth community' *Report to Heads of Government by the Secretary-General* (London, August 1966).

13. This categorisation is by no means exhaustive. Conflicts can involve parties other than formal governments, communities or groups of insurgents and it is both theoretically possible for Commonwealth organs to act in a conflict handling capacity and historically the case that they have done so. The Secretary-General acted in such an intermediary capacity during the dispute between the Nigerian Federal Government and Shell/BP over the payment of royalties to the Biafran regime during the Nigerian civil war.

14. Another instance of a Commonwealth agent being involved in an 'Outsider v. Outsider' dispute is reported very briefly and tantalisingly in the Secretary-General's report of 1975, when he refers to talks he had had with the President of Frelimo 'at a critical moment in exchanges between his movement and the Portuguese authorities' Mr Smith's report continues; 'I hope that this meeting and other meetings and contacts with the Portuguese Foreign Ministry were helpful to both sides as a contribution to achieving a negotiated independence for Mozambique' *Report to Heads of Government by the Commonwealth Secretary–General, April 1973–March 1975* (London, 1975, p. 13). It could be argued that the struggle for independence in Mozambique was intimately connected with the Rhodesian problem, so that the Commonwealth was hardly completely 'outside' the former dispute.

15. [*Seventh*] *Report by the Secretary-General to Heads of Government* (London, May 1979) p. 18.

16. Ibid.

17. Ibid., pp. 18–19.

18. *Report by the Secretary General to Heads of Government* (London, 1973) p. 6. Pakistan withdrew from the Commonwealth on 30 January 1972.

19. This account is based largely upon John J. Stremlau *The International Politics of the Nigerian Civil War* (Princeton, 1977) who, in turn, bases his version of the London talks upon interviews with participants and a *Summary Record of Discussions* made at the time by the Commonwealth Secretariat.

15 Migration in the Commonwealth

HUGH TINKER

Speaking in 1943, Lord Cranborne (later Lord Salisbury) declared 'I believe that Imperial overseas settlement and the interchange of populations between one part of the British Commonwealth and the others is essential to the future happiness and prosperity and even the survival of the British Empire.'[1] This resounding declaration was actually on behalf of *white*, mainly United Kingdom, emigration and settlement; nobody (except the Indians) was particularly enthusiastic about Indian colonisation in so many parts of the Commonwealth. Nevertheless, this was a period of mobility within the Commonwealth, a mobility which continued at a high level through the 1950s and into the 1970s. In some countries gradually, in others abruptly, the free flow of inter-Commonwealth migration was replaced by rigid immigration controls. As we begin the 1980s we enter a phase (likely to be permanent) in which almost all the Commonwealth countries will strengthen the barriers against new arrivals.

However, in every case, the door is being slammed shut after hundreds or thousands have passed through. Every country in the Commonwealth, with the important exception of India (and to some extent West Africa), has its communities of recently-arrived outsiders: that is to say, immigrants or their progeny who have settled within the last hundred years. Almost all these countries share the characteristics of the plural society in which people of different cultures reside in quite close proximity, take part in common economic activities (trade and industry), and in many common public activities, such as politics, health services, welfare, and education – and yet go their separate ways in all matters of the family, religion and (predominantly) in culture and language. The characteristics of the plural society link those who are

244

otherwise divided between rich and poor, North and South. And yet this common heritage is not perceived as a unifying feature; immigration is almost universally perceived as having created a 'problem'. Important political elements in almost all countries acquire popularity by insisting that immigration must be totally barred and by suggesting that the immigrants, or their descendants, can be persuaded to return to their ancestral homes. Those few political leaders who adopt a liberal attitude to immigration (as some did in Canada in the 1960s) almost all pay in loss of electrical support for their liberalism.

This hostility to the newcomer (albeit often one whose family has been around more than half a century) is a feature of the new sense of separate national identity which has followed the emergence of the forty new states created out of the former British Empire since the Second World War. This nativism has centred upon a slogan which has been echoed in many lands, that of the 'Sons of the Soil'. This slogan, enunciated in ever more narrow terms, seems much more potent than the vaguely supra-national or international concept of the Commonwealth. It may not be an exaggeration to suggest that the Commonwealth is perceived as a negative force, even a threat to the aggressively chauvinistic 'Sons of the Soil'.

Having suggested that migration has come to be identified as a 'problem', let us inquire more closely into how the situation has been created. Migration often developed because in certain 'old' countries there is very heavy population pressure upon natural resources while in others the population is thin in relation to resources. In association with this imbalance, a second type of migration has followed when certain areas have a shortage of commercial, professional and technical skills while others have a surplus. This is the classic form of emigration to 'the new land', the 'land of opportunity'. However, a counter-movement has also developed which in time has replaced the flow from the 'full' to the 'empty' lands by a flow from the less developed periphery to the more developed centre. This counterflow has undoubtedly been accentuated by the imperial factor – and the post-imperial Commonwealth factor. Lenin perceived this over sixty years ago, writing: 'Another of the peculiarities of Imperialism ... is the decline in emigration from Imperialist countries and the increase in immigration (influx of workers and transmigration) to these countries from the more backward countries where wages are lower.'[2]

The first form of migration was given impetus by the progressive development of the 'new' 'empty' lands – Canada, Australia, Malaya, etc. – as producers of raw materials consumed by the metropole, with its massive industrial capacity: cereals, sugar, meat, rubber, tin, and other minerals were all in demand. Countries with the natural or climatic resources to meet the demand lacked a labour force. Certain 'old' countries had a surplus of labour, created by the conversion from traditional to modern modes of production, a surplus increased in certain periods by calamities (famine and flood), by the trade cycle which created slumps, and by deliberate policy (e.g. the evictions in the Scottish Highlands and in Ireland). The main countries of population surplus were the United Kingdom, India, and China, which, through Hong Kong and the Treaty Ports was part of the imperial periphery. These countries, then, witnessed the 'classic' forms of emigration: that of unskilled or semiskilled labourers, mostly male, providing the recruits for 'industrial agriculture', i.e. production of natural products for the export market.

During the early phase of migration to the New World and to the Antipodes it appeared possible that all the above sources of emigration might contribute to imperial settlement. Not all United Kingdom emigrants were eager to be off. From 1850 to 1890, the Irish out-numbered English, Scots and Welsh in the outflow from the United Kingdom: they were not grateful to the 'mother country' for making them go. Moreover, before the First World War 70 per cent of UK emigrants chose to settle in the United States (of the remainder about half went to Australasia, a quarter to Canada). Australia, Canada, South Africa all needed workers to labour in the fields, on the building of railroads and on other construction work. India and China could produce all the workers needed, and at first the employers were glad to take advantage of their numbers. However, very rapidly an organised white working class emerged in these countries, determined to preserve the superior standard of living which their scarce numbers had helped to provide. By the 1890s the white colonies of settlement had devised immigration rules which effectively excluded all non-whites and (by such devices as language tests) favoured the UK immigrant. However, there were still the tropical colonies requiring plantation workers and to East Africa, Malaya, Ceylon, the Pacific, and the Caribbean went thousands of semi-free workers from India and China.

The new economic order in the lands producing export products required not merely a basic labour force but also the infrastructure of development. Many English emigrants (as opposed to the Irish) carried overseas skills which enabled them to obtain a good standard of living immediately on arrival, supplying locomotive engineers, factory man-agers, doctors, or the many other technical and professional qualifications in demand. The tropical colonies could not afford the luxury of employing British professionals, except in small numbers at the very top. Fortunately, there was an alternative source of recruitment. The first universities on the model of the University of London were established in India in 1857, and by the beginning of the twentieth century there were sufficient numbers of Indian teachers, doctors, lawyers, journalists, accountants, and other professionals to meet the demands of the colonial administration and business network.

All the migration data demonstrates that when a 'trail' is well established it perpetuates a particular kind of emigration and settlement. If most of the clerks, mechanics, dispensers, and teachers in Malaya on the rubber plantations and in the government offices in 1910 were from India or Ceylon, fifty years later the same situation still prevailed, even though qualified candidates from among the 'Sons of the Soil' were beginning to emerge. As the immigrants established what seemed to be an exclusive monopoly in most sectors of business and administration in British tropical colonies, so resentment increased.

This deteriorating situation became much worse when the world slump of 1929–30 hit the prices of export materials such as rubber, sugar and rice. In Burma in 1930 resentment of the outsider exploded over the issue of Indian labourers replacing Burmese labourers in the Rangoon docks. This limited grievance became the cause for general anti-Indian rioting in which some 7000 Indians were made homeless, shops were wrecked and 2000 Indian rickshaws were smashed. The same month (June 1930), 33 000 Burma Indians abruptly went back to India. The longer-term effect of the slump was also to reverse migration flows and send recent migrants back 'home'.[3] This return affected not only the Asians but also emigrants from the United Kingdom to Canada and Australia, many of whom decided that privation was more bearable back in the mother country.

The Second World War brought about an unprecedented intercontinental movement of men in the armed forces, affecting almost every corner of the Empire. Canadians came to Britain and Europe; Australians went to Malaya and North Africa; Indian soldiers were sent almost everywhere (to Malaya, Burma, East and North Africa, and even to Britain), soldiers from the Gold Coast, Sierra Leone, Nigeria, Kenya and Uganda were sent to fight in Burma. Even small territories such as Trinidad, Mauritius and Bechuanaland sent contingents across the seas. Although there were some conflicts between the servicemen and the local population (as between Australians and Afrikaners in South Africa) in general this massive intermingling of the peoples of the

Empire created a strong sense of comradeship, intermixed with a restless urge to leave home when the soldiers were demobilised.

The sense of Commonwealth solidarity was somewhat diminished by the Canadian Citizenship Act of 1946. This provided for Canadians to have their own, exclusive political status as Canadian citizens. The 1946 Act made it very simple for any *white* immigrant (from Britain or one of the white dominions) to acquire Canadian citizenship and also re- cognised the special status of (white) British subjects in Canada. This move to promote a national (implicitly racial) exclusiveness within the Commonwealth ran counter to all thinking in the United Kingdom, where such a forward-looking statesman as Stafford Cripps could declare:

> The fundamental basis of the Commonwealth at the present time was common allegiance to the Crown and a common citizenship. If some other form of association was to be devised it would be necessary to find something which would have equal strength as a cohesive force.[4]

An extension of this principle was devised by the British Nationality Act of 1948, which created Commonwealth citizenship, and the Declaration of London in April 1949 whereby republican India was recognised, while the British Monarch was accepted as Head of the Commonwealth.[5] The concept of unity and free association was preserved, and with it the theory of the free movement of peoples as a vital Commonwealth element.

However, there still remained the belief in Britain that such movement was exclusively *outward* (despite the resettlement of 114 000 Polish ex-servicemen and 24 000 former East European prisoners of war in Britain immediately after the war). British emigration rapidly regained momentum. The Empire Settlement Act of 1922 (renewed in 1937) provided a framework for assistance to those moving from Britain to areas of white settlement. Before 1939, Canada had been the most popular destination; after 1945, Australia was the Mecca of British emigrants.

The Japanese invasion of South East Asia in 1942, and their advance through New Guinea almost to Australia's shores, had made leaders of all parties conscious of the weakness of a country of 3 million square miles with 12 210 miles of coastline and a population (1943) of 7 229 864. From 1947 a vigorous policy of attraction helped to almost double the population within thirty years (1971: 12 728 461). This entailed bringing in between 100 000 and 180 000 'New Australians' every year. The United Kingdom contributed about half the new arrivals, many coming under the '£10 Passage' scheme. The Labour victory in the British general election in 1964 helped to accelerate the exodus: 73 501 persons took advantage of the £10 scheme in 1965.

The traditional White Australia policy continued to be enforced during these decades of mass immigration. When preferred sources (such as Britain, the Netherlands and Scandinavia) did not produce sufficient numbers, the immigration agencies turned to Southern Europe – Greece, the Balkans, and southern Italy. The door against non-white members of the Commonwealth remained firmly shut[6] – and this, despite vigorous Australian participation in Commonwealth aid and development schemes, such as the Colombo Plan, and the provision of higher education to hundreds of students from Asia and the Pacific (especially from Malaya and Singapore). During the Gough Whitlam premiership the full severity of the White Australia policy was relaxed, but only in favour of special cases, more particularly individuals from Fiji and Polynesia.

A 'White Canada' policy had never been so explicitly enunciated, though equally rigorously enforced from the days of the Komagata Maru incident (1914) onward. The mainly Sikh community of British Columbia was denied equal civic rights and was unable to bring relatives into Canada. The independence of India in 1947 coincided with the emergence of a new spirit in the Canadian Liberal Party, symbolised by the appointment of Lester Pearson to the portfolio of External Affairs in the government of Louis Sant Laurent. The 6000 Canadians of 'East Indian' origin now obtained full civic rights, while sizeable numbers came from Asia to study, though not yet to settle. The first major change came with amendments to the immigration rules in 1962 which lifted the embargo on entry from all countries outside Europe and the United States. The situation was further transformed in 1967 when Canada scrapped all existing regulations in favour of a points system. This linked immigration closely to manpower requirements: admission was regulated by Canada's need for certain kinds of skill. In the late 1960s, the Canadian economy was entering a period of expansion, while in the sphere of education and public welfare Canada was moving to catch up with the United States. Canada needed doctors, architects, engineers, accountants, schoolteachers and college professors. If Asia could provide qualified people they were freely admitted.

Even in moments of crisis, the Canadians operated their system skilfully and gainfully. When Idi Amin announced that the entire Asian community must get out of Uganda, Canada sent recruiters to Kampala. They screened the applicants and picked the best: notably, the followers of the Aga Khan, the Ismailis, with their financial and commercial skills and their substantial resources. Britain reluctantly and belatedly accepted most of the remaining Uganda Asians, including many who were elderly, unfamiliar with English, and commanded no skill except that of the petty trader.

The Asian newcomers in Canada were predominantly professional people. Large numbers also arrived from the former British West Indies and from former British Guiana. Some of these brought professional skills; many were prepared to enter Canada's service sector as menial workers in hospitals, hotels and schools: a sector from which native Canadians, responding to wider opportunities, were moving out fast. If Australia was the Mecca of the white European migrant in the 1960s and 1970s, Canada was the promised land for enterprising people who were brown or black.

While one door was opening for non-white migrants in North America, others were closing in Africa. Asian emigration to South Africa was terminated before the First World War. On one side, the Government of India banned all emigration under indenture – the system of bondage whereby the sugar planters of Natal had recruited a helot labour force. On the other side, the Government of the Union of South Africa prohibited the entry of any person from India. This included all relatives or fiancées of Indians domiciled in South Africa, and also affected any South African Indian who left the country for all but a brief period. However, with South Africa closed, Indians were still able to enter East Africa. Many did so before and immediately after the Second World War.

When postwar emigration from Britain was resumed, some joined the white settler community in Kenya (indeed, government assistance was available to help them). The total white population of Kenya in the late 1950s was double its pre-1939 size, but was only about one-quarter the Asian total.[7] The whites controlled the colonial legislature. They did not perceive the Africans (only just 'emerging from barbarism') as a threat, but they were frightened of the Asians. They attempted to enforce severe restrictions upon Indian immigration, planning to bring in workers from Southern Europe to provide the basic technical skills which they had so far to obtain from the *fundi* (Swahili term for artisan). Indian ingenuity largely overcame the barrier erected by the white settlers; but white attempts at exclusion were soon overtaken by black protection of the Sons of the Soil as the East African territories moved with unexpected celerity into independence (1961: Tanganyika, 1962: Uganda, 1963: Kenya). The new regulations effectively closed Indian immigration and also severely restricted the business and other activities of all those Asians who did not immediately acquire the citizenship of the new states.[8]

As the 1960s went on, and ever more colonial territories acquired independence, those doors which were not already shut were now slammed tight. Throughout the Commonwealth, most countries recognised the passports of fellow-members for the purpose of tourist entry, but soon none allowed in the would-be resident without preliminary documentation. Most countries required the production of a work-permit (only issued in exceptional circumstances) from all but the short-stay visitor. In the Caribbean, movement from one island to another is limited to the tourist or the seasonal worker required to harvest the sugarcane crop, although Guyana does encourage immigration by blacks (Afros) because the Burnham government hopes to correct the imbalance between the East Indian majority and the black minority. Malaysia and Sri Lanka (Ceylon) whose doors had been open before the 1930s, and whose plantation economies had gained so much from immigrant labour, now imposed total restrictions on entry from India of an almost South African severity. India and Pakistan even went to the extreme limit of mutual exclusiveness in requiring visas before allowing entry of the other's citizens (India also required a visa for entry from Sri Lanka). Among these new barriers against the entry of fellow members of the Commonwealth, none were so resented as the restrictions imposed by Britain from 1962 onward.

The process whereby Britain changed from being a society of emigration into one of immigration was totally unexpected to the native British. Whereas the ethos or ideology of the United States (and also Canada and Australia) is to regard immigration as an essential element in national development

> Give me your tired, your poor,
> Your huddled masses, yearning to breathe free –

British ideology, if it were ever expressed in poetry, would echo the words of Kipling:

> Winds of the World give answer!
> They are whimpering too and fro –
> And what should they know of England
> Who only England know?[9]

Britishers move outward: other folk do not move inward. Yet the 1948 Act recognised the right of all Commonwealth citizens to enter freely, and in the 1950s and early 1960s the British economy was short of labour. The brief British boom was based upon high wages in the new industries (cars, aircraft, electronics) and low wages in older sectors (textiles, iron and steel, public transport). The native British were moving out of the old into the new industries. Manpower for the old woollen mills and iron foundries as well as for the buses and the railways and also for the swiftly expanding health services and hospitals was desperately short. The need was filled from the poor (non-white) Commonwealth. Some of the newcomers came without prior induce-ment: Sikhs, who had already found their way to East Africa, Malaya, Hong Kong, and a score of other territories, now came to Britain, to London and the Midlands. Pakistanis from the North-West Frontier, accustomed to visiting British ports as sailors, entered the West Riding textile industry. But some arrived in response to recruiting campaigns launched from Britain. London Transport kept its buses moving and opened up new underground lines by a massive recruiting campaign in Barbados and other Caribbean islands. The Health Service found much-needed hospital nurses among educated West Indian girls, and others from Hong Kong. Mental health nursing (the 'Cinderella' of the service) drew almost all its new recruits from Mauritius.

The influx of black and brown people was viewed with alarm by the native British of all classes. The 'open door' into the motherland, of which so many had been proud, was first wedged ajar and then closed almost absolutely. Legislation between 1962 and 1971 made it difficult even to enter as a declared tourist or student. Britain's accession to the EEC produced a remarkable situation at British airports where those arriving for disembarkation see two sets of signs: 'British and EEC Passports' (the easy way) and 'Commonwealth and Foreign Passports', signifying a tough time ahead. British immigration legislation had unexpected consequences. Before the introduction of controls, many of the new 'immigrants' were in reality transients. Their purpose was to work hard for a few years, save as much as possible, and return to their homes as 'big men'. The controls made that impossible. The newcomers sent for wives and children; more children were born in Britain; transients had become settlers.

The 1971 Act attempted to bring Britain into line with Western Europe where manpower shortages had been met by encouraging short-stay workers, the so-called 'guest workers'.[10] The process of acquiring UK citizenship was made tougher, the penalties against illegal entry and residence were increased, and the number of offences and misfortunes (e.g. mental illness) rendering someone liable to expulsion were intensified. The immigration controls were not really directed against white Commonwealth members at all, but they also applied to them and created strong resentment in Australia, New Zealand and Canada. The 'grandfather' clause in the 1971 Act relaxed the severity of the controls: any person, one of whose grandparents had been born in the British Isles (including the Republic of Ireland) was deemed to be *patrial* and to possess a 'right of abode'. This provision, however, only made the racist basis of British attitudes more sharply obvious.[11]

As British controls were intensified on lines intended to exclude non-whites, their severity was almost totally relaxed in respect of certain categories of non-white. Any person able to show a bank balance of a certain size (£30 000 at one time) had a free right of entry. Also, professional people with skills in short supply could enter, on the lines of the Canadian system. During the 1950s and early 1960s there was a steady emigration of highly qualified British people – aircraft designers, film producers, production managers, even university professors – to the United States. The largest group were British medical men, often departing immediately after qualifying, in response to the insatiable American demand for medicine. This 'brain drain' was a frequent subject of editorials in the quality newspapers. It was not so frequently observed that the shortages so created were being made up by Britain imposing a brain drain upon India, Pakistan and other Third World countries.

It has to be accepted that India and Pakistan, especially, have overproduced doctors, economists, and even engineers in terms of what their impoverished economies can sustain. The opportunities for an Indian doctor in the rural areas are exiguous. Hence, a form of 'circulation of élites has seemed almost inevitable, in which the most highly qualified Indians end up in the United States (like Nobel prize-winner Dr Gobind Khorana), and the next-highest come to Britain.[12] However, even this avenue into Britain may soon be closed. In 1980, with the increased training of medical students in Britain in the 1970s, there were for the first time more doctors than posts available. For several years, overseas doctors had been compelled to accept the least prestigious positions in the least desirable areas. In 1980, it appeared that there were no posts of any kind available to Indians and Pakistanis, even to those qualified in Britain. The British Medical Association has tightened up on overseas entry by introducing English language tests and other regulations designed to make entry into the profession difficult. The 'circulation of élites' seems finished, so far as overseas Commonwealth professionals are concerned.

As immigration into Britain comes to a halt,[13] so emigration – the traditional safety-valve in times when the British economy comes under strain – is no longer readily available. Australians have always regarded the Pommies as their best 'new chums': but no longer. From the 1970s onward, British immigrants began to acquire an unenviable reputation for being work-shy and for intensifying the troubles in Australia's strike-torn industries. The Whitlam Labour government abolished the special privileges: from 1974 all persons arriving from the United Kingdom were required to produce visas; the days of free entry were over. By 1977 immigrants from the British Isles formed less than 18 per cent of new entrants.

Canada also began to close its doors to British immigrants (and to other immigrants). The Canadian economy had been buoyant during the 1960s and early 1970s, and the long-standing problem of the continual 'seepage' of Canadian talent south of the border ceased (it may be recalled that the economist, John Galbraith, and the strategist, Zbigniew Brzezinski, are only two of Canada's more notable exports to the United States). Indeed, during the later stages of the Vietnam war, Canada took in thousands of protesters from the United States. However, the Canadian capacity to absorb new arrivals began to contract in the late 1970s. The world recession hit Canada like the other industrialised countries and the programme of active immigration was drastically cut. Problems were piling up. Many students and short-stay visitors were failing to leave on time. The Canadian regulations were so liberal that almost all those who stayed on unlawfully could expect to oppose extradition successfully (at the expense of the Canadian taxpayer). Resentment against non-white immigrants was assuming unpleasant forms. Toronto, a city which had become cosmopolitan through the many avenues of immigration, saw nasty scenes of violence, particularly directed against the immigrant Pakistanis. 'Paki-bashing', it was said, was fomented by settlers from Britain; but the evidence suggested that native Canadians were every bit as racist as immigrants from the United Kingdom.

As the economy flagged, so the need for skills dwindled. Total immigration shrank, but the Liberal philosophy insisted that those who had been permitted to enter should be allowed to sponsor their own relatives for entry. Because there were many more recent immigrants from South Asia, the Caribbean and Guyana than from Britain, sponsorship meant that the available permits went increasingly to these countries and only a limited number was available to the British. In 1976, out of a total immigration of 149 429 there were 21 548 from the United Kingdom. (In 1966 the UK share of a total of 194 793 new arrivals was 63 291.)

Paradoxically, there remained one opening for the would-be British emigrant: a country which historically played an important role in the Empire story, but which had severed all links with the Commonwealth in 1960: South Africa. The South African economy continued to prosper while others were languishing. Gold, diamonds and other scarce minerals benefited from a steady (sometimes dramatic) rise in world prices. South Africa's industries were increasingly diversified. South African apartheid ideology required that whenever an industry expanded, all but the basic, unskilled jobs must be filled by whites, though there were not enough native South African whites to go round. 'Dilution' was one solution: upgrading blacks and coloureds without explicitly acknowledging that they had been given skilled jobs. But the preferred solution was to bring in white workers from outside. Hence, the redundant British worker from a shipyard or a steel mill or a textile factory could move to South Africa, confident that he would be engaged as a supervisor or charge-hand and automatically become a member of the privileged middle class. These British settlers helped to reinforce the beleaguered English-speaking minority (a minority which still continued to dominate business and industry) so everyone was happy – except the Africans. The worries about the possible threat to white hegemony which surfaced with the Soweto riots led to a temporary falling-off of immigration from Britain, but the appalling effects of monetarist policy on the British economy from 1980 onward seem likely to stimulate British working-class (and maybe professional) emigration to South Africa to new heights: so long as that inherently unstable situation continues to preserve the appearance of stability.[14]

Migration, then, has ceased to be a major element in the continuing evolution of the Commonwealth. But it remains a major factor in the politics of intra-Commonwealth relations. From time to time the Commonwealth Secretariat has tried to obtain information on the actual scale of the continuing migration and also upon the norms which the various member countries apply in their migration policies. Each time, the Secretariat gets a frosty reception from virtually every member country and is compelled to abandon any attempt to rationalise intra-Commonwealth policies. Even information-gathering is frowned upon. Migration never features upon any conference agenda; it is too combustible for sober consideration. Nevertheless, grievances about the practices of individual countries – above all, those of the United Kingdom – are very much part of the emotional undercurrent which shapes Commonwealth relations. Resentment of British immigration practices – especially the infamous virginity tests – has soured India's relations with the UK. It seems as though the application of an overt, explicit policy of exclusion on racial lines – such as the White Australia policy – is resented less than an assurance of liberal, non-racial immigration intentions when these are merely the cloak for racially-motivated exclusion. Britain, in some sense still the 'mother country', is the most vulnerable to this diffuse emotional resentment. Nevertheless, almost all the other members have reasons for avoiding discussion of their policies and attitudes so that overall a 'softly softly' tone pervades the whole subject of migration.

Must we, therefore, accept that there can be no Commonwealth response to this question in which all, by a common history, are so closely involved? As regards the larger countries, we may have to accept what are now regarded as the realities. For India, Bangladesh, Nigeria, or other large entities, emigration is not really important as a solution to any of their problems. Other strategies, such as freer trade or better commodity agreements offer much greater advantages. For the small territories, the so-called mini-states and micro-states, emigration is essential for survival. When Britian first introduced controls on Commonwealth settlement, this was recognised by the fixing of a special annual quota for immigration from Malta. For the small states of the Caribbean (such as Barbados), for Mauritius, and for the newly-independent island-states of the Pacific, outlets are vital for their more enterprising citizens. The mini-states of Southern Africa – Lesotho, Botswana, Swaziland – all exist as clients of South Africa, dependent on the temporary export of their labour. Their problems also deserve to be considered within a wider Commonwealth context. It should not be beyond even the limited amount of Commonwealth agreement on this subject to produce a measure of combined support for the admission of emigrants from the small islands and territories into the larger, more affluent Commonwealth countries.[15]

If it is necessary to acknowledge that the era of Commonwealth migration is virtually finished, we still might find mutual benefit in exploring on more positive lines the implications of living in a plural society. Although this term is employed with glib frequency, very few public persons or social scientists have actually defined what they mean. The plural society can mean a more or less benign form of apartheid, in which the different cultures and religions of monorities are fostered in separate schools, with separate examination systems; illness is treated in separate clinics and hospitals where the languages and dietary and other needs of a minority can be catered for; separate housing areas can be provided by public authorities for different communities; and perhaps separate representation is accorded to the minorities in the legislature. This would be one extreme. The other would accord with what prevails at present in Britain, where freedom of worship is acknowledged, the state schools make some limited provision for minority religions and cultures, and the law lays down a code of practice concerning employment, accommodation, and other areas of discrimination which can (theoretically) be policed and enforced by specialist agencies or the judiciary.

If we survey the situation in different parts of the Commonwealth we find that the treatment of minorities follows the 'minimum' standard of Britain rather than the 'maximum' application of 'separate development' policies. Only in Canada is an attempt made to provide equal, and separate status for the French-speaking minority; many Commonwealth countries fall far short of United Kingdom standards. Malaysia has reinforced the privileges which the independence constitution gave to the Malay Muslims by subsequent legislation which makes it an offence to question these privileges. India, with a liberal constitution, in actual practice treats certain minorities – Muslims, Christians, the Animists – as second-class citizens. The founding of a toothless Commission for the Minorities has only drawn attention to their underprivileged status. The helpless plight of the aboriginal people of Australia has not as yet been ameliorated by their newly-found enhanced political consciousness. Given these realities, it seems unlikely that any broad Commonwealth initiative towards defining and giving dignity to minorities in a plural society will happen.

Perhaps Britain as the 'mother country' (albeit a mother who excludes her children from the home) can play some part in adopting a more positive attitude to minorities in a plural society. Parliament and the political parties have proved largely negative in their approach: their role confined mainly to going along, reluctantly or actively, with the racism endemic in British society. Thus far, Britain has moved cautiously in bringing the law into the area of race. Most British judges and lawyers take a passive view of their role. Their job is to uphold the status quo; it is not to become involved in social or political reform. This is in striking contrast to the United States where the 'crusading lawyer' is to be found almost everywhere, and if the politicians lack nerve, then the Supreme Court may take the initiative. One leading British judge, Lord

Scarman, sees the same answer as relevant in Britain through a legally enforceable Bill of Rights.[16] Possibly this is a development which might have a wider Commonwealth application.

Even in those member countries where parliament has been dissolved, and open politics denied, the courts still continue to try to uphold the rule of law. They cannot oppose a naked tyranny, such as that of Amin in Uganda, but they can require the executive to pause and reconsider in circumstances less extreme. If it were considered appropriate to bring in a Bill of Rights in Britain, this should be done without regard for any spin-off effect. Yet gradually this might come: after all, most (though not all) Commonwealth countries have subscribed to the United Nations Declaration on Human Rights.

Meanwhile, we shall all have to live with the consequences of the migration so massively encouraged within the Empire and Commonwealth in the past. Those consequences will not go away, however much some politicians may suggest that they might be made to do so. The challenge to be more humane, more tolerant, more enlightened, more generous is so urgent that surely some must take heed?

NOTES AND REFERENCES

1. *Migration within the British Commonwealth*, Cmd. 6658 (London, 1945).
2. V. I. Lenin, *Imperialism* (Petrograd, 1917; English edn, London: Lawrence & Wishart, 1933).
3. See the present author's *Separate and Unequal: India and the Indians in the British Commonwealth, 1920–1950* (London: C. Hurst, 1976) especially pp. 115 and 125.
4. Speaking to the India and Burma Committee of the Cabinet, 1 July 1947.
5. These questions are considered at length in *Separate and Unequal*, chapter 10.
6. The ban affected any black or brown Britisher applying at Australia House, London.
7. The population of the capital, Nairobi, was about 10 per cent white, 30 per cent Indian and 60 per cent African in the 1950s. Of the land within municipal limits, 2700 acres out of a total 6400 acres was specifically reserved for white occupation.
8. For a full account of this process, see the present author's *The Banyan Tree; overseas emigrants from India, Pakistan, and Bangladesh* (London: Oxford University Press, 1977) especially chapters 4 and 5.
9. Rudyard Kipling, *The English Flag*. Perhaps British sentiment is even more directly expressed in the famous:

> East is East and West is West,
> And never the twain shall meet.

10. The irony of the term *Gastarbeiter* is accentuated when it is recalled that this same term was applied to the slave labour which the Nazis conscripted from their conquered territories.

11. In the Committee stage of the 1971 Bill the 'Grandfather' clause was deleted by the unexpected combination of Enoch Powell (in the belief that it would let in thousands of Eurasians and others of mixed blood) and progressive Tories and Liberals who saw the clause as racist. The clause was restored at the Third Reading. Under this clause, white Rhodesians were able freely to enter Britain although the Smith regime was regarded as illegal. They just went to Pretoria, displayed a birth certificate of a forebear, and obtained a passport from the British consulate.

12. A special study of the role of the 'East Indian' professional man in the USA has been made by Manindra Kumar Mohapatra. One survey showed that of his respondents 26 per cent were academics, 17 per cent engineers, and 21 per cent medical men. Over 63 per cent were home-owners. Over half had incomes of over $25 000 per annum in 1976. See his *Orientations of Overseas Indians Toward Discrimination in American Society*, 1977 (available in a photocopy in the library of Old Dominion University, Virginia, USA).

13. There may be one last sudden influx into Britain if the tenuous balance in Zimbabwe between the wealthy white minority and the impoverished black majority is overturned. Most of the white minority can claim entry into Britain as patrials. It seems more likely that most of them will choose to settle in South Africa, which is where most of the present stream of white departures are heading.

14. In 1975, out of the total of 50 337 whites entering South Africa, immigrants from UK numbered 25 387 (50.3 per cent). In the next three years, total numbers fell to one-third of the 1975 total and British immigrants (1978) numbered only 3672 (19.8 per cent of the total). By this time, the largest numbers of whites entering South Africa were from Rhodesia (Zimbabwe) and Mozambique.

15. As one Barbadian leader wryly observed to the present writer: 'Why not some discrimination in discrimination?'

16. Lord Scarman, *Minority Rights in a Plural Society* (London: Minority Rights Group, 1977).

16 The Existing Dependencies

L. S. TRACHTENBERG

As regards the self-governing colonies, we no longer talk of them as dependencies. The sense of possession has given way to the sentiment of kinship. We think and speak of them as part of ourselves, as part of the British Empire, united to us although they may be dispersed throughout the world, by ties of kindred, religion, history, and of language, joined together by the sea that formerly seemed to divide us.

(Joseph Chamberlain, Secretary of State for the Colonies, 31 March 1897)

Eighty-five years later, things have come to be viewed differently from Chamberlain's day and now we speak no longer of colonies but instead of dependent territories and associated states. But whatever the name, these actors are still a corporate part of the true spirit of kinship to which Chamberlain referred, a spirit which is today embodied in the Commonwealth. Along with the name by which we refer to these territorial actors, much has changed and evolved since 1897, but this basic spirit of fraternity which created the Commonwealth is as alive today as ever. These territories are no longer referred to as 'ours' and if anything the Commonwealth spirit has done a great deal to perpetuate itself through the rapid dismantling of Britain's colonial possessions and the creation of the contemporary Commonwealth. But is the burgeoning membership of the Commonwealth in the best interests of the remaining dependencies?[1]

Britain's colonial history can be taken as starting with the establishment of the Virginia colony, its first permanent settlement, in 1607. During the remainder of the seventeenth century, new colonies were created and proliferated throughout the eastern portion of North

America and in parts of the West Indies. Trading posts were also established in India, and to a lesser extent in Africa. Into the eighteenth century Britain found itself in conflict with France over many of these possessions and this ultimately led to the British conquest and retention of Canada, along with the securing of a controlling portion of the Indian sub-continent. Following closely on the heels of these commanding victories, however, came the loss of the thirteen American colonies. Lessons were learned from the American War of Independence when in 1839, a report on the causes of discontent and civil disobedience in the Canadian colonies was published. This report affirmed that the principles of 'responsible government' were appropriate in Canada as well as in those larger colonies where significant European settlement had taken place, for example, Australia, New Zealand and South Africa. A new distinction arose between those 'colonies of settlement' and all the other colonial possessions, found almost entirely in the tropical regions. The colonies of settlement had effectively achieved independence by the beginning of the First World War and this was to be formalised in the Statute of Westminster in 1931, while the remaining colonies were gradually evolving from their original roles as trading and/or military settlements. These latter could be divided into two different categories, protectorates and crown colonies, with the distinction relating to the law by which the British established authority, rather than to any particular form of government. Each territory was looked at individually and the degree to which authority was delegated from governor down to the local level was based on the circumstances extant at the time.

By 1917, the principle of preparing dependent territories for self-government was accepted with respect to India, and during the 1920s and 1930s, advances in political development were made in a number of other possessions as well as in India. By the Second World War, this pace of development had been greatly accelerated. Colonel Oliver Stanley, Secretary of State for the Colonies, noted in a speech to the House of Commons on 13 July 1943 that:

... the central purpose of our colonial administration has often been proclaimed. It has been called the doctrine of trusteeship ... We are pledged to guide colonial people along the road to self-government within the framework of the British Empire. We are pledged to build up their social and economic institutions, and we are pledged to develop their natural resources.

In 1947 India, Pakistan, Burma and Ceylon, in the first realisation of this policy, were granted independence, and with the independence of Ghana in 1957 this policy was extended from Asia to Africa and other parts of the globe. As one observer has lightly noted, 'After 1947, with considerable *sang-froid* the governors (of the colonies) set about liquidating their powers – imprisoning the revolutionaries one moment, making them prime ministers the next, and then retiring to the English countryside.[2]

The movement gathered momentum following Ghana's independence, and by the end of the 1960s most of the African colonies (by now referred to as dependencies) had gained independence, as had many territories in Asia and the Caribbean. This policy was extended to the Pacific in the 1970s, and by 1982 only a handful of economically unviable micro-territories belonging to Britain, Australia and New Zealand remained in that region.

In the Caribbean region during the 1960s some of the smaller dependent territories, the Leeward and Windward Islands, felt that they were unable to cope with the problems of full independence and to meet this special need, associated statehood was created.[3] This was a constitutional status amounting to slightly less than independence and it gave each territory full responsibility for its own internal affairs, while Britain remained responsible for defence and external affairs. This new status was put into effect in Antigua, Dominica, Grenada, St Christopher-Nevis-Anguilla, St Lucia, and St Vincent (Montserrat, also in this island grouping, retained crown colony status by choice).

Associated statehood is a completely voluntary status and is terminable by either party at any time. These territories can choose independence without further recourse to the British parliament, on the condition that legislation to this effect receives two-thirds of the vote in a popular referendum and the approval of two-thirds of the elected members of the local legislature. This association can also be terminated by British legislation in the form of an Order in Council, a procedure which has been followed at the request of all five associated states which have become independent: Grenada in 1974, Dominica in 1978, St Lucia and St Vincent in 1979 and Antigua and Barbuda in 1981. The British Government will only use this method of granting independence when it is satisfied that the majority of the population in a territory desires independence and that a proper constitution has been drafted and accepted. Today, only the associated state of St Kitts-Nevis remains and it is likely that it, too, will shortly seek its independence, though perhaps as two separate territories.[4]

THE POLICY ON THE GRANTING OF INDEPENDENCE

The British government has maintained the policy for several years that it is not their intention to delay independence for those who want it, nor to impose independence on those who do not. The government's guiding principle has basically been the desires of the peoples concerned. In many instances, though a goal of independence has been declared the actual timing of the vital decision has been left to the people of the territory concerned and their elected leaders.

The fundamental policy attitude of the United Nations is embodied in General Assembly Resolution 1514 of 14 December 1960, entitled 'Declaration on the Granting of Independence to Colonial Countries and Peoples'. This Declaration states that the subjection of peoples to subjugation, domination and exploitation constitutes a denial of fundamental human rights, is contrary to the Charter and is an impediment to the promotion of world peace and co-operation; and that

> immediate steps shall be taken, in ... all territories which have not yet attained independence, to transfer all powers to the peoples of those territories, without any conditions or reservations, in accordance with their freely expressed will and desire, without any distinction as to race, creed or colour in order to enable them to enjoy complete independence and freedom.[5]

The United Nations General Assembly's Special Committee of 25 (originally the Special Committee of 17 in 1961) is the main watchdog of this policy and examines on a regular basis the application of Resolution 1514, as well as makes specific recommendations to assist the implementation of the Declaration. Most recently it has been examining the role of foreign economic and other interests operating in dependent territories which may present a major obstacle to political independence. All of the UN efforts in this field find their roots in the Charter, which asserts the principle of 'equal rights and self determination' in Article 1, as well as three specific chapters – 11, 12 and 13 – all devoted to the interests of dependent people. But it was not until Resolution 1514, that the UN actually took a firm stand on the granting of independence.

The activities of the special committee created a climate of opinion in many dependent territories that, despite their size, it was desirable to achieve independence within a new state. The territorial size of a new unit became irrelevant to independence at this point and Resolution 1514 notes that the inadequacy of political, economic, social or educational preparedness should never serve as a pretext for the delay or denial of independence. As one commentator notes with regard to the Caribbean, 'with Jamaica's lead, Trinidad soon followed. It was not so much a case of Trinidad's "size" being seen as having increased as Trinidad's perceptions that the concept of the size required for an independent nation had altered.'[6] As significantly, it has also been stated that, 'no political change of our time is more striking than the erosion of the criteria essential to self government'.[7]

It should also be noted that, until the 1960 Declaration, the United Nations was relatively uninvolved in the 'Commonwealth decolonisation process'. As T. B. Millar has pointed out, the UN was not involved in the decolonisation of India, Pakistan, Ceylon and Burma, and it exerted only a minimal influence on British Somaliland.[8] In the case of Cyprus there would seem to be little evidence of UN involvement regarding independence, and in the cases of Ghana, Malaya, Nigeria, Sierra Leone, Jamaica, Trinidad and Tobago, Uganda and Malta, the UN was uninvolved in the independence process, though many of these states were associated with some of the specialised agencies prior to independence. It is only since Resolution 1514, with the creation of the special committee, that the UN has adopted a more 'aggressive' role.

The Commonwealth policy on the granting of independence is embodied in the *Declaration of Commonwealth Principles*, drafted in 1971. This states that

we oppose all forms of colonial domination and racial oppression and are committed to the principles of human dignity and equality. We will therefore use all our efforts to foster human equality and dignity everywhere, and to further the principles of self-determination and non-racialism.

This policy has been reaffirmed on numerous occasions, most recently at the Commonwealth Heads of Government Meeting in October 1981 where, in the 'Melbourne Communiqué', it is noted in paragraph 7 that 'Heads of Government asserted the right of all peoples freely to determine their destiny' and 'they recognised an obligation to work for conditions more conducive to respect for sovereignty, independence, territorial integrity and the right to self-determination'. This is a policy based, no doubt, on the fact that all Commonwealth countries except Britain have been colonies, as well as commonsense. Compared to the current UN stand, the Commonwealth policy would seem to be a rather 'limp-wristed' one for what is so clearly a shared experience. But as will be seen, much of the Commonwealth policy on this and related issues tends to be rather insubstantial, at best, unclear.[9] Much of this has to do with the fear of offending the British Foreign and Commonwealth Office (the main body with which the commonwealth Secretariat would have to contend vis-a-vis dependent territories and independence issues) as well as an apparent lack of clarity in FCO policy when it actually comes to taking action on a particular independence issue. Before proceeding to an examination of the role the Commonwealth plays in existing dependent territories, the development of membership criteria in the Commonwealth and the existing dependent territories themselves will be examined.

Following the Second World War, responsibility for membership in the Commonwealth fell on the Colonial Office, which evolved into the Commonwealth Relations Office and eventually, following some internal mergers, into the FCO. By the 1950s, though, it became established, with the membership of Republican India in 1949, that a constitutional monarchy was not a prerequisite for remaining a member, the recognition of the British monarch as head of the Commonwealth and as a symbol of the free association of its members remained a necessity for members even though for the majority the monarch was not head of state.

There was a gap of some eight years before the admission of Ghana and Malaya in 1957. During this time the older, original members had come to terms with the presence of India, Pakistan and Ceylon and were almost looking forward to the eventual admission of the Africans. With the obvious exception of Britain, all members in 1957 had been former dependencies and it was never assumed that all dependencies would automatically become members upon attaining independence any more than independence was a certain future for all or even most of the dependencies.

The prospect for the Commonwealth of a significant increase in the numbers of British colonies gaining independence stimulated a degree of discussion during the 1950s. At first, especially in 1954, when it appeared that South Africa might attempt to block the admission of newly-independent African states it appears that discussions were held on the idea of a two-tier Commonwealth of senior and junior members.[10] This system was envisioned as a core of close-knit members surrounded by a number of others which, while having the same formal status, would not be involved in the close co-operation of those at the core. The idea lapsed when South Africa's attitude changed towards the membership of black states, though this idea was again put forward in 1965 as a possible means of dealing with the then perceived problem of British colonies which, while anxious to acquire self government, were not large enough to become sovereign states.[11]

As far as membership was concerned in the 1960s there was no change in principle, merely great changes in numbers and in relations between members. The recognition that large numbers of colonies wanting to seek independence might overcrowd the Commonwealth caused Commonwealth Heads of Government Meeting in 1960 to agree a 'detailed study' of the constitutional development of the Commonwealth, with particular reference to the future of the smaller dependent territories. It would appear that this question was also studied at the official level but no further mention of it was made in communiqués from Heads of Government Meetings. Instead, colonies continued to seek and gain membership as they became independent until, in the beginning of the 1970s, Tonga with a population of less than 90 000 was accepted. Nauru, with a population of about 6000 became a 'special member' in 1969.[12] The need for a special status for Nauru was recognised as early as 1967 by the island's leadership, and together with Arnold Smith and the Commonwealth Secretariat, they developed the new category of 'special member'.

The larger and older members decided not to bar the way for such small fellow members, although at an earlier stage the organisation was unwilling to accept the New Zealand dependency of Western Samoa, which became independent in 1962. In due course, and with the acceptance of Nauru in 1968, and Tonga and Fiji in 1970, Western Samoa was eventually accepted for full membership in 1970. The six West Indian associated states, autonomous, though still British dependencies, were permitted access to Commonwealth functional meetings, but like the 'special members' these states did not attend CHOGMs.

The main effects of this increase in numbers has been on the conduct and concerns of Commonwealth meetings and on the Commonwealth Secretariat, a body which was and still is rather more favoured by the smaller members than some of the older, larger members. In all Commonwealth meetings, like the United Nations General Assembly, the members, no matter how small they are, are 'equal in status' both by tradition and as universally recognised sovereign states.

It is important to note that the Commonwealth has not been a magnet for all of Britain's former possessions, nor have all of its members stayed with the organisation. In 1947, Burma became independent outside of the Commonwealth, followed by Israel (Palestine) in 1948, while in 1949 the Ireland Act recognised Eire as a republic outside of the Commonwealth. This was followed by the Sudan in 1956; the Somali Republic in 1960 (made up of British Somaliland and the United Nations Trust Territory of Italian Somaliland); the Federal Republic of Cameroon (formerly the dependency of South Cameroon and the neighbouring French Cameroon) in 1961; and the Maldive Islands in 1965. The Peoples Democratic Republic of South Yemen (including Aden), then part of the South Arabian Federation, became independent outside the Commonwealth in 1967 (though prior to independence Aden had approached the organization for consideration as a member).[13] Other former protectorates which never applied for membership include Kuwait and the United Arab Emirates. From an earlier age neither Iraq nor Transjordan, both British-administered League of Nations mandates, had any ties with the then British Commonwealth.

Two states are notable for having left the organisation following long periods of membership. When South Africa became a republic on 31 May 1961, she ceased to be a member of the Commonwealth, due primarily to the state's racial policies (discussed extensively at the Prime Ministers' Meeting in March 1961). Over ten years later, in January 1972, Pakistan withdrew from the Commonwealth after the recognition of Bangladesh by increasing numbers of Commonwealth members. The government had been saying for over two years, that it would 'quit the Commonwealth at the appropriate opportunity' and this was apparently considered to be the right time.

One side-note of interest, is the case of Mozambique, a state which has come closer to being integrated into the Commonwealth than any other non-ex-British colony. Arnold Smith was involved in the Mozambique peace negotiations from early 1979 and also offered to assist Portugal in setting up a 'Commonwealth type of system' for her ex-colonies. He was instrumental in seeing that Mozambique received considerable assistance from the Commonwealth (and the United Nations) while Mozambique supported the economic blockade of Rhodesia. No other state outside the Commonwealth has ever received this degree of assistance from the organisation but even without non-ex-colonies as members, the Commonwealth remains a large and complex organisation.[14]

THE EXISTING DEPENDENCIES AND THEIR FUTURE

There are currently forty-six Commonwealth members. The majority of existing dependencies and territories are likely to achieve independence at some point in the future since it is generally accepted that there can be no practical reason for denial of this status to any but a few territories under very special circumstances.

Britain in the early 1980s has one associated state and thirteen dependent territories under its control, though two of these dependencies, the British Antarctic Territories and the British Indian Ocean Territory have no permanent population and can be immediately dismissed as no more than a scientific station and a US/UK military facility respectively, with no independence prospects. The populated dependencies are Anguilla, Bermuda, The British Virgin Islands, The Cayman Islands, The Falkland Islands and Dependencies, Gibraltar, Hong Kong, Montserrat, The Pitcairn Islands, St Helena and Dependencies, and the Turks and Caicos Islands.

New Zealand possesses the self-governing territories of the Cook Islands and Niue both considered in a situation similar to the associated state of St Kitts-Nevis, as well as the non-self-governing territory of the Tokelau Islands and an uninhabited territory in the Antarctic region called the Ross Dependency.

Australia's external territories include seven different units, though four of these are not permanently inhabited (Coral Sea Island Territories, the Australian Antarctic Territory, Heard Island and MacDonald Islands, and the territory of Ashmore and Cartier Islands). The remaining three territories, Norfolk Island, Cocos (Keeling) Island and Christmas Island are all inhabited.

A brief survey of the populated territories should provide some assistance in helping to secure a picture of the dependencies in the late twentieth century. One must bear in mind when examining these potential states what one observer of the scene has noted, that we 'must mark with reverence the feeling of a people that they *are* a people however absurd their claims or definitions may seem to others'.[15]

The Associated State of St Kitts-Nevis (formerly St Christopher-Nevis-Anguilla)

Location: Northern part of the Leeward Group of the Lesser Antilles in the Eastern Caribbean

Size: Two islands, with a total land area of 101 square miles, separated by a channel two miles in width (St Kitts is approximately twice the size of Nevis)

Population: 50 000 (December 1980), with St Kitts having approximately 80 per cent of the population (St Kitts also
carries the distinction of being the first island in the West
Indies to be colonised by the English in 1623.)

On 27 February 1967, St Christopher-Nevis-Anguilla assumed the
status of association with Britain, under the West Indies Act of 1967.
This association was free and voluntary, and terminable by either side at
any time with the territory being fully self-governing in all of its internal
affairs. In 1967, the British had to send troops to the island to restore
order following strong feelings on the part of Anguillans that they were
being dominated by St Kitts. In 1969 following two referenda, in which
the people declared that they would not be ruled by St Kitts, Anguilla
fell under the temporary administration of a British commissioner, an
arrangement which ultimately ended in Anguilla becoming a separate
British dependency on 19 December 1980.

St Kitts-Nevis, as with Antigua, prior to its independence, has its
external and defence affairs run by the British government representative in Bridgetown, Barbados. It was anticipated that with the
formal separation of Anguilla, St Kitts-Nevis would proceed smoothly
to independence. Numerous obstacles to this smooth transition exist,
however, and the problem lies in a longstanding desire by Nevis to
secede from the association as did Anguilla. On the basis of the influence
of two very senior politicians, St Kitts had long been opposed to any
plan that further divided the future state. This intransigence ended in
1979 when both of these men died and the new leadership in St Kitts
adopted a more compromising attitude towards Nevis. An agreement
with the British government was reached in December 1979 under which
St Kitts and Nevis were to be granted independence as one unit in 1980.
Nevis, however, was to be permitted to hold a referendum within
eighteen months of the achievement of independence to determine the
secession issue.

In its first election defeat in twenty-seven years, the ruling St Kitts
Labour Party (SKLP) lost power only months before independence was
scheduled. The new coalition government of St Kitts Conservatives and
Nevis Reformists decided to focus efforts on the securing of national
unity and they subsequently postponed independence. Though this was
not the end of the seccession issue, the Nevisians were sharing power for
the first time and seemed content with the primary goal of developing the
economy of the two islands.

Late in 1981, however, it became apparent that the coalition government was encountering serious problems when the 'ideal' situation of the post-election period came to an end. A new call for seccession had been sounded by 'Nevisian nationalists' and it is quite probable that unless this rift is healed, it could eventually lead to a separate call for independence by St Kitts without Nevis.[16] In a territory which is already largely financed by external aid (primarily British) this division would only tend to make the long-term viability of St Kitts and Nevis as sovereign states increasingly suspect. But of all the territories currently queuing for independence, St Kitts-Nevis stands clearly, if shakily, at the front.

Anguilla

Location: The most northerly part of the Leeward Islands in the Eastern Caribbean

Size: A single island of 35 square miles

Population: 7000 (1980 estimate)

Anguilla separated by choice from St Kitts-Nevis in 1969, under the Anguilla (Temporary Provision) Order-in-Council and a commissioner was appointed to administer the island. In 1971, the British parliament passed the Anguilla Act and Britain assumed direct control of the island. On 10 February 1976, the Anguilla (Constitution) Order came into effect, giving a new status and a separate constitution to Anguilla though it remained formally part of the associated state of St Kitts-Nevis-Anguilla, until 19 December 1980 when, with the agreement of the associated state's government, it became a separate dependency. It is still administered under the 1976 Constitution with executive power invested in the Commissioner who is appointed by the Queen.

The small island territories of the Caribbean have always exhibited a great apprehension about being dominated by their larger, more powerful, island neighbours. As two observers of the area have succinctly noted,

Most of the former and present associated states comprise two or more islands whose links are forged less by ties of sentiment than by propinquity and Colonial Office administrative needs. But large islands will not undertake responsibility for financing the development of small partners, while small island misgivings over suzerainty and neglect have led to inter-island estrangement, even political fragmentation, and times of crucial constitutional change, as in the late 1960s when the associated states were created and the late 1970s as they became independent.[17]

The motive ascribed above, 'notably fear of dictation' caused Anguilla to seek separation from St Kitts-Nevis. The renewal of dependency status for Anguilla was 'just the outcome that Anguillans had sought all along' and any future independence is definitely ruled out.[18] This trend towards fragmentation has been on the increase among small island territories since the 1970s, especially in the Caribbean, and will be discussed in more detail below.

Three of Britain's dependent territories face special problems in the future, due primarily to the territorial claims of other states on these dependencies.

The Falkland Islands and Dependencies

Location: In the Southwest Atlantic 300 miles off the coast of Argentina

Size: Two large islands and numerous small ones covering an area of 4700 square miles (The dependencies, South Georgia and South Sandwich Island, have an area of 1580 square miles and no permanent population.)

Population: 1800 (1980)

The Islands' present constitution came into force in 1949, and the government has been administered by a governor since that time. At the centre of the life of all Falkland Islanders is a longstanding territorial claim by Argentina on the Islands, a dispute which came to a head on 2 April 1982 when Argentina invaded the Islands.

Over the past few years, the British and Argentinian governments have periodically discussed the future of the Falklands, including bringing the dispute before the United Nations in 1965 (where it remains on the agenda). Some minor agreements had been reached (i.e. in 1974 regarding the supply of petroleum products to the Islands by Argentina), but in 1981, these talks broke down following Britain's announcement that, in accordance with the wishes of the Islanders, the dispute was to be frozen. The new Argentinian government of General Leopoldo Galtieri rejected this proposal and noted that, unless Britain was willing to make significant concessions at bilateral talks scheduled in New York at the end of February 1982, Argentina was ready to consider military alternatives to solving the dispute.

Despite a joint statement issued in New York, that the talks had been 'cordial and positive',[19] the Foreign Ministry in Buenos Aires issued another statement at the same time that, unless a solution was quickly found to the problem, negotiations would end and Argentina would consider itself free to choose 'a procedure which better suits our interests'.[20] The sudden impatience of Argentina was a result of the suspected presence of oil off the coast of the Falklands – reserves estimated at 2.4 billion barrels – as well as increasing domestic unrest in Argentina. This unrest culminated in large-scale disturbances at the end of March and it is widely believed that this prompted the invasion on 2nd April, though it is clear from certain reports that such an invasion had been probable since the end of January.[21] It is also clear that while Britain often viewed the Falklands situation as a minor foreign policy problem, it has always been one of the major policy orientations of all Argentinian governments. Shortly after the invasion, the United Nations Security Council met and passed a resolution (502) calling on Argentina to withdraw and continue negotiations with Britain.

By 14 June, British troops had regained control of all the Islands and were holding over 9000 Argentines as prisoners of war, while two days later, on 16 June, General Menendez, Argentine Governor of the Islands, signed an act of surrender. Mrs Thatcher seemed quite unprepared to negotiate on the issue of sovereignty and her government was examining the different options for the future of the islands.

The first of these was large-scale economic development with the ultimate aim being the independence of the Islands, backed by a 'multinational security agreement'. This idea, while popular in Whitehall, was strongly rejected by United States' officials, who did not see the Islands as viable independent entities under any circumstances, and were proposing a 'multinational administration', to include members of the Islands population, but also probably representatives of Argentina. This latter point was unlikely to be popular among many members of the government or public, and its acceptance was doubtful.

Britain's only apparent option to an independent Falklands appeared to be 'Fortress Falklands', a maintenance of the status quo, backed by a large British garrison (6000 to 7000 strong). This option seemed to be the one most likely to gain immediate acceptance from the Government and its supporters, if for no other reason than the 'Fortress' is already largely established.

The government was also under growing pressure from the Opposition to consider other proposals: from the Labour Party, the idea of a United Nations Trusteeship for the Islands, and from the Liberal-SDP Alliance, the idea that the OAS should be used to persuade Argentina not to re-invade, thus allowing the United States to become involved in an OAS force on the Islands. Other ideas at this time included splitting the Islands and giving the West Falklands to Argentina and the East Falklands to Britain. This idea would allow Britain to retain that portion of the islands most heavily populated with Falklanders, and also perhaps go some way to solving the sticky question of sovereignty. There had been no mention of any Commonwealth involvement in mediation, and two obstacles existed to hinder any active participation.

First, most of the larger members of the Commonwealth had come out strongly in favour of 'economic measures' against Argentina and this would potentially damage the credibility of the organisation in a mediatory role. Further, along the same lines, the Commonwealth Secretariat had informally requested all members to support Britain in the dispute. But it is quite possible that, as Britain attempts to provide future security arrangements for the Islands, the Commonwealth could step in as a guarantor that Britain's interests were not 'colonial' in nature. This guarantee by the Commonwealth may make future arrangements easier for Britain to sell to both her allies and the international community as a whole.

The Islanders, almost exclusively of British birth or descent, have expressed a desire that any solution should include the preservation of British administration, law and way of life. The economy is 99 per cent based on exports resulting from the tenant farming of 650 000 sheep and not much else (the dispute has, over the years, caused numerous disruptions to the Island's already small economy). Unlike most of its other dependent brethren, the Falklands' viability as an independent state rests equally on the questions of security as well as of the more common concerns of internal economic standards. The recently published Shackleton Report calls for relatively large scale economic development, but such development would bring thousands of workers and new residents to the Islands, while 'Fortress Falklands' would mean thousands of military personnel. The fact is that, whatever choice is eventually made by the Islanders, and the British government, the Islanders will be quickly outnumbered. The Islands will change irrevocably, as will the Islanders' way of life. Regardless of the outcome of the crisis, the Islanders face many difficulties in a future which suggests that independence, though conceivable at this time, would be fraught with irresolution and very high human costs.

Hong Kong

Location: Lies off the southeast coast of China

Size: Hong Kong consists of the island of Hong Kong and a portion of the Chinese mainland to the north, together with 236 adjacent islands. These range from Lan Tau with an area of 54.7 square miles to a large number of uninhabited rock islets. The total area is approximately 409 square miles which includes 5.6 square miles reclaimed from the sea since 1945. Hong Kong has an area of approximately 30 square miles, while the New Territories account for over 375 square miles.

Population: 5.1 million (1980). 98 per cent of the population is Chinese (though 57 per cent is British by virtue of Hong Kong birth and the status of these people now comes under question with the new British Nationality Act)

Hong Kong has been a free port since 1842, when it was ceded in perpetuity to Britain by the Treaty of Nanjing. The area of neighbouring Kowloon, Stonecutters Island, Ap Lei Chau and Green Island were ceded by the Convention of Peking in 1860. The New Territories, which consist of the islands around Hong Kong and the rural area north of Kowloon, were leased to Britain for 99 years in the year 1898, the lease expiring in 1997. By the mid-1980s over 2.5 million people will live in the New Territories, which many see as an expression of confidence in the future as this land lies in the territory under lease from China. On the other hand, leases on all property in the New Territories are only being granted by the government for a period of 99 years, less the last three days, from 1 July 1898; in other words, in 1982, leases will only be granted for fifteen years, a clear expression of caution and, perhaps, doubt.

The status of Hong Kong will of course be clarified by 1997 and much will depend upon any number of political machinations which could unfold in the coming years. The Falklands crisis has little relevance here, as, if the Chinese 'chose to abrogate the treaties and pour across the borders that would be the end of Hong Kong and everyone has always known it'.[22] The People's Republic of China has, however, invested heavily in Hong Kong and over fifteen of the major banks in the territory are owned and operated by Peking. The most likely scenario to come about is a future Hong Kong which is a Chinese free trade zone under British management. But whatever government eventually wrests control of the territory, it is highly improbable that independence is included in Hong Kong's future.

Gibraltar

Location: Southwest Europe, occupying a narrow peninsula on the southern coast of Spain

Size: 2.25 square miles

Population: 29 787 (1980)

Gibraltar has a long and involved history dating back to 1160 and the founding of a city by Arabs on the Gibraltar peninsula. Gibraltar was ceded to Britain in 1730 under the Treaty of Utrecht and following the great siege of 1779–83, during which Britain successfully defended the peninsula against a combined Spanish and French assault, Britain has continued to remain peacefully in control. Though Spain had long contested British control of Gibraltar, it was not until 1964 that Spain acted by imposing severe restrictions on border-crossing movements at its frontier with Gibraltar.

In 1967, a referendum was held and 96 per cent of the electorate voted; 12 138 Gibraltarians voted to retain their link with Britain and 44 voters supported a change to Spanish sovereignty. In the summer of 1969 Spain closed its borders with Gibraltar entirely and discontinued the ferry service between Algeciras (a port west of Gibraltar in southwest Spain) and the peninsula. It also cut all public telephone and telegraph lines between Gibraltar and Spain.

At roughly the same time as this isolation was being imposed on Gibraltar by Spain, the peninsula received a new constitution which came into force on 11 August 1969. The preamble of this constitution stated that Britain will retain sovereignty over Gibraltar unless and until an act of parliament provides otherwise; and then it would never enter into arrangements whereby the people of Gibraltar would pass under the sovereignty of another state against their freely and democratically expressed wishes.

The situation created in 1969 lasted until mid-1977, when telephone links were again restored. The following year, Britain and Spain established their first official working groups on areas of mutual interest concerning Gibraltar. These ties continued to become closer, especially with Spain's attempts to gain full membership in the European Community and NATO. In late 1981 the Spanish Prime Minister announced plans to reopen the Gibraltar–Spanish border on 20 April 1982, though this and planned talks on the future of the peninsula were postponed pending the outcome of the Falklands crisis.

Despite the fact that Britain's longstanding dispute with Spain over Gibraltar's status appears to be showing signs of conciliation, the basic issue of sovereignty over the territory remains. The Falklands crisis will have an obvious impact on Gibraltar, and one can be certain that the future of the 'Rock' will appear much higher on the list of current British foreign policy priorities. Although the right wing in Spain has taken to referring to the Falklands as 'Argentina's Gibraltar', Spain is doubly constrained by its applications to both NATO and the EEC. With Britain able to block both of these applications at any point in the future, Spain is much more likely to attempt to resolve the Gibraltar situation peacefully rather than using the 'Argentinian method'.

Brunei

Located on the northwest coast of Borneo, Brunei, a former Malay State, is a country of 2226 square miles with a population in 1980 of 213 000. Britain has been responsible for the external affairs of Brunei, a sultanate since the mid-1800s. Following negotiations in June 1978 the Sultan and the British Government signed a new treaty in January 1979 under which Brunei will become fully sovereign and independent on 31 December 1983.

The remaining British dependencies are all rather small and at this time, there is no immediate prospect of any of these territories gaining their independence. They are however, briefly surveyed below.

Bermuda

Location: Western Atlantic Ocean

Size:	150 islands and islets, a total area of 20.95 square miles (the principal ten islands are connected by bridges). The United States Government leases 2.3 square miles for use as a military base

Population: 55 000 (1980)

The British Virgin Islands

Location: Lies 50 miles east of Puerto Rico and a part of the larger Virgin Islands group

Size: A group of 36 islands covering approximately 55 square miles

Population: 11 000 (1980)

The Cayman Islands

Location: Northwest of Jamaica in the West Indies

Size: Three islands with a total area of approximately 100 square miles

Population: 17 340 (1980)

Montserrat

Location: A part of the Leeward Islands Group in the Eastern Caribbean

Size: A single island of 39 square miles

Population: 12 100 (1980)

The Pitcairn Islands Group

Location: In the Pacific Ocean midway between Panama and New Zealand

Size: One main island (Pitcairn Island) with an area of 1.75 square miles and three small uninhabited islands

Population: 61 (1980). The Island was first colonised by the
                  descendents of the ten mutineers from HMS *Bounty* along
                  with six Tahitian men and twelve Tahitian women in 1790
                  and following several complete removals to other islands
                  for fear of over-population, the Pitcairns received official
                  recognition as a colony in 1877.

St Helena and Dependencies

Location: St Helena lies 2000 kilometres west of Angola in the South
                  Atlantic; Ascension Island lies 1100 kilometres to the
                  northwest of St Helena; Tristan da Cunha 2400 kil-
                  ometres to the southwest of St Helena.

Size: St Helena, the main island of the group, is 47 square miles;
                  Ascension is 34 square miles; Tristan da Cunha is 38
                  square miles (Tristan da Cunha also has three small
                  uninhabited neighbours which are also dependencies of St
                  Helena).

Population: St Helena: 5147 (1976); Ascension: 1022 (1980); Tristan
                  da Cunha: 323 (1980). St Helena was made a colony in
                  1834 but is more famous for having been Napoleon
                  Bonaparte's place of exile from 1815 until his death in
                  1821. Ascension Island has recently gained international
                  recognition as a crucial staging point for British naval and
                  air forces travelling to the Falkland Islands.

Turks and Caicos Islands

Location: In the southeast end of the Bahamas group

Size: The dependency is made up of two groups, the Turks,
                  consisting of two inhabited islands, six uninhabited quays
                  and large numbers of rocks, while the Caicos has six
                  principal islands. The total land area of this group is 193
                  square miles.

Population: 7500 (1980)

The Australian External Territories

There are seven territories under the control of Australia, though as noted earlier, four of these are uninhabited. The following is a brief description of the status of the three inhabited territories.

Norfolk Island

Location: Southwest Pacific

Size: 14 square miles

Population: 2190 (1979), including visitors

Cocos (Keeling) Islands

Location: East India Ocean

Size: Two separate atolls comprised of 27 small coral islands with a total area of 5.5 square miles. Only the two main islands, Home and West, are inhabited.

Population: 487 (1980)

Christmas Island

Location: East Indian Ocean, a few hundred miles east of the Cocos (Keeling) Islands

Size: 52 square miles

Population: 3184 (1980)

The New Zealand External Territories

There are three inhabited territories under various forms of control by New Zealand, two of which are in 'free association' and the other as a dependency. These are:

Cook Islands

Location: South central Pacific

Size: Fifteen islands, spread over an area of some 775 000 square miles, though with a total land area of only 93 square miles

Population: 18 200 (1980) but down 2.4 per cent on the 1970 population and exactly the same as the 1960 population

The Cook Islands became a New Zealand possession in 1901 and their status has evolved over the years to that of full self-government and association. New Zealand remains responsible for external affairs, though a special feature of this relation is that the Islanders can, at any time, move into full independence through unilateral action should they choose to do so. Although a small territory, the Cook Islands have seen their share of political problems, more normally associated with larger territories. In 1978, the courts ruled that eight of the winners of the general election, the Cook Island Party (which had been in continuous power since 1965), had been elected as a result of bribery and that it should be replaced by candidates from the Democratic Party which had contested the seats.

The Islands' economy is heavily based on agricultural exports and a developing tourist industry (which has been aided by an international airport on the main island of Rarotonga). There are also substantial invisible earnings from Cook Islanders working in New Zealand and sending their wages home.

Following St Kitts-Nevis, these islands would seem to be the most likely candidates for independence. The current policy calls for continued association, but as with their Caribbean cousins, the Cook Islands might find themselves under pressure from other island states in the region to seek their independence regardless of the consequences.

Niue

Location: Southwest Pacific (originally called Savage Island), and discovered by Captain Cook in 1774

Size: 100 square miles

Population: 3000 (1979), and rapidly declining since 1970 (5000)

Tokelau

Location: Southwest Pacific

Size: Three islands with a total area of 3.9 square miles

Population: 1620 (1980), up from 1575 in 1976. This was a result of the suspension of a resettlement programme begun by the islanders in 1965 due to fears of over-population. It is now hoped that migration alone will help to stem any possible over-population problem.

Namibia

One last territory which needs mention here is Namibia. While Namibia is not formally a possession of any Commonwealth country, its future is an obvious concern to all members. Though the issue of membership is never raised in any of the official literature published by the Commonwealth Secretariat, there is an assumption that on attaining complete independence, Namibia will join the Commonwealth.

In 1982, then, there were 27 dependent territories, though seven of these have no permanent populations[23] and can be dismissed for the future as no more than the sole resting place for exotic flora and fauna and odd weather stations or missile tracking sites. Of the remaining twenty dependent territories, three will obtain independence by the end of the decade. St Kitts-Nevis (either together or separately), the Cook Islands and Brunei. One can be optimistic about these territories on the basis of their current status as fully self-governing.

Another three territories are just as unlikely to achieve independence due to political problems: Hong Kong because of the Chinese claim on this territory; Gibraltar because of the Spanish claim; and the much-discussed Falkland Islands and the Argentinian claim.

While size and population have recently become relatively unimportant to the granting of independence, the ability to maintain an independent state in the cases of the Pitcairn Islands (population 70), Norfolk Island (population 2190), the Cocos (Keelings) Islands (population 487), Christmas Island (population 3150), Niue (population 3000) and Tokelau (population 1620) is highly questionable. Not only is their small size and population a problem, but most of these territories face serious resource/population depletion over the next 20–50 years.

A good example of this problem is Nauru, which expects its sole industry, phosphate, to last only until the year 2000. In the meantime it is rapidly attempting to expand its shipping and air services and plans are under way to develop the island as a tax haven and tourist centre. Nauru may win this race as it has an extremely high gross domestic product (100 million dollars in 1976) for its size (population 10 000), the highest *per capita* standard of living on the globe and, for now, the resources to finance its internal development. Other micro-states might not be so fortunate, and it is clear that the territories mentioned above could become an increasing burden on the states responsible for them as well as on international organisations, such as the United Nations and the Commonwealth.

This leaves eight territories, one of whose fate, Namibia, will ultimately be left to the political machinations of power politics played out both inside and outside international organisations. The other seven territories, all British dependencies, of various sizes and situations, are all on a route which undoubtedly leads to independence, though perhaps not until the 1990s or even longer. There are those observers who feel that dependencies such as Montserrat, the British Virgin Islands and the Turks and Caicos are just too small to be wholly self-governing, let alone sovereign, and they imply that this is also currently agreed to by the rest of these territories.[24] There is never any guarantee of achieving this status, but the pressure from independent neighbours will be great, as noted earlier, and it is likely that all seven of these states will eventually succumb, whether it is in their best interest or not.

Elmer Plischke wrote in 1977 that the main question regarding micro-states is 'not whether people are entitled to manage their own affairs and enjoy political independence, but whether, irrespective of their size and ability to fulfil their responsibilities, they should also be entitled to sovereign equality in the affairs of the community of nations'.[25] He went on to propose the creation of new forms of international participation which he claimed were vital in dealing with the problems of micro-states lest the rule of sovereign equality swamp international organisation. It would appear that Plischke is attempting to put out a fire that has long raged out of control and will only end when there is nothing left to burn. Rather than propose new methods by which potential candidates for statehood would become second-class citizens in the international system, one needs to examine the existing frameworks of co-operation and make them stronger and better able to assist potential and actual newcomers.

THE COMMONWEALTH ROLE IN DEPENDENT TERRITORIES

The official British position on independence is stated by the Foreign and Commonwealth Office (FCO):

The Government respects the wishes of the people of the British Dependent Territories to determine their own future in accordance with the principles of the United Nations Charter. We are committed to the policy followed by successive governments since 1945 of giving every help and encouragement to those Dependent Territories who wish to become independent while not forcing independence on those who do not want it. Once a Dependent Territory indicates that it wishes to move to independence, we help the Territory achieve this in as rapid and orderly a manner as possible.[26]

The FCO has also noted that while independence is not presently foreseen for any of the existing dependencies except the associated state of St Kitts-Nevis, 'it is eventually inevitable' for all with the timing to be decided by each individual territory. The FCO also points out that the one clear exception to 'inevitable independence' is Hong Kong, which it claims will never achieve independence.

Dependent territories, with a few minor exceptions, seem not to be recognised as part of the Commonwealth as an organisation. The organisation's activities tend to focus solely on independent membership despite the fact that dependencies are 'embraced' in the Commonwealth and do take part in many of its activities. Officially, however, this participation is limited. The Commonwealth Secretariat has noted that there is no direct political relationship between the dependent territories and the Commonwealth Secretariat.[27] They do concede that in exceptional circumstances, assistance has been given to territories during the requisite constitutional conference that always precedes independence. The legal division of the Secretariat has pointed to the case of Belize, where considerable legal assistance was provided during the constitutional conference held in April 1981. This advice had to do primarily, though not exclusively, with the question of difficulties over nationality problems in that country. The Secretariat points out that assistance of a political or legal nature is only given if asked for and that requests are made through the independent state on which the territory in question is dependent.

The FCO and Commonwealth Secretariat (to the extent to which they were able) both declared that there is no timetable for future decolonisation or independence, and despite the Declaration of Commonwealth Principles and United Nations Resolution 1514, the two bodies have emphasised that the decision of independence is up to the territory in question and not the state which controls the territory in question. The same applies with the territories of New Zealand and Australia.

Though the position is somewhat unclear, the Commonwealth Secretariat would appear never to have actually restricted itself to dealing with states will full membership and it has always served from the beginning, in one way or another, both emerging states and adjuncts of existing members in consultation with those members. But to what degree is the Commonwealth Secretariat able to assist these territories in achieving their goals, whether these be independence or continued dependence?

The Commonwealth's greatest potential contribution to dependent territories would appear to be in the areas of economic development. It is only since the late 1970s that the Commonwealth Secretariat would appear to be coming out of its shell regarding its numerous economic activities in dependent territories. This has been primarily due to Britain's own involvement in the economic affairs of these territories and the degree to which this has overshadowed Commonwealth programmes.

The British government has long recognised the need to establish the economic and social bases for political advances and the improvement of living standards of dependent territories. It is the Overseas Development Administration (ODA) that deals with the provision of economic assistance to dependent territories. The FCO claims to have relatively little to say on economic matters in dependencies except to provide the ODA with information requested. The ODA places aid to dependencies high on its list of priorities, with funds largely committed to such important sectors as communications, education, health services, water supplies, housing, agriculture and development, as well as research into these areas. Nearly all of this aid takes the form of grants, though a primary exception to this is investment finance provided through the Commonwealth Development Corporation (CDC).[28] Dependent territories and associated states have also been able to benefit indirectly from British contributions to such multilateral aid-giving agencies as the United Nations Development Programme (UNDP), as well as the various specialised agencies of the United Nations, the European Community and the Regional Development Banks.

In the past few years, however, Britain has begun to reduce its direct grant to dependencies through both the ODA and CDC and these territories have become more involved in Commonwealth aid development programmes. While not full members, dependencies have the right to participate in most Commonwealth activities (the main exception to this is attendance at Commonwealth Heads of Government Meetings), including the various technical co-operation projects. The largest and most important of these programmes is the Commonwealth Fund for Technical Co-operation (CFTC).

The CFTC has a range of programmes for the benefit of both full members and dependent territories, especially in the areas of technical assistance, education, training and health. In the late 1970s, the CFTC also had projects in a number of dependent territories, for example, a Malaysian expert was working in Montserrat advising on the production of dairy goods and their by-products, while during the same period a Jamaican specialist was in the Gilbert Islands (shortly afterwards this territory became independent as Kiribati) providing assistance on how to establish a small defence force that could also function in a developmental role. Although agriculture and development of natural resources are CFTC's primary work, they have assisted dependencies in a variety of other areas, such as helping to arrange hotel management and radio technician courses and provided advice on their development of legal procedures in territories well advanced towards independence.

CONCLUSIONS

Arnold Smith, former Secretary-General of the Commonwealth, has noted that the issue of a minimum population for Commonwealth members arose in 1960 when the organisation had only 10 members.[29] At that time, Cabinet Secretaries from the member states met the British Prime Minister and 'concluded that the Commonwealth should do nothing to exclude countries for reasons of size'.[30]

Earlier in this Chapter, some of the very smallest territories were noted as having little realistic hope of attaining independence, i.e. Pitcairns, Cocos, Tokelau, etc. Unlikely as it is, should some of these very small territories ever gain independence, the floodgates would be open to an increase in the fragmentation of large states and small states made up of large numbers of inhabited islands (e.g. the Cook Islands with 15 inhabited islands in the group). This is a situation which could one day lead to an international system of well over 300 states. Many critics scoff at such a suggestion, yet we have reached a situation today almost unthought of by experts 20 years ago, and there is no reason why, 20 years in the future, the number of states in the system should not have doubled again. Given perhaps the independence of territories of less than 3000 people, what is to stop the increased fragmentation of territories such as the above mentioned Cook islands, or Kiribati (with

28 islands), or Tuvalu (with 9 main islands), or the breaking away of Tobago from Trinadad, or Barbuda from Antigua? Following this line of thought, one could envision the secession of Hawaii or Alaska from the United States, territories which have been part of America for far less time than any of these other groups have been together. As independence is granted to smaller and smaller territories, the claims will become more absurd but the older established members of the international community will have little recourse; in a system of 300 states it is estimated that over 50 per cent would have populations of under 300 000 and would obviously be sympathetic to their smaller brethren. It is this threat of increased fragmentation which the Commonwealth must make some attempt to halt.

Looking at the problem from the perspective of the 1980s, the new international economic order can be seen as one expression of small, less powerful states' attempts to join in what Alfred Cobban called 'a co-ordinated economic system',[31] though another and perhaps better example is the apparent growth of regionalism in those regions where these small territories and states are most abundant, i.e. the Caribbean (CARICOM) and the Pacific (South Pacific Commission and South Pacific Forum). Membership in these organisations is allowing dependent territories a voice in regional affairs (along with many reciprocal benefits) without having to put an unprepared foot through the independence door.

The British Government would also appear to be increasingly willing to allow the United Nations to participate in the decolonisation process for its remaining dependencies and has passed much of the responsibility for assisting the dependent territories to become more self-sufficient over to the United nations and the Commonwealth. As has been seen, the Commonwealth is beginning to work directly with dependent territories and it is clear that the organisation has evolved since those days in the early 1960s when membership stood at 10. It is true that in that early period the growth of the organisation did not appear as a potential problem. But ironically it is growth that is one of the main problems the Commonwealth will have to face in the future. In the next twenty years the Commonwealth will face a whole range of new challenges from dependent territories and small states and as the Commonwealth has dealt so successfully with its own evolution as an international organisation so should it face up to this task which confronts it and help to prepare dependent territories now for a more secure future, whether as dependencies, as states, or perhaps in some new, as of yet not conceived, state of existence.

Of course, what we may be seeing is a reaction in exactly the opposite direction as to that noted above; towards increased integration, due to the failure of a state to succeed because of its small size and lack of economic viability. This would bring a resurgence of links between small states and territories so that they may return to that status of being linked to islands from which they have broken off during the 1960s, 1970s and 1980s in assertion of their independence. One recent example, on a larger scale, is the new federation announced between Gambia and Senegal. The Gambian Government has stated that this federation, dubbed 'Senegambia' has been under consideration for several years and involves no real change of status for either state but is rather an attempt to increase the economic viability and regional security of both. All they are doing apparently is 'jumping the gun on previous ECOWAS proposals and providing a testing ground for future federation on a larger scale'.[32]

The Commonwealth seems to be aware of the problems of small states and territories, and at Melbourne in 1981 Heads of Government made a special point of noting the situation in the Caribbean and Pacific regions, as well as that of island developing states.[33] But it also continues to put forward the right of self-determination as laid down by the United Nations Charter.[34] As long as the Commonwealth continues to support that policy, it must provide increased levels of support of a long-term nature to both dependencies and states in those areas where serious fragmentation is a potential problem.

The British Government would also appear to be increasingly willing to allow the United Nations to participate in the decolonisation process for its remaining dependencies and has passed much of the responsibility for assisting the dependent territories to become more self-sufficient over to the United Nations and the Commonwealth. As has been seen, the Commonwealth is beginning to work directly with dependent territories and it is clear that the organisation has evolved since those days in the early 1960s when membership stood at 10. It is true that in that early period, the growth of the organisation did not appear as a potential problem. But ironically, it is growth that is one of the main problems the Commonwealth will have to face in the future. In the next 20 years the Commonwealth will face a whole range of new challenges from dependent territories and small states and as the Commonwealth has dealt so successfully with its own evolution as an international organisation so should it face up to this task which confronts it, and help to prepare dependent territories now for a more secure future, whether as dependencies, as states, or perhaps in some new, as yet unconceived, state of existence.

NOTES AND REFERENCES

All references to information from the Commonwealth Secretariat and Foreign and Commonwealth Office stem from the official publications of these bodies as well as conversations with the staff of these organisations. I would like to thank the following people for their assistance and patience in my constant questioning: Ms Battan (FCO), Ms Brett-Rooks (FCO), Mr Hay (FCO), Mr Baltrop (FCO), Mr Dickson (Commonwealth Secretariat), Mr Enerum (Commonwealth Secretariat), Ms Gunthorp (Commonwealth Secretariat). Special thanks also go to Mr Anthony Payne and Mr A. Trevor Clarke for their comments and suggestions.

1. See Appendix. There are also the 'Crown Colonies' of the Isle of Man and the Channel Islands, but these are not usually considered 'colonies' or 'dependencies' in the sense of this paper and are therefore excluded.
2. Anthony Sampson, *The Anatomy of Britain* (London: Hodder and Stoughton, 1962).
3. Embodied in the West Indies Act, 1967. The scheme is based on an earlier precedent established between the Cook Islands and New Zealand.
4. See W. Gilmore, 'Requiem for Associated Statehood?' in *Review of International Studies*, 8:1 (January 1982), pp. 9–25.
5. United Nations General Assembly, Resolution 1514, 14 December 1960.
6. B. Coard, 'The meaning of political independence in the Commonwealth Caribbean' in *Independence for Grenada – Myth or Reality?* (St Augustine, Trinidad: Institute of International Relations, 1974) p. 70.
7. D. Lowenthal and C. Clarke, 'Island Orphans: Barbuda and the rest', *Journal of Commonwealth and Comparative Politics*, November 1980, p. 294.
8. T. B. Millar, *The Commonwealth and the United Nations* (Sydney: Sydney University Press, 1967).
9. In his book *One World to Share* (London: Hutchinson, 1979), S. S. Ramphal, Secretary-General of the Commonwealth, only makes one brief mention of the problem of dependent territories within the Commonwealth (p. 326), despite his having been Secretary-General for several years. This is probably less reflective of Ramphal's personal attitude as it is the attitude of the organisation as a whole.
10. See *Observer*, 4 April 1954, and *The Times*, 16 December 1954.
11. J. D. B. Miller, *The Commonwealth in the World*, 3rd edn (London: Duckworth, 1965), pp. 271–3.
12. 'Special Membership' is currently held by Nauru, Tuvalu and St Vincent and the Grenadines, and allows these states to participate in all Commonwealth activities except Heads of Government Meetings.
13. Arnold Smith, *Stitches in Time: The Commonwealth in World Politics* (London: Andre Deutsch, 1981) p. 158.
14. Ibid., pp. 220–4.
15. Bernard Levin, *The Times*, 23 February 1977, p. 14.
16. Anthony Payne, *Change in the Commonwealth Caribbean*, Chatham House Papers No. 12 (London: Royal Institute of International Affairs, 1981), and conversations between Mr Payne and the Author.

17. D. Lowenthal and C. Clarke, 'Island Orphans', p. 295.
18. Ibid., For further details of this separation see W. J. Bush, *Anguilla and the Mini-State Dilemma*, Policy Paper No. 5 (New York: Center for International Studies, 1971).
19. *Guardian*, 3 March 1982, p. 6.
20. Ibid.
21. *Observer*, 31 January 1982, p. 15; see also *Observer*, 4 April 1982; and *The Sunday Times*, 11 April 1982.
22. *Guardian*, 10 April 1982, p.10.
23. These are: British Antarctic Territory, British Indian Ocean Territory, Australian Antarctic Territory, Heard and McDonald Islands, Coral Sea Island Territory, Territory of Ashmore and Cartier Islands and the Ross Dependency.
24. Lowenthal and Clarke, 'Island Orphans'.
25. Elmer Plischke, *Micro-states in World Affairs: Policy Problems and Options* (Washington, D.C.: American Enterprise Institute, 1977) p. 9.
26. Letter from Ms B. Brett-Rooks, Hong Kong and General Department, Foreign and Commonwealth Office, 27 November 1981.
27. Conversation with officials of the Commonwealth Secretariat during months of November and December 1981, and January 1982.
28. The Commonwealth Development Corporation (CDC), established in 1948 by the British government, was set up to assist the then dependent territories in economic development by providing funds for development schemes of a commercial nature. This assistance was later extended to independent areas both within and outside the Commonwealth. By mid-1976 the CDC had committed some £276.1 million of which £228.4 million had been invested in about 260 projects in 40 states. CDC during the 1970s was to direct aid to the very poorest states in its target areas. For the first six months of 1976, all of the £13 million committed went to the poor states and nearly 70 per cent went to agricultural projects.
29. Smith, *Stitches in Time*, p. 154.
30. Ibid.
31. Alfred Cobban, *The Nation-State and National Self-Determination*, revised edn (London: Collins, 1969) p. 280.
32. Conversation with Dr A. C. Bundu, Gambian High Commission, London, on 5 January 1982.
33. Commonwealth Heads of Government, *The Melbourne Communiqué*, October 1981 (London: Commonwealth Secretariat, 1981) paras 27, 35–7, 71–4.
34. Ibid., para. 35.

Part IV
Conclusions

17 The Commonwealth as an International Organisation

A. J. R. GROOM

There are those for whom it is almost an article of faith that the Commonwealth is *sui generis*, and to be cherished as such, while for others, if it is anything at all, the Commonwealth is a peripheral, slightly odd international organisation with a vestigial role sustained by atavistic attitudes of a somewhat distasteful character. How, then, does the Commonwealth fit into the range of international organisations?

The official Commonwealth is clearly inter-governmental, rather than supranational in character and it abjures constitutional formulae. At the unofficial level the Commonwealth reveals a high degree of integration and community in which state structures are by-passed and penetrated in flows of goods, services, people and ideas which spill over beyond the bounds of the official Commonwealth in some functional dimensions to include actors from countries such as the USA, Ireland, the Sudan and, through regional ties and overlapping membership, most areas of the world. In some aspects the unofficial Commonwealth departs far from the territorially based state-centric form of an INGO with its constituent national and geographically regional branches, to embrace a form in which the unit membership is entirely functional, as in the case of the Association of Commonwealth Universities (individual universities are members). The unofficial Commonwealth is also well ensconced in the political domain, where the Commonwealth Parliamentary Association is particularly influential and penetrates the heart of the state structure with transnational linkages. Thus the Commonwealth is an example of intergovernmental adjustment at the official level and of integration at the unofficial level, while the total absence of a Commonwealth constitution is a good indication of the relative absence of the constitutional state-building approach.

Like every other organisation the Commonwealth must, if it exists and if it is to survive, fulfil four functions. The measure of the strength of the Commonwealth as an organisation is the degree to which and the manner in which it fulfils these functions. They are simply an empirical guide, pointing to strengths and weaknesses of use to those who wish to promote or obstruct a particular organisation. The four functions are: a capacity to adapt to the social and physical environment as a coherent unit; the ability to integrate sub-units; a sense of identity; and sufficient self-knowledge to enable goals to be set. All organisations attempt these functions, but the structures through which and the process by which they are performed are legion. To what extent does the Commonwealth fulfil these functions and what are the processes by which, and the structures through which, it does so?

One of the great strengths of the Commonwealth as an organisation is its manifest ability to adapt to its environment. From Empire to Commonwealth is a massive adaptation, not only in institutions but also in mores. Indeed, the frequency with which a premature obituary for the Commonwealth has been written is a testament to its ability to adapt. Adaptation is facilitated by a pragmatic approach to problems and opportunities allied with an abhorrence of legalism and no truck for formal constitutions, all of which stem from habits built up consensually, and relate to a penchant for flexibility and diversity. Adaptability, however, has its drawbacks: it can lead to drift and anarchy. It is not therefore the only requisite for survival: sub-units must be integrated so that, no matter how great the adaptability, flexibility and diversity, a discernible whole remains.

The Commonwealth is not strong at integrating its sub-units. Indeed, three countries have withdrawn from the official Commonwealth, and parts of the unofficial Commonwealth have become moribund and whole functions have decayed. But new functions have grown and other sectors flourish. Nevertheless, the history of the Commonwealth is a story of the loosening of ties between the sub-units, although without the evolution from Empire to Commonwealth the organisation would have collapsed in violent conflict which, in any case, was far from being absent. In short, the organisation could only continue to exist if it adapted by weakening and changing the method by which it integrated its sub-units. Colonies became independent, and the Commonwealth lost both a leader and a centre as Britain abdicated and Anglocentricity declined, yet the recognition of sovereign equality and the notion of a transregional, open organisation enabled it to survive at the price of a loss of cohesion.

Survival has in no small part been due to the strength of loyalty and affective attachment to the Commonwealth. The obituaries of the Commonwealth have been premature because they concentrated upon the growing inability of the organisation to integrate its sub-units, particularly in utilitarian dimensions such as trade, a common foreign policy and security. They ignored the less tangible affective ties and the less salient utilitarian ties in a variety of functional dimensions. There is an impressive loyalty to and affection for the organisation, giving rise to a reluctance, even in times of great tension, to be done with it, and an evident desire to look for new roles for the Commonwealth and for new ways of performing old functions. Such loyalty is clearly not an exclusive loyalty to the Commonwealth and, if forced to choose between the Commonwealth and other fora, participants might frequently not have chosen the Commonwealth. But they were not forced to choose and the flexibility, diversity and adaptability of the Commonwealth, coupled with its ability to command loyalty, enabled it to survive.

Survival, however, implies setting goals – survival for what? – and this connotes a sufficient degree of self-knowledge to enable goal-setting to take place. Without values to point to desired goals, values which are derived from past experience, there can be no goal-setting, and an organisation without values and therefore without goals will hardly survive, for it will have no way of knowing how to utilise its ability to adapt, to integrate its sub-units and to command loyalty. Has the Commonwealth been able to generate sufficient self-knowledge to set goals?

The existence of a shared past in the Empire is ambiguous because experiences varied – and so did the lessons learned. Despite this, shared assets and values grew out of the relationship. The assets include a working knowledge of English, and compatible administrative methods which go some way to establishing a decision-making style the envy of other international organisations. But is it style without substance? What does the Commonwealth consensus produce? Is there a sufficient communality of values to permit the setting of goals and an action policy? The Singapore and Lusaka Declarations are statements of consensus on fundamental values, and the relationship with South Africa exemplifies fundamental aspects of these values. They have given rise to an action policy in Southern Africa and also more recently in the North-South context in the negotiating fora, through the CFTC, and by the special concern with the problems and interests of very small states.

Yet for the most part the Commonwealth cannot take decisions; it can, however, help to clarify issues and to create a conventional wisdom based on a set of shared values. It is an undramatic but worthwhile achievement in a world riven with dissension. At the unofficial level the Commonwealth can go further, since many functional bodies have significant action programmes. As an organisation, therefore, the Commonwealth has displayed a degree of self-knowledge sufficient to enable it to set goals and to implement a modest action-policy for their achievement.

The Commonwealth, broadly defined at its official and unofficial levels, is a system capable of fulfilling its functional requirements in a manner commensurate with its future survival, at least in the medium term. It is strongest in its adaptability and possibly weakest in its ability to integrate its sub-units, with modest capabilities (greater at the unofficial than the official level) to inspire loyalty, to set goals and implement an action policy. Its performance is good when compared with many other frameworks, particularly regional ones, and its significance and relative success in the difficult North-South dimension deserves special mention. However, at the institutional level the Commonwealth has its peculiarities which, although not sufficient to make it different in kind, do, nevertheless, make it an unusual institution. The normal institutional structure of an international organisation comprises a general assembly, a secretariat, a budget, and voting procedures set out in a constitution which attributes rights and duties to the members and functions to the various bodies. How do these work in the case of the Commonwealth?

The Commonwealth has no general assembly in the manner of most international organisations. However, to balance this it has regular Heads of Government Meetings every two years and meetings of senior officials in the intervening years. The salient characteristics of meetings of the official Commonwealth whether at Heads of Government, ministerial (in numerous functional dimensions) or official level are felicitous. What 'gives commonwealth consultations their unique character' is

— the avoidance of set speeches: prepared texts would be circulated; interventions would be succinct and pithy, not in the nature of *tours d'horizon:*
— occasional restricted sessions would be held limited to heads of delegations alone and with discussion off the record:
— there would be maximum opportunities for informal discussion over

coffee, at the end of the day and during the weekend retreat, but a minimum of formal social occasions:
—everything possible would be done to strengthen the character of the occasion as a meeting of political leaders, with its Chairman charged to prevent the discussions becoming stylised; to encourage a free exchange of ideas and opinion and to promote a meeting of minds.[1]

There is thus little of the parliamentary diplomacy that characterises many institutions which have a general assembly in frequent and lengthy session. Nor is there any great manipulation of procedures or voting trade-offs since sessions are short and informal. There is no legislation as such, merely a directive to the Secretariat or a pledge to act in a particular way which reflects a consensus from which members can demur, so much of the life of a typical international institution is missing – not at all. Heads of government and ministers are not usually political babes in the wood, so that there is political substance and sophistication to their deliberations, which can be of great moment. The Lusaka discussions on Southern Africa are a case in point, in which real political pressure was exerted, and successfully, perhaps because of, rather than despite, the unusual institutional setting. However, if there is no general assembly in the Commonwealth in the usual international institutional sense, there is the traditional secretariat familiar from other international institutions.

The Secretariat came through its cathartic experiences of birth and the Anglo-African confrontation over Southern Africa and helped to bring about the emergence of the contemporary Commonwealth. It now acts in all aspects of the official Commonwealth's activities and it is relatively loosely controlled by member states so that it has the necessary leeway to develop initiatives. Besides servicing meetings and implementing directives (not least on Southern Africa) the main activities of the Secretariat have been political and economic. At the most general level the Secretariat has sought to promote a Commonwealth spirit and way of doing things which forms a practical and pragmatic, if evolving, ideology. Of politico-economic importance is the Secretariat's current stress on the North-South relationship and its programme for the small and the weak.[2] The Secretariat, in devising and implementing its programmes, makes considerable use of non-Secretariat personnel both for the conceptualisation of needs and policy and in their accomplishment. In particular, the CFTC is what Mr Ramphal has rightly called 'a unique instrument of co-operation for development'.[3] While it is very small in financial terms it is very good in developmental terms – small beer, perhaps, but a good local brew. Its chief merits are its flexibility, particularly its willingness to contemplate small unusual requests, its efficiency both in performing its tasks and in keeping administrative costs down and its acceptability, which is doubtless aided to no small degree by its policy of using experts from one developing country to help another developing country, thereby taking the edge off some of the neo-colonial aspects of international stratification.

The Commonwealth, not surprisingly, has more demands made on it than it has the financial resources to meet. The major financial supporters are Australia, Britain, Canada, India and Nigeria, but all members make a contribution. There is tension between the needs, as stressed by the most deprived, and the financial constraints about which members are reminded by the principal donors. Nevertheless, worthwhile programmes are funded and, by international standards, the Secretariat, and especially the CFTC, is excellent value for money. Once agreed by the consensus procedures a Commonwealth programme is usually adequately funded, at least at the official level. Such is not the case with the unofficial Commonwealth: although parts of the system work well in the sense of tailoring their aspirations to a realistic budget, other parts of the system are woefully under-financed and under-manned. Doubtless there are unofficial Commonwealth institutions that are deservedly moribund but there are others of great potential worth that cannot function adequately for lack of finance. With this in mind the Commonwealth prime ministers, when setting up the Secretariat, also established a Commonwealth Foundation through which Commonwealth governments could help the unofficial Commonwealth, particularly in the Third World and in a North-South dimension. It is a particularly happy instance of that rare integration of the IGO, INGO, and NGO worlds.

Among the many ways of classifying international institutions that have gained currency is one between forum and service organisations. Forum organisations provide a meeting place, the classic 'good offices', but do not make a tremendous independent institutional impact upon the processes that take place within them. Service organisations, on the other hand, do have an active institutional role, often with a strong and independent Secretariat having a significant budget and expertise at its disposal for its own action programmes. Like most other organisations the Commonwealth has elements of both conceptions. The functional divisions of the Secretariat and many parts of the unofficial Commonwealth have a strong service orientation, but the Commonwealth system as a whole also has strong forum tendencies at all levels, from the meetings of Heads of Governments to the Commonwealth Carnival at the Commonwealth Games. Moreover, it is the special character of forum activity – its freedom, flexibility, frankness but usual friendliness, among almost as heterogeneous collection of actors as the world can provide – that is of special value. In Commonwealth forums 'different' does not mean 'hostile' or even 'strange', it means open association and exchange without fear in a psycho-social community.

Membership in the Commonwealth is no impediment to membership of other institutions which are based on principles compatible with those of Commonwealth declarations, but does it signify a duplication of the work of other organisations in a wasteful manner in any significant areas? At the time of the creation of the Secretariat, which also involved the incorporation of several existing secretariats of different functional bodies, a study was undertaken of the likely extent of duplication, actual and potential.[4] The findings suggested that the activities of the Commonwealth were not superfluous or a wasteful duplication but that they were useful, complementary and supplementary and, given the expansion in Commonwealth activities, it seems fair to say that they are now more so. However, in some areas the Commonwealth has lost a role.

In the early years of the UN the Commonwealth was a recognisable unit in the political affairs of the organisation to the extent of a 'Commonwealth' seat on the Security Council and frequent Commonwealth caucusing. These practices faded out as the Third World joined the organisation in force and developed its own procedures and as the British Commonwealth gave way to the contemporary Commonwealth. While the Commonwealth Secretariat has observer status at the United Nations, no serious attempt has been made to develop a Commonwealth position on issues in the General Assembly or Security Council except in isolated cases. Movement in the other direction has been more significant when issues from those bodies – such as Southern Africa and the NIEO – have spilled over, sometimes acrimoniously sometimes happily, into the Commonwealth framework. The Commonwealth does not act as a unit in the UN but it can, on occasion, through its own unique forum and by its own special processes, help the world to negotiate. In the Specialised Agencies matters are somewhat different, since Commonwealth ministerial meetings are frequently held immediately before the main annual meeting of the particular agency. However, this does not presage a Commonwealth line or concerns, but merely consultation with an exchange of views on issues and of information – a process not without its subsequent influence on the proceedings of the agency. The Commonwealth Secretariat maintains a listening post in Geneva where there is much UN activity, and it is thus better able to respond to the needs of its members, particularly the smaller members. However, the direct role of the Commonwealth in UN affairs is not great.[5]

The Commonwealth has developed as an important trans-regional organisation whose significance is magnified by there being few other such organisations. Its trans-regionality and the benefits therefrom can be illustrated by the role of the Commonwealth Secretariat was able to play in the Lomé negotiations between the EEC, including a Commonwealth member, and the ACP countries, many of whom are from the Commonwealth. There is an important trans-regional supportive role for which the Commonwealth is well-fitted and one which it is increasingly playing. However, regionalism was not without its traumas for the Commonwealth. The developing regional ties of the newly-independent countries in the mid-sixties were at cross-purposes with a British-led 'British Commonwealth' as world actor such as was conceived by Mr Wilson's government in the mid-1960s. When Britain changed direction and espoused regionalism by plunging into Europe, difficulties of an economic nature arose for many Commonwealth countries. The outcome of both these instances of the strengthening of regional ties was the transformation of the British Commonwealth into the Commonwealth – a Commonwealth that was now genuinely trans-regional, rather than inter-continental but Anglocentric. The association, if it was to survive, had to be open and not exclusive. It also had to prove its worth and relevance in a new context of growing regionalism and declining Anglocentricity. Without the active British connection, was there anything left worth bothering about? Governments have come to think that there is, and have shown it by their commitment to and use of Commonwealth enterprises. The Secretariat in its activities has demonstrated that there is a felt need and has responded to it. And the unofficial Commonwealth has, in many instances, flourished. Furthermore, the Commonwealth has also responded to the challenge of regionalism by adopting a regional mode for some of its own activities.

While the IGO world is the superstructure of the Commonwealth, the foundations lie buried in the less glamorous, but nevertheless fascinating and largely unknown 'unofficial' Commonwealth of INGOs and NGOs. These bodies create a 'complex network of relationships' which involve both the Secretariat and, particularly, the Commonwealth Foundation.[6]

The unofficial Commonwealth complements the official in a number of ways. It underpins and reinforces the official Commonwealth by helping to keep it in touch with public opinion in member countries and relaying back to the public the changing nature of government's priorities and objectives. NGOs offer an avenue for the expression of common concerns and for action to meet specific needs. In other words, they constitute an important channel for direct communication with the people which governments, by their nature, cannot provide. NGOs are also in a position to move ahead of official policy and to point the way to innovation and change.[7]

And that is part of the trouble. Some governments view with a degree of circumspection, or worse, any organisation which has a direct link with the people which is in a position to 'move ahead of official policy and to point the way to innovation and change'. Such bodies could constitute a threat to governments; they could subvert government policies and usurp the government's right and responsibility to take the lead in promoting the well-being of its society; they could reflect the vested interests of unrepresentative minorities or be manipulated by foreign interests and thereby constitute a threat to a new and hard-won independence. But this is a 'worst case' analysis, and worst cases are not the usual case. Indeed, although the unofficial Commonwealth has been growing and constitutes a network, it is not an organised network. INGOs and NGOs are often ignorant of each others' activities and are sometimes wilfully unconcerned about wasteful duplication. They each have their own public, clientele and experts and are sometimes oblivious to the outside world unless threatened with institutional catastrophe. Little wonder then that they are urged to 'establish closer links and extend co-operation among themselves, as well as with the official Commonwealth'.[8] Most governments have little to fear from them and could make good use of them. Governments, too, have been encouraged to 'make a conscious drive to establish regular exchanges with the unofficial sector . . .',[9] which would be furthered by 'the setting up of an NGO desk within the Secretariat'.[10]

Governments have not acted upon these proposals, which is not surprising since they are quite radical in a world context. Few IGOs have a full relationship with 'their' INGOs and NGOs. However, the Commonwealth NGO and INGO worlds could help themselves by increasing their own mutual ties. An occasional Commonwealth Assembly of NGOs and INGOs whose purpose would be to examine the state of the unofficial Commonwealth as a system, supported, in the meantime, by a NGO desk in the Secretariat (as a link point for the unofficial Commonwealth and Liaison officer with the official Commonwealth in those areas not covered by other methods) might be helpful. Even such modest proposals must, however, come to terms with differing conceptions of NGOs.

The governments of developing countries need, cultivate and respond to grassroots support, but they conceive it in terms of national development, and often a national development plan, for which *they* are primarily responsible. Their framework is different: they are states trying to become nations; they are seeking to mobilise their people and also to assimilate them; for them unity is the pressing need, not diversity. Thus the pluralism of the NGO and INGO world of developed countries is anathema to the extent that it may prejudice unity. NGOs which work with the governmental framework for national development, and which do not pose any threat to what is often no more than a nascent unity, are acceptable; others, which for good reasons or otherwise do not accept such a framework or which pose an actual or potential threat to unity, are regarded with considerable suspicion. The context in the developed countries is very different and it behoves NGOs in those countries to recognise the differences.[11]

The conception of the Commonwealth as having two parts – official and unofficial each acknowledging the other as significant and integral to the whole, despite current differences as to the exact relationship, is one way in which the Commonwealth differs from other international institutions. Moreover, the Commonwealth is unusually trans-regional and open. Furthermore, it has no centre in the sense of a quasi-legislating general assembly or politically, economically, socially or culturally. While the Secretariat is located in London, it is in no sense dominated by the British. London is a good centre for communications and has an excellent representation of Commonwealth governments: it is a convenience, and one that can be utilised by the Secretariat better to organise its activities in other parts of the Commonwealth. In decision-making procedures other international institutions are moving towards the consensus method of the Commonwealth but few, as yet, have been able to develop the freedom and frankness without fear of its exchanges. When compared with the UN the Commonwealth is speedier in its processes because of the absence of a constitution or elaborate rules, and becuase of a common working language and compatible administrative procedures. It also works better than many regional organisations because it has the necessary financial basis, and when agreement is called for it can usually be achieved. Although the Secretariat may wish the Commonwealth to become more of a regular institution this could destroy some of its utility and attraction to governments. There is, therefore, a latent struggle between the nebulous but effective form valued by some and the notion of the Commonwealth as an international institution. The Secretariat has been invaluable in enabling the Commonwealth to be both institutional but different. If the Commonwealth moves to become a normal institution it may not survive, as there is no need for a mini-UN. However, a Secretariat, not too strong but competent, flexible and efficient, can be a device for facilitating consensus and acting as a barometer and bridge transregionally, between official and unofficial, between dimensions and above all, between North and South.

The Commonwealth is part of the nervous system of world society. It is not particularly salient but it usually manages to be a haven of relative sanity in a difficult and dangerous world. The world could survive without it, but not as well. It leads to a modest exchange of people, ideas, goods and services transregionally and between North and South on a basis more acceptable to the participants than many other institutions. Moreover, it is capable of genuine discussion of differences and even of their resolution. It is not overtly coercive and its structures are not oppressive. It brings a sense of community into the struggle to control coercion and dismantle oppressive world structures. In short, it is an unusual but legitimised and useful part of the institutional structure of contemporary world society.

NOTES AND REFERENCES

1. S. S. Ramphal, 'Relations on Lusaka', speech to the Royal Institute of International Affairs, London, 21 September 1979, memeo, pp. 5–6.
2. See *Report of the Commonwealth Secretary-General* (London: Commonwealth Secretariat, 1979) pp. 8–9, and *Report of the Commonwealth Secretary-General* (London: Commonwealth Secretariat, 1977) p. 32.
3. See the 1979 *Report of the Commonwealth Secretary-General*, p. 10.
4. See *Report of the Review Committee on Intra-Commonwealth Organisations* (London: Commonwealth Secretariat, August 1966).
5. In a recent somewhat nostalgic article some practical suggestions have been made for the Commonwealth Secretariat to play a supportive role at the UN. See Samar Sen, 'The Commonwealth Role at the United Nations', *Round Table*, January 1980.
6. From *Governments to Grassroots*, Report of Advisory Committee on Relationships services. Official and Unofficial Commonwealth (London: Commonwealth Secretariat, 1978).

7. Ibid., para. 19.
8. Ibid., para. 22.
9. Ibid., para. 23.
10. Ibid., para. 33.
11. See Dr A. Bolaji Akinyemi in *The Commonwealth and NGOs*, Dalhousie University Conference, October 25–29, 1976, Halifax N.S. mimeo.

18 The Commonwealth in the 1980s: Challenges and Opportunities

PAUL TAYLOR

Relations between states, like other social relationships, may be judged in terms of their approximation to one or other of two models of society. In the community model actors identify strongly with each other and expect that their interests will converge in the long run. Indeed they may postpone the settlement of short-term disagreements in the expectation that this will happen, and stress shared values and experiences as the main justification of the relationship. On the other hand, in the pluralist model relationships are justified primarily in terms of their utilitarian rewards to the actors, and the satisfaction of interest is less frequently postponed as there is no agreement upon priorities among them. The central principle of the first model is emotional, psychological, or identitive; that of the second is utilitarian, calculative, and concerned with the balancing of accounts in the short term.[1]

International relations are generally thought usually to be closer to the second model. But relations between governments may sometimes have something of the character of the first model. Indeed, it is one of the distinctive characteristics of the Commonwealth that it moves some way towards the model of community. Relations between its members show elements of mutual identification and shared values, perhaps more so than between most members of the international system – although there is also a pluralist element in that it provides a framework for the satisfaction of some of the members' separate interests. Certainly the Commonwealth is regarded by members as being not simply a community, but also an organisation which is capable of satisfying the different interests of its member states. This chapter analyses the strength of the community and pluralist aspects of the Commonwealth, and considers some of the challenges to both in the early 1980s.

The emergence of a Commonwealth possessing a degree of community from an empire which was widely interpreted as being in Britain's self-interest, but not that of the colonies, in the relatively brief period between the end of the Second World War and the mid-1960s, is indeed astonishing. It developed so quickly and in the circumstances of de-colonisation could so easily have destroyed the potential for community building. Yet the identitive factor, which had been reinforced by the common language, similar governmental and administrative patterns, the education of elites from the new states and the old in the same educational establishments in Britain and elsewhere, and the monarchy, more often than not proved strong enough to survive the strains of the struggle for independence. After independence the 'pluralist' advantages of membership in the Commonwealth impressed themselves on the majority of the new states. One measure of the interest of the new states in preserving the Commonwealth link was the growth of international organisations among its members. In 1979 there were twenty-three pan-Commonwealth or Commonwealth regional intergovernmental organisations and over ninety such non-governmental organisations.[2] In addition, there were numerous national organisations which dealt with a more limited number of Commonwealth countries and Commonwealth groupings act together in several universal international organisations. Ten of the Commonwealth or regional governmental agencies were established in 1964 or later – including the organisation which is perhaps the central institution, the Secretariat established in London in 1965, and which was to become the second largest international organisation (after the International Maritime Consultative Organisation) in that city. Eight of the sixteen Commonwealth or regional educational or research non-governmental organisations were formed in or after 1964. In 1971, less than ten years after the majority of Commonwealth members had escaped from a relationship judged by their leaders as oppressive – the colonial relationship with Britain – the head of the New Zealand Ministry of Foreign Affairs could assert that the Commonwealth had five advantages: its meetings of heads of government conveyed a sense of intimacy; activity within it was facilitated by a common heritage of constitutional and administrative institutions; it was the framework within which useful cross-relationships could develop, such as that between Australia and New Zealand and Malaya and Singapore (and later between Australia and Jamaica, Canada and the Caribbean); and the co-operative action of the specialised bureaux covered a vast range.[3] The first two of these advantages are derived from the existence of the sense of community among the members; the others refer to the existence of a belief that there are pluralist advantages in membership though it is apparent that these are built upon the elements of community.

The Commonwealth as it emerged after the mid-1960s was, however, based upon two hypocrisies, although these may indeed – in the circumstances of the time – have been forgivable. These may be called a hypocrisy of structure, and a hypocrisy of ideology. The convention emerged that the structure of the Commonwealth was not hierarchical and that Britain was merely a member like any other. The creation of the Secretariat was perhaps the major institutional expression of this convention: after its establishment various activities, particularly the arrangement and servicing of the biennial meetings of the heads of government, were handled by the international organisation rather than by the British government. Indeed, it has been argued that without the Secretariat the meetings of the heads of government would have been discontinued in the late 1960s. It was also agreed that there would no longer be a British Commonwealth; the label 'British' was to be discarded in favour of the generic type. There came a point, indeed, when the question arose among some members in the context of the Rhodesian problem, as to whether Britain itself could not be deprived of membership. Yet despite this convention of equality Britain has remained the focus of the enterprise, particularly at the non-governmental level. It is, after all, British culture (broadly-defined), and the common heritage of British administration and government, which provide the main fibres of these identitive ties. Britain remains the identitive focus of the system, although this in no way precludes the identification and development of the cultures of the others. But in this sense the members of the Commonwealth are not equal.

When the Commonwealth is judged as an agency for satisfying the more tangible interests of its members it is apparent that all are not equal in the sense that each has the means and inclination to meet the needs of the others. One indication of this is that the thirteen pan-Commonwealth governmental organisations are all based in Britain, as are sixty-one of the ninety-six Commonwealth or regional non-governmental organisations.[4] As a pluralist organisation, indeed, the Commonwealth has profound inequalities: the interest of the majority is to organise themselves in order to put pressure upon the stronger minority, and amongst the latter group Britain has remained the most important. This pressure is not intended only to effect the redistribution of wealth from richer to poorer, although this is certainly one of its purposes. Rather, it is intended to push the states which, because of their diplomatic status and position in the international system, are able to effect outcomes in the direction desired by the majority. Britain is capable of taking a lead in shaping the development policy of the richer states, and of increasing her own aid to the poorer states; but she is also capable of exercising a greater influence than most of the others, if she can be suitably motivated, upon, for instance, the internal policies of South Africa and upon the future of Namibia. In this sense the Commonwealth is interesting to the majority of its members because it is a channel of influence upon its leading state, although that influence has to be suitably dressed up so that its object does not seek to escape. Similarly the majority of states are anxious to maximise their utilitarian returns from Britain.

When compared with the pluralist model it is the inequalities among the members of the Commonwealth which are striking: the assumption of equality is a convenient fiction. That Britain has a greater capacity to resolve problems within the Commonwealth and disagreements between its members, and a greater capacity to provide than most, lends validity to the aphorism that the organisation is held together by the problems which divide it. Britain is also capable of exercising greater influence than most other members within other organisations, such as the United Nations and the International Monetary Fund, and in general diplomacy.

A second hypocrisy concerns the ideology of the Commonwealth, particularly as it affects questions of racial integration and of constitutional democracy. The Commonwealth is officially firmly committed to these principles and has proclaimed them on at least three occasions in communiqués and programmes; at the CHOGMs in 1971 at Singapore, at Gleneagles in 1977 – when members agreed to take all necessary steps to outlaw apartheid in sport; and, again at Lusaka in 1979 when racialism was roundly condemned.[5] The problem is that these great causes are espoused in ringing tones in public, at a time when developments in a number of member states seem flatly to contradict them. At the same time no state can bring itself to accuse others of flouting the official ideology, lest it be accused itself, or lest it appear guilty of intervention in the domestic affairs of sovereign states, in contravention of the domestic jurisdiction clauses of the United Nations' Charter. The two great exceptions to this unstated agreement to ignore the various affronts to the official ideology are, of course, the issue of apartheid in South Africa, and the decision by Tanzania, backed by other members, to assist in the removal of Idi Amin's disgraceful regime in Uganda. Members went to the extent of formally condemning the Amin regime and implicitly sanctioned the Tanzanian invasion.[6]

The hypocrisy of ideology in the Commonwealth is that, whilst constitutional democracy is affirmed and anti-racialism acclaimed, in practice a number of states are one-party systems and others are ruled by or have had military regimes. Although there is currently only one military regime – Ghana – among the forty-four member states, and only one – Grenada – had no parliament,[7] quite a few could only be described as fairly repressive one-party systems. The assumption that there was a general inclination towards democratic practice seemed rather generous. Furthermore, an increasing number of states, black and white, have discriminatory internal policies, and exclusive immigration laws. The tendency within the Commonwealth, despite the proclamation of the right of citizens to move freely between states, is increasingly towards the exclusion of foreigners even when these are Commonwealth citizens. Moreover, 'discrimination of various kinds had come to be an accepted part of the law in many Commonwealth countries'.[8] One of the best illustrations of the tension between ideology and practice seems to be Britain's own immigration laws as they developed through the 1970s. In 1972 in an editorial on proposed legislation to reduce immigration to Britain *The Times* commented: 'This is and always has been a colour problem: the application of similar rules to the old and new Commonwealth has been a fundamentally hypocritical attempt to pretend that colour was not the issue.'[9] David McIntyre concluded that 'On few subjects has so much hypocrisy been in evidence as on the question of Commonwealth immigration into the United Kingdom'.[10] The policy was intended to have the effect of keeping blacks out, whilst avoiding charges of racial discrimination and allowing in citizens from the white Commonwealth. It could not be denied that black Commonwealth states have complained about British immigration policy, but many are also vulnerable to accusations of discrimination of various kinds.

There were complaints against countries whose players, particularly cricketers and rugby players, had had sporting links with South Africa, but such complaints were at the risk of generating a storm of mutual accusations of intolerance, or of unacceptable intervention in the business of sporting organisations within states, such as team selection. There was the continuing risk that the attempt to apply a sporting boycott of South Africa would lead to divisions in sports on racial lines in the Commonwealth itself. For instance, in 1981 there seemed to be a real risk that international cricket in the Commonwealth would be racially defined: teams from black and brown states would play each other, and white teams would do the same. In the autumn of 1981 a tour of India by an English cricket team was under threat of abandonment for several weeks because of the Indian government's doubts about two English players who had sporting links with South Africa, though it eventually took place. In 1981 the decision by the New Zealand government, despite the Gleneagles agreement, not to go beyond condemning the invitation to the South Africa rugby team to visit their country by acting to exclude them, again promised before the Commonwealth meeting in Australia to lead to profound disagreements and disruption. When the heads of government met at Melbourne in October 1981 the New Zealand Prime Minister, Mr Muldoon, was involved in acrimonious exchanges with, in particular, African leaders. It seemed increasingly difficult to sustain the hypocrisy that the norm in the Commonwealth was harmony between the races.

The code of practice of the central institution of the contemporary Commonwealth, the biennial Meeting of the Heads of Government (CHOGM), rests upon these two hypocrisies: that the members are equally important in the structure of the system, and that they are united in the pursuit and practice of racial equality, and constitutional democracy. The sense of intimacy to which the New Zealand foreign ministry official referred depends upon the ability of the members to act as if the Commonwealth had no hierarchy, as if British experience and culture were not the identitive cement of the system, and as if all states were equally petitioners and providers. On the surface at least the behaviour of Commonwealth members at their meetings is a model for meetings between heads of government: the maintenance of the hypocrisies which we have mentioned has allowed the identitive elements to emerge although they also help to explain the occasional deviant behaviour.

The achievements of these meetings, both in terms of style and in terms of substance, should not be underestimated. The Singapore meeting was undoubtedly instrumental in persuading the British government of Edward Heath that there would be unacceptable costs in providing arms to South Africa in the teeth of the opposition of the greater number of the Commonwealth states.[11] The Lusaka meeting of 1979 was the occasion of considerable progress towards a settlement of the Rhodesian question. Mrs Thatcher was reportedly persuaded there that the Muzorewa constitution could not work, and it provided a suitable framework in which the frontline states, together with the

Commonwealth secretariat, and the governments of Australia and Jamaica, could work out a satisfactory approach.[12] But there were ominous intimations of the fragility of the community aspects of the meeting. Edward Heath caused considerable animosity at Singapore by sailing with white chums rather than socialising with Commonwealth prime ministers and presidents. Harold Wilson was accused of manipulating the timing and agenda of the meetings to suit his own interest. And, before the Lusaka meeting, although in the event everything went well, there seemed to be a real possibility that the community sentiment would be destroyed in a sudden exposure of the hypocrisies already discussed, in a display of anger by Mrs Thatcher.[13] It seemed all too possible that she would tell the others that Britain could not be pushed around, that the idea of equality was a sham, and that others were equally guilty of transgressions. There was a sense of skating on rather thin ice. The community element is a real aspect of the meetings of Commonwealth heads of state; in the early 1980s its appearances should be judged as a striking and heartening development in a world so profoundly divided. Yet the factors which threaten it should not be ignored.

The main difficulty in the Commonwealth in the late 1970s and early 1980s may be explained in general terms as follows: in any social relationship the identitive community element needs to be reinforced by the pluralist aspect in the sense that community needs to be sustained by a measure of satisfaction of the separate interests of states. Whilst community can compensate for inadequate utilitarian returns, if the latter declined too far community would also be eroded. More specifically: the Commonwealth now seems to have reached the point at which the utilitarian rewards of membership for its leading members, particularly Britain, are declining and may reach a level at which the community relationship can no longer be sustained. Both the Conservative Party and the Labour Party continued to express support for the Commonwealth from their different perspectives, yet both parties were in a period of major change: the depth and durability of their attachment was uncertain. Aspects of an attitude in Britain which illustrates this were discussed in a speech on 11 December 1980 by the Commonwealth Secretary-General, Shridath Ramphal. He said that

Britain pays its dues and does, more often than not, what is asked of it: but sometimes in a detached and seemingly uncaring way. . . . My point is . . . to plead for greater acknowledgement, greater evidence, greater assurance, that for Britain too, the Commonwealth does

matter . . . In the years ahead there will be need to preserve balance –
to ensure that Britain's relationship with the Commonwealth does not
swing from dominion to detachment, but steadies to a sense of
fraternity.[14]

The Secretary-General clearly fears that the tendency in Britain's policy
which needs to be countered leads away from involvement with the
Commonwealth. There does indeed seem to be a feeling amongst the
major sections of the politically relevant elites in Britain that the
Commonwealth is becoming less capable of providing tangible rewards,
and this is both a reflection of a decline in identity with the Commonwealth – a weakening of the community element – and a cause of
further decline.

From the time of the founding of the United Nations until the late
1950s the Commonwealth link was a source of strength to the British in
that organisation and outside it; indeed, one of the justifications for their
permanent membership of the Security Council was their leadership of a
group of nations, and of the Empire. But by the 1970s attitudes amongst
Commonwealth governments had so changed that the British were
anxious to avoid accusations of throwing their weight about: they were
vulnerable to the charge of neo-imperialism, of bullying their offspring.
One commentator added that 'Other Commonwealth countries are even
more cautious on the question of taking on "leadership" '.[15] In
consequence 'As a group the Commonwealth does not exist at the UN
and since 1964, even the "gentlemen's agreement" that allowed some
kind of Commonwealth representation in the Security Council, the
Economic and Social Council, [and so on] has hardly been evoked in
practice.'[16] One cause of this lack of leadership, and the subdued
posture of the Commonwealth as a group in the UN and elsewhere is the
ideological hypocrisy: things cannot be brought out lest quarrels ensue.
But the British government cannot avoid accusations of failing to act to
protect the interests of Commonwealth members: from their point of
view the situation is fraught with enfeebling paradoxes. The British have
responsibility without leadership; blame without power. There are great
problems in creating an adequate consensus among Commonwealth
members on any major issue. The Commonwealth has a peculiar form of
inbuilt *immobilisme* which has become a burden to the British: yet
Britain certainly acquires an increment of diplomatic weight because of
that connection, and is moved by this at the moment to continue to play
the game. Yet she dare not lead except with great timidity for fear of
being accused of intolerable arrogance.

In the 1970s the attention of the British government was also diverted from the Commonwealth to the European Communities: its interest in managing the complications of responsibility without leadership was declining. Whilst it is probably true, as Ramphal pointed out, that Commonwealth countries are happy to see Britain in Europe, membership has certainly proved to be a distraction from the other enterprise. Commonwealth members are aware of the importance of developing links with the world's largest trading unit, and of making the best possible arrangements for their exports and for aid with that group. Britain is seen as their agent in these matters and in this context 'the Commonwealth wants to see Britain more effective in Europe'.[17] One problem, of course, is that Britain's obligations in this area are based as much upon old loyalties and duties – the identitive aspect – as upon a careful calculation of self-interest, and are liable to be seen as less binding if the sense of community fades. All the indications are that the attention of the British Foreign and Commonwealth Office is increasingly focused upon the system for European Political Co-operation and that the Commonwealth connection, accordingly, gets less attention,[18] though it has been argued that Commonwealth members meet each other as frequently in the capitals of third states as do the members of the European Communities. The range of meetings, the development of an extensive infra-structure and the diplomatic weight of the European Communities in the international system, all reinforce the new enthusiasm at the expense of the old. The Communities have become an important part of the daily diplomatic life of Britain, whereas the Commonwealth, even when it acts successfully, as in Lusaka, is increasingly a less involving and even an occasional enterprise. The British government usually gives responsibility for Commonwealth relations to a junior minister at the FCO and the largest single briefing for the Prime Minister by the FCO is for the meetings of heads of government. But the status of the official responsible for Commonwealth business has probably declined, and the scale of the Prime Minister's briefing is a reflection of the unusually wide range of business with which she then has to deal rather than a measure of its salience. The scale of the briefing might also be a reflection of her relative unfamiliarity with the business of the Commonwealth.

An underlying difficulty in reinforcing Britain's attachment to the Commonwealth is that as her economic circumstances worsen it is increasingly difficult to convince her government that there is much to be gained by further investment in the Commonwealth in the form of special aid. During the 1970s the proportion of Britain's trade with the

Communities steadily increased while that with the Commonwealth declined: by 1981 nearly 50 per cent of Britain's total trade was with the EEC and around 60 per cent was with the EEC and European states linked with it.[19] In the early 1960s the Commonwealth contained a number of important trading partners for the United Kingdom, but Commonwealth trade subsequently declined in importance compared with that with the EEC. This decline in Commonwealth trade with Britain – mainly from the older Commonwealth – is matched by an increasing reluctance on the part of the British government to provide adequate aid for the poorer members. Britain has failed to respond to the kind of arguments presented in the Brandt Report except at the non-governmental level, and in 1981 was one of the states named by the World Bank as having devoted an unsatisfactory proportion of Gross National Product to helping the developing countries. Although around 80 per cent of British aid went to Commonwealth countries in the late 1970s, this amounted to only £500 million and total aid was a mere 0.4 per cent of GNP.[20] These figures compared with around £7000 million spent on defence, and £1000 million in gross contributions – around £600 million net – to the EEC in 1980. One of the complaints made about the otherwise highly successful meeting of heads of government at Lusaka in 1979 was that there was a reluctance of governments to produce even small amounts of funds for the modest programmes of such bodies as the Commonwealth Fund for Technical Co-operation, the Commonwealth Foundation, and the Commonwealth Youth Programme, though Britain later somewhat increased her contributions. Secretary-General Ramphal charged more specifically that 'Britain has reduced support for CTFC at the time when it could not hurt more'.[21] It seemed that through the 1970s Britain's declining trading interdependence with the Commonwealth was matched by a declining enthusiasm on the part of its government for giving aid to its members. The Commonwealth was also declining in importance as a framework of economic independence for the British.

As the perception of the inadequacy of Britain's specific rewards from the Commonwealth grew amongst her political elites, so the government's preparedness to devote resources to the identitive elements declined. Ramphal pointed out the damaging effect upon the sense of community of Commonwealth citizens of the immigration systems at points of entry, where Commonwealth citizens were now required to pass through the gates labelled with that dreadful term 'alien'. The British government also decided that Commonwealth students at British universities should be asked to pay full overseas fees, which were approaching £3000 per annum in some subjects in some universities in Britain in the academic session 1981–82. The government seemed to be completely impervious to the argument that concessions should be made to Commonwealth students as this reinforced their goodwill towards the British, reinforced their sense of community with other Commonwealth citizens, and was a valuable diplomatic resource for the British government. The British government also seemed to be incapable in the early 1980s of understanding that the British tertiary eduction system was regarded by many Commonwealth states as a natural extension of their own schools; it was seen to be in some sense part of a unified Commonwealth system of education. The governments of Malaysia and Singapore made their displeasure about the new discriminatory fee structure clear to the British government and there was considerable lobbying behind the scenes at Lusaka.[22] In January 1980 a delegation of parents from Cyprus came to Britain to tell the government about their alarm: where else could their sons and daughters find the education they preferred and which they had learned to expect in their association with the Commonwealth?[23] At their Melbourne meeting in 1981 the Heads of Government 'recognised that there was widespread and serious concern that the recent very substantial increases in overseas student fees in some countries were creating impediments to the movement of students and teachers' (from the *Communiqué*, October 1981). It was reported that the number of students from the poorer member-states of the Commonwealth had declined significantly in the late 1970s: in 1978–80 the numbers from Tanzania, Malawi and Bangladesh taking places at British universities fell by 23 per cent.[24] Some states reacted angrily by deciding that students who until then had been trained in Britain, for instance in shipping control and navigation, should now be sent to the USA or Australia. There was evidence of a reaction based upon a sense of betrayal of a mutual trust. Others, such as India, had decided earlier to increase the level of their provision for postgraduates in their own countries, but this trend was accelerated by the decisions of the British government. Fewer Commonwealth military were also sent for training in Britain.[25]

The changing attitude was also reflected in the British government's continuing threat to cut spending on the BBC's overseas broadcasting, including that to the Commonwealth. In 1978 it was reported that

the BBC's services to Commonwealth countries in English, Hindi, Urdu, Tamil, Bengali, Hausa, Swahili but alas, no longer in Sinhala, attract some of our largest audiences: 20 per cent of the adult population of Nigeria are regular listeners to the World Service in English, 30 per cent of Northern Nigerians listen to the Hausa service, and in Northern Indian cities 15 per cent listen to broadcasts in Hindi and in West Bengal 16 per cent listen to those in Bengali.[26]

Yet the Central Policy Review Staff suggested in that year that broadcasting to the Commonwealth should be severely cut. Although their proposals were modified, further cuts were proposed in 1981 which were likely to be implemented. At that time it looked likely that there would be cuts in the BBC's broadcasting in the English language to the Commonwealth. The Government also proposed to reduce its contribution to the transcription service from £1 million to £500 000 per annum: this service was extensively used by member states and constituted a form of indirect broadcasting to them from Britain. The various sections of the BBC concerned with broadcasting in indigenous Commonwealth languages were also consistently short of funds: there were pressures to contract. The Foreign Secretary, Lord Carrington, insisted that cuts should be made despite a clear vote against them in the House of Lords in the summer of 1981: the argument put by him was that broadcasting was essentially an act of foreign policy and should be determined by criteria laid down by those responsible for foreign policy. Commonwealth broadcasting was not to be allocated a high priority in the new scheme of things: the resources had become scarce and were to be spent on persuading 'our enemies'. Unfortunately, as Gerald Mansell pointed out, 'The argument that we do not need to cultivate our friends is flawed'.[27] In this area, too the British government seemed unable to see the benefit of devoting more resources to consolidating relations with old friends, something which has a particular importance in view of Britain's declining ability to provide them with tangible benefits. Friends might be satisfied with less, and prepared to give more. A greater proportion of the effort to maintain relationships seemed to be made by non-governmental organisations, and with declining effect. These tended to be the descendants of the philanthropic organisations of the old empire.

There is, then, evidence to suggest that the British government has become careless about forms of behaviour which are offensive to Commonwealth citizens are which undermine their sense of community. It has also become less willing to spend money on activities which sustain the identitive links, although some of these may also have facilitated more tangible short-term returns. For instance, the real cost of a subsidised university place is hard to calculate, because the sums which students spend in local shops, on accommodation, and so on, can be set against the subsidy, although again the government has decided to ignore this calculation. These changes have been allowed in part because political elites have found the tangible rewards of the Commonwealth increasingly difficult to identify, and the costs increasingly apparent, and in part because it is easy to take community for granted. On the other hand British actions which weaken the identitive links also make it more likely that the other members will look for tangible rewards – ways of satisfying their own interests in the shorter term – as a justification for membership. The weaker the identitive elements, the stronger the utilitarian rewards need to be. The question of how much the members of the Commonwealth other than Britain get out of the organisation in practical terms has therefore also become a more important one in the early 1980s precisely because of Britain's declining commitment to the identitive elements.

It is, however, difficult to formulate an answer to this question with much detail or precision, though it seems that only the smallest and poorest among the member states receive a significant proportion of their resource transfers from the Commonwealth. For most of the others the broad function of its organisations is to provide expertise – the necessary human skills – but to seek major resources from elsewhere. Commonwealth organisations are not ways of providing but rather of arranging for provision from outside. Hence the Commonwealth Science Council is concerned to identify projects which can be run in collaboration with others, including international organisations in the United Nations framework, or national governmental organisations; it is, as Ramphal pointed out, a priming group. The Commonwealth health organisations have rather small numbers of staff, but start projects which may be run in collaboration with, or even taken over by, organisations like the World Health Organisation. (The Commonwealth is capable of acting as a lobby there.) The CFTC also focuses upon plugging gaps in other people's enterprises rather than in carrying through its own. No Commonwealth organisation, therefore, is a significant channel of resources, although they may make a real contribution to the initiation of activities and to their organisation. While this contribution should not be undervalued there are dangers in treating modest size as a virtue: the rhetoric of the admirers of the CFTC, for instance, is that its resources are modest but that all its members contribute to its finances and its slimness is an aid to efficiency. There is, however, a danger that the rhetoric could merely provide a cover for the rich states keeping their contributions at a modest level.

The image of the Commonwealth is perhaps that of a family organising to get more out of the outside world: if the emotional and psychological links of the family weaken, however, and its members begin to expect to get more tangible returns from each other, the disappointment will be greater than if the links had never existed. But the level of practical support in aid of various kinds within the Commonwealth itself is rather low (the organisation does not add much to general sources), and donor states, particularly the British, are rather reluctant to increase their contributions. Indeed, the proportion of Britain's total aid which goes to the Commonwealth is likely to go down in the 1980s.

I have already mentioned another tangible benefit of membership, that of putting pressure upon Britain to follow an approved line in tackling internal problems, and of representing the interests of partners in other fora, like the European Communities and the international financial institutions. Both of these interests of membership have a certain decomposable character: when the problems are solved this reason for preserving the relationship is removed; the biggest problem of all, the issue of South African race relations, may prove more divisive than uniting; and the British government is increasingly finding it difficult to convince itself that it would act as a Commonwealth agent, as its political elites, particularly those concerned with foreign policy, are now attracted more by European political co-operation. For some member states the Commonwealth is valued in part because it is a way of countering less desirable attractions: for both Canada and Australia it is a distancing from the American connection. There is a risk, however, that such a negative motive, if lacking reinforcement by identitive elements and practical interest, will prove rather fragile. The conclusion seems unavoidable when stripped of the rhetoric of Commonwealth community, which in any case rests on the hypocrisies mentioned above, that the practical benefits of membership are rather slender, for members other than the group of poorest states, in the early 1980s. This is not to suggest that the Commonwealth is liable to disintegrate overnight. But the level of practical utilitarian reward for a large number of states may be inadequate to make up for the challenge to the identitive elements and may lead to less restrained mutual recrimination. One manifestation of this could be the exposure of the hypocrisy of ideology in the Commonwealth.

The Commonwealth is still an unusual partnership and its members have retained a sense of mutual obligation. But the weaknesses in the pattern of their relations should not be ignored by those who would wish the Commonwealth to prosper. One fundamental need is for member states to ponder deeply upon the implications of that 'sense of fraternity' which the Secretary-General wished to see more evident in Britain. It seems that Britain is sometimes expected to be more fraternal than others – there is underneath the assumption of equality an inequality of obligation and expectations. Fraternity needs, however to involve a more balanced partnership in the common enterprise amongst those states which have the resources to make a contribution. States such as Nigeria and India, and others with a comparatively greater range of resources, should be prepared to make a proportionately equal invest-ment with the 'older dominions', and there should be no appearance of the white nations doing more. There are signs that they are beginning to do this, and this should be welcomed and encouraged. One condition of the sharing of obligations is probably the acceptance, particularly by the newer members, that the identitive links are important and that they are indeed based on versions of British culture and political experience. The Commonwealth needs to develop a new kind of cultural enthusiasm, namely a concern with a local, indigenous culture but not at the expense of a full acknowledgement of the value of the common cultural experience which the members share.

If a group of richer states involving both the new members and the older ones came to accept more fully the need to share equitably the obligations and duties of membership, and recognised more fully the value of the common elements in their cultures, a number of useful changes could be more easily introduced. For instance, intra-Commonwealth broadcasting could be greatly expanded if more money was available: one of the main difficulties with BBC external services at the moment seems to be that funding is inadequate to allow expansion. But attention could be paid by the slightly better-off states together to the problem of extending educational broadcasting to the worst-off states, and not just through the BBC; and to broadcasting which stressed the common cultural heritage. Another great need is for much more common funding of education for students from the poorer states, and also for students from states where internal problems have made financing temporarily difficult. In the early 1980s, for instance, students from Uganda in Britain had difficulty in moving funds, even when available, from their own country, and there were great difficulties in obtaining grants. Students from Nigeria have also found difficulty in funding their education in Britain. One possibility would be a Com-monwealth Student Fund with sufficient resources in readily convertible currencies to make a real contribution to the financing of students with adequate qualifications, regardless of the whims or difficulties of particular governments. The policy of the British government towards Commonwealth students in the early 1980s was a mistaken one, and greater efforts could be made by the other members to remedy the situation: the losers should not be the good students from the worst-off states. There should be more common funding which would reduce the dangers and inefficiences from an imperfect system of separate national funding.

I have pointed out that the development of links which sustained the identitive elements is to some extent an alternative to the provision of tangible rewards as a way of reinforcing the cohesion of a group such as this. Ideally, of course, the two should go together. For the British there are enormous long-term costs in excluding Commonwealth students: identity with and sympathy for Britain which often results from study here is a long-term diplomatic asset which should not be thrown away lightly. But in the longer term there is the possibility of evolving a more developed Commonwealth university system, possibly including a number of Commonwealth universities with common funding and admissions policies, and an integrated administrative structure. Indeed, something positive should be done to build upon the remnants of the educational organisations which have survived from the days of the British Empire and which in fact are surprisingly widespread. The other members also have a powerful incentive to help to strengthen the identitive links in that their strength ensures that Britain will act as their agent, for instance, in the European Communities. Britain and the new members find different difficulties (rival interests, and declining enthusiasm in Britain, and a reluctance by the others to accept that British culture broadly-defined is a common link in the Commonwealth) in the way of devoting more resources to the sustaining of the identitive elements, but for both this would be rewarding.

There are also several ways of increasing the number of utilitarian rewards to members, thereby strengthening the Commonwealth as a pluralist organisation. It would certainly be much easier to defend the retention by Britain, as her power declines, of a permanent seat in the Security Council of the United Nations, if she could be seen in the context of a more coherent group. It seems increasingly peculiar that Britain should retain her permanent seat in the Security Council, but the translation of the British place in the Council into a Commonwealth seat is also an attractive option. This could not happen, however, until the difficulties of managing the Commonwealth group in the UN and of identifying the principles underlying its cohesion have been overcome. It is hard to see the Secretariat taking on such a position as has been suggested by Samar Sen. The precise details of the manner of Commonwealth representation in the United Nations would need to be carefully worked out: possibilities include a rotating six-monthly presidency analagous with that of the European Communities, but advised by standing committees of government representatives. This would obviously involve an expansion of the Commonwealth's institutional arrangements beyond its Secretariat, the biennial meetings of heads of government, and the meetings of senior foreign office officials in the 'off' years. The Secretariat would also need to be expanded from its present rather slender resources, and the present move towards extending its co-ordinating role in relation to the United Nations specialised agencies should be encouraged. The United Nations, and the UN system, seems to be an appropriate point of focus of such institutional development. The Commonwealth has developed a myth that there is a virtue in slender means and slim institutional facilities: this myth should be examined more critically by supporters of the Commonwealth.

As regards aid-provision there is probably no alternative in the short term to an increase in the level of aid and other support from Britain above the present abysmal 0.4 per cent of GNP. Given existing links and traditional sensibilities the British excuse for ignoring the suggestions of the Brandt report, particularly as these are based on intelligent self-interest, are singularly feeble. In the longer term, however, more should be done to involve the wealthier states in the Commonwealth more actively in common support activities. The former President of the World Bank, Robert McNamara, has recently argued that there would be advantages in a system of aid to the poorer countries which included donations from the medium poor. The latter would then be compensated by the developed states. The Commonwealth could work more towards that system. The CFTC has done good work, but is far too small an operation. The Commonwealth should certainly continue to act as an agency for attracting support from elsewhere, but it needs greatly to develop its role as a channel for resource transfers. This does not just mean that Britain should give more, but rather that there should be a realistic evaluation of the capacity of all members to provide support.

This is but a brief sketch of some of the things which could be done. But if the Commonwealth is to maintain its cohesion, current weaknesses need to be recognised and remedied. In particular it is important to recognise the relationship between the identitive elements and the pluralist elements in the Commonwealth, and the way that changes in the level of either are liable to affect the other. As the Secretary-General put it, there is a need to ensure that Britain's relationship with the Commonwealth does not swing from dominion to detachment, but steadies to a sense of fraternity. But it is also important to recognise that there are good reasons for Britain's hesitation in the 1980s, although there has also been a degree of carelessness and a large amount of hypocrisy. Some of the remedies are, however, in the hands of Britain's partners. There needs to be a greater understanding on their part of the nature of fraternity and the obligations which it involves. There are difficult adjustments to be made on all sides if the appearance of community in the Commonwealth is to be given more solid foundation and to flourish.

NOTES AND REFERENCES

1. See Karl Deutsch, *Tides Among Nations* (New York: Free press, 1979) especially chapters 1 and 6.
2. Figures calculated from Commonwealth Secretariat, *Commonwealth Organisations: a handbook of official and unofficial organisations active in the Commonwealth* (London: Commonwealth Secretariat, 1979).
3. Reported in W. David McIntyre, *The Commonwealth of Nations: origins and impact 1869–1971* (Minneapolis: University of Minnesota Press, 1977) p. 473.
4. Figures calculated from *Commonwealth Organisations: a handbook of official and unofficial organisations active in the Commonwealth* (London: Commonwealth Secretariat, 1979).
5. See *The Round Table*, issue no. 242, April 1971, pp. 191–8; issue 267, July 1977, pp. 215–29; See the Appendix for texts.
6. See Noreen Burrows, 'Tanzania's Intervention in Uganda: some legal aspects', *The World Today*, July 1979, pp. 306–10.
7. Reported in Commonwealth Notebook, *The Round Table*, April 1981, Issue 282, p. 196.
8. W. David McIntyre, *The Commonwealth of Nations*, p. 468.
9. *The Times*, November 24, 1972, p. 15.
10. W. David McIntyre, *The Commonwealth of Nations*, p. 466.
11. See Derek Ingram, *The Imperfect Commonwealth* (London: Rex Collings, 1977).
12. See Derek Ingram, 'Lusaka 1979: a significant Commonwealth meeting,' *The Round Table*, No. 276, Oct. 1979, pp. 278–9.
13. Ibid.
14. From a lecture by Shridath S. Ramphal, the Focus Lecture 1980, *The Commonwealth in the 1980s: the Need to Care*, issued by Commonwealth Secretariat, p. 9.

15. Samar Sen, 'The Commonwealth Role at the United Nations,' *The Round Table*, Issue 277, June 1980, p. 14.
17. S. S. Ramphal, *The Commonwealth in the 1980s*, p. 8.
18. See Christopher Hill, 'The British Experience of European Political Cooperation, 1970–81', paper for RIIA TERSA Conference, 20–4 July 1981, cited with the author's permission.
19. See figures quoted *Europe 81*, no. 7, July 1981, p. 6.
20. See Andrew Walker, *The Commonwealth: a new look* (Oxford: Pergamon, 1978).
21. Ramphal, *The Commonwealth in the 1980s*, p. 3.
22. See John O'Leary, 'Britain puts up the fees for overseas students', *The Round Table*, Issue 278, April 1980, pp. 170–1.
23. Ibid., p. 169.
24. Ibid., p. 169.
25. See above.
26. Gerard Mansell, 'The Voice of Britain in the Commonwealth', *The Round Table*, No. 269, January 1978, p. 49.
27. Ibid., p. 52.

Appendices

Appendix A:
The Commonwealth – Members and Organisations

THE COMMONWEALTH

Member Country (Capital)	Population (thousands)
Antigua and Barbuda (St Johns)	74
Australia (Canberra)	14 300
Bahamas (Nassau)	234
Bangladesh (Dacca)	88 934
Barbados (Bridgetown)	248
Belize (Belmopan)	131
Botswana (Gaborone)	773
Britain (London)	55 900
Canada (Ottawa)	23 700
Cyprus (Nicosia)	618
Dominica (Roseau)	82
Fiji (Suva)	619
The Gambia (Banjul)	587
Ghana (Accra)	11 313
Grenada (St George's)	109
Guyana (Georgetown)	834
India (New Delhi)	659 217
Jamaica (Kingston)	2 159
Kenya (Nairobi)	15 274
Kiribati (Tarawa)	56
Lesotho (Maseru)	1 309
Malawi (Lilongwe)	5 817
Malaysia (Kuala Lumpur)	13 137
Malta (Valletta)	340
Mauritius (Port Louis)	941
Nauru (Nauru)	10

New Zealand (Wellington)	3 200
Nigeria (Lagos)	82 603
Papua New Guinea (Port Moresby)	2 930
St Lucia (Castries)	122
St Vincent and the Grenadines (Kingstown)	106
Seychelles (Victoria)	64
Sierra Leone (Freetown)	3 381
Singapore (Singapore)	2 361
Solomon Islands (Honiara)	221
Sri Lanka (Colombo)	14 542
Swaziland (Mbabane)	541
Tanzania (Dar es Salaam)	18 030
Tongo (Nuka' alofa)	100
Trinidad and Tobago (Port of Spain)	1 150
Tuvalu (Funafuti)	10
Uganda (Kampala)	12 797
Vanuatu (Port Vila)	105
Western Samoa (Apia)	155
Zambia (Lusaka)	5 580
Zimbabwe (Harare)	7 146

Figures above are for mid-1979. Figures below are projections for mid-1982.

Special Members

Nauru	7
Tavalu (Funafuti)	6

UK Associated States

St Kitts-Nevis (Basseterre)	54

UK Protected State

Brunei (Bandar Seri Bagawan)	180

UK Dependencies

Anguilla (The Valley)	7
Bermuda (Hamilton)	60
British Antarctic Territory	0.1
British Indian Ocean Territory	0.1
British Virgin Islands (Road Town)	11.5
Cayman Islands (Georgetown)	13.5
Falkland Islands and Dependencies (Stanley)	2
Gibraltar	30
Hong Kong (Victoria)	5 000
Monserrat (Plymouth)	12.4
Pitcairn Islands (Adamstown)	0.074
St Helena and Dependencies (Jamestown)	6.5
Turks and Caicos Islands (Cockburn Town)	8

Australian Dependencies

Australian Antarctic Territory	
Christmas Islands	3.5
Cocos (Keeling) Islands	0.65
Heard and McDonald Islands	
Norfolk Island	1.5

New Zealand Associated State

Cook Islands (Avarua)	22

New Zealand Dependencies

Niue	3.8
Ross Dependency	0.050
Tokelau Islands	1.6

EXTRACT FROM THE COMMONWEALTH SECRETARIAT PUBLICATION
COMMONWEALTH ORGANISATIONS

Classification of Organisations

The following list is designed to help users identify at a glance those areas of activity with which each organisation is concerned.

Functional areas of activity are defined as follows:

Funding agency: grants for development projects (both technical assistance and capital aid); scholarships and awards for education and training; sponsorship schemes

Co-ordination: agencies which draw together and liaise among a group of like organisations

Information exchange: resource centres, audio-visual services; libraries; publications; speaker services; discussion meetings, seminars and conferences

Research: pure and applied

Development assistance: technical advice and expertise; material aid (including emergency relief); overseas voluntary workers

Education and training: exchange of personnel; formal and non-formal education programmes; technical and vocational training courses; youth training programmes; development education

Professional standards: improvement of professional standards; codes of conduct; equivalence of qualifications

Geographical area: area in which each organisation has, by membership or activity, a presence

Headquarters: country in which the organisation is officially based

Abbreviations to the Figure

Admin	Administration
Adv	Advisory
Agric	Agricultural
AFR/Afr	Africa/n
AS	Asia
Assoc	Association
AUS/Aus	Australia/n
BAR	Barbados
BRI/Bri	Britain/British
CAN/Can	Canada/Canadian
CAR/Car	Carribean
Coun	Council
Cttee	Committee
CW	Commonwealth
Dev	Development
Educ	Education/al
Fed	Federation
Fdn	Foundation
GHA	Ghana
GUY	Guyana
IND	India
INT/Int	International
JAM	Jamaica
KEN	Kenya
Lang	Language
Lit	Literature
NAT	National
NC	New Caledonia
NIG	Nigeria
NZ	New Zealand
Org	Organisation
PAC	Pacific
Ser	Service/s
SRI	Sri Lanka
TAN	Tanzania

CLASSIFICATION OF ORGANISATIONS

Organisation	Funding agency	Co-ordination	Information exchange	Research	Development assistance	Education and training	Professional standards	Geographical area	Headquarters
OFFICIAL: Commonwealth									
CW Advisory Aeronautical Research Coun			●	●			●	CW	BRI
CW Agricultural Bureaux		●	●		●		●	CW	BRI
CW Air Transport Council			●				●	CW	BRI
CW Assoc of Tax Administrators		●	●				●	CW	BRI
CW Cttee on Defence		●					●	CW	BRI
CW Cttee on Mineral Resources and Geology			●	●				CW	BRI
CW Defence Science Organisation							●	CW	BRI
CW Foundation	●						●	CW	BRI
CW Scholarship and Fellowship Plan	●	●	●		●	●		CW	BRI
CW Science Council		●	●	●	●	●	●	CW	BRI
CW Secretariat (inc CFTC)		●	●			●	●	CW	BRI
CW Telecommunication Bureau			●			●	●	CW	BRI
CW War Graves Commission						●		CW	BRI
OFFICIAL: Regional									
Caribbean Community Secretariat		●	●			●		CAR	GUY
Colombo Plan	●	●	●	●	●	●		AS/PAC	SRI
Cttee for Co-ordination of Joint Prospecting for Mineral Resources		●	●			●		PAC	FIJI
CW Regional Health Secretariat	●	●	●		●	●	●	AFR	TAN
Economic Community of W African States		●	●					AFR	NIG
S Pacific Bureau for Economic Co-operation		●	●					PAC	FIJI
S Pacific Commission		●	●	●	●	●		PAC	NC
University of the S Pacific		●	●		●	●		PAC	FIJI
W African Health Community		●	●			●		AFR	NIG

Organisation	Funding agency	Co-ordination	Information exchange	Research	Development assistance	Education and training	Professional standards	Geographical area	Headquarters
OFFICIAL: National development agencies									
Aus Dev Assistance Bureau	●	●			●	●		INT	AUS
British Council	●	●	●	●	●	●		INT	BRI
Canadian Int Dev Agency	●	●		●	●	●		INT	CAN
Centre for Int Research Co-op		●			●	●		INT	AUS
CW Dev Corporation	●				●	●		INT	BRI
Crown Agents	●	●				●		INT	BRI
Ministry of Overseas Dev, Britain	●	●						INT	BRI
Technical Educ and Training							●	INT	BRI
UNOFFICIAL: Agriculture and forestry									
CW Assoc of Scientific Agric Societies		●		●	●	●	●	CW	CAN
CW Forestry Association			●				●	CW	BRI
CW Forestry Institute			●				●	CW	BRI
CW Veterinary Association		●	●			●	●	CW	CAN
Royal Agric Society of the CW		●	●			●		CW	BRI
Standing Cttee on CW Forestry		●	●			●		CW	BRI
UNOFFICIAL: Culture									
Assoc of CW Lit and Lang Studies								CW	AUS
CW Arts Association		●	●			●	●	CW	BRI
CW Arts Cttee		●	●			●	●	CW	BRI
CW Assoc of Museums		●	●			●	●	CW	BRI
CW Philharmonic Orchestra Trust			●					CW	BRI
Org for Museums, Monuments and Sites of Africa		●	●	●			●	AFR	GHA
Development co-operation									
Afro-Asian Rural Reconstruction Org		●			●	●		AFR/AS	IND
All Africa Conf of Churches		●			●	●		AFR	KEN
Archbishop of Sydney's Overseas Relief Fund	●				●			AS	AUS
Asian Bureau Australia								AS/PAC	AUS
Assoc of Apex Clubs	●		●	●	●			AS	AUS

Organization		Region	Country
Aus Baptist World Aid and Relief Cttee		INT	AUS
Aus Care for Refugees (Austcare)		AS/PAC	AUS
Aus Catholic Relief		INT	AUS
Aus Coun for Overseas Aid		INT	BRI
British Executive Ser Overseas		NAT	BRI
British Volunteer Programme		NAT	CAN
Canadian Council for Int Co-op		INT	CAN
Canadian Executive Ser Overseas		INT	CAN
Canadian University Ser Overseas		INT	CAN
Catholic Fund for Overseas Dev		INT	BRI
Catholic Institute for Int Relations		INT	CAN
Centre D'Etude et de Co-op Int		INT	BRI
Christians Abroad		INT	BRI
Community Aid Abroad		INT	AUS
Food for the Hungry		INT	CAN
For Those Who Have Less		AS	CAN
Fdn for the Peoples of the S Pacific		PAC	AUS
FRIDA		AFR	BRI
Int Coalition for Dev Action		INT	BRI
Int Dev Action		NAT	AUS
Int Dev Research Centre		INT	CAN
Int Voluntary Service		INT	BRI
Inter Pares		INT	CAN
Match Int Centre		INT	CAN
NZ Assoc for Int Relief, Rehabilitation and Development		INT	NZ
North-South Institute		NAT	CAN
Overseas Book Centre		INT	CAN
Overseas Dev Institute		NAT	BRI
Overseas Service Bureau		INT	AUS
Oxfam		INT	BRI
Primates World Relief and Dev Fund		INT	CAN
Project Concern Australia		AS/PAC	AUS
Ranfurly Library Service Ltd		INT	BRI
Society of St Vincent de Paul		AS/PAC	AUS
TEAR Fund Ltd		INT	BRI
Unitarian Ser Cttee of Canada		INT	CAN
United Nations Assoc (UK)		INT	BRI
United Society for the Propagation of the Gospel		INT	BRI

Organisation	Funding agency	Co-ordination	Information exchange	Research	Development assistance	Education and training	Professional standards	Geographical area	Headquarters
Voluntary Service Overseas	●		●					INT	BRI
Volunteer Service Abroad	●			●	●	●		AS/PAC	NZ
Volunteer Missionary Movement	●				●	●		INT	BRI
War on Want	●				●	●		INT	BRI
UNOFFICIAL: Education and research									
African Adult Educ Assoc		●	●		●	●	●	AFR	KEN
Asian-S Pacific Bureau of Adult Educ		●	●			●	●	AS/PAC	AUS
Assoc of African Universities		●	●			●	●	AFR	GHA
Assoc of CW Universities		●	●			●	●	CW	BRI
Bransons CW Educ Trust Ltd						●		CW	BRI
Budiriro Trust						●		AFR	BRI
Center for CW and Comparative Studies		●		●			●	CW	USA
Center for Int Briefing			●			●		INT	BRI
CW Assoc of Science and Maths Educators		●	●			●		CW	BRI
CW Consultative Space Research Ctee		●	●	●				CW	BRI
CW Coun for Educational Admin						●	●	CW	AUS
CW Geographical Bureau			●			●	●	CW	BRI
CW Institute, London			●			●		CW	BRI
CW Institute, Scotland			●			●		NAT	BRI
Coun for Educ in the CW				●		●		NAT	BRI
Inst of CW and Comparative Studies		●		●		●		NAT	CAN
Inst of CW Studies, London				●		●		NAT	BRI
Inst of CW Studies, Oxford				●		●		NAT	BRI
Int African Institute				●		●		AFR	BRI
Int Council for Adult Education	●		●			●	●	INT	CAN
Inter-University Council		●	●			●	●	INT	BRI
Queen Elizabeth House			●	●		●		NAT	BRI
Royal Institute of Public Admin			●	●		●	●	INT	BRI
Sir Ernest Cassel Educ Trust	●			●		●		CW	BRI
United World Colleges	●					●		CW	BRI
World Educ Fellowship			●			●	●	INT	BRI

UNOFFICIAL: Environment

Organisation								Region	Country
Caribbean Conservation Assoc	•	•			•	•	•	CAR	BAR
CW Assoc of Architects	•	•			•	•	•	CW	BRI
CW Assoc of Planners	•	•			•	•	•	CW	BRI
CW Assoc of Surveying and Land Economy		•			•	•	•	CW	BRI
CW Human Ecology Coun	•	•			•	•	•	CW	BRI

UNOFFICIAL: Health

Organisation								Region	Country
African Medical and Research Fdn	•	•	•	•				AFR	KEN
Assistance Medicale Internationale	•	•	•	•				INT	CAN
CW (and Int) Medical Adv Bureau	•	•	•	•	•	•	•	NAT	BRI
CW Medical Association	•	•			•	•	•	CW	BRI
CW Nurses Federation	•	•			•	•	•	CW	BRI
CW Pharmaceutical Association	•	•			•	•	•	CW	BRI
CW Society for the Deaf	•	•			•	•	•	CW	BRI
Int Confederation of Midwives	•	•	•	•	•	•	•	INT	BRI
LEPRA	•	•						AFR/AS	BRI
Operation Eyesight Universal	•	•						AFR/AS	CAN
Royal CW Society for the Blind	•	•	•	•	•	•	•	CW	BRI
St John Ambulance Assoc and Brigade	•	•	•	•	•	•	•	INT	BRI

UNOFFICIAL: Industry and commerce

Organisation								Region	Country
CW Sugar Exporters Assoc		•			•	•	•	CW	BRI
E Africa and Mauritius Assoc		•			•	•	•	AFR	BRI
W Africa Cttee		•			•	•	•	AFR	BRI
W India Cttee		•	•		•	•	•	CAR	BRI

UNOFFICIAL: Information and the media

Organisation								Region	Country
CW Broadcasting Assoc	•	•			•	•	•	CW	BRI
CW Journalists Assoc	•	•			•	•	•	CW	BRI
CW Library Assoc	•	•			•	•	•	CW	JAM
CW Press Union	•	•			•	•	•	CW	BRI
Diplomatic and CW Writers Assoc	•		•		•	•	•	NAT	BRI
Working Party on Library Holdings of CW Literature	•		•		•	•	•	CW	BRI

Organisation	Funding agency	Co-ordination	Information exchange	Research	Development assistance	Education and training	Professional standards	Geographical area	Headquarters
UNOFFICIAL: International understanding									
Associated Countrywomen of the World	●	●	●			●		INT	BRI
Assoc of CW Teachers		●	●			●		NAT	BRI
British Assoc of the Experiment in Int Living			●					INT	BRI
British Caribbean Association			●			●		CAR	BRI
CW Assoc of Canada			●			●		CW	CAN
CW Countries League			●			●		CW	BRI
CW Friendship Movement			●			●		CW	BRI
CW Linking Trust			●					CW	BRI
CW of Nations Day Movement			●					NAT	AUS
CW Resettlement Association		●		●				CW	BRI
CW Society of N America		●●	●			●		CW	USA
CW Society of Singapore						●		CW	SIN
English Speaking Union of the CW		●	●			●●		INT	BRI
Friends World Cttee of Consultation								INT	BRI
Fund for Int Student Co-operation	●					●		INT	BRI
Joint CW Societies Council			●					NAT	BRI
League for the Exchange of CW Teachers		●	●	●				CW	BRI
Royal CW Society			●			●		CW	BRI
Royal Overseas League			●			●		CW	BRI
Society for CW Friendship			●					CW	IND
Victoria League for CW Friendship			●			●		CW	BRI
Women's Corona Society			●					INT	BRI
UNOFFICIAL: Law and parliament									
CW Legal Adv Service		●	●				●	CW	BRI
CW Legal Bureau		●	●			●	●	CW	NZ
CW Legal Educ Association		●	●				●	CW	BRI
CW Magistrates' Association			●			●●	●	CW	BRI
CW Parliamentary Association			●				●	CW	BRI

UNOFFICIAL: Science and technology

Achievement		
Intermediate Technology Dev Group	INT	BRI
Royal Society	INT	BRI
Royal Society of Arts	NAT	BRI
UNOFFICIAL: Social welfare and human rights		
Amnesty International	INT	BRI
Anti Slavery Society	INT	BRI
British CW Ex-Ser League	CW	BRI
CW Students' Children Society	CW	BRI
Fairbridge Society	CW	BRI
Int Alliance of Women	INT	BRI
Int Planned Parenthood Fed	INT	BRI
IODE	CW	CAN
Leonard Cheshire Fdn	INT	BRI
Minority Rights Group	INT	BRI
Project Trust	INT	BRI
Royal Canadian Legion	INT	CAN
Save the Children Fund	INT	BRI
UNOFFICIAL: Sport and leisure		
CW Games Federation	CW	BRI
CW Heraldry Board	CW	NZ
CW Weightlifting Federation	CW	BRI
World Expeditionary Association	INT	BRI
UNOFFICIAL: Youth		
African Centre for Educ Exchange	AFR	NIG
Boys' Brigade	INT	BRI
Canada World Youth	INT	CAN
CW Youth Exchange Council	CW	BRI
Comex	CW	BRI
Duke of Edinburgh's Award Scheme	INT	BRI
Educ Interchange Council	INT	BRI
Girls' Brigade Int Council	INT	BRI
Girl Guides Association	CW	BRI
Int Youth Hostel Federation	INT	BRI
Scout Association	INT	BRI

Appendix B: The Agreed Memorandum on the Commonwealth Secretariat

I. ESTABLISHMENT OF THE SECRETARIAT

(1) Pursuant to their decision announced after the conclusion of the Commonwealth Prime Ministers' Meeting in July 1964 the Commonwealth Prime Ministers have decided to establish forthwith a Commonwealth Secretariat. As envisaged in the communiqué issued at the close of the 1964 Meeting, the Commonwealth Prime Ministers see the Secretariat as being at the service of all Commonwealth Governments and as a visible symbol of the spirit of co-operation which animates the Commonwealth.

II. SITE OF THE SECRETARIAT

(2) The British Government will arrange for the Secretariat to be accommodated in Marlborough House.

III. FUNCTION OF THE SECRETARIAT

(3) The Commonwealth Prime Ministers have given further consideration to the role of the Commonwealth Secretariat, and the following paragraphs record the functions which they have agreed it should perform.

(4) The Secretary-General and his staff should approach their task bearing in mind that the Commonwealth is an association which enables countries in different regions of the world, consisting of a variety of races and representing a number of interests and points of view, to exchange opinions in a friendly, informal and intimate atmosphere. The organisation and functions of the Commonwealth Secretariat should be so designed as to assist in supporting and building on these fundamental

elements in the Commonwealth association. At the same time the Commonwealth is not a formal organisation. It does not encroach on the sovereignty of individual members. Nor does it require its members to seek to reach collective decisions or to take united action. Experience has proved that there are advantages in such informality. It enables its members to adapt their procedures to meet changing circumstances; conversely there would be disadvantages in establishing too formal procedures and institutions in the association.

General Considerations

(5) Both the Secretary-General and his staff should be seen to be the servants of Commonwealth countries collectively. They derive their functions from the authority of Commonwealth Heads of Government; and in the discharge of his responsibilities in this connection the Secretary-General should have access to Heads of Government, who will indicate the appropriate channels of communication to them.

(6) The Secretariat should not arrogate to itself executive functions. At the same time it should have, and develop, a relationship with other intra-Commonwealth bodies.

(7) The Secretariat should have a constructive role to play. At the same time it should operate initially on a modest footing; and its staff and functions should be left to expand pragmatically in the light of experience, subject always to the approval of Governments.

(8) Against this background and in the expectation that, as its contacts spread, the Secretariat could expect to receive increasing calls on its resources, the various functions which it will exercise fall under the following broad headings: international affairs, economic affairs and general and administrative functions.

International Affairs

(9) Consultation is the life blood of the Commonwealth association. At their Meeting in July 1964, the Commonwealth Prime Ministers expressed the view that on matters of major international importance a fuller exchange of views could very appropriately be promoted on an increasingly multilateral basis through the agency of the Secretariat. They were particularly anxious to ensure that there should be opportunity for fuller participation by all member countries in the normal processes of Commonwealth consultation. At the same time they showed themselves conscious of the importance of maintaining the unwritten conventions which have always determined those processes. The Secretary-General will observe the same conventions and act in the same spirit.

(10) In so far as Commonwealth Governments agree that the Secretariat should discharge any specific task, it will be fully at their disposal. In general, however, its purpose will be to serve them by facilitating and

promoting consultation on matters of common concern. To this end, subject to the general principles set out in paragraphs 12 and 13 below, the Secretary-General will arrange to prepare and circulate papers on international questions of common concern to all Commonwealth Governments where he considers it useful to do so. It may also prove helpful if, in consultation with the Governments concerned, he arranges occasional meetings of officials of member Governments for the exchange of information and views on agreed subjects. Such meetings might on occasion, if member Governments agreed, take place in various Commonwealth capitals or elsewhere.

(11)   The general principles which the Secretary-General will observe are set out in the following paragraphs.

(12)   The functions of the Secretariat are envisaged as being *inter alia* the dissemination of factual information to member countries on matters of common concern. 'Factual' information cannot be precisely defined; but, provided that the Secretary-General proceeds with circumspection in the exercise of this function, he is authorised, where he thinks it useful to do so, to prepare and circulate, either on his own initiative or at the request of a member Government, papers on international questions of common concern, provided that these papers do not propagate any particular sectional or partisan points of view, contain no policy judgments or recommendations by the Secretariat and do not touch upon the internal affairs of a member country or disputes or serious differences between two or more member countries. In addition, the Secretary-General will, on the request of a member Government, circulate papers submitted by that Government on international questions of common concern, provided that, if these touch upon the internal affairs of member countries or disputes between two or more member countries, they will not be circulated without prior concurrence of the country or countries concerned. The Secretary-General has discretion to refuse to prepare or circulate any paper, whatever its origin, which in his view propagates any sectional or partisan point of view or would for any other reason be liable to be offensive to any member country or countries.

(13)   The position of the remaining dependent territories within the Commonwealth is one matter which continues to command lively interest among member countries. The Secretariat could play a role in this field; and it might circulate to member Governments balanced papers on the constitutional advance of the remaining territories or on their progress towards independence, on the understanding that the responsible member Governments would always be closely consulted in the preparation of the papers.

(14)   The Secretariat will be guided by the principles outlined in the preceding paragraphs because it is important that it should develop as a unifying element within the Commonwealth. But, provided that it begins modestly and remains careful not to trespass on the independence and sovereignty of the member Governments whose servant it will be, it will be possible for

it to grow in the spirit of the Commonwealth association itself. All Commonwealth Governments wish to contribute to this process and will be ready to assist the Secretary-General in every possible way. In particular the Secretary-General will from the outset establish close relations with Commonwealth Governments and with their representatives in London; and Governments will arrange to keep the development of the Secretariat's functions under regular review, by means of an annual report on its work. By these means the Secretariat will gradually accumulate, with the passage of time, a body of knowledge and experience which will contribute to an even closer understanding among member Governments on those major international issues which are of common and continuing concern to all the members of the Commonwealth.

Economic Affairs

(15) The Secretariat will discharge several valuable roles in the economic field, the more important of which are outlined in the following paragraphs. Several intra-Commonwealth bodies are already actively at work in this field, and their relationship to the Secretariat is to be examined in accordance with the arrangements set out in paragraphs 23 to 26.

(16) The Secretary-General will initiate, collate and distribute to member Governments material bearing not only on economic problems, but also on social and cultural issues in respect of which the potential value of his work could be considerable. He is authorised to follow up the specialised factual reports of the various agencies already at work in these fields by promoting wider ranging studies on e.g. the inter-relationship of agricultural and industrial growth in the new Commonwealth. In this connection the Secretary-General may implement such tasks by commissioning, within the limits prescribed by his approved budget, specialist studies from outside expert sources rather than by engaging additional permanent staff.

(17) Apart from servicing meetings of the various Commonwealth economic bodies, the Secretariat may, as appropriate, be represented at meetings of these specialised agencies in order to keep in close touch with their activities; and it will also keep in touch with the various United Nations agencies whose work in Commonwealth countries will on occasion be of direct concern to it.

(18) In connection with the general economic aspects of the Secretariat's work, the proposals advanced at the last meeting of Commonwealth Prime Ministers for the initiation of joint Commonwealth Development Projects in individual Commonwealth countries are relevant. The passage from the 1964 communiqué reads:

> In particular they considered a proposal that development projects might be launched in individual Commonwealth countries, which would be implemented by various members acting in close col-

laboration and contributing whatever resources – in men, money, materials and technical expertise – they could most appropriately provide. Such projects, which would be additional to the support which Commonwealth countries already provide to the United Nations Special Fund and Expanded Programme of Technical Assistance, could be directed to a number of different purposes – the improvement of agricultural production and the development of natural resources through extension services, training and research; the enlargement of professional and technical training: the development of new industries; and so forth. But they would all be inspired by the common purpose of promoting the development of the Commonwealth by a co-ordinated programme of joint or bilateral projects. The British Government said that they would be prepared to make a substantial contribution to projects of this kind within their expanding programme of development aid. The other member Governments expressed support for the objective of the proposal and agreed that further consideration should be given to the basis on which such a programme might be established.

(19)   As regards the Secretariat's general functions and, in particular, its activities in the economic field, it is important that nothing should be done which might disturb the existing channels of economic and technical assistance to member countries or duplicate the present bilateral and multilateral links. The functions of the Secretariat in connection with the Commonwealth Development Projects are therefore expert and advisory and will not detract from the right of member countries to determine their own aid and development programmes.

(20)   Subject to these basic considerations the Secretariat will be able to play a valuable part in assisting member Governments, at their request, in advancing, and obtaining support for, development projects and technical assistance in a variety of fields on a multilateral Commonwealth basis, as appropriate. It will also help in the expeditious processing of requests for such assistance made by one Commonwealth country to another. In this connection, it will prepare and make available to Commonwealth Governments up-to-date information on the possibility of securing aid and technical assistance in various fields from individual countries of the Commonwealth.

(21)   Thus the Secretariat, by accumulating a reliable body of knowledge on the aid potential of the Commonwealth to which member countries can usefully have recourse for the purpose of promoting their own development, will enable Commonwealth countries generally to co-operate to the maximum extent possible in promoting the economic development of all.

(22)   In general, the Secretary-General, in discharging his functions in this field of economic and related affairs, will be guided by the principles set down in paragraphs 12 and 13.

Proposed Review of Intra-Commonwealth Organisations

(23)   A comprehensive review of existing intra-Commonwealth organisations concerned with economic and related affairs will be carried out, in view of the changing nature of the Commonwealth and of the fact that the multiplicity of organisations working in these fields has crreated problems of staff and finance.

(24)   The main purpose of this review will be to examine whether existing work on economic and related affairs is being unnecessarily duplicated; how far the activities of the Specialised Agencies of the United Nations now supersede those of existing intra-Commonwealth bodies; what Commonwealth bodies might usefully be absorbed within the Secretariat; which have functions so specialised that they cannot profitably be so absorbed; and how close co-operation between these latter and the Secretariat, particularly in the light of the needs of the changing Commonwealth, can most effectively be achieved.

(25)   In order to secure an impartial appraisal and to protect the future relationship between the Secretariat and other Commonwealth organisations this review will be carried out by a small committee, appointed by Commonwealth Governments, under an independent Chairman. In order to safeguard the Secretary-General's position he will not be a member of the Committee. Nevertheless, he will have the right to be present or to be represented throughout the proceedings of the Committee and to participate in its discussions. The Commonwealth organisations concerned will, of course, have the right to submit evidence to the Committee.

(26)   Pending the outcome of the review the Secretariat and the Commonwealth Economic Committee will work in the closest consultation. Again without prejudice to the review, the Secretariat will take over from the Commonwealth Relations Office as soon as convenient the secretarial functions which that Department at present carries out on behalf of the Commonwealth Liaison Committee.

Servicing of Commonwealth Meetings

(27)   The Secretariat, operating as the visible servant of the Commonwealth association, will carry out the task of servicing future meetings of Commonwealth Heads of Government and, where appropriate, other Ministerial and official meetings open to all members of the Commonwealth. The Secretariat will be able to rely on the host country for such secretarial help as it cannot itself provide and for assistance in matters of accommodation, hospitality, transport and the like.

(28)   The Secretariat will service the annual conferences of the Commonwealth Economic Consultative Council and meetings of the Commonwealth Liaison Committee. The more technical or specialised

organisations e.g. the Commonwealth Education Conference, the Commonwealth Education Liaison Committee or the Commonwealth Telecommunications Board will, pending the proposed review of Commonwealth organisations, continue to organise their own meetings.

(29)   As regards Meetings of Prime Ministers the Secretary-General will henceforth serve as Secretary-General to each Meeting. Subject to the principles set out in paragraphs 12 and 13 above, his duties will include the preparation, collation and circulation of papers on agenda items, together with such background papers as appear appropriate; the production of minutes; and, with the assistance of the host Government, the general organisation of the Meeting.

(30)   As the preparation of the agenda itself, the Secretary-General will be responsible for co-ordinating this process in the light of such direct discussions as Commonwealth Heads of Government may find convenient. Heads of Government will maintain the practice whereby the provisional agenda is drawn up, after consultation among themselves, in the form of a list of broad headings for discussion and they also reserve to themselves decisions on the timing and location of their Meetings.

IV. ADMINISTRATIVE ARRANGEMENTS

(31)   In consonance with the above functions of the Secretariat, its administrative organisation will be as follows.

(32)   The Chief Officer of the Secretariat will be the Secretary-General, and all members of the staff of the Secretariat will be responsible only to him.

(33)   The Secretary-General will be appointed by Commonwealth Heads of Government collectively. He will be a man of high standing, equivalent in rank to a Senior High Commissioner. A significant part of his duties will be visiting member countries of the Commonwealth.

(34)   The Deputy Secretaries-General will be appointed by Commonwealth Heads of Government acting through their representatives in London. One Deputy Secretary-General will have the necessary qualifications and special responsibilities for economic matters and should deal, on request, with development projects. As the work of the Secretariat expands, it may become necessary to appoint a second Deputy Secretary-General who will be primarily concerned with the other functions of the Secretariat.

(35)   The paramount consideration in the selection of staff and in the determination of conditions of service will be the necessity of securing the highest standards of efficiency, competence and integrity, due regard being paid to the importance of recruiting the staff on as wide a geographical basis as possible within the Commonwealth. The Secretary-General will have discretion, in the light of the above considerations, to appoint senior staff to the service of the Secretariat from among panels of

names submitted by Commonwealth Governments, who need not feel themselves limited to Government servants in submitting nominations.

(36) The Secretary-General has authority to make appointments of junior staff, subject to the approved budgetary limitations.

(37) All persons appointed to the staff of the Secretariat must be subject to clearance to the extent that their own Governments raise no objection to their suitability for employment. All members of the Secretariat, whatever their origin, must be strictly impartial in the discharge of their functions and place loyalty to the Commonwealth as a whole above all other considerations.

(38) Senior officers, including the Secretary-General and Deputy Secretaries-General, will be appointed in the first instance for not more than five years and preferably not less than three in order to ensure continuity of administration. In determining the period of tenure of other individual officers, the Secretary-General will no doubt wish to have regard to the need to stagger appointments in order to avoid a complete change of senior staff at any one time.

(39) The British Government will introduce legislation in order to give the Secretariat a legal personality under United Kingdom law and to accord to the Secretariat and its staff the immunities and privileges which are set out in Annex A.

(40) Other Commonwealth Governments will take steps to accord corresponding immunities and privileges to the staff of the Secretariat when visiting their territories, subject to whatever constitutional processes are required.

(41) The cost of the Secretariat will be borne in agreed shares by Commonwealth Governments; the scale of contributions is set out in Annex B.

(42) The annual budget will be considered by the Commonwealth High Commissioners in London or their representatives, together with a United Kingdom representative, meeting as a Finance Committee. The budget will then be submitted to Commonwealth Governments for their approval. The Senior Commonwealth High Commissioner in London or a representative of the British Government will be responsible for convening the Finance Committee as necessary.

Appendix C: The Declaration of Commonwealth Principles

When Commonwealth Heads of Government met in Singapore in January 1971 they agreed on a set of ideals which are subscribed to by all members and provide a basis for peace, understanding and goodwill among all mankind. They are expressed in the Declaration of Commonwealth Principles:

The Commonwealth of Nations is a voluntary association of independent sovereign states, each responsible for its own policies, consulting and co-operating in the common interests of their peoples and in the promotion of international understanding and world peace.

Members of the Commonwealth come from territories in the six continents and five oceans, include peoples of different races, languages and religions, and display every stage of economic development from poor developing nations to wealthy industrialised nations. They encompass a rich variety of cultures, traditions and institutions.

Membership of the Commonwealth is compatible with the freedom of member governments to be non-aligned or to belong to any other grouping, association or alliance. Within this diversity all members of the Commonwealth hold certain principles in common. It is by pursuing these principles that the Commonwealth can continue to influence international society for the benefit of mankind.

We believe that international peace and order are essential to the security and prosperity of mankind; we therefore support the United Nations and seek to strengthen its influence for peace in the world, and its efforts to remove the causes of tension between nations.

We believe in the liberty of the individual, in equal rights for all citizens regardless of race, colour, creed or political belief, and in their inalienable right to participate by means of free and democratic political processes in framing the society in which they live. We therefore strive to promote in each of our countries those representative institutions and guarantees for personal freedom under the law that are our common heritage.

We recognise racial prejudice as a dangerous sickness threatening the healthy development of the human race and racial discrimination as an unmitigated evil of society. Each of us will vigorously combat this evil within our own nation. No country will afford to regimes which practise racial discrimination assistance which in its own judgement directly contributes to the pursuit or consolidation of this evil policy.

We oppose all forms of colonial domination and racial oppression and are committed to the principles of human dignity and equality. We will therefore use all our efforts to foster human equality and dignity everywhere, and to further the principles of self-determination and non-racialism.

We believe that the wide disparities in wealth now existing between different sections of mankind are too great to be tolerated. They also create world tensions. Our aim is their progressive removal. We therefore seek to use our efforts to overcome poverty, ignorance and disease, in raising standards of life and achieving a more equitable international society.

To this end our aim is to achieve the freest possible flow of international trade on terms fair and equitable to all, taking into account the special requirements of the developing countries, and to encourage the flow of adequate resources, including governmental and private resources, to the developing countries, bearing in mind the importance of doing this in a true spirit of partnership and of establishing for this purpose in the developing countries conditions which are conducive to sustained investment and growth.

We believe that international co-operation is essential to remove the causes of war, promote tolerance, combat injustice, and secure development among the peoples of the world. We are convinced that the Commonwealth is one of the most fruitful associations for these purposes.

In pursuing these principles the members of the Commonwealth believe that they can provide a constructive example of the multi-national approach which is vital to peace and progress in the modern world. The association is based on consultation, discussion and co-operation.

In rejecting coercion as an instrument of policy they recognise that the security of each member state from external aggression is a matter of concern to all members. It provides many channels for continuing exchanges of knowledge and views on professional, cutural, economic, legal and political issues among member states.

These relationships we intend to foster and extend, for we believe that our multi-national association can expand human understanding and understanding among nations, assist in the elimination of discrimination based on differences of race, colour or creed, maintain and strengthen personal liberty, contribute to the enrichment of life for all, and provide a powerful influence for peace among nations.

Appendix D: Commonwealth Statement on Apartheid in Sport (The Gleneagles Agreement)

The member countries of the Commonwealth, embracing peoples of diverse races, colours, languages and faiths, have long recognised racial prejudice and discrimination as a dangerous sickness and an unmitigated evil and are pledged to use all their efforts to foster human dignity everywhere. At their London Meeting, Heads of Government reaffirmed that apartheid in sport, as in other fields, is an abomination and runs directly counter to the Declaration of Commonwealth Principles which they made at Singapore on 22 January 1971.

They were conscious that sport is an important means of developing and fostering understanding between the people, and especially between the young people, of all countries. But, they were also aware that, quite apart from other factors, sporting contacts between their nationals and the nationals of countries practising apartheid in sport tend to encourage the belief (however unwarranted) that they are prepared to condone this abhorrent policy or are less than totally committed to the Principles embodied in their Singapore Declaration. Regretting past misunderstandings and difficulties and recognising that these were partly the result of inadequate inter-governmental consultations, they agreed that they would seek to remedy this situation in the context of the increased level of understanding now achieved.

They reaffirmed their full support for the international campaign against apartheid and welcomed the efforts of the United Nations to reach universally accepted approaches to the question of sporting contacts within the framework of that campaign.

Mindful of these and other considerations, they accepted it as the urgent duty of each of their Governments vigorously to combat the evil of apartheid by withholding any form of support for, and by taking every practical step to discourage contact or competition by their nationals with sporting organisations, teams or sportsmen from South Africa or from any other country where sports are organised on the basis of race, colour or ethnic origin.

They fully acknowledged that it was for each Government to determine in accordance with its law the methods by which it might best discharge these commitments. But they recognised that the effective fulfilment of their commitments was essential to the harmonious development of Commonwealth sport hereafter.

They acknowledged also that the full realisation of their objectives involved the understanding, support and active participation of the nationals of their countries and of their national sporting organisations and authorities. As they drew a curtain across the past they issued a collective call for that understanding, support and participation with a view to ensuring that in this matter the peoples and Governments of the Commonwealth might help to give a lead to the world. Heads of Government specially welcomed the belief, unanimously expressed at their Meeting, that in the light of their consultations and accord there were unlikely to be future sporting contacts of any significance between Commonwealth countries or their nationals and South Africa while that country continues to pursue the detestable policy of apartheid. On that basis, and having regard to their commitments, they looked forward with satisfaction to the holding of the Commonwealth Games in Edmonton and to the continued strengthening of Commonwealth sport generally.

London, 15 June 1977

Appendix E: The Lusaka Declaration of the Commonwealth on Racism and Racial Prejudice

At their meeting in Lusaka in August 1979 Commonwealth Heads of Government, building on the 1971 Declaration of Commonwealth Principles and the statement on Apartheid in Sport issued at their London meeting in 1977, adopted a Declaration on Racism and Racial Prejudice.

We, the Commonwealth Heads of Government, recalling the Declaration of Commonwealth Principles made at Singapore on 22 January 1971 and the statement on Apartheid in Sport, issued in London on 15 June 1977, have decided to proclaim our desire to work jointly as well as severally for the eradication of all forms of racism and racial prejudice.

The Commonwealth is an institution devoted to the promotion of international underuing and world peace, and to the achievement of equal rights for all citizens regardless of race, colour, sex, creed or political belief, and is committed to the eradication of the dangerous evils of racism and racial prejudice.

We now, therefore, proclaim this Lusaka Declaration of the Commonwealth on Racism and Racial Prejudice.

United in our desire to rid the world of the evils of racism and racial prejudice, we proclaim our faith in the inherent dignity and worth of the human person and declare that:

(1) the peoples of the Commonwealth have the right to live freely in dignity and equality, without any distinction or exclusion based on race, colour, sex, descent, or national or ethnic origin;

(2)   while everyone is free to retain diversity in his or her culture and lifestyle, this diversity does not justify the perpetuation of racial prejudice or racially discriminatory practices;

(3)   everyone has the right to equality before the law and equal justice under the law;

(4)   everyone has the right to effective remedies and protection against any form of discrimination based on the grounds of race, colour, sex, descent, or national or ethnic origin.

We reject as inhuman and intolerable all policies designed to perpetuate apartheid, racial segregation or other policies based on theories that racial groups are or may be inherently superior or inferior.

We reaffirm that it is the duty of all the peoples of the Commonwealth to work together for the total eradication of the infamous policy of apartheid which is internationally recognised as a crime against the conscience and dignity of mankind and the very existence of which is an affront to humanity.

We agree that everyone has the right to protection against acts of incitement to racial hatred and discrimination, whether committed by individuals, groups or other organisations.

We affirm that there should be no discrimination based on race, colour, sex, descent or national or ethnic origin in the acquisition or exercise of the right to vote; in the field of civil rights or access to citizenship; or in the economic, social or cultural fields, particularly education, health, employment, occupation, housing, social security and cultural life.

We attach particular importance to ensuring that children shall be protected from practices which may may foster racism or racial prejudice. Children have the right to be brought up and educated in a spirit of tolerance and understanding so as to be able to contribute fully to the building of future societies based on justice and friendship.

We believe that those groups in societies who may be especially disadvantaged because of residual racist attitudes are entitled to the fullest protection of the law.

We recognise that the history of the Commonwealth and its diversity require that special attention should be paid to the problems of indigenous minorities. We recognise that the same special attention should be paid to the problems of immigrants, immigrant workers and refugees.

We agree that special measures may in particular circumstances be required to advance the development of disadvantaged groups in society. We recognise that the effects of colonialism or racism in the past may make desirable special provisions for the social and economic enhancement of indigenous populations.

Inspired by the principles of freedom and equality which characterise our association, we accept the solemn duty of working together to eliminate racism and racial prejudice. This duty involves the acceptance of the principle that positive measures may be required to advance the elimination of racism, including assistance to those struggling to rid themselves and their environment of the practice.

Being aware that legislation alone cannot eliminate racism and racial prejudice, we endorse the need to initiate public information and education policies designed to promote understanding, tolerance, respect and friendship among peoples and racial groups.

We are particularly conscious of the importance of the contribution the media cao make to human rights and the eradication of racism and racial prejudice by helping to eliminate ignorance and misunderstanding between people and by drawing attention to the evils which afflict humanity. We affirm the importance of truthful presentation of facts in order to ensure that the public are fully informed of the dangers presented by racism and racial prejudice.

In accordance with established principles of International Law and, in particular, the provisions of the International Convention on the Elimination of all Forms of Racial Discrimination, we affirm that everyone is, at all times and in all places, entitled to be protected in the enjoyment of the right to be free of racism and racial prejudice.

We believe that the existence in the world of apartheid and racial discrimination is a matter of concern to all human beings. We recognise that we share an international responsibility to work together for the total eradication of apartheid and racial discrimination.

We note that racism and racial prejudice, wherever they occur, are significant factors contributing to tension between nations and thus inhibit peaceful progress and development. We believe that the goal of the eradication of racism stands as a critical priority for governments of the Commonwealth, committed as they are to the promotion of the ideals of peaceful and happy lives for their people.

We intend that the Commonwealth, as an international organisation with a fundamental and deep-rooted attachment to principles of freedom and equality, should co-operate with other organisations in the fulfilment of these principles. In particular the Commonwealth should seek to enhance the co-ordination of its activities with those of other organisations similarly committed to the promotion and protection of human rights and fundamental freedoms.

Lusaka, August 1979

Appendix F: The Melbourne Declaration

We, the Heads of Government here assembled, drawn from the five continents representing a quarter of the world's entire population:

(1) Affirm our strong and unanimous conviction that all men and women have the right to live in ways that sustain and nourish human dignity;

(2) Believe that this right imposes obligations on all states, large and small, not only in respect to their own people but in their dealings with all other nations;

(3) Assert that the gross inequality of wealth and opportunity currently existing in the world, and the unbroken circle of poverty in which the lives of millions in developing countries are confined, are fundamental sources of tension and instability in the world;

(4) As a consequence, assert our unanimous conviction that there must be determined and dedicated action at national and international levels to reduce that inequality and to break that circle;

(5) Believe that for all these reasons it is imperative to revitalise the dialogue between developed and developing countries;

(6) Declare that this will require a political commitment, clear vision and intellectual realism which have thus far escaped mankind and to all of which the Commonwealth can greatly contribute;

(7) Believe that the dialogue must be conducted with a genuine willingness to accept real and significant changes commensurate with the urgency of the problems we now face;

(8) Firmly believe that the choice is not between change and no change but between timely, adequate, managed change and disruptive, involuntary change imposed by breakdown and conflict;

(9) Maintain that success will only be achieved as states recognise and give due weight to the essential inter-dependence of peoples and of states;

(10) Declare that, while the most urgent humanitarian considerations demand action, self-interest itself warrants a constructive and positive approach to these great human problems by all governments;

(11) Recognise that in the process of negotiations, nations must cast aside inhibitions and habits which have thwarted progress in the past and find new ways of talking constructively to one another so as to reach agreement on effective joint action;

(12) Note that, as well as technical economic considerations, it is imperative that states keep in the forefront of their attention the larger moral, political and strategic dimensions of what is at stake;

353

(13)   Maintain that while the problems are formidable, they are not of such a weight that they will defeat our purpose, given political will and an understanding of the needs of different countries and groups;

(14)   Assert that what is at stake – in terms of how hundreds of millions will live or die; of the prospects for co-operation or conflict and of the prospects for economic advance or stagnation – is of such vital importance in human terms that it would be an indictment of this generation if that political will and the readiness to find a creative compromise were not found;

(15)   Firmly believe that the issues are so important that they require the personal commitment and involvement of political leaders who, representing the will of their people, have the greatest power to advance the common cause of mankind;

(16)   Attaching the highest importance to the principles and objectives of this document, recognising the mutual interests and interdependence of all nations, declare our common resolve: to end the present impasse: to advance the dialogue between developed and developing countries: to infuse an increased sense of urgency and direction into the resolution of these common problems of mankind: and solemnly call on all leaders of all countries to join us in a commitment to taking prompt, practical and effective action to that end.

Issued by Commonwealth leaders, 3 October 1981

Bibliography

PREPARED BY L. S. TRACHTENBERG

OFFICIAL PUBLICATIONS OF THE COMMONWEALTH SECRETARIAT

Reports of the Secretary-General
  First   July 1965–August 1966
  Second   September 1966–October 1968
  Third   November 1968–November 1970
  Fourth   December 1970–March 1973
  Fifth   April 1973–March 1975
  Sixth   April 1975–March 1977
  Seventh April 1977–March 1979
  Eighth   April 1979–June 1981
Commonwealth Heads of Government Communiqués
Notes on the Commonwealth (a series of approximately 15 leaflets)
The Commonwealth Today (1979)
Commonwealth Organisations (1979, 2nd end)
Commonwealth Skills for Commonwealth Needs (1979, 2nd edn)
Towards a New International Economic Order: The Final Report of the Commonwealth Group of Experts (1977)
Commonwealth National Bibliographies: An annotated directory (1977)
Training for Agricultural Development: A directory of resources in the Commonwealth (1976)
Appropriate Technology in the Commonwealth: A directory of Institutions (1977)
The Front-Line States: The Burden of the Liberation Struggle (1978)
Southern Rhodesia Elections: Report of the Commonwealth Observer Group (1980)
International Activities in Science and Technology: A register of organisations of interest to Commonwealth countries
The above represents only a sample of the many publications of the Commonwealth Secretariat, and all should be available from the Secretariat in London. Also available are reprints of the speeches of the Commonwealth Secretary-General.

BOOKS AND MONOGRAPHS

Aiyar, S. P., *The Commonwealth in South Asia* (Bombay: Lalvani Publishing House, 1969).

Annual Survey of Commonwealth Law, 1976 (Oxford: Clarendon Press, 1978).

Arnold, G., *Economic Co-operation in the Commonwealth* (Oxford: Pergamon Press, 1967).

Arnold, G., *Towards Peace and a Multiracial Commonwealth* (London: Chapman & Hall, 1964).

Attlee, Earl, *Empire into Commonwealth* (Oxford: Oxford University Press, 1961).

Austin, D., *The Commonwealth in Eclipse?* (Accra: Ghana University Press, 1972).

Ball, M. M., The 'Open' Commonwealth (Durham, NC: Duke University Press, 1972).

Beaton, L., *Commonwealth in a New Era* (London: Trade Policy Research Centre, 1969).

Bloomfield, V., *Commonwealth Elections, 1945–1970: a bibliography* (London: Mansell, 1976).

Bradley, K. (ed.), *The Living Commonwealth* (London: Hutchinson, 1961).

Bradley, Sir K., *What is the Commonwealth?* (London: Commonwealth Institute, 1968).

Brookfield, H., *Colonialism, development and independence: the case of the Melanesian islands in the South Pacific* (Cambridge: Cambridge University Press, 1972).

Carrington, C. E., *The British Overseas*, 2nd edn (London: Cambridge University Press, 1968).

Choix (special issue), *Francophonie et Commonwealth: Mythe ou réalités?* (Quebec: Centre quebecois de relations internationales, 1978).

Cowen, Z., *The British Commonwealth of Nations in a changing world: law, politics and prospects* (Evanston, Ill.: Northwestern University Press, 1965).

Cross, J. A., *Whitehall and the Commonwealth: British Departmental Organisation for Commonwealth Relations, 1900–1966* (London: Routledge, Kegan Paul, 1967).

Dawson, R. B., *Commonwealth Immigrants* (London: Oxford University Press, 1964).

DeSmith, S. A., *The New Commonwealth and its Constitutions* (London: Stevens, 1964).

Eayrs, J. (ed.), *The Commonwealth and Suez: A Documentary Survey* (London: Oxford University Press, 1964).

Fawcett, J. E. S., *The British Commonwealth in International Law* (London: Stevens, 1963).

Ganjal, S. C., *India and the Commonwealth* (Agra: Shiv Lal Agarwal, 1970).

Garner, J., *The Commonwealth Office, 1925–1968* (London: Heinemann, 1978).

Gordon-Walker, P., *The Commonwealth* (London: Mercury Books, 1965).

Gordon-Walker, P., *The Commonwealth* (London: Secker and Warburg, 1962).

Hall, H. D., *Commonwealth: A history of the British commonwealth of nations* (New York: Van Nostrand, 1971).

Hamilton, W. B., *et al.* (eds), *A Decade of the Commonwealth, 1954–1964* (Durham, NC: Duke of University Press, 1966).

Harris, P. B., *The Commonwealth* (London: Longman, 1975).

Ingram, D., *The Commonwealth Challenge* (London: Allen and Unwin, 1962).

Ingram, D., *Commonwealth for a Colour-Blind World* (London: Allen & Unwin, 1965).

Ingram, D., *The Commonwealth at Work* (London: Pergamon Press, 1969).

Ingram, D., *The Imperfect Commonwealth* (London: Rex Collings, 1977).

Institute of Commonwealth Studies (London University), *The Changing Role of the Commonwealth Economic Connections* (London: Institute of Commonwealth Studies 1971).

Josey, A., *Lee Kuan Yew and the Commonwealth* (Singapore: Donald Moore Press, 1969).

MacDonald, M., *The Evolving Commonwealth* (Ditchley Foundation Lecture 9) (Oxfordshire: Ditchley Foundation, 1970).

McIntyre, W. D., *The Commonwealth of Nations: Origins and Impacts, 1869–1971* (London: Oxford University Press, 1978).

Macmillan, H., *Britain, the Commonwealth and Europe* (London: Conservative and Unionist Central Office, 1962).

Mansergh, N. (ed.), *Documents and Speeches on British Commonwealth Affairs, 1931–1952*, 2 vols (London: Oxford University Press, 1953).

Mansergh, N. (ed.), *Documents and Speeches on Commonwealth Affairs, 1952–1962* (London: Oxford University Press, 1963).

Mansergh, N., *The Commonwealth Experience* (London: Weidenfield and Nicolson, 1969).

Mazrui, A., *The Anglo–African Commonwealth: political friction & cultural fusion* (Oxford: Pergamon Press, 1967).

Menzies, R. G., *The Changing Commonwealth* (Smuts Memorial Lecture) (Cambridge: Cambridge University Press, 1960).

Millar, T. B., *The Commonwealth and the United Nations* (Sydney: Sydney University Press, 1967).

Miller, J. D. B., *Britain and the Old Dominions* (London: Chatto and Windus, 1966).

Miller, J. D. B., *Survey of Commonwealth Affairs: Problems of Expansion and Attrition, 1953–1969* (London: Oxford University Press, 1974).

Nyerere, J., *South Africa and the Commonwealth* (Dar es Salaam: Government Printers, 1971).

Payne, A., *The Politics of the Caribbean Community, 1961–1979* (Manchester: Manchester University Press, 1980).

Rajan, M. S., *The post-war transformation of the Commonwealth* (New Delhi: Asia Publishing House, 1963).

Ramphal, S. S., *One World to Share: Selected Speeches of the Commonwealth Secretary-General, 1975–1979* (London: Hutchinson, 1979).

Sandys, D., *The Modern Commonwealth* (London: HMSO, 1962).

Smith, A., with C. Sanger, *Stitches in Time: The Commonwealth in World Politics* (London: Andre Deutsch, 1981).

Smith, T. E., *Commonwealth Migration* (London: Macmillan, 1981).

Streeten, P., and H. Corbet (eds), *Commonwealth Policy in a Global Context* (London: Frank Cass, 1971).

Study Group of the Conservative Commonwealth and Overseas Council, *Policy for the Commonwealth* (London: SGCCOC, 1967).

Taylor, P., and A. J. R. Groom (eds), *International Organisation* (London: Frances Pinter, 1978).

Tinker, H., *Separate and Unequal: India and the Indians in the British Commonwealth, 1920–1950* (London: C. Hurst, 1976).

Uri, P. (ed.), *From Commonwealth to Common Market* (Harmondsworth: Penguin, 1968).

Walker, A., *The Modern Commonwealth* (London: Longman, 1976).

Walker, A., *The Commonwealth: a New Look* (Oxford: Pergamon Press, 1978).

Watson, J. B., *Empire to Commonwealth, 1919–1970* (London: Dent, 1971).

Watts, R. L., *New Federations: Experiments in the Commonwealth* (Oxford: Clarendon Press, 1965).

Wheare, K. C., *The Constitutional Structure of the Commonwealth* (Oxford: Clarendon Press, 1960).

Williams, P., *Aid in the Commonwealth* (London: Overseas Development Institute, 1965).

Williamson, J. A., *A Notebook of Commonwealth History*, 3rd edn (London: Macmillan, 1967).

World Bank, *The Commonwealth Caribbean: The Integration Experience* (Baltimore: John Hopkins University Press for World Bank, 1978).

ARTICLES

Austin, D., 'The Commonwealth turned upside down', *World Today*, October 1966, pp. 418–26.

Ball, M., 'Regionalism and the Pacific Commonwealth', *Pacific Affairs*, 46 (1973).

Barber, J., 'The impact of the Rhodesian crisis on the Commonwealth', *Journal of Commonwealth Political Studies*, July 1969, pp. 83–95.

Beloff, M., 'Dream of Commonwealth: decline and fall of an ideal', *Round Table*, 1970, pp. 463–70.

Boulding, K. E. & T. Mukerjee, 'Unprofitable Empire: Britain in India, 1800–1967: A Critique of the Hobson-Lenin Thesis on Imperialism', *Peace Research Society (International) Papers*, vol. 16, 1971.

Bull, H., 'What is the Commonwealth?', *World Politics*, July 1959, pp. 572–87.

Charlton, E., 'The Commonwealth in the 80s: Principles and Prospects', *Round Table*, 284, October 1981, pp. 334–7.

Derbyshire, J., 'The Commonwealth', *Australian Foreign Affairs Record*, April 1977, pp. 172–7.

Desmith, S. A., 'Fundamental Rules Forty Years On', *International Journal*, Spring 1971, pp. 347–60.

Doxey, M., 'Strategies in Multilateral Diplomacy: the Commonwealth, Southern Africa, and the New International Economic Order', *International Journal* 35, Spring 1980.

Dutt, R. P., 'Britain's Commonwealth Contradictions', *International Affairs* (Moscow), May 1969, pp. 18–23.

Eayrs, J., 'The Overhaul of the Commonwealth', *Round Table*, January 1967, pp. 48–56.

Elvin, L., 'Teaching the Commonwealth to the Commonwealth', *Round Table*, January 1974, pp. 109–16.

Foot, D., 'A Commonwealth of Law: A Spiritual home in Westminster Hall', *Round Table*, 1970, pp. 417–23.

Garner, P., 'The Commonwealth Under Strain', *Round Table*, January 1974.

Goodwin, G. L., 'The Commonwealth and the United Nations', *International Organisation*, Summer 1965, pp. 678–94.

Gordon-Walker, P., 'The British Labour Party and the Commonwealth', *Round Table*, November 1970, pp. 503–10.

Groom, A. J. R., 'Commonwealth Arts: an emerging dimension', *Round Table*, April 1983, pp. 153–81.

Gupta, S., 'Commonwealth South-Asia and the Enlarged Community: the continued value of the Commonwealth link', *Round Table*, October 1971.

Harnetty, P., 'Canada, South Africa and the Commonwealth', *Journal of Commonwealth Political Studies*, November 1963, pp. 33–44.

Henry, K. S., 'Language, Culture and Society in the Commonwealth Caribbean', *Journal of Black Studies*, (7:1) September 1976, pp. 79–94.

Holmes, J. W., 'The impact of the Commonwealth on the emergence of Africa', *International Organization*, 16, 1962, pp. 291–302.

Holmes, J., 'A Canadian Commonwealth: Realism out of Rhetoric', *Round Table*, October 1966, pp. 335–49.

Hosein, E. N., 'The Problem of Imported Television Content in the Commonwealth Caribbean', *Caribbean Quarterly (Jamaica)*, 22 (4) 1976, pp. 7–25.

Ingram, D., 'Ten Turbulent Years: the Commonwealth Secretariat at Work', *Round Table*, April 1975, pp. 139–48.

Ingram, D., ' "A Quiet Conference": an interview with Shridath Ramphal', *Round Table*, October 1977.

Ingram, D., 'The Commonwealth Meeting in Lusaka', *Round Table*, July 1979, pp. 204–10.

Ingram, D., 'Lusaka 1979: A significant Commonwealth Meeting', *Round Table*, October 1979, pp. 275–83.

Ingram, D. and A. Walker, 'Commonwealth Conference 1979', *Round Table*, July 1979, pp. 215–30.

Jackson, R., 'The Question of Commonwealth Values', *Round Table*, October 1974, pp. 359–67.

Jesling, T., and S. Harris, 'The Devaluation in World Commodity Prices: A problem for the Commonwealth', *Round Table*, April 1974.

Johnson, H., 'The Commonwealth Preferences: a system in need of analysis', *Round Table*, October 1966, pp. 363–76.

Kumar, D., 'The New Community and the Developing Commonwealth: Problems of Trade and Aid', *Round Table*, October 1971.

Leach, R. H., 'The Secretariat', *International Journal*, Spring 1971, pp. 373–400.

Leslie, S. C., 'The Unknown Secretariat: Three Years of Remarkable Achievement', *Round Table*, 233, January 1969, pp. 21–8.

Lewis, R., 'Commonwealth Africa and the Enlarged Community: political, cultural and economic impact', *Round Table*, October 1971.

Lipton, M., and C. Bell, 'The Fall in Commonwealth Trade', *Round Table*, January 1970.

'Love Me, Love My Commonwealth', *The Economist*, 4 August 1979, pp. 33–5.

Lyon, P., 'The Commonwealth's Jubilee Summit', *World Today*, July 1977, pp. 250–8.

Lyon, P., 'The Commonwealth in the 1970s', *World Today*, April 1971, pp. 174–85.

Mansell, G., 'The Voice of Britain in the Commonwealth', *Round Table*, January 1978, pp. 48–54.

Marshall, W. K., 'A Review of Historical Writing on the Commonwealth Caribbean', *Social & Economic Studies (Jamaica)*, 24 (3) 1975, pp. 271–307.

Millar, T. B., 'Empire into Commonwealth into History', *International Organization*, Winter 1970, pp. 93–100.

Miller, J. D. B., 'British Interests and the Commonwealth', *Journal of Commonwealth Political Studies*, November 1966, pp. 180–90.

Miller, J. D. B., 'Britain and the Commonwealth', *South Atlantic Quarterly*, Spring 1970, pp. 186–204.

'More Than a Bosses Club', *The Economist*, 4 June 1977, pp. 14–15.

Morris-Jones, W. H., and T. J. Johnson, 'A Commonwealth of Learning', *Round Table*, November 1970, pp. 385–96.

'Nationality and Citizenship', *Round Table*, October 1980, pp. 357–9.

Oxtoby, R., 'Vocational Education and Development Planning: Emergent Issues in the Commonwealth Caribbean', *Comparative Education*, October 1977.

Peacock, A., 'Australia in the Modern Commonwealth', *Round Table*, July 1978, pp. 269–79.

Polhemus, J. H., 'The Important Commonwealth: A Behavioral Indicator', *International Studies Quarterly*, September 1981, pp. 469–90.

Ramphal, S. S., 'The Focus Lecture: The Commonwealth in the 1980s', *Round Table*, April 1981, pp. 170–8.

Richardson, B. C., 'Presenting the Commonwealth Caribbean with and Extraregional Point of View', *Journal of Geography*, December 1976.

Round Table (unsigned), 'Immigration and the Ideal of Commonwealth', *Round Table*, 1973, pp. 139–44.

Sen, S., 'The Commonwealth Role at the United Nations', *Round Table*, January 1980, pp. 10–17.

Smith, A., 'The Need for Commonwealth', *Round Table*, July 1966, pp. 219–27.

Smith, A., 'The Modern Commonwealth', *New Commonwealth*, 9 (1970), pp. 3–5.

Smith, A., 'Commonwealth of Nations after Twenty-Five Years of Change', *International Perspectives*, November/December 1975.

Springer, H., 'Problems of Aid in Education in the Commonwealth', *Round Table*, July 1970.

Thomas, P. J., 'Women in the Military: America and the British Commonwealth', *Armed Forces and Society*, 4:4 Summer 1978, pp. 623–46.

Thorpe, J., 'A Liberal Looks at the Commonwealth', *Commonwealth Journal*, 11, April 1968.

Trudeau, P. E., 'The Commonwealth after Ottawa', *Round Table*, 253, January 1974, pp. 38–41.

Vivekanandan, B., 'The Commonwealth Secretariat', *International Studies* (New Delhi), January 1968, pp. 301–31.

Welch, (Jr), C. E., 'Civil–Military Relations in Newer Commonwealth States: The Transfer and Transformation of British Models', *Journal of Developing Areas*, 12:2, January 1978, pp. 153–70.

PERIODICALS (with special interest in Commonwealth questions)

ART Links. Published by the Commonwealth Arts Association

Commonwealth. Published by the Royal Commonwealth Society until January 1982, and now published by Longman

Commonwealth and Colonial History Newsletter. Published by the History Department, University of Canterbury, Christchurch, New Zealand

Commonwealth Currents. Published by Commonwealth Secretariat

Commonwealth Law Bulletin. Published by the Commonwealth Secretariat

Commonwealth Record of Recent Events. Published by the Commonwealth Secretariat

Journal of Commonwealth and Comparative Politics. Formerly Journal of Commonwealth Political Studies, published by Institute of Commonwealth Studies, London

The Parliamentarian. Journal of the Parliaments of the Commonwealth, published by the Commonwealth Parliamentary Association

Round Table. Published by Butterworth Scientific on behalf of The Round Table

Index of Authors, Politicians, etc.

Akinyemi, A. B.   304n
Amin, Idi   6, 7, 8, 201, 211, 236, 309
   and Ugandan Asians   249–50
Anderson, J. N.   138n
Ankrah, General   229
Arndt, H.   156
Arnold, G.   163n

Bailey, M.   39n
Ball, M. M.   36n
Bell, P.   163n
Bingham, T. H.   39n
Blake, D. H.   182n
Bull, H.   36n
Burnham, P. M.   47, 50
Burrows, N.   322n

Callaghan, James   201, 211
Cameron, J.   35
Carrington, Lord   316
Castel, J.   138n
Chamberlain, Joseph   260
Clarke, C.   288n, 289n
Coard, B.   288n
Cobban, A.   286, 289n
Connell-Smith, G.   51n
Cooper, R.   222n
Cooper, T. M.   139n
Cosgrave, P.   224n
Cox, R. W.   36n, 38n
Cross, J. A.   36n, 37n

Dalton, M. C.   138n
Darby, P.   221n
Derrett, J. D.   138n
Deutsch, K.   322n
Dobell, P.   221n
Douglas-Home, A.   220n
Drummond, I.   145, 163n

Earys, J.   218n
Epstein, L.   187, 219n

Fawcett, J.   138n
Foccart, J.   173, 177
Fraser, M.   229
Freedman, P.   92n
Frey-Wouters, A.   165n

Gardner, R.   163n
Garner, J.   36n, 37n
Gaulle, Charles de   168, 173
Gilmore, W.   288n
Giscard d'Estaing, V.   173, 178
Golan, T.   182
Gore-Booth, Lord   37n
Gray, S. M.   39n
Gupta, A.   223n
Gupta, S.   220n

Harris, S.   222n
Harvey, H.   36n, 138n
Hatch, J.   223n
Haydon, E. S.   138n
Hazard, J.   138n
Heath, Edward   9, 189, 192, 205, 310,
   311
Henig, S.   222n
Hill, C.   323n

Ingram, D.   163n, 322n

Jacobson, H. K.   36n
Jagan, C.   47
Jennings, I.   138n
Jennings, R. Y.   139n
Josling, T.   222n

Kaunda, K.   59, 196, 197, 200, 215

362

Keynes, J. M. 163n
Khama, S. 191
Khorana, G. 253
Kumar, D. 220n
Kyemba, H. 223n

Lee Kuan Yew 45, 194–5, 198, 200
Lenin, V. I. 258n
Levin, B. 288n
Lewis, R. 220n, 223n
Little, R. 182n
Lowenthal, D. 288n, 289n

Macleod, A. 221n
Mahler, V. A. 164n
Manley, Michael 50, 58, 64n, 200, 207, 222n, 229
Mansell, G. 316, 323n
Mansergh, N. 51n, 163n
Marten, N. 151
Martin, G. 222n
Mazrui, A. A. 13n, 220n
McIntyre, W. D. 162n, 309, 322n
McKinlay, R. D. 182n
McNamara, R. 321
Menendez, General 272
Menzies, R. 201, 221n
Meyers, B. D. 36n, 37n, 38n
Millar, T. B. 264, 288n
Miller, J. D. B. 36n, 37n, 164n, 288n
Mirdha, R. N. 221n
Mitterrand, F. 173
Mohapatra, M. K. 258n
Morgan, D. J. 163n
Morritt, J. 63n
Mortimer, M. 221n
Moynagh, M. 164n
Muldoon, R. 216, 310
Muzorewa, A. 31

Nehru, P. 3, 13n
Nettleford, R. M. 83, 92n
Noorani, A. G. 223n
Normanbrook, Lord 36n
Nyerere, J. 192–4, 200, 228

Obote, M. 196, 229, 238
O'Leary, J. 323n

Panter-Brick, S. K. 182n
Payne, A. 165n, 288n
Pearson, Lester 194, 200, 249
Pinder, J. 222n
Plischke, E. 282, 289n
Polk, J. 163n
Powell, E. 259n

Ramphal, Shridath 14n, 24–5, 38n, 46, 215, 224n, 236, 242n, 288n, 303n
and Britain's role in Commonwealth 311–12, 313, 314
and Rhodesian problem 30, 31, 228
and role of Commonwealth 10, 11, 89, 94, 99, 148, 162, 212, 228–9, 297
Rao, S. K. 29
Rivers, B. 39n
Roberts-Wray, K. 138n

Sampson, A. 288n
Sandys, D. 219n
Sanger, C. 37n, 38n, 164n
Scarman, Lord 258, 259n
Schlesinger, R. B. 138n
Schuster, G. 143
Schwebel, S. M. 36n
Seers, D. 34
Sen, S. 303n, 321, 323n
Senghor, L. 170
Smith, Arnold 11, 18, 24, 28, 29, 37n, 38n, 40, 162, 164n, 221n, 233, 267, 288n, 289n
and Commonwealth membership 266, 285
and Rhodesia 29, 30
and role of Commonwealth 7, 148, 205–6, 228–9
Smith, Ian 31, 236, 238, 243n
Smith, T. B. 138n
Smyth, D. 222n
Stanley, O. 261
Strange, S. 163n
Stremlau, J. L. 243n

Tenaille, F. 182n

Thatcher, M.   201, 215, 272, 310, 311
Thordasson, B.   221n
Toré, S.   177
Trudeau, P.   7, 13n, 38n, 151, 194,
    199, 201, 221n, 224n

Vivekanandan, B.   37n

Walker, A.   323n
Walters, R. S.   182n
Whitlam, Gough   249, 254

Wight, M.   36n
Williams, E.   49, 161
Wilson, D. A.   51n
Wilson, Harold   191, 192, 201, 202,
    209, 206–7, 234, 300, 311
Winham, G.   220n
Wright, M.   15

Young, S.   219n

Zacher, M. W.   36n

Index of Subjects

ACP (African, Caribbean and Pacific)
 states 28, 29, 154, 156–7
 and EEC 46, 160, 300
 and trade 145, 180
African countries
 and Commonwealth 43, 187, 265
 at CHOGMs 197–8, 210 (Ottawa 203; Singapore 190–1,
  198)
 culture in 84, 89
 education in 74, 77
 and health 110, 111
 independence 262
 and India 209
 law in 128, 129, 135
 military training 119, 120
 and New Zealand's sporting links
  with South Africa 213, 215–16
 and trade 147
 and Uganda 211–12
 and Zimbabwe 240
 see also under individual countries
African Financial Community
  (CFA) 176, 177, 179, 180
aid
 from Britain 151–2, 158, 318, 321
 from France 173–4
Algeria 170, 171, 175, 178
 independence 167–8
alternative energy programme 99–
  100
Anguilla 269, 270–1
ANZUS 42
apartheid 43, 190, 256
 and Gleneagles Agreement 4, 6,
  308, 348–9
Argentina, and Falkland Islands 271–3
arms issues
 British sale of arms to South Af-

rica 24, 190–7
 in India 120
arts 83–93
 Britain's influence on 83, 84
 developments in 89
 after independence 84–5
 and politics 88
Asia/Pacific countries
 and CSC programmes 100
 education in 74, 75
 independence 262
 law in 128, 129, 135
 see also under individual countries
associated statehood 262
Association for Commonwealth
  Literature and Language Studies
  (ACLALS) 90–1
Association of French and Partially
  French Universities (AUPLF)
  170
Association of South-East Asian
  Nations (ASEAN) 42, 44–5
 Treaty of Amity and Co-
  operation 45
Australia 17, 117, 142–3, 145, 248–9
 and British migration laws 253
 external territories 268, 279–83
 and immigration 246, 248, 249,
  250, 254
 and South Pacific Forum 49
 views on Commonwealth 37n,
  201, 318

Bali Concord 45
Bangladesh 237, 257
Barbados 44
Belize 44, 283
 dispute with Guatemala 230, 234,
  235
Biafra 238–9

Bingham Report 30
Boys' Brigade 61
'brain drain' 113–14, 252
Brandt Report 153, 314, 321
Bretton Woods institutions 146
Britain
  aid from 151–2, 158, 318, 321
  and CFTC funds 151–2
  colonial history 260–1
  cultural influence 83, 84
  dependencies of 268–78, 284
  and developing countries 206–8
  educational influence 65–9, 70
  and EEC 18, 49, 69, 74, 147, 154, 159, 179, 201, 203, 205, 206, 208, 252, 300, 313–14
  and emigration 246–7, 250, 252, 254, 255
  and immigration 252–4, 256, 257, 309, 314
  independence policies 263–4, 286
  legal influence 126–32
  and military training 116–17, 119
  monetary policy 142–3, 146
  and Rhodesia 5, 191, 192, 307
  role in Commonwealth 9–10, 11, 12, 141, 153, 185–9, 193, 300, 307–8, 311–12, 322
  and sale of arms to South Africa 24, 190–7
  and trade with Commonwealth 153, 158–9, 313–14
  views on Commonwealth 18, 198, 314–17
  and Zimbabwe 240
British Guiana 47
British Nationality Act (1948) 248, 252
broadcasting 315–16, 319
Brunei 276
Burma 262, 266

Campbell Report 155, 156
Canada
  and Caribbean countries 49–50, 200
  and CFTC funds 151
  and Commonwealth 17, 19, 37n, 200, 318

  and French language 257
  law in 128, 132
  and migration 245, 246, 247, 248, 249–50, 253, 254–5
  military training 120
  and OAS 43
Canadian Citizenship Act (1946) 248
Caribbean countries
  and CSC programmes 100–1
  education in 74, 78–9
  and emigration 256
  independence 262, 270–1
  and health 110, 111
  legal training 135
  and trade 147
  see also individual countries
Caribbean Community and Common Market (CARICOM) 28, 41, 46–8, 160, 161, 286
Caribbean Examination Council (CXC) 79
Caribbean Free Trade Area (CARIFTA) 47
Ceylon 262, 265
CRA *see* African Financial Community
Colonial Office 17, 265
colonialism 4, 5, 43, 188, 260–1
  and arts 84–5
  and education 66–8
  French 166–82
  law under 128–9
Common Fund 155–6
Commonwealth
  changing nature of 10, 15–19, 24, 140–1, 147, 185–9, 221n, 299
  characteristics of 3–13, 126, 137–8, 305–11
  decision-making process 6, 8, 13
  and dependent territories 265–7, 282–5, 286–7
  economic co-operation in 140–65
  economic system 158–61 (changes in 142–7; and information exchange 153–8)
  as international organisation 293–303

and international relations 27–31, 187, 225–42, 305
members and organisations of 307–8, 327–37
membership of 195, 265–6, 285, 299, 317–21
and migration 244–59
military aspects 116–24, 180–1
role and functions of 67, 192–3, 204–5, 216–17, 294–6, 306–7
and United Nations 299–300, 302, 312, 320–1
unofficial 112–13, 293, 298, 300, 302, 332–7
see also Secretariat
Commonwealth Agricultural Bureaux 102
Commonwealth Arts Association (CAA) 86, 89
Commonwealth Arts Organisation (CAO) 85, 86–90
Commonwealth Association of Museums 88, 89, 90
Commonwealth Bursaries for Youth Personnel Scheme 57, 59
Commonwealth Centre for Advanced Studies in Youth Work 57, 59
Commonwealth Committee on Defence 121
Commonwealth Committee on Mineral Resources and Geology (CCMRG) 101
Commonwealth Defence Science Organisation 122
Commonwealth Development Corporation (CDC) 77, 284
Commonwealth Economic Committee (CEC) 154
Commonwealth Education Liaison Committee (CELC) 72
Commonwealth Engineers' Council (CEC) 103
Commonwealth Foundation 69, 70–1, 300, 314
and arts 88–9, 90, 91
and health 110–11
Commonwealth Fund for Technical Co-operation (CFTC) 5, 12, 21, 148, 149, 208, 314

and Britain 151–2
and dependent territories 285
and economic programmes 11, 149–53
and education 69, 70, 71–2
and examination councils 79
funding of 150–2
and health 109, 110–11
Industrial Development Unit 34
and law 135–6
role of 31–4, 149, 295, 297–8, 317–18, 321
Commonwealth Games Federation 62
Commonwealth Geological Liaison Office (CGLO) 101
Commonwealth Heads of Government Meetings (CHOGMs)
Singapore (1971) 4–5, 16, 24, 28, 55, 150, 186, 189–201, 219, 226, 295, 308, 310, 311 (Declaration of Commonwealth Principles 4, 5, 226, 346–7)
Ottawa (1973) 40, 55, 201–5
Kingston (1975) 96, 154, 200, 202, 205–10, 235, 237
London (1977) 25, 31, 41, 155, 208–14, 240 (Lancaster House Agreement 123, 229)
Lusaka (1979) 34, 88, 89, 156, 157, 201, 229, 214–15, 240, 295, 297, 308, 310, 311, 314, 315 (Declaration on Racism and Racial Prejudice 350–2)
Melbourne (1981) 25, 87, 91, 151, 213, 215–19, 264, 287, 310, 315 (Declaration 353–4)
and conflict management 225, 227–8, 229–30, 236
division of interests at 206–8
legal effect of 126
nature of 8–9, 198–9, 211, 213–14, 296–7, 310
and nuclear tests 202–3
role of 11, 185–9, 196, 202–3, 206, 217–19, 310
and 'special members' 266
Commonwealth Heads of Government Regional Meetings

Commonwealth Heads – *cont.*
(CHOGRMs) 41, 46, 210, 227, 242n
Commonwealth Institute 91
Commonwealth Institute for Applied Research in Social and Economic Development 57, 58
Commonwealth Legal Bureau 136
Commonwealth Legal Education Association 135, 136
Commonwealth Magistrates' Association 137
Commonwealth Relations Office (CRO) 16, 17, 18, 37n, 265
Commonwealth Science Council (CSC) 69, 94–105, 317
Commonwealth Study Fellowship Fund 57, 58
Commonwealth Sugar Agreement 146
Commonwealth Youth Affairs Council 57, 60
Commonwealth Youth Affairs Information Service 57
Commonwealth Youth Exchange Council 61–2
Commonwealth Youth Programme (CYP) 55–63, 109, 314
Commonwealth Youth Service Awards Scheme 57, 58
conflict
management 225–43
types of 233–9
Conservative Party, and Commonwealth 187, 188–9, 190, 214, 311
Cook Islands 280, 285
Crown, and Commonwealth 16, 126, 131, 137, 211, 248, 265
Cultural and Technical Co-operation Agency of French-speaking Countries 170
Cyprus 230, 237, 315

Declaration of Commonwealth Principles (1971) 4, 5, 226, 346–7
Declaration of London (1949) 248
defence 18, 116, 117–18
dependencies 260–89

Commonwealth role in 282–5
future of 267–82
and Commonwealth membership 265–7
see also under individual countries
developing countries 194–6, 302
CHOGM and 206–8
and education 68
and health 114
inflation in 204
LDCs and MDCs 47
technical co-operation between 152
dominions 17, 142, 147
Duke of Edinburgh's Award Schemes 62

Economic Community of West African States (ECOWAS) 43, 177
economic co-operation in Commonwealth 140–65
economic policies
of Britain 142–3, 146
of France 173–9
economic programmes of Commonwealth 149–73
education 56, 58–9, 65–82
of Commonwealth students in Britain 314–15, 319–20
and emigration 247
during Empire 65–7
exchanges 66, 67, 70, 74, 75–7
in French ex-colonies 170–1, 178
health education 109
in India 247, 315
influences on 65–9
market 73–5
emigration
from Britain 246–7, 250, 252, 254, 255
from Canada 247
from India 247, 250–1, 253, 256
from Nigeria 256
from Pakistan 251, 252, 253
from United States 254
Empire (British)
change to Commonwealth 294, 295, 306

compared with French 166–7 (*see also* French colonialism)
decline of 140–1
education under 65–7
English language
and arts 84, 85, 90
and education 68, 76
role in Commonwealth 9, 171
European Economic Community (EEC) 47, 125, 211
and ACP 46, 160, 300
Britain's entry into 18, 49, 69, 74, 147, 154, 159, 179, 201, 203, 205, 206, 208, 252, 300, 313
and Commonwealth Youth Programme 61
examination councils 77–9

Falkland Islands 281
war 44, 235, 271–4
Foreign and Commonwealth Office (FCO) 17, 18, 233, 313
Commonwealth Co-ordination Department 17
and independence 265, 282–3, 284
Foreign Office 17
franc zone 176–7
France
cultural influence 169–71
economic relations 174–9
and immigration 178–9
influence of institutions in 172–3
influence of legal system 128
military influence 180–1
nuclear testing 48, 202
treaties with ex-colonies 179–80
see also French colonialism
French colonialism 166–82
independence from 167–9
policy of 166–7

General Agreement on Tariffs and Trade (GATT) 28, 146–7
Ghana 18, 265, 309
Gibraltar 229, 235
future of 275–6, 281
Girl Guides' Association 62
Gleneagles Agreement (on apartheid

in sport) 4, 6, 213, 215, 308, 310, 348–9
gold standard, abandonment of 141, 143
Guatemala 44, 234, 235
Guinea 177–8
Gulbenkian Foundation 88, 89
Guyana 44, 48, 208, 251

HABITAT 104
health issues 107–15
Hong Kong 252
future of 274–5
independence 281, 283
and law 127
Hong Kong Supreme Court Ordinance (1950) 127
House of Lords 133

immigration
and Australia 246, 248, 249, 250, 254
and Britain 252–4, 256, 257, 309, 314
and France 178–9
and India 244, 251, 257
and Malaysia 251, 257
and South Africa 246, 250, 255, 256, 259n
and United States 253
Immigration Act (1971) 252, 259n
Imperial Agricultural Bureaux 94
Imperial Economic Conference (1932) 143, 144
imperial preference system 144, 145
independence 17, 261–5
British policy on 263
Commonwealth policy on 264–7
and size of country 285–6
UN policy on 263–4
see also under individual countries
India 319
and arms transactions 120
army 121
arts in 83
and Commonwealth 19, 143, 144, 186, 209–10, 248
and conflict with Pakistan 236, 237–8

India – *cont.*
  education 247, 315
  emigration from 247, 250–1, 253, 256
  immigration to 244, 251, 257
  independence 3–4, 16, 17, 249, 261, 262, 265
India Office 17
information exchange 153–9
Integrated Programme for Commodities (IPC) 155, 156
Intermediate Technology Development Group (ITDG) 103
International Court of Justice 131–2
International Monetary Fund (IMF) 104, 146
international relations and Commonwealth 27–31, 187, 225–42, 305
International Youth Year (IYY) 60, 61

Jamaica 48, 50, 264
  banana industry 159
Japan 145, 248
Judicial Committee of the Privy Council 132–4

Kashmir 226, 230, 242n
Kenya 167, 250

Labour Party
  and Commonwealth 187–8, 189, 311
  and EEC membership 206
  and emigration 249
  and Falklands dispute 273
  and Nigerian independence 239
  and Vietnam 234
Lancaster House Conference 25, 31, 41, 123, 155, 208–14, 229, 240
language, influence of
  English 9, 68, 76, 84, 85, 90, 171
  French 169–71
Latin America and OAS 44
law 125
  British 126–32
  Chinese 126
  French 128
  and migration 257

  Roman–Dutch 128, 129, 130, 131
  Scottish 130
League of Nations 107
Lomé Convention 28, 46, 159, 160, 177, 179, 207, 300
Lusaka Declaration on Racism and Racial Prejudice 4, 6, 24, 25, 28, 31, 350–2

Malaysia 18, 45, 235, 315
  and migration 251, 257
Mauritius 208, 252
McIntyre Report 154
membership of Commonwealth 195, 265–6, 285
  benefits from 317–21
  'special membership' 266
metrology and quality control programme 100
migration 244–59
  causes of 245
  patterns of 245–8
  see also under individual countries
military co-operation 116–24
military influences
  of Britain 116–17, 119
  of France 180–1
Ministry of Overseas Development 17
Morocco 171, 172
Mozambique 29, 46, 231, 243n, 267

Namibia 43, 281, 282, 308
NATO 42, 117, 118
natural products programme 101
Nauru 266, 281–2
New International Economic Order (NIEO) 28, 29, 154
New Zealand
  and Commonwealth 117, 201
  external territories of 268, 279–81, 283
  and migration 253
  and South Pacific Forum 48–9
  sporting links with South Africa 213, 215–16, 310
Nigeria 18, 34, 123, 207, 319
  and arms transactions 120
  civil war 237–9

and emigration 256
law in 130, 132
and OAU 43
North–South dialogue 6, 10, 11, 147, 151, 153, 154, 156, 162, 218, 296, 297, 303
nuclear energy 160n
nuclear tests 48, 202–3

Orders in Council 262
Organisation for African Unity (OAU) 43, 211, 213
Organisation of American States (OAS) 42, 43–4, 211
Organisation for Economic Co-operation and Development (OECD) 28, 61
Overseas Development Association (ODA) 284

Pakistan 38n, 213, 264, 267
civil war 231
conflict with India 236, 237–8
and emigration 251, 252, 253
independence 17, 28, 132, 262
Pan American Health Organisation (PAHO) 107
Phelps–Stokes missions 67
Plowden Report 17, 37n
Prime Ministers' meetings 16, 17, 18, 30, 116, 125

Queen, The *see under* Crown

racialism
and British sale of arms to South Africa 190–7
and Commonwealth 5, 6, 16, 43, 213, 215, 308–10, 318, 347
Gleneagles Agreement 4, 6, 213, 215, 308, 310, 348–9
Lusaka Declaration 25, 350–2
and migration 248, 249–50, 252, 256–7
and Rhodesia 29, 34, 43, 46, 51, 123, 202, 203, 209, 213–14, 231, 232
and South Africa 4, 5, 6, 8, 43, 190, 191, 256, 308, 348–9
regionalism 40–51

Rhodesia 18, 201, 210
and Britain 5, 191, 192, 307
racialism in, and Common-wealth 5, 6, 29, 34, 43, 46, 51, 123, 202, 203, 209, 213–14, 231, 232
sanctions 30–1, 50, 231
UDI 24, 30, 215, 230, 231
rural technology 34

St Kitts-Nevis 262
independence 268–70, 280, 283
sanctions 30–1, 50, 231
Sanctions Committee 30
science 94–105
Secretariat 4, 6, 9, 11, 27, 50, 199, 283
budget 20–1, 151
and Commonwealth Youth Pro-gramme 56, 57
and co-operation 31–5
divisions of: Economic Affairs 29, 156; Education and Train-ing 31, 32, 69, 70, 72–3; Export Market Development 153; Food Production and Rural De-velopment 100; General Tech-nical Assistance 31; Medi-cal 108–9, 110–11
and economic matters 147, 148–9
establishment of 11, 15–19, 307
and health 108–9, 114
and law 134–6
memorandum 19–20, 338–45
and migration 255–6
and report commissioning 154–8
resources of 20–3
role 11–12, 18, 21, 23–5, 26, 29–30, 147–9, 162, 226, 227, 228, 233
and science and technology 102
and World Health Organi-sation 111–12
Secretary-General
and conflict management 228–9
role 11–12, 18, 21, 23–5, 26, 29–30, 147–9, 162
Shackleton Report 273
Singapore 45, 51, 315

South Africa　265, 295, 297
　British sale of arms to　24, 190–7
　and Commonwealth　17, 117, 267
　and immigration　246, 250, 255,
　　256, 259n
　and racialism　4, 5, 6, 8, 43, 191,
　　308, 318
　sporting links with　210, 213,
　　215–16, 309–10
South-East Asia　44, 248
South Pacific Bureau for Economic
　Co-operation　49
South Pacific Forum　46, 48–9, 286
sport, and racialism　210, 213,
　215–16, 309–10
Sri Lanka　17, 153, 251
Statute of Westminster　16, 141,
　145–6, 154
Sterling Area　142–3, 145–6, 154
Sugar Agreement　208

Tanganyika　193
Tanzania　30
　invasion of Uganda　236, 309
　and OAU　43, 234
tariffs　144, 147
technology　94–105, 178
　rural　34, 100
Telecommunications Bureau　69
trade
　agreements　144
　between Britain and Common-
　　wealth　313–14
　changes in　146–7
　between France and ex-
　　colonies　174
　and information exchange　153–8
　preferences　144, 145
Tonga　266
Trinidad　18, 264

Uganda　6, 7, 8, 18, 34, 201, 211–12,
　225, 229, 234, 283, 319
　Asian population　249–50
　Tanzanian invasion　236, 309
United Nations　28, 29, 43, 50, 123,
　124, 237
　and Commonwealth　299, 302,
　　312, 320–1

and conflict management　230
Declaration on the granting of
　Independence to Colonial
　Countries　263, 264
Declaration on Human Rights
　258
Development Programme (UNDP)
　284
and Falklands dispute　271, 273
and independence　263–4, 286, 287
and International Youth Year　60,
　61
peacekeeping forces　122, 123
UNCTAD　28, 148, 155, 207, 211
UNESCO　61, 89, 91, 104
UNIDO　104
United States
　atom-testing　48
　economic dominance of　140, 146,
　　161
　economy of　144
　and education　66, 68
　and Falklands dispute　272
　and Guatemala　44
　legal influence　130
　and migration　253, 254
　military　117, 118
　and Vietnam　168–9

West African Examination Council
　(WAEC)　77
West Indies Act (1967)　269
World Bank　156–7
World Health Organisation
　(WHO)　71, 107, 111–12, 113,
　317

Yaoundé Convention　179–80
Youth Project Scheme　58
Youth Study Fellowships　58
youth training　55–9

Zambia　29, 30, 120
Zimbabwe　259n
　arms transactions　120
　conflict, and Commonwealth　239–
　　42
　independence　167, 203
　legal system　130–1